PRAISE FOR

BATTLE FOR THE BIRD

"*Battle for the Bird* is an absolute triumph of reporting and storytelling. Kurt Wagner puts the reader into the room—all the rooms—as one of the great business dramas unfolds and provides an unmatched account of the chaos, power struggles, and excitement that have defined the company's existence."

— Ashlee Vance, *New York Times*
bestselling author of *Elon Musk* and
host of Bloomberg's "Hello World"

"*Battle for the Bird* is a meticulous and riveting account of how one of the world's most critical communications platforms has become collateral damage in a one-sided love affair gone awry. Kurt Wagner reveals new, shocking details about how this power transferred from one billionaire to the next and fresh insights on whether Twitter, now X, can be saved."

— Emily Chang,
bestselling author of *Brotopia* and
host of Bloomberg's "The Circuit"

"If you want to understand how one of the most powerful social networks in history managed to be such a dramatic corporate disaster, you must read Kurt Wagner's deeply reported inside story. *Battle for the Bird* is a warning for Elon Musk: running Twitter is not rocket science."

— Sarah Frier, author of *Financial Times*
and McKinsey 2020 Business Book of the Year
No Filter: The Inside Story of Instagram

"In *Battle for the Bird*, Kurt Wagner tells a gripping tale of the high-stakes struggle to control Twitter, one of the world's most influential companies, and the insane, mind-boggling, chaotic battle between Elon Musk, the Twitter board, and Jack Dorsey, as the entire concept of free speech hung in the balance."

— Nick Bilton,
author of *Hatching Twitter* and
special correspondent for *Vanity Fair*

"Solid business and tech journalism about how a public good became a nuisance in the hands of a reckless billionaire."

— *Kirkus Reviews*

"A riveting account of how 'hubris and resentment and naïveté' drove Elon Musk's tumultuous 2022 takeover of Twitter . . . This is *Barbarians at the Gate* for the social media age."

— *Publishers Weekly,* starred review

BATTLE FOR
THE BIRD

JACK DORSEY, ELON MUSK,
AND THE $44 BILLION
FIGHT FOR TWITTER'S SOUL

KURT WAGNER

ATRIA PAPERBACK

NEW YORK   AMSTERDAM/ANTWERP   LONDON
TORONTO   SYDNEY/MELBOURNE   NEW DELHI

ATRIA
PAPERBACK

An Imprint of Simon & Schuster, LLC
1230 Avenue of the Americas
New York, NY 10020

For more than 100 years, Simon & Schuster has championed authors and the stories they create. By respecting the copyright of an author's intellectual property, you enable Simon & Schuster and the author to continue publishing exceptional books for years to come. We thank you for supporting the author's copyright by purchasing an authorized edition of this book.

First Atria Paperback edition April 2025

ATRIA PAPERBACK and colophon are trademarks of Simon & Schuster, LLC

Simon & Schuster strongly believes in freedom of expression and stands against censorship in all its forms. For more information, visit BooksBelong.com.

For information about special discounts for bulk purchases, please contact Simon & Schuster Special Sales at 1-866-506-1949 or business@simonandschuster.com.

The Simon & Schuster Speakers Bureau can bring authors to your live event. For more information or to book an event, contact the Simon & Schuster Speakers Bureau at 1-866-248-3049 or visit our website at www.simonspeakers.com.

Interior design by Timothy Shaner, NightandDayDesign.biz

Manufactured in the United States of America

1 3 5 7 9 10 8 6 4 2

Library of Congress Control Number: 2023951241

ISBN 978-1-6680-1735-7
ISBN 978-1-6680-1736-4 (pbk)
ISBN 978-1-6680-1737-1 (ebook)

For Jess, Jack, and Payton—my favorite people.

CONTENTS

PART III: BATTLE FOR TWITTER

PART IV: TWITTER 2.0

AUTHOR'S NOTE

This book is based on conversations and interviews with more than 150 people, including more than 115 people who worked for or advised Twitter. Almost everyone I spoke with for this book requested anonymity in order to speak freely, so while I cannot name most of my sources, I spoke to people from almost every stage of the company's history, including senior executives, managers, and board members. As of December 2023, many former employees were still in active legal disputes with Twitter or Elon Musk, which impacted their willingness to go on the record.

I also benefited from several years of additional reporting on Twitter well before I ever decided to pursue a book. I watched and listened to dozens of hours of publicly available interviews from people described in this book, and read hundreds of pages of court documents, financial filings, and internal emails and presentations.

Despite several attempts to reach them, both Jack Dorsey and Elon Musk chose not to participate for this book.

I'm grateful to all the people who trusted me to tell this story.

INTRODUCTION

On April 25, 2022, the day Jack Dorsey finally sold Twitter to the world's richest person, he opened up Tidal, the music streaming service he bought from Jay-Z for almost $300 million, and dialed up Radiohead's "Everything in Its Right Place."

Dorsey had been thinking about this day for years. It wasn't because he wanted to rid himself of Twitter. Quite the opposite. Dorsey had always loved Twitter and fought like hell to stay involved in the company from its earliest days, even when others had tried to kick him out. But Twitter had morphed into something that saddened Dorsey. The product was founded in 2006, as a simple way to share what you were up to in 140 characters or less. Twitter then immediately fell into a trap that Dorsey, as a co-founder and Twitter's first CEO, was at least partially responsible for setting. As the product grew and added more users, the company behind it added more employees, more offices, and took hundreds of millions of dollars from venture capitalists to keep things growing. In 2013, Twitter, Inc. went public on the New York Stock Exchange, joining the never-ending race to make even more money for even more investors. That part of Twitter's story wasn't unique. Companies take venture capital money and go public all the time. That was how businesses were made, especially in the competitive and lucrative world of Silicon Valley. It was also how everyone got rich, Dorsey included.

What made Dorsey sad was his firm belief that Twitter didn't belong on the Wall Street hamster wheel. Twitter had the potential to be something more than just a profit machine: It was the world's *global consciousness*—a direct line into the way that people think and communicate and solve problems. Twitter reflected humanity in short, snackable snippets, and was the fastest way for news to travel online. There was nothing else quite like it.

As time wore on, Wall Street started ruining that—at least as far as Dorsey was concerned. Being a business meant placating advertisers by fact-checking posts and filtering out offensive tweets that made people uncomfortable. It also meant dealing with lawmakers who liked to apply pressure on the company and make demands about what Twitter could or couldn't do. If Dorsey could invent a time machine, he could go back to 2006 and build Twitter as an internet protocol, a technology layer similar to what allows anyone to build on the world wide web. In Dorsey's alternate universe, there would be no "company" for investors to pressure, and no "owner" responsible for making the impossible decisions, such as what kinds of posts should and shouldn't exist in the world. Twitter's transformation from an idea to a company had been the "original sin," Dorsey thought. It was his biggest regret.

This is why Dorsey was so very happy on Monday, April 25, 2022. One of his idols, Elon Musk, was buying Twitter for $44 billion, snatching the company away from Wall Street and taking it private. Musk was adding Twitter to his growing collection of world-changing businesses, which already included the electric car company Tesla and rocket company SpaceX. As the world's richest man, he claimed he didn't care about Twitter's finances; his goal was to make Twitter "maximally trusted and broadly inclusive," a bastion of free speech that would help preserve civilization in much the same way Tesla would by eliminating the need for fossil fuels, or SpaceX would by transforming humans into an interplanetary species. "Civilizational risk is decreased," Musk said, "the more we can increase the trust of Twitter as a public platform."

Musk checked all of Dorsey's boxes. He didn't just care about Twitter's role in humanity; he was also an avid Twitter user himself. He understood all the quirks and nuances that made the service great. "I don't believe anyone should own or run Twitter," Dorsey tweeted the day the deal was announced. "Solving for the problem of it being a company however, Elon is the singular solution I trust. I trust his mission to extend the light of consciousness."

Musk's decision to buy Twitter hadn't happened by accident. Dorsey had been privately pushing Musk to get involved at the company for weeks, bad-mouthing Twitter's board of directors both privately and publicly and sharing his own belief that Twitter needed to be a private company to properly accomplish its goals. Musk clearly agreed, making Twitter a "seller-friendly" offer and then pushing and prodding the company until it was his.

Four minutes after the deal was officially announced, Dorsey sent his pal a private message. "Thank you" ♥, he wrote. "I basically followed your advice!" Musk wrote back. "I know and I appreciate you," Dorsey replied. "This is the right and only path. I'll continue to do whatever it takes to make it work."

Twitter is often mentioned in the same sentence as other major internet companies such as Google, Amazon, Apple, or Meta. In some ways, that's appropriate. Twitter's social and cultural influence was prominent enough for years to merit inclusion with the other tech giants. By mid-2022, the year Elon Musk bought the company, Twitter had almost 240 million daily users, a small fraction of the global population, but tweets were virtually everywhere. TV networks displayed them during news reports, newspapers and magazines put them into print, and radio broadcasters read them over the airwaves. If it happened on Twitter, it typically found its way to the masses.

For years Twitter punched above its weight, spurring seismic shifts in culture and politics. It was a powerful source of news during uprisings in the Middle East, known as the "Arab Spring," and helped spur cultural movements such as #BlackLivesMatter and #MeToo. Twitter was a megaphone for the rich and powerful and a connective tissue between world leaders and their constituents. From 2017 until 2021, Twitter delivered a daily stream of consciousness from a sitting U.S. president, a live, digital journal published every day for the entire world to read. News moved so quickly on Twitter that the media industry was changed forever. For most of Twitter's existence, it wasn't even a debate: Twitter was the absolute quickest way to find out what was happening in the world *right now*.

That all meant that running Twitter came with an immense amount of power and control over global speech, a power that made Dorsey deeply uncomfortable and pushed Musk to shell out a fortune. Both men would learn the hard way that policing the global conversation is a thankless and impossible job.

As a business, though, Twitter largely underachieved. For years it captured the world's attention but didn't really know what to do with it. Most people don't realize just how small Twitter is when compared to other tech giants. When Musk spent $44 billion to overpay for Twitter in April 2022, Facebook was worth $540 billion, which was half of what it had been just seven months earlier. Google parent-company Alphabet was worth almost $1.5 *trillion*. Influence, it turns out, does not always equate to value.

In some ways, Jack Dorsey was right. Twitter was always going to struggle to live up to Wall Street's expectations. It carried similar ambitions as companies ten times its size, which also meant it dealt with lots of the same problems but without nearly as many resources to solve them. A lot of this was on Dorsey, who ran Twitter as CEO for eight years, and sat on its board from the very beginning. Twitter was on its deathbed in 2015 when Dorsey returned as CEO, and he coaxed the company back to life. For that he deserves credit. But for all his complaints about Wall Street and the construct of Twitter's business, it was a relationship Dorsey helped create. Plus, colleagues were disappointed that he never seemed interested in making money while he was in charge. The Wall Street game may be hard, but it's even harder when you aren't interested in playing.

By that measure, taking Twitter private wasn't necessarily a bad idea. Dorsey may have simply bet on the wrong billionaire. After he called Musk the "singular solution I trust," almost everything started to unravel. Musk spent months publicly ravaging Twitter and its executives, eventually trying to abandon the deal entirely before it officially closed. Twitter's warm and fuzzy corporate culture Dorsey helped build was undone by Musk in a matter of weeks. Twitter's small but stable advertising business eventually came close to bankruptcy. Musk's promise to deliver a service that is "maximally trusted and broadly inclusive" still hasn't materialized. Jason Goldman, one of Twitter's earliest executives and board members, later called Dorsey's "light of consciousness" tweet "one of the worst-aged tweets of all time." Dorsey himself admitted in April 2023, one year after the Musk deal was signed, that things didn't go the way he'd expected. "It all went south," he said.

There isn't a single explanation for *why* Musk bought Twitter. The reality is there were several factors. Twitter banned President Donald Trump for life in 2021, a decision that left both Dorsey and his company forever scarred, and left Twitter's critics convinced that the company was out to destroy one of the most precious freedoms in the world: the freedom of speech. In the two years before Musk arrived, Dorsey started to check out in favor of other interests, like the cryptocurrency Bitcoin, which opened the door for someone else to come in and take control. And then there was Twitter's business, which was a disappointment for years. The company was ripe for some kind of drastic change when Musk showed up on its doorstep.

When Dorsey's successor, Parag Agrawal, was asked by an employee shortly after the Musk deal was announced whether the takeover could have been avoided, he reflected on the reality that Twitter let too many opportunities slip by. "I think so, right?" he replied in front of the entire company. "If we look back five years, could we have made Twitter even better than it is today? Could we have been stronger technically? Could we have made better choices around the product? Could we have done better on monetization? Could we have done things differently to earn more trust around our policies? Yes. We could have done things differently and better."

It didn't have to be this way. The Twitter story is one of deception, bad decisions, and misguided trust. It's a story of hubris and resentment and naïveté. But most of all it's a story about a business and product that never lived up to expectations, and the two men who led Twitter down a road to the craziest business deal corporate America has ever seen.

PART I

TWITTER 1.0

ONE

JACK IS BACK

Dick Costolo was trying his very best not to cry. It was June 2015 and hundreds of Twitter employees had crammed into the ninth-floor cafeteria of the company's San Francisco headquarters for an unexpected company-wide meeting scheduled that very morning. Costolo, in a navy blue sport coat and light gray pants, stood on a makeshift stage, looked out over hundreds of familiar faces, and steadied himself by making eye contact with a couple of apathetic-looking infrastructure engineers sitting near the back of the room. Then he delivered the surprising news: After almost five years running one of the most influential companies in tech, Costolo was stepping down at month's end. Twitter's thirty-eight-year-old cofounder and chairman, Jack Dorsey, would take over as interim CEO until the company found someone permanent.

For the most part, employees were sad to see Costolo go. At fifty-one years old with a bald head, black rectangular glasses, and a quick wit, Costolo was both incredibly funny and easy to talk to, which made him almost universally well liked in the world of corporate America. In his twenties, he'd dreamed of a career in comedy, performing improv with the likes of Steve Carell at Second City in Chicago. He even auditioned twice for *Saturday Night Live* before tossing away the dream and diving into tech. Costolo started multiple companies and eventually sold a startup to Google for $100 million in 2007. A few years later, in 2009, he joined Twitter as chief operating officer, and was promoted to CEO just one year later. As Twitter grew from a couple hundred employees to several thousand under his watch, Costolo still felt accessible, joining regular CrossFit classes in the office with junior employees and earning respect by remembering almost every employee by name (at least until head count started creeping above two thousand people).

But the past five years had also been a challenge. When Costolo first got the CEO job in late 2010, Twitter was a well-known albeit still misunderstood player in the world of media and politics. The service let people post short snippets of text to anyone who chose to follow them. It quickly became popular with politicians, journalists, and celebrities looking for a direct line to communicate with their fans. Barack Obama had an account. So did Taylor Swift, Ashton Kutcher, and Oprah Winfrey. In 2009, a NASA astronaut sent a tweet from the International Space Station. Just few years later, Twitter would play a key role in helping protesters organize during the Arab Spring.

Despite Twitter's global influence, the service made almost no money. The year Costolo took over, Twitter had just $28 million in revenue, a figure he was tasked with growing considerably. He largely succeeded, taking Twitter public in late 2013 and making many of its executives, investors, and early employees very rich. By the time Costolo stepped down, the company was pulling in more than $500 million in revenue in a single quarter, most of it from advertising. At the very least, Costolo had turned Twitter into a legitimate business that traded on the New York Stock Exchange.

Still, the job had worn him down, and the fun-loving CEO was tired. Wall Street investors were growing increasingly frustrated with Twitter, which was often compared to its much larger social media peer, Facebook. Even though Facebook was almost five times Twitter's size, Mark Zuckerberg's service was still growing like a weed in almost every country around the world. Facebook added 43 million new users during the final three months of 2014; Twitter added just 4 million. It was a stark contrast, and one that posed a major problem for Twitter since advertisers wanted to spend money where they could reach as many people as possible, and investors wanted to buy stock in companies that were still growing. The general belief was that Twitter was too confusing for regular people to use. A lot of people didn't even know what they should be tweeting about. The company needed a product facelift to win people over and keep its user base growing, and Costolo was a business guy, not a product guy.

The job was hard in other ways, too. Twitter's role as a megaphone for famous people meant that the company was in the news constantly, which meant that Costolo was in the news constantly. He took much of it in stride, like when he got a phone call from his daughter in late 2014. "Hey, Dad, I have bad news and good news," she said. "The bad news is Yahoo Finance says you're one of the five worst CEOs of the year." *What is the good news?* Costolo asked. "Well, no one reads Yahoo Finance is part of the good news, and the other part of the good news is you're number five. So there's four people who are ahead of you." Sometimes the job was downright terrifying. In late 2014, Twitter started suspending accounts that were supporting the Islamic State terrorist organization, also known as ISIS. Costolo received so many death threats that Twitter hired full-time security to sit outside his house. "Running Twitter is like running any other company in dog years," he'd say years later. "A year at Twitter is like being C.E.O. of any other company for seven years . . . it's just a wacky company to run."

At the end of 2014, with both ISIS and the media out to get him, Costolo told Twitter's board that he was done, and that they'd better start looking for a replacement. By the summer of 2015, the board still hadn't found a successor. Instead they asked Jack Dorsey to temporarily step in until the group could conduct a more thorough search. Some on the board would have liked Dorsey to take the job full-time. He was Twitter's cofounder, after all, and many people considered him the type of product savant that Twitter clearly needed. But Dorsey's track record at Twitter was also spotty. As the company's first CEO during its founding days, he'd been a disaster, and was eventually fired by the board and replaced by another cofounder in a tangled mess of corporate and personal drama. Dorsey had certainly grown up since then, but he was also running another company, the payments firm Square, which meant the full-time Twitter job was probably out of the question. Twitter was on track to make more than $2 billion in revenue when Costolo resigned; it had grown too big and influential to have a part-time CEO.

Still, Square's office was literally across the street from Twitter's, and as chairman, Dorsey knew everything that was going on anyway. He and Costolo had dinner every week at Zuni Café, just three blocks down the road on Market Street; they met on Tuesday nights at the same table in the upstairs dining room to talk about the company and anything else that came to mind. If anyone could keep Twitter going for a few months while the board figured out a plan, it was Dorsey.

After Costolo delivered his news from the cafeteria stage, employees rose to their feet and offered a thunderous ovation. Dorsey, in black from head to toe with a sport coat, jeans, and boots, stood onstage just a few feet away, applauding alongside everybody else for the man he was about to replace. As the ovation subsided, an employee asked Costolo what he planned to do after his resignation became official. "Sleep," Costolo said. He planned to go to bed early and sleep until ten thirty the next morning. "It's gonna be the best sleep of my life," he quipped.

Costolo was free. Twitter was Jack Dorsey's problem now.

As a kid, Jack Dorsey never dreamed about being a CEO, and he certainly never dreamed about being the CEO of two companies at once. Dorsey fashioned himself an artist from a young age, and he spent his childhood in St. Louis, Missouri, drawing, painting, and daydreaming about getting a cat and sailing around the world by himself. He was a serious introvert, a quality that was magnified as a young child because of a speech impediment that, at one point, got so severe he stopped speaking. But Dorsey was also infinitely curious and loved to create new things.

As he grew older, he developed an obsession with cities and the infrastructure that made them work, spending time at the railyard taking pictures of trains, or jumping on the city bus to explore new parts of town.
When his dad brought home the family's first computer—an IBM PC
Junior in the mid-1980s—Dorsey started to write software code for the
first time. He'd listen to the family's police scanner, plotting the coordinates of local fire engines and police cars onto the computer, eventually
manipulating the homemade map so that he could watch the digital dots
move across the screen from one emergency to the next. As his talent and
interest in coding expanded, Dorsey started exploring the internet more
broadly, hanging out in online chat rooms and bulletin boards where he
read about the ideals of an open internet and learned about new topics
like cryptography. Dorsey would reminisce about this early introduction to the internet for years to come, proudly owning the fact that he'd
grown up immersed in the "hacker" culture that helped form the basis
of the modern internet age.

That hacker mentality paid off as a college student at the University
of Missouri–Rolla, when Dorsey discovered a security hole on a website
for a New York–based dispatch company called Dispatch Management
Services. Still passionate about maps and cities, he loved the idea of
working in dispatch, and emailed the company's chairman, Greg Kidd,
to both warn him about the vulnerability and, perhaps subconsciously,
show off his hacking skills. The stunt landed Dorsey his first job in tech.
He dropped out of school in Missouri to move to New York and start coding full-time for Kidd's company. For a twenty-year-old obsessed with
cities, New York was a dream come true. At first Dorsey lived in an old
Scottish manor out on Long Island that Kidd used for corporate housing.
With several themed bedrooms and a shag carpet bathroom, employees referred to the building as the "Swamp House," and Dorsey was its
youngest resident. He wanted to be even closer to the city, though, and
soon moved to a different loft that Kidd rented on John Street in lower
Manhattan, just a block away from the World Trade Center. Known as

the "Crash Pad," the bedroom came with a shared bathroom and several eclectic roommates, "other outcasts who shouldn't have been in the wall street district after 8," Dorsey later wrote. He'd spend hours at the Borders bookstore, listening to music, or just walking the city and thinking.

Dispatch Management Services went public in 1998, and Kidd quit shortly after. He was the kind of guy who enjoyed eating the hot dogs from New York street vendors, and the company had quickly become too corporate, with too many suits suddenly hanging around. Kidd convinced Dorsey to move with him to San Francisco, where he planned to start another company. What Kidd came up with was called "DNet," a precursor to the world of immediate online delivery, which let people buy local products and have them delivered directly to their home the very same day. It was a great idea, but DNet was about twenty years too early. Dorsey was laid off as the dot-com bubble burst, and the company folded less than a couple of years after it started. But the move to California hadn't been fruitless. A few years after his arrival, Dorsey was living at an old biscuit factory in Oakland during the summer of 2000 when he took out a notebook and sketched out the idea for a service he called STAT.US. The point was for people to update their friends about what they were doing from a mobile phone—"real-time, up-to-date, from the road"—similar to the status feature popularized by AOL's Instant Messenger. That summer Dorsey went for a walk in San Francisco's Golden Gate Park, pulled out his new BlackBerry, and tested the idea by sending a status. "I'm at the bison paddock," he wrote. Very few of Dorsey's friends had a BlackBerry; even fewer cared where Dorsey was hanging out. Like DNet, STAT.US had also arrived before its time.

Still, the idea stuck with Dorsey. He spent the next several years bouncing around the country pursuing various passions and trying to figure out his life. He met a girlfriend in an online chat room while still in California and followed her to Cambridge, Massachusetts, where he spent his days hunched over a laptop in Kendall Square near the Massachusetts Institute of Technology campus, seemingly picking up ideas and inspiration through osmosis. He was still an introverted loner at heart, happy to spend hours reading or walking or experimenting with different ideas on his laptop. He maintained his passion for art, and for a short time would fold origami cranes and leave them hidden in places around town for others to find. At one point Dorsey got a tattoo on his left forearm that read "0Daemon!?" It had several meanings, the most obvious being the reference to a daemon, which is a computer program that runs silently in the background. It was symbolic of how Dorsey viewed his own existence.

After a year in Cambridge, at twenty-five years old, Dorsey moved back to St. Louis, where he started working for his dad's mass spectrometer business and dove headfirst into other new hobbies, like botanical illustration. After a bout with carpal tunnel syndrome, he became so obsessed with massage therapy that Dorsey enrolled in the Healing Arts Center in St. Louis and took a thousand hours of training to get his massage therapy license. Maybe, he thought, he would start a business where he massaged computer programmers while they worked, offering up advice or coding assistance at the same time. *Massage therapy and code therapy together.* Everyone he told thought it was a dumb idea.

Eventually, Dorsey's wanderings brought him back to California. In late 2004, he moved into a small cottage behind Kidd's house in Berkeley and started nannying for Kidd's infant daughter. He pierced his nose and picked up odd jobs here and there, including a job writing ticketing system software for a company that offered tours of Alcatraz.

One afternoon, Dorsey was working from a coffee shop in South Park, a popular neighborhood for startups in San Francisco's growing tech scene, when he saw a familiar face walk by the window and into the café to order a drink. Dorsey didn't know Ev Williams, but he knew *of* him from the news. Just a few years earlier Williams had sold his blogging service, Blogger, to Google for millions of dollars, and was now running a podcasting startup called Odeo. Dorsey didn't approach Williams in person, but pulled out his laptop, found Williams's email, and sent him a copy of his resume, which only included his first name. Within weeks, Dorsey had a job writing code for a podcasting company. He was finally working at a real startup.

Dorsey was adopted into Odeo almost immediately. He was a strong coder and got his work done without complaint, which meant he was significantly easier to work with than most of the other engineers at the company. Dorsey became friendly with several folks on the team, attending concerts in the city and going out for drinks. He rekindled his childhood interest in sailing, volunteering one weekend to help a coworker pick up their new boat and sail it into the bay, where they accidentally ran it aground. He was still quiet, but he was witty and intriguingly weird. At one point he walked around San Francisco with his phone number stitched onto his T-shirt to see if anyone would call. They did, and it was awkward. He could also take a joke. Shortly after joining Odeo, Dorsey posed as a model for a local department store, Jeremy's. Dorsey had always been handsome; at around five feet ten he wasn't particularly tall, but he was slender with blue eyes, a heavy brow, and a slight chin dimple visible before he began rocking a ZZ Top beard. The photo shoot led to an email thread from colleagues who couldn't wait to give him shit. "JACK IS SOOOO HOT!" wrote one coworker who forwarded the photos to the rest of the team. "Meow," replied another.

While Dorsey had found his footing, Odeo was far from crushing it. Shortly after he joined, Steve Jobs decided to get into podcasting, too. In mid-2005, Apple launched an update so people could discover and listen to podcasts directly within iTunes, planting the kiss of death upon the much smaller Odeo. The team still had money from Williams and other investors, but morale was decimated since everyone knew that Odeo was dead in the water. The team needed another idea.

In February 2006, Dorsey's crude vision for an on-the-go status product was reawakened after a late night out drinking. Dorsey sat in the car in San Francisco with one of his new friends, Odeo's cofounder Noah Glass, talking about the company that was crumbling around them and brainstorming ideas to try to salvage their jobs. As they threw stuff against the wall, Dorsey brought up the status concept that he'd scribbled onto a sheet of paper inside the biscuit factory five years earlier. Whether it was the booze, the fatigue, or some other whiff of inspiration, the idea made more sense than ever, especially to Glass. The two presented it to Williams and another employee, Biz Stone, the next morning. After a few more weeks of brainstorming and an employee "hackathon" to come up with as many new ideas as possible, Williams decided the status product, which Glass had dubbed "Twitter," was the best one they had. He assigned Dorsey and Stone to build the original prototype.

Twitter officially came to life in March 2006, and for much of the next year it was all Dorsey could think about. The product let people send short text updates that were then delivered to their followers' phones as a text message. The 140-character limit on tweets ensured that they could be delivered within a single text, and even provided Twitter a little extra room that was eventually used to include a person's username. The team's original tweets read like bite-sized diary entries.

"having some coffee"

"heading home"

"sleep"

But like most startups, the product growth moved slowly and the internal politics got messy. Even though the team was obsessed with tweeting, Twitter had fewer than five thousand users roughly six months after launch. Glass, something of a loose cannon who had started rubbing some of his colleagues the wrong way, was also pushed out of the company a few months after the first Twitter prototype was built, a decision made by Williams but with Dorsey's support. (Glass would later be referred to in the press as "Twitter's forgotten co-founder.") Several other employees were also pushed out as Williams bought out their Odeo shares and formally pivoted the company toward Twitter. Dorsey remained the new product's technical leader, writing and managing much of the software that kept Twitter operational.

It took an entire year before Twitter had its true coming-out moment. In March 2007, at the South by Southwest tech conference in Austin, Texas, Twitter was the talk of the town. The team had arranged so that feeds of tweets were displayed on video screens at the conference and attendees used the new service to figure out what everyone else in Austin was up to during nights full of parties and debauchery. Twitter won an award for the best blogging startup, and Dorsey's acceptance speech was incredibly on-brand; it was fewer than 140 characters. Within three months, more than 100,000 people had signed up for Twitter, which was getting regular attention from the tech press.

That summer, Williams appointed thirty-year-old Dorsey as the company's first CEO. Dorsey had not only been instrumental in coming up with the idea, but he'd been the one building Twitter throughout and was completely infatuated with the product. The problem, of course, was that Dorsey had never been the CEO of anything—he had barely been a manager of other engineers. As a creator and inventor, Dorsey had excelled. As a CEO, he struggled. His quiet, soft-spoken demeanor didn't lend to the kind of confident and decisive decision-making that startups typically need, and Twitter's now-rapid growth meant that the site was crashing constantly. On top of that, Dorsey was still pursuing several other passions and hobbies, including a sewing class. He eventually hoped to make his own jeans. He wasn't even convinced that Twitter should be a real company. Dorsey wanted Twitter to be some kind of public service product that didn't need to make a lot of money. As a hacker, he thought Twitter might be better as some kind of internet protocol—a technology layer that other people could then build on top of in much the same way that email worked.

That wasn't what Twitter was building, though. It was building a real company, with real investors who expected returns. Williams, who had taken on the role of chairman, took issue with the fact that Dorsey would leave work to do yoga or attend his sewing classes. "You can either be a dressmaker or the CEO of Twitter," Williams told him. "But you can't be both."

The ultimatum didn't work. As Twitter grew, Dorsey's inexperience running a company was magnified. He struggled to manage people, made major decisions without alerting Twitter's small board of directors, and tracked Twitter's expenses—incorrectly, it turns out—on his own laptop. By fall of 2008, just over a year after giving Dorsey the job, Williams had seen enough. So had Twitter's board, which also included two venture capitalists who had invested in Twitter, Bijan Sabet from Spark Capital and Fred Wilson from Union Square Ventures. The small group decided that Dorsey was out, and Williams should take over. Dorsey got the news over breakfast at the Clift hotel in San Francisco on October 15, 2008. They wanted him to stay on as chairman, a purely ceremonial title without any real responsibility. His short time as CEO was over.

Dorsey was devastated. Twitter was his baby and working at the company had provided a sense of stability and purpose that he'd struggled to find anywhere else. He also felt furious and betrayed. Williams and the rest of Twitter's board had pushed him out of a job, and there was nothing he could do to stop them. Even as a cofounder, Dorsey didn't have any significant control over the company; that belonged to Twitter's investors and to Williams, who had financed Twitter from the beginning with the money he made from selling Blogger. It was a harsh introduction to the reality that a company's investors often get what they want. Whoever brings the money has the power.

Dorsey hid his anger well, at least publicly. Even though he was no longer running Twitter, he was still doing interviews and widely playing the role of Twitter cofounder at high-profile events. He joined a delegation of tech executives for a three-day tour of Iraq with the U.S. State Department to explore "high-tech business ventures." Later, he sat next to Secretary of State Hillary Clinton at a State Department dinner party in Washington, D.C. Dorsey joined a panel with famed Chinese artist and activist Ai Weiwei, and even threw out the first pitch at a game for his hometown St. Louis Cardinals. What people largely didn't realize was that Dorsey's role inside Twitter was essentially nonexistent. The company was moving on without him, and the cofounders who remained, Ev Williams and Biz Stone, were annoyed that Dorsey was doing so much press without their approval.

His lack of influence would change in the summer of 2010. The full story, as detailed by Nick Bilton in the book *Hatching Twitter*, goes something like this: Dorsey, still Twitter's chairman, started meeting with senior Twitter executives to offer advice, and more importantly, listen to their complaints and grievances about Williams. Many believed he was indecisive and moving too slowly. Dorsey started encouraging those executives to voice their concerns to the board directly, gently funneling those complaints to Williams's bosses. As the summer wore on and the complaints started to pile up, Dorsey arranged a series of secret meetings with several top Twitter executives and board members at his own San Francisco apartment to discuss Williams's job. Williams, of course, was not invited and had no idea what was happening behind his back. As Bilton, a former *New York Times* journalist, described it, "Ensuring that the right things landed in the right people's ears, Jack had spent the summer moving people around like pawns in a chess match against his nemesis. The problem was, Ev had no idea he was playing."

Unsurprisingly, Dorsey won. In October 2010, two years after pushing Dorsey out, Williams was fired and replaced by Dick Costolo. Williams had pushed out Dorsey, and now Dorsey had returned the favor.

If people were sad to see Costolo step aside in June 2015, they may have been just as equally shocked to see Dorsey walking back through the door considering all the baggage he carried with him. Suddenly Twitter's board of directors included three former CEOs: Dorsey, Williams, and Costolo, each of whom had replaced one of the others. As uncomfortable as that dynamic may have been, it wasn't Twitter's biggest issue in finding a full-time CEO. Ironically, the reason that Twitter's board felt Dorsey could do the job on an interim basis was the same reason that nobody thought Dorsey could do the job on a full-time basis: He already had another CEO job at Square.

Shortly after Dorsey had been fired from Twitter, he reconnected with an old friend from St. Louis named Jim McKelvey. Dorsey had worked for McKelvey as a teenager, doing a series of odd jobs for his startup that helped businesses put the glossy brochures they typically handed out at conferences onto CD-ROMs. Fifteen years later, in 2008, the two got together in St. Louis over the holidays and Dorsey told his friend about being fired. "I felt like someone had beaten up my younger brother, and I was furious," McKelvey later wrote. The two decided to brainstorm new business ideas together, and briefly considered building an electric car or an app for journaling. One day, McKelvey, who was working as a glass artist at the time, sold a glass faucet he'd made for $2,000. Except the sale fell through once the buyer realized McKelvey couldn't accept her American Express card. McKelvey called Dorsey to commiserate, and they decided that there needed to be an easier way for small businesses to accept credit cards. The Apple iPhone had been unveiled just a few years earlier, and they came up with an ingenious idea: They built a small credit card reader that plugged into the iPhone's headphone jack, transferring the card's information to the phone as it was swiped. The card reader turned any iPhone into a mobile cash register. They called the company Square, short for "square up."

By 2015, Square had morphed into a legitimate business. The company had almost 1,200 employees, had raised $150 million from several investors, and was valued at $6 billion. Square's original credit card reader was a staple at coffee shops and farmers' markets around the country, and the company had since launched a product for turning an iPad into a cash register at physical retail locations. Square was even offering small business loans. The Jack Dorsey running Square in 2015 was much more mature, responsible, and experienced than the Jack Dorsey who had been fired from Twitter in 2008 for mismanaging funds and spending too much time sewing. He'd also learned a couple very valuable lessons. Dorsey wasn't just CEO, he was also Square's largest shareholder. If he was going to give up his job, it was going to be on *his* terms.

Dorsey's role at Square was a problem from the moment he was named interim CEO of Twitter. The assumption, at least initially, was that Dorsey might leave Square behind. The Twitter job was significantly higher profile, and the social network's market value was almost four times higher than Square's. Plus it would be a chance for Dorsey to recoup his first love.

What people didn't know was that Dorsey's role at Square was more important than ever. The payments company was privately preparing paperwork for an initial public offering (IPO) in the fall, which meant that it was out of the question for its cofounder and CEO to walk out the door months before going public. It would have been a disaster for Square investors, including Dorsey.

Still, some inside Square were worried. Even though Dorsey had told employees internally that he wanted to stay at Square, most of them also knew how much he loved Twitter. Among those concerned was Aaron Zamost, the head of Square's PR team, who was getting dozens of questions per day from the press asking about Dorsey's future. Zamost wanted to put the issue to rest to try to eliminate the now-daily distractions, especially with the looming IPO. A few days after Dorsey was announced as interim CEO at Twitter, Zamost put out a statement from Square with Dorsey's name attached. "As I said last week, I'm as committed as ever to Square and its continued success," the statement read. "I'm Square CEO and that won't change." It was the kind of statement Zamost would usually give Twitter a heads-up about, but not this time. He was worried that Twitter's board would try and kill the statement before it went live.

Now that Dorsey was digging in his heels, Peter Currie, the chairman of Twitter's board, felt compelled to apply some pressure of his own. Currie was part of a faction of directors that had hoped Dorsey would eventually cave and give up his job at Square to return to Twitter full-time. He released his own statement a few days later, and the language was unequivocal. "The Committee will only consider candidates for recommendation to the full Board who are in a position to make a full-time commitment to Twitter," it read.

The game of chicken was on. Dorsey wasn't leaving Square, and the board wasn't entertaining part-time candidates. If Dorsey was going to return to Twitter full-time, somebody was going to have to blink.

With Dorsey seemingly out of contention, Twitter's board of directors hired a well-known executive search firm, Spencer Stuart, to help them find a permanent replacement. The search firm had actually been Plan B. For much of the spring, Twitter's board had worked on recruiting another candidate who was already inside the building: Adam Bain, Twitter's head of sales and partnerships, and one of the most likable people at the whole company.

Twitter's board, including Dorsey and Williams, had been leaning on Bain for months to try to convince him to take the job. As the head of sales, he was running the part of Twitter that seemed to be working the best. Twitter's user base grew less than 10 percent in 2015, but Twitter's revenue grew 58 percent. The problem was that Bain didn't want the job. He knew he was good at running Twitter's business, but like everyone else, he believed Twitter's problems were primarily related to the product, which wasn't his strength. He floated the idea of taking a second-in-command position, working as the business lead alongside a more product-minded CEO, like Dorsey or Williams, similar to the

Mark Zuckerberg–Sheryl Sandberg relationship that everyone seemed to admire over at Facebook. Of course, Dorsey's other job stood in the way.

The team at Spencer Stuart scoured Silicon Valley for anyone with a big tech or media job. The initial list of candidates reviewed by the board included almost two hundred names, many of them already holding major positions and thus highly unlikely to be interested. The list included people like Susan Wojcicki, who was running YouTube; Tim Armstrong, the CEO of AOL; Jason Kilar, who had recently been head of Hulu; and Angela Ahrendts, the head of retail for Apple.

As the weeks ticked by and phone calls were made, the list began to narrow significantly. Omid Kordestani, a longtime and well-liked Google executive credited with building the company's massive search ads business, was one potential target, though he bowed out after meeting with Dorsey; he walked away convinced that the Twitter cofounder was both interested and committed to the job despite the board's claim that it wouldn't hire a part-timer. The board also talked to Tony Bates, who had worked at Microsoft and Cisco and was the president of the camera company GoPro.

As summer morphed into fall, one candidate emerged from the pack: Andy Jassy, the head of Amazon Web Services, the retail giant's incredibly successful and underrated cloud computing division. Jassy had been at Amazon since 1997, earning the trust of CEO Jeff Bezos and building a reputation as someone who embodied Amazon's hard-core culture by working long hours and requiring his teams to do the same. In 2015, the year he was considered for the Twitter job, Jassy's AWS division did nearly $8 billion in sales, and was on pace to reach $10 billion in sales faster than Amazon's commerce business had. From a business standpoint, Jassy was everything that Twitter needed and more. He met with several Twitter board members individually throughout the process, including at least one trip from Seattle down to San Francisco. But it wasn't a given that Jassy would leave Amazon, and Twitter's board was also worried that he wasn't the product expert the company needed. He'd signed up for Twitter early on, way back in 2009, but Jassy hadn't started tweeting until that fall, when he was considered for the job. Building AWS was impressive but a completely different beast than building a consumer product for 300 million people.

In late September, Twitter's board blinked first. The group decided that getting half of Dorsey's time was better than 100 percent of anybody else, including Jassy. It also meant eating crow on its statement about only considering full-time candidates. On Thursday, October 1, the board told Dorsey on a conference call that the job was his. He'd been running Twitter for exactly three months, and now he would get to run Twitter for the long haul. The news of his appointment had already leaked to the press one day earlier, but Twitter's board waited a few more days before going public with the news. Currie acknowledged the fact that the board had been forced to backtrack on its pledge to hire a full-time CEO. "We assumed we would only consider a candidate who could make an undivided commitment to be our CEO," he said when Dorsey was announced. "But over time it became apparent to us that Jack was not just meeting but surpassing the expectations we had of him as interim CEO, while also running Square."

Still, the board made arrangements to try to accommodate for the unique setup. Twitter made Bain the company's chief operating officer, solidifying him as Dorsey's number two and the top business exec in the way he'd envisioned it several months earlier. The board also brought on Kordestani, the Google veteran, just a few weeks later in a new role as executive chairman to help Dorsey run the business and serve as an unofficial executive coach. If Dorsey was going to keep two jobs, he'd have to do so with a few other seasoned business executives hovering nearby to ensure things wouldn't run off the rails.

Dorsey celebrated his new job on the day it was formally announced, attending a VIP dinner at Bar Tartine in San Francisco with celebrities like actor Bradley Cooper, Metallica drummer Lars Ulrich, and close friends Rick Rubin, the record producer, and Vivi Nevo, the Hollywood investor. Dorsey had outlasted Twitter's board, and now he was back atop the company he cofounded with a second chance to prove he could run one of the world's highest-profile businesses. There was a lot to celebrate.

As everyone would learn soon enough, there was also a lot to fix.

TWO

#ITSJUSTFUCKINGUS

Jack Dorsey's day usually started around 5 a.m. He began with thirty minutes of meditation followed by several iterations of the seven-minute workout, a high-intensity training routine that required nothing but a chair and a wall. After that Dorsey would make coffee, perhaps taking a moment to watch the sun rise from his back patio that sat on the edge of a cliff overlooking the Golden Gate Bridge, then he'd check in at work. He'd strap on a pair of running sandals, grab his phone, and make the five-mile walk through the streets of San Francisco to Twitter's downtown headquarters—rain or shine. Sometimes he'd listen to podcasts, other times audiobooks, but for Dorsey the morning routine became a constant and important start to his day. As an introvert, this quiet time was how he got his energy. As the CEO of two publicly traded companies, it was how he kept his sanity.

Dorsey needed those sanity tools, because life had become incredibly stressful since taking over Twitter again. He spent almost all his time working. It was a lifestyle that was borderline unsustainable, but aided by the fact Dorsey wasn't married and didn't have any kids. To cope, he started the new routine and leaned heavily into meditation, a practice he'd dabbled with for years but had never taken seriously until now. On a typical day he'd spend his mornings at Twitter and his afternoons and evenings at Square, but typical days were not very "typical" considering his travel schedule and the unexpected demands that came with running two companies with completely different business models.

As exciting as it was to be back at Twitter, the timing of his new job was complicated. When Dorsey got the nod from Twitter's board, Square was in the final stages of prep for its planned IPO, which meant Dorsey was soon on the road pitching bankers and Wall Street investors about his other company. The IPO happened the week before Thanksgiving, and Square's stock price jumped 45 percent on the initial trading day. The pop was misleading. Square had priced its shares at a valuation that was much lower than what private investors had given the company just one year earlier. In the days leading up to the IPO, the situation looked so bleak that Square's advisors even floated the idea of postponing the deal altogether. Still, Dorsey made the most of Square's first day as a public company, which was also his thirty-ninth birthday. Square set up a street market outside the New York Stock Exchange where people could buy products from vendors using Square's mobile register. Dorsey also rejected the tradition of ringing the bell from the balcony overlooking the trading floor, and instead arranged for the bell to ring when his mom, Marcia, used her Apple Watch to buy a bouquet of flowers from one of Square's earliest sellers on the street outside. Dorsey was another year older, but he remained as unconventional as ever.

Reviving Twitter was proving to be more difficult. Just one week after getting the CEO job, Dorsey laid off more than three hundred people—8 percent of the workforce—in the first round of layoffs in the company's decade-long history. He called the cuts "tough but necessary," believing they would help Twitter move faster and make quicker decisions, but they also set a depressing mood for his return. To perk everybody up, Dorsey decided to give back $200 million of his Twitter stock to the employee equity pool, a rare and generous gift meant to show his belief in the company.

The good vibes were short-lived. Dorsey's permanent appointment had generated tons of excitement in the press, but that excitement didn't translate to new users for Twitter. In the final three months of 2015, which was Dorsey's first official quarter in the job, Twitter's user base didn't grow at all. By early January, investors were growing impatient as the Facebook comparisons grew more and more unflattering. Twitter's stock was trading near an all-time low. If the layoffs had made Twitter faster, it wasn't obvious from the outside. The company was secretly working on several new features, including longer tweets so people could post more than 140 characters at a time and a new algorithm for reordering the tweets in the feed, but those changes were taking several months to finish.

The final week of January was a pivotal one for Twitter. Dorsey had arranged for a multiday "retreat" for the top one hundred senior leaders at the company, who all convened in San Francisco to talk about strategy, discuss product initiatives, and sing kumbaya in preparation for the year ahead. Dorsey even bought everyone a book called *Mindset: The New Psychology of Success*, by Carol Dweck, who also had a TED talk titled "The Power of Believing That You Can Improve." But the weekend before the event started, news leaked that several of Twitter's most senior leaders had resigned, including the head of product, Kevin Weil; the head of engineering, Alex Roetter; the head of media, Katie Stanton; and Jason Toff, the head of Twitter's short-form video app, Vine. Losing that many senior executives at once would be a tough blow for any company. For Dorsey, who was desperate to improve Twitter's product, it was a real punch to the gut. Even though Dorsey knew about the departures, the timing of the leak just days before his leadership confab was not ideal. The excitement that had first manifested around Dorsey's return was quickly fading. Many employees, including senior executives, were frustrated things weren't changing faster.

One of those departing, Weil, had climbed the ranks internally over a seven-year career to become the top product executive a year before Dorsey's return. Weil was incredibly smart, with physics degrees from both Harvard and Stanford, but more importantly he felt like a perfect fit for Dorsey. While he wasn't known as a product inventor in the way Dorsey was, Weil was considered a strong "operator" who could execute whatever vision Dorsey ultimately came up with. Weil's departure stung, but the specifics made it hurt even worse: He was leaving Twitter for Instagram, owned by Facebook, and Twitter's archrival. Instagram cofounder Kevin Systrom had recruited Weil hard over the holidays, eventually winning him over. Weil had told Dorsey he was planning to leave before Systrom ever approached, but now he had to give his boss an update in early January: he wasn't just leaving, he was leaving for Instagram. The Twitter CEO stopped inviting Weil to executive team meetings but agreed he should stay at the company for a few more weeks to ease the transition. By the first day of the leadership retreat, Twitter's executive team knew that Weil was leaving for Instagram, but almost no one else at the company was aware.

That night, as the Twitter "Top 100" convened for a special dinner, news leaked in the press that Weil was headed to Instagram. Weil hadn't attended the retreat but was invited to the dinner, and someone quickly pulled him aside and showed him the news article on their phone. Crestfallen, Weil spoke to Dorsey, who told him that he should probably leave. As the news spread throughout the room, Weil left the dinner and spent the evening walking alone around the streets of San Francisco. Shortly after, in a rare moment of spite, Dorsey sent an email to the entire company.

Subject: KW
I know we all read of the disappointing and confusing news about a really lame move by a former colleague. I'm going to be very candid with you all Thursday at Tea Time about my feelings on this. Would rather do it in person. Just wanted to let you know I'm thinking about it, and thinking about you all. Onward!
Jack

Even though he'd known for weeks and kept Weil on for a transition period, Dorsey acted betrayed and offended by the news. He would later apologize for the email, but it was clear that Twitter wasn't just struggling; its new CEO was growing increasingly frustrated as well.

Twitter's senior executives spent the next two days discussing the company's looming challenges, first with the Top 100, and then later in the week with the entire company at a regular all-hands meeting known as "Tea Time." At one point, an employee asked Twitter's chief financial officer, Anthony Noto, why the company didn't just look for a buyer. *If turning Twitter around is going to be so hard, why not find a way out?*

Noto was unlike any other executive at Twitter, and in many ways, he was Dorsey's opposite. As a former academic All-American football player at the U.S. Military Academy at West Point, Noto was clean-shaven, broad-shouldered, and square-jawed. He didn't like nonsense, and he didn't like excuses, but he did like swearing, and had a tendency of dropping f-bombs in front of the entire company. Where Dorsey was often quiet and conflict-averse, Noto was hard-charging and opinion-ated. He had joined Twitter after several high-profile stops, first as a well-respected Wall Street analyst at Goldman Sachs, then as the CFO of the National Football League, where some speculated that he might one day make a good commissioner. At the end of Twitter's leadership week, with a slumping stock price and executives racing for the exits, Noto had little patience for the employee's question. Even the *idea* of sim-ply giving up and selling the company had left him personally offended.

"Nobody is coming to save us," he barked back. "It's just fucking us!"

Noto's Tea Time tirade quickly became a rallying cry for Twitter employees. They jumped at the idea of adopting a new underdog mental-ity. They tweeted using the hashtag #itsjustfuckingus and made printouts with the phrase to hang around the office and in the elevators. Much to the HR department's dismay, somebody even ordered #itsjustfuckingus stickers to pass around to employees. A week that had started with the doom-and-gloom departures of several key executives had ended on a more positive, combative note.

Two months later, Dorsey was in New York to celebrate Twitter's ten-year anniversary with a special appearance on NBC's *Today* show. Dressed in a trim black sweater and black jeans paired with bright orange leather sneakers, Dorsey stood in the "Orange Room" across from Matt Lauer and Carson Daly, his sleeves rolled up and a coffee cup in hand. Lauer wanted to know about one of Twitter's new, big product changes, and jumped in with a question about Twitter's 140-character limit.

"A hundred and forty characters, the limit," Lauer said. "Is it staying? And if it's going away—when?"

News had leaked months earlier that Twitter was planning to remove the limit to give people more space to share their thoughts. It was considered a pretty bold move. The 140-character limit had been around since Twitter's founding, and short, pithy tweets had become a signature part of Twitter's identity. Internally, a team of employees using the code name "Beyond 140" had already built several iterations of a feature to expand the length of tweets, including one that gave people 10,000 characters to post. The product had been near the top of Twitter's priority list, and the group thought that everything was close to launch.

But then Lauer asked his question.

"It's staying," Dorsey said with a chuckle. "It's a good constraint for us and it allows for of-the-moment brevity."

The Beyond 140 team was shocked when they found out that Dorsey had apparently killed their project on live TV. They later learned that Dorsey had gotten cold feet after initial news of the change had sparked lots of user criticism. Twitter would eventually launch Beyond 140, but not for another twenty months.

The incident highlighted a major dilemma happening inside Twitter when Dorsey first returned. Everyone agreed that Twitter needed drastic change to jump-start user growth, but there was also a fear of straying too far from what had made the service popular to begin with. It was a constant tug-of-war that slowed everything down and highlighted one of Dorsey's biggest flaws as a manager: that he didn't like making decisions. Dorsey had matured significantly since the last time he was in charge at Twitter, but he had a hands-off management style that infuriated people. Dorsey would rarely speak in meetings, often just sitting and listening, occasionally chiming in to ask a high-level or abstract question. ("Why?") Executives would often leave these meetings unsure about what to do next or how Dorsey actually felt about whatever it was they were working on.

Even when Twitter did finally ship things, users were quick to complain publicly and stridently, which gave employees pause. A month earlier, Twitter had started using an algorithm to determine the order that tweets would appear in users' feeds. It was a strategy that had been incredibly successful at Facebook but was a departure from Twitter's reverse-chronological feed, which always showed the most recent tweets first. Users were so upset that the hashtag #RIPTwitter started trending on the service. Lauer had even alluded to the backlash during Dorsey's *Today* show appearance, asking whether he thought Twitter would survive until its fifteenth birthday. "We'll be here on the twentieth," Dorsey replied.

While Twitter was still struggling to figure out how to change the product, Dorsey was at least homing in on a clearer idea of what Twitter was for. Throughout his first six months on the job, Dorsey and the rest of Twitter's executives started repeating one word over and over again: *live*. "Live commentary, live connections, live conversations," Dorsey said during one of the company's earnings calls. "We really want to focus on live because we think it's the fastest and easiest way to understand the power of Twitter and get into it," he added. Twitter's reputation as the service for posting about your breakfast or sharing the music you were listening to had long since evolved. It was now the place you went to find the score of the game as it was happening, or to talk about who got snubbed during the Oscars while the show was still on-air. The company was trying to lean harder into that new reality. On Twitter's earnings call in February 2016, executives used the word *live* 36 times in just 54 minutes. In April, it rebranded itself on Apple's App Store; instead of appearing under the "social networking" category alongside rivals like Facebook and Instagram, Twitter switched to the "news" category, further signaling its renewed purpose.

This fresh focus got a major jolt in the spring of 2016 when Twitter shockingly won the streaming rights to ten of the NFL's *Thursday Night Football* games. NFL streaming rights were both incredibly expensive and difficult to come by. Broadcast networks CBS and NBC had paid $450 million apiece for the right to broadcast Thursday night games in 2016 and 2017, or roughly 20 percent of Twitter's annual revenue. But the NFL had carved out separate rights for a streaming deal with a digital partner, and Twitter had an advantage that other tech companies didn't: Noto, Twitter's CFO, had also been CFO of the NFL a few years earlier. He pitched NFL commissioner Roger Goodell on the idea of a tie-up over lunch at the Yale Club in New York City, and later followed up with a formal bid that included a general promise that Twitter would build the streaming product however the NFL wanted. Twitter beat out Facebook and Amazon to win the streaming rights for a paltry $10 million.

The deal quickly pushed Twitter into a new direction that made the company look and feel a lot more like a traditional media company. By late summer, Twitter had an entire lineup of live sports and shows you could watch inside the app, including some professional hockey and baseball games, plus other programs with partners like CBS, Bloomberg, and the NBA. Outside of *Thursday Night Football*, few of the videos Twitter streamed were considered *must-watch TV* that people would schedule their evening around. But Twitter rode the powerful wave created by the NFL, and the company's sales team started dangling *Thursday Night Football* games like a carrot in front of advertisers. Anyone who wanted to buy ads to run alongside the NFL games also had to buy other, less popular ad placements. Twitter's $10 million deal with the NFL led to more than $50 million in revenue.

The company also came out with a new marketing campaign to try to capitalize on the renewed strategy. Twitter ran video ads that tried to explain what the service was for—and how it was different than other social networks, like Facebook. The ads jumped between video clips of

Donald Trump and Hillary Clinton giving campaign speeches, LeBron James blocking a shot during the NBA playoffs, and Black Lives Matter protesters. "What's everyone talking about?" the video's narrator asked. "What's trending? How did it start? When will it end?" The idea was that Twitter was *the* place you went to discover what was happening in the world around you. It was a free global news source in your pocket. The campaign got positive reviews. For perhaps the first time in company history, ten years after it launched, Twitter had finally articulated what the service was actually for.

Inside Twitter, though, the transition toward streaming was bumpier than most people realized. While Noto was pushing hard to turn Twitter into a digital television, other top executives had been against the NFL deal from the start, including Chief Technology Officer Adam Messinger who oversaw product and engineering, and Kayvon Beykpour, who ran Twitter's livestreaming video app, Periscope.

It wasn't that Beykpour didn't like live video; Periscope, which he'd founded years earlier and later sold to Twitter for $120 million, allowed anyone to stream video directly from their phone. He was a huge believer that live video belonged on Twitter. But what made Twitter (and Periscope) unique was that it felt raw and authentic. Becoming yet another place to stream packaged NFL games, on the other hand, felt both boring and off-brand. An even bigger issue, though, was that Beykpour and Noto disagreed on the product details for this new idea. Beykpour wanted to use Periscope's streaming technology to power NFL games and make sure that all of Twitter's livestreaming features were consistent. Noto wasn't convinced Periscope could handle it.

Dorsey settled the dispute by largely stepping aside and giving Noto free rein. The CFO even spun up his own product team inside Twitter to build the streaming feature. Beykpour and Messinger weren't thrilled. Not only did Twitter now have two completely distinct teams building streaming features, but Noto, a finance guy with no product experience, was suddenly leading the biggest product effort in company history.

Shareholders seemed similarly blasé about the streaming strategy. When the football season kicked off, Twitter's stock price was still
down more than 30 percent since Dorsey's return as CEO. Twitter was
redefining itself, but pressure was building to move quicker. The executive team and the board started discussing the harsh reality of more
layoffs, and maybe even selling off parts of the company that weren't
making money, like its stand-alone video app, Vine. Even with the NFL
and a slew of other partners on board, it seemed like no one outside of
Twitter was sold on the company's potential.

Well, almost no one. It turns out Twitter still had one major booster,
and he was eager to make a deal.

Like most billionaires, Marc Benioff didn't lose very often. The Salesforce
CEO ran one of the most successful tech companies in the world, which
he founded in 1999 and had since grown into a $50 billion behemoth.
Salesforce's success had made Benioff incredibly rich, and he knew how
to enjoy the perks of a $4 billion fortune. He owned a five-acre estate
on the Big Island in Hawaii and multiple homes in San Francisco's ritzy
Sea Cliff neighborhood, which was across town from the local children's
hospital that bore his name thanks to a $100 million donation. In 2014,
Fortune readers selected Benioff as the magazine's "Businessperson of
the Year." Benioff lived a good life.

But in the summer of 2016, Benioff was furious. A few weeks earlier,
he had been spurned when he tried to buy LinkedIn, the professional social
network that instead sold to rival Microsoft for an eye-popping $26 billion
in cash. Benioff had made the decision difficult at least, bidding up the
price repeatedly before eventually losing out despite a final offer that was
actually a few bucks per share higher than Microsoft's bid. The rejection
left Benioff desperate for another deal, and that summer he texted Jack
Dorsey, whose own Sea Cliff mansion was visible from one of Benioff's
windows, and inquired about buying Twitter instead.

To a lot of people, including many of Benioff's top lieutenants, a Twitter-Salesforce marriage didn't make much sense. Salesforce was an enterprise software company, meaning it didn't build products for every-day internet users like Twitter or Facebook, but instead made a killing selling software that other businesses used to manage their sales and customer relationships. It was a lucrative business, but not necessarily an obvious fit for a social network where people posted about politics and trolled celebrities. To Benioff, though, a Twitter-Salesforce marriage was all that made sense. He started calling Twitter an "unpolished jewel" and thought Twitter was a perfect way for Salesforce's clients to get feedback from their customers. Twitter was sitting on a "treasure trove of data" that businesses could use to improve everything from their marketing strat-egy to product development, he thought. "Plus, Twitter was struggling," he would later write in his memoir, "and the way I saw it, the merging of our two companies would be beneficial for us both."

Benioff had approached Twitter first, but surprisingly, he wasn't the only suitor. Shortly after Benioff texted Dorsey, Disney also approached Twitter about a deal. Disney executives had watched in earnest over the summer as Twitter tried to reposition itself as a live video service and thought that the company might be the solution to one of its newest problems. Netflix and Hulu were proving that streaming video directly to viewers was the future, and while Disney owned some of the most valuable video content in the world, it had largely relied on partners to deliver it into people's homes. Buying Twitter would cut out the middle-man, giving Disney the technology to stream its catalog of movies, TV shows, and live sports directly to its audience. Disney CEO Bob Iger had considered building his own streaming platform, but his chief strategy officer, Kevin Mayer, estimated that it could take five years. Buying a company like Twitter, while more expensive, would expedite that time-line significantly. Plus, the Disney executives had an in: Dorsey sat on Disney's board of directors and considered Iger a mentor.

Dorsey and the rest of Twitter's board weren't looking for a buyer when Salesforce and Disney first approached, but the idea of finally selling the company wasn't a bad one given the way things had been going. A sale would relieve the constant pressure from Twitter's slumping stock price, and might help the company avoid a second round of job cuts, which no one was excited about.

Both suitors floated unofficial bids: Salesforce was considering a price around $29 per share, which valued Twitter just north of $20 billion; Disney came in a few dollars lower, somewhere in the mid to high 20s, closer to $17 or $18 billion. Twitter's market cap earlier that summer had fluctuated between $12 billion and $14 billion, which made both options seem appealing. Twitter and its board hired bankers from Goldman Sachs and Allen & Company to advise them on what to do. As fiduciaries, the board had a responsibility to Twitter's shareholders to look for the best possible deal, so they decided to run a formal "process" and see if anyone else was interested in buying the company.

They got a lot of nibbles. Twitter's executive team, including Dorsey, Noto, COO Adam Bain, and general counsel Vijaya Gadde, met with a laundry list of prominent tech executives over several weeks. There was Jeff Blackburn from Amazon, who didn't seem that interested, and Eddy Cue and Adrian Perica from Apple, who seemed very interested but couldn't figure out how Twitter fit into Apple's broader strategy. Twitter chairman Omid Kordestani spoke with YouTube boss Susan Wojcicki and other Google execs, old friends and colleagues who were also interested but worried about antitrust issues. Brian Roberts at Comcast and Steve Burke from NBCUniversal took meetings but were never serious buyers. Microsoft CEO Satya Nadella and his top dealmaker Peggy Johnson also met with Twitter but had just bought LinkedIn for $26 billion; Twitter, perhaps, was a few months late.

It became clear after weeks of meetings that Salesforce and Disney were the only two serious contenders. What wasn't clear was whether Dorsey actually wanted to sell. The Twitter CEO was a relatively small shareholder—he controlled just over 3 percent of Twitter's voting power, which meant he couldn't make a decision on his own even if he wanted to. But as a cofounder and the recently appointed CEO, his voice carried more weight than anybody's, and it was apparent to those around him that Dorsey wasn't excited about the Salesforce bid. Benioff's vision for Twitter as a data gold mine to fuel better customer service felt like a sad reality for a product that had once helped orchestrate uprisings in the Middle East and reshaped the global media industry. Dorsey wasn't sold on the idea, and his indifference was shared by several other senior members of Twitter's team and board.

Almost everyone, though, liked the idea of a Twitter-Disney deal, including Dorsey. He'd joined Disney's board in 2013 and was a huge fan of Iger. If Twitter could live inside Disney, it would likely mean Dorsey could stay at the helm but without the added pressure of running a public company. The idea of Twitter joining the likes of Pixar, ESPN, and Lucasfilm under the broader Disney umbrella sounded really appealing.

Then, after months of secret meetings and dinners and brainstorming, everything abruptly unraveled. The same week that Twitter's bankers were expecting formal bids, both Disney and Salesforce balked. Benioff had spent weeks getting blowback from Salesforce's investors and his own management team, who all thought buying Twitter was a massive mistake. After news of a possible deal leaked, Salesforce's stock fell 8 percent over a two-week span. Benioff couldn't justify the deal and, despite his initial outreach, chose to save his money and walk away.

Iger got closer, and even had approval from Disney's board of directors to finalize a deal. After spending a final weekend thinking it over, though, he had a change of heart. "The troubles were greater than I wanted to take on, greater than I thought it was responsible for us to take on," he'd later say. More specifically, Iger started to fret about the prevalence of hate speech on Twitter—the racists and the trolls and the spam that had earned Twitter a reputation as being one of the internet's most widely used cesspools. Disney had spent decades cultivating a family-friendly brand; it was the home of Mickey and Minnie and Pluto. Twitter would put all that in jeopardy. "The nastiness," Iger confessed, "is extraordinary." Iger picked up the phone and called Dorsey with the

news. Twitter's CEO was stunned. After months of meetings and nego-
tiations, both Disney and Salesforce were out.

A few weeks later, Noto flew back to Los Angeles for a last-ditch
effort to bring Disney back to the table. It almost worked. The two sides
discussed a second, lowball bid around $21 per share, or a total price of
about $15 billion. Disney, it seemed, was interested to see just how des-
perate Twitter was, and the number was so low that some on Twitter's
board didn't even take the discussions seriously. During a board meeting to talk about it, Kordestani asked everyone in the room to weigh in
with their opinion. Given how intimately involved he'd been in the process, Noto was in the room and shared his feelings. "Tell them to fuck
off," he said. The deal talks were officially over. Twitter was on its own.

After months of distractions and now without a buyer, Twitter's
management team pivoted. It was time to cut costs. Twitter had never
been profitable in its ten-year existence, and turning a profit suddenly
became a top priority to win back investors and hopefully jump-start
the stock price. On October 27, for the second year in a row, Twitter laid
off roughly 350 employees, or 9 percent of the staff, and closed several
international offices.

In a decision that would be second-guessed for years to come, Twitter also shut down Vine, its video app that had popularized the concept
of short, bite-sized videos. Dorsey had discovered Vine years earlier
when he was still Twitter's chairman and pushed hard for the company
to acquire it. The app was a cultural phenomenon, turning hundreds of
unknown internet creators into stars with massive followings and lucrative brand deals. But Twitter never prioritized Vine's business. The service never made meaningful money for the company, and the Vine team
never built features so that popular users could get paid for their videos. Vine's internet stars soon left for YouTube and Instagram, where it
was easier to make money. By the time Vine was shuttered, most of its
homegrown creators were already gone, and Twitter was left wondering,
What if? A few years later, another app called TikTok would become

one of the most popular social media apps in the world by focusing on
similar short-form videos.

The mood inside Twitter was as dark and depressing as it had ever
been. Bain, the COO, had spent the past three months imagining a world
where Twitter was part of a larger company, shielded by the pressures
of Wall Street. When the deals fell apart and Twitter had to cut more
jobs, he was deflated. After more than six years at the company, Bain
left Twitter just a few weeks after the layoffs.

It had been almost a year since Noto had dropped an f-bomb at Tea
Time, telling Twitter's employees that there was no one coming to save
the company. At the time, that statement was mostly motivational, but it
had also been prophetic. Twitter was indeed on its own. If it was going
to turn things around, it would have to do so as an independent company
with Jack Dorsey as the CEO.

As 2016 came to a close, Dorsey spent time reflecting on a difficult
year. Not everything had been bad. The NFL deal had elevated Twitter's profile, and Dorsey was making quick work on a personal project
of his—remaking Twitter's board of directors. The board morphed significantly after Dorsey returned as CEO as he worked to install new
members whom he trusted and enjoyed working with. In just eighteen
months, Twitter added five new board members, all of them vetted and
approved by the CEO.

Those victories, though, were hard to appreciate after a failed sale,
more layoffs, and the decision to shut down Vine. On New Year's Eve,
Dorsey sent an email to the whole company to share his reflections.
The subject line just said "Trust." He thanked everyone for their effort
and sacrifice and acknowledged Twitter's yearlong attempt to explain
why people should use the product to begin with. This focus and dedication to "live" was working, he promised. Then Dorsey got critical.
"We aren't moving fast enough and we aren't trusting ourselves enough

to show real courage," he wrote, blaming himself for the same short-comings and adding that Twitter needed to take bigger swings even if it meant potential failure.

"I want Twitter to be the most essential news and talk network *ever,*" he wrote. "And there's never been a better time. Look at what's happening. Look at the trends. Trust is eroding. Trust in the media. Trust in the news. Trust in our governments. Trust in each other. The only thing that builds trust is openness."

Look at what's happening.

Dorsey didn't mention Donald Trump by name, but he didn't have to. Everyone knew what the CEO was alluding to. Trump's shocking victory over Hillary Clinton in the U.S. presidential election a few months earlier had thrown the country into chaos. Trump was already one of the service's loudest and most controversial users, and now he was president of the United States. Twitter's role on the global stage was about to change forever, and Dorsey's job was about to get a whole lot harder.

THREE

@REALDONALDTRUMP

A s Donald Trump strolled through Twitter's New York City office in a dark navy suit and a powder blue tie, he definitely had the look of a presidential candidate. He just wasn't acting like one.

It was September 21, 2015, just a few months after declaring his campaign for president. Trump was in the Chelsea section of Manhattan for a live Twitter Q&A with his 4.2 million followers. The visit was part of a broader campaign strategy to reach voters through his favorite social network. Several Twitter employees were on hand to show him around and help with the logistics. The group was generally happy to have him there. Twitter had entire sales and partnerships teams dedicated to getting politicians onto the service to tweet and, hopefully, spend money on campaign ads. No one knew what to make of Trump's run for president, or whether those ad dollars would eventually come. He was polling well, but he was also an outsider—a reality TV star who didn't come from the traditional Washington establishment and certainly didn't speak like a politician. It seemed most likely that his campaign would fade as the race wore on, but that was fine. Trump was still a prolific tweeter and understood the service better than all the other candidates, which made him a fun guest at the office.

Unlike other politicians who had visited Twitter over the years, including folks like Secretary of State Hillary Clinton and Senator John McCain,

Trump wasn't rolling with a large posse of aides and didn't make idle chatter about Twitter's operations, its corporate culture, or how many employees were on H-1B visas. Instead, as he walked past glass-walled conference rooms and Twitter's cafeteria stocked with free snacks, he dissected the building like a New York City real estate developer. Who had supplied the concrete? he asked. What was the square footage? Trump fixated on the fire doors, a brand that he had used in one of his own New York City buildings and found to be inadequate. He promised to get Twitter the number for his "fire door guy." As the crew moved through the building to a conference room for the Q&A, one of Twitter's political lobbyists, Maryam Mujica, mentioned her father had lived in Trump Tower when she was growing up and that she'd visited the building often. "Isn't it a fantastic building? It's the best, it's the best," Trump remarked before unintentionally embarrassing her. "She clearly has a lot of money," he said to the group.

During the Q&A, employees asked Trump questions that had been submitted on Twitter and recorded his answers so he could post the videos to his account, re-recording if he didn't like the delivery on the first take. He took questions from all over the political map.

"I will totally protect Israel. They've been let down badly by the Obama administration."

"First thing I'd do on my first day as president is close up our borders so that illegal immigrants cannot come into our country. We have tremendous problems."

"Very pro–Second Amendment."

At the end of the visit, Twitter's employees took a group photo with Trump in the conference room, some flashing Trump's signature thumbs-up to the camera with several others wearing red or black MAKE AMERICA GREAT AGAIN hats. The Twitter employees went home that night assuming it would probably be the most they'd ever deal with Trump. He was popular, sure, but he wasn't going to win.

In the run-up to the 2016 presidential election, Twitter's government and elections teams shared a digital manual with U.S. political candidates running for office. The *Twitter Government and Elections Handbook* was 133 pages long and included everything from advice on how to tweet before and after a debate to how to protect your account from getting hacked. At its most basic level, it was a guide explaining how Twitter worked and what it was for. Tips included things like "be personal in your tweets," hold Twitter Q&As to interact with followers, and "be bold and engaging."

Donald Trump embodied the Twitter handbook better than any other political candidate in history. He'd joined Twitter in 2009 to help promote his reality TV show, *The Apprentice*, and learned over time the value of having a free megaphone to reach millions of people. Trump tweeted constantly, often dictating tweets to his aides, or posting them personally from his home or one of his many golf courses. He used his Twitter account to promote his TV interviews and campaign events and often retweeted his followers and fans, which was a smart way to encourage more people to reply to him on the off-chance he might blast their post to his millions of followers. Most importantly, his tweets felt *authentic*. He used ALL CAPS and exclamation points and made up his own hashtags; reading his tweets felt like tapping directly into his brain. If you were looking for the kind of watered-down, PR-approved statements that most political candidates offered up, you wouldn't find them on the account of @realDonaldTrump.

At first, the reality of having a leading political candidate adopt the service so faithfully seemed like a major win for Dorsey and Twitter. Trump's freewheeling style was a perfect fit for Twitter's short, pithy format, and his account served as a kind of blueprint for other politicians hoping to stand out in the noisy world of social media. Trump's Twitter following nearly doubled from 3 million when he announced his candidacy in June 2015 to 5.7 million just six months later. Just as important was that Trump's engagement, which is the number of likes and retweets he got on his posts, was blowing up at an exponential rate. He was getting more attention and distribution on Twitter than ever before. In January 2016, Trump was being retweeted 28 times more often than he was one year earlier. He loved the attention, fascinated by the ability to measure his growing popularity in real time as the notifications poured in.

The problem was Trump's very popular tweets could also be pretty nasty. He attacked his political opponents with a vengeance, ruthlessly mocking anyone who criticized him, and pushed the boundaries of basic decorum on a daily basis. Former Florida governor Jeb Bush was "a basket case," a "loser," and "really pathetic." Texas senator Ted Cruz was a "cheater," a "liar," and "a true low life pol!" He tweeted that if you listen to Republican candidate and businesswoman Carly Fiorina "for more than ten minutes straight, you develop a massive headache." Trump loved to give his opponents nicknames, which he would tweet out regularly to his growing audience. Cruz was "Lyin' Ted," and Florida senator Marco Rubio was "Little Marco." Nothing, it seemed, was off-limits, including attacks on women he found unattractive, which he did often in the years before his candidacy. He once tweeted that Arianna Huffington, who founded the media outlet Huffington Post, was "unattractive both inside and out" and that "I understand why her former husband left her for a man." When he saw eighty-one-year-old actress Kim Novak on his television in 2014, he tweeted that she should "sue her plastic surgeon!" The retort cut Novak so deeply she didn't leave her house for days.

Inside Twitter, employees watched with unease as Trump's campaign picked up steam. Twitter workers were predominantly liberal; almost 93 percent of employee political donations went to Democratic candidates in 2016. The vast majority of employees probably wouldn't vote for Trump anyway. But his tweets were also morally repugnant and offensive to most Twitter employees who were proud to work for a company that was openly focused on improving diversity and social issues. Twitter had resource groups for Black, Latin, and LGBTQ employees and set public hiring goals to diversify the company's workforce; Dorsey, the CEO, wore T-shirts emblazoned with the hashtag #StayWoke, and had marched a few years prior in Ferguson, Missouri, after police officers there shot and killed an eighteen-year-old black man, Michael Brown. One of Dorsey's friends, DeRay Mckesson, was an unofficial leader of the Black Lives Matter movement; when he was arrested during a protest in the summer of 2016, Dorsey emailed the company with pictures of Mckesson being handcuffed in a #StayWoke Twitter T-shirt. "It's important everyone at Twitter feels safe and supported," Dorsey wrote at the time, recommending folks reach out to the HR department if needed.

Trump, meanwhile, was the antithesis of Twitter's "woke" corporate culture. He openly objectified women and made veiled, racist comments about immigrants and other minorities. When asked about his stance on same-sex marriage in 2015, Trump responded by saying, "I'm [for] traditional marriage." Trump had tweeted ugly things long before he showed up at Twitter's office in September, but he'd felt like a long shot during that visit. He seemed like a reality TV businessman just looking for a little notoriety. But by the summer of 2016, everything had changed. Trump had won the Republican nomination, rising to prominence thanks in part to a service that Twitter employees built and supported day in and day out. For many of them, it was an uncomfortable reality.

Twitter had a set of rules that users had to follow to keep their accounts active, which included policies against posting "targeted abuse or harassment" of another user. Twitter had struggled for years to walk the thin line between upholding the freedom for people to say whatever they wanted and ensuring other people weren't bullied off the service entirely. "Freedom of expression means little as our underlying philosophy if we continue to allow voices to be silenced because they are afraid to speak up," Twitter's general counsel, Vijaya Gadde, wrote in *The Washington Post* in 2015. There was no doubt Trump was harassing and insulting other Twitter users, but the company's rules were vague and seemed to be intended for more egregious attacks on ordinary users, like someone using a racial or ethnic slur. They certainly hadn't been written for the purpose of policing schoolyard taunts between celebrity politicians.

Dorsey didn't seem bothered by Twitter's role in distributing Trump's rhetoric. He thought it was important that people hear directly from Trump.

If anything, his Twitter adoption highlighted the product's importance in the world of global politics even if he did push the envelope. Dorsey argued that the point of Twitter was to give people a chance to speak and let the world decide what messages to amplify. "A platform has to be free to every opinion and every voice and I think we need to hear them all," he said in June 2016 from the stage at Code Conference, a popular tech conference where he wore the #StayWoke T-shirt. "I think we need to hear every extreme to find the balance." The thought of using his role as CEO to silence Trump made Dorsey very uncomfortable.

That outward confidence hid the reality that Twitter was navigating uncharted waters. The service had never had a user quite like Trump; most Twitter trolls didn't have millions of followers, and definitely weren't running for president of the United States. For the most part, the company didn't know what to do with him or how to handle his posts within the confines of their existing rulebook. So they mostly left him alone.

As the campaign got closer to election night, though, Twitter stumbled. In August 2016, the Trump campaign committed major advertising money to Twitter. It signed a contract to spend $5 million on Twitter ads in exchange for some discounts and special ad units that Twitter's sales team cooked up. (Hillary Clinton's campaign was offered a similar package, but declined.) Included in the ad package was a set of "custom hashtag emojis," which Twitter could set up so that anytime somebody tweeted a specific hashtag, an emoji would be automatically added to the end of it. These hashtag emojis had been around for a few years, and Twitter often used them for major sporting events. If someone tweeted #USA during the 2014 World Cup, for example, an American flag emoji was automatically added to the tweet. The custom hashtags were so popular that the company began selling them for over $1 million to major advertisers, such as Coca-Cola and Starbucks.

Most brands that paid for these campaigns used innocuous emojis, like their corporate logo, for example. Trump, of course, pushed the envelope. Ahead of the first presidential debate against Hillary Clinton in September, Trump's campaign put in their order for a custom emoji to go along with the hashtag #CrookedHillary. As part of the ad package, Twitter employees created the custom emoji, and the company sent the Trump campaign a series of options, including a hand holding a green moneybag. The Trump team didn't think the emoji was provocative enough, and asked Twitter to try again. This time Twitter drummed up an emoji of a stick figure running away with a bag of money. "Sure, it was more aggressive and eye-catching," wrote Gary Coby, the digital director for Trump's campaign, "but that was the goal." Everything seemed set.

A few days before the debate, Twitter called the Trump campaign with news that the emoji had been blocked by senior leadership. According to Coby, Twitter didn't want to "accuse someone of committing a crime they did not commit or were not under investigation for," and feared legal retaliation from the Clinton campaign. Coby, upset and incredulous, pulled the ad campaign entirely.

A few weeks later, he tried again, this time before the second presidential debate in early October. Twitter's team came up with another set of custom emoji options to go along with the hashtag #CrookedHillary, including a moneybag with wings on it, which Coby described as representing "govt waste and money flying away from taxpayers." The hashtag and emoji were approved by Twitter's policy and legal teams, and Twitter even prepared its PR team to handle a media blitz around the emoji. The company wanted to showcase the kinds of ads that marketers could buy on the service.

A few nights before the second debate, Coby got another call. Twitter's senior leaders had again squashed the emoji campaign, and this time the explanation was different. Twitter executives were worried because there was no way to distinguish a hashtag emoji that was an ad from one that had been created by Twitter for free, like the country flags during the World Cup. The company feared that users would see the #CrookedHillary emoji and assume Twitter was behind the promotion. Dorsey and Twitter's COO, Adam Bain, got on a call with Coby and a livid Sean Spicer, communications director for the Republican National Committee, to explain the company's thinking and announce that it was ending hashtag emoji ads for all politicians moving forward. "We told them it was BS and what they were doing with a public platform was incredibly reckless and dangerous," Coby later wrote. "We voiced that it was clearly a political move and telling us otherwise was just insulting." The Trump campaign pulled several of its planned advertisements for the final weeks before the election, and ultimately paid Twitter millions less than the $5 million it had originally committed to.

For Dorsey and Twitter, it was an embarrassing and costly introduction to dealing with Trump. It was also a reminder of the power it suddenly had when it came to global politics. Twitter's concern that the promoted hashtag looked like a company endorsement was a valid one, but Twitter had also been naïve. It never considered that an advertiser might use a paid emoji to target or attack a political rival—at least not until Trump showed up. It was the first time that Trump's aggressive approach to campaigning and politicking forced Twitter to change its company policies, but it wouldn't be the last.

Trump was elected president of the United States on November 8, 2016, shocking the world and devastating many of Twitter's employees. Trump had bullied, attacked, and belittled his opponents all the way to the White House, and he'd largely done so using Twitter and Facebook. By election night, Trump had 13 million Twitter followers—more than four times as many as when he started his campaign. He proved the ugly reality that controversy and conflict were a great way to succeed on Twitter.

The next morning, Dorsey emailed employees.

Subject: Yesterday
There are a lot of emotions after the US Election. Let's show empathy and support for each other. It you need to take time for yourself to process everything, please do that.

A lot of people are focusing on who won, but that's done. I think we should focus on why. A vote is a voice and a desire to be heard. What are the underlying root causes people are facing? What are the issues in this country we need to fix? And how can we as individuals, and as an organization of individuals, help? Let's listen, learn, and unify.

Twitter is even more critical today than it was yesterday. We have a role to continue amplifying people's voices. We have a role to help people find and speak truth to power. And we have a role to provide a venue for dialogue that empowers people.

And I want to be clear about my own stance and what matters to me. All people are equal. I will fight every day for our shared humanity, and constantly seek to provide for our common good here in the US, and for all people. And I commit to using my position and self to speak truth to power, and call-out and fight injustice wherever I see it. I will be more vocal.

We're all in this together. If you want to talk about anything, I'm available and always listening (and learning).

Thank you all,

Jack

The following month, the president-elect hosted several prominent tech and business executives at Trump Tower in New York City to discuss working together after he was sworn in. The attendees included some of the most powerful people in the world: Amazon CEO Jeff Bezos sat next to Google cofounder Larry Page, who sat next to Facebook COO Sheryl Sandberg. Apple CEO Tim Cook sat to Trump's left, and just a few feet away sat Tesla CEO Elon Musk.

Dorsey didn't receive an invite. Twitter was undeniably smaller than most of the other companies in attendance that day, but few were more influential, especially for Trump. Back at Twitter's office, some on the team believed that Dorsey had been snubbed because of the #CrookedHillary advertising incident. Trump and his aides clearly believed Twitter was biased against him, and real or perceived, it sure seemed like Twitter was being punished in turn. Spicer, who helped arrange the meeting, denied the accusation that Dorsey had been snubbed. "The conference table," he said, "was only so big."

Dorsey liked to say that Twitter was a reflection of the world. It was, after all, "what's happening," and in 2017 the world became more complicated and divisive than it had been in years. Trump entered the White House as the most politically polarizing president in decades. His decision within days of his inauguration to close American borders to several predominantly Muslim countries escalated an already simmering culture war.

Any hope that Trump would tone down his tweets once he became *President* Trump were quickly dashed as he used the service to lash out at anybody who criticized him. He tweeted that mainstream media outlets like *The New York Times* and CNN were "the enemy of the American People!" and used Twitter to announce a ban on transgender people serving in the military, claiming that they would be a "burden." In August, when a group of white supremacists marched in Charlottesville, Virginia, and one of them rammed his car into a group of counterprotesters, killing a woman, Trump said there were "very fine people on both sides" of the incident. The comments earned a tweet of praise from David Duke, a former grand wizard of the Ku Klux Klan.

The tweets were causing anxiety inside Twitter's headquarters, but Trump wasn't the company's only problem. Twitter executives were also coming to terms with the reality that a Russian propaganda firm with ties to the Kremlin had used its service to try to influence the 2016 election in Trump's favor. Russia's Internet Research Agency had created nearly 4,000 Twitter accounts before the election to sow discord among voters, mostly pushing pro-Trump messaging. It did the same on Facebook, too. Around 1.4 million people interacted with the accounts on Twitter, and some were even retweeted by Trump's sons and other members of his campaign staff. Twitter didn't even realize the accounts existed until after the election, at which point the only thing the company could do was conduct an autopsy.

A team of Twitter lawyers and policy officials coordinated by Colin Crowell, the company's vice president of public policy, spent much of 2017 trying to understand the gravity of the Russian campaign. In San Francisco, an impromptu "war room" was set up in a vacant conference room on the fifth floor to scour the site for Russian bot accounts and figure out what had happened. Twitter also had to deal with the fallout from a very unhappy Congress. When Twitter in September delivered its initial set of findings about the Russian campaign to U.S. senator Mark Warner, the top Democrat on the Senate Intelligence Committee, Warner called the report "deeply disappointing." Twitter had only presented a small part of its findings, and much less than what Facebook had handed over to the senator's office. Warner was none too pleased, calling it "an enormous lack of understanding from the Twitter team of how serious this issue is."

Between Trump's constant tweeting and Twitter's unexpected role in a Russian election scandal, employees were losing their minds. Like the rest of the country, Twitter's workforce had spent the first nine months of Trump's presidency fixated on everything that he tweeted, often discussing his latest posts on internal message threads and debating the company's role as Trump's favorite broadcast channel. Almost nobody understood all of Twitter's rules, which were at times purposefully vague to give the company more leeway to make decisions on a case-by-case basis, but Trump's first few months in office had put the Twitter rulebook under a microscope. Trump's opponents looked for reasons that he should be punished or suspended for his often ugly and controversial tweets.

Writing and enforcing the rules for Twitter users was a generally terrible and thankless job. Inside Twitter, that job belonged to Del Harvey, who ran the company's Trust and Safety group that was responsible for, in her words, "predicting and designing for catastrophes." In practice that meant creating rules to weed out tweets peddling child nudity, terrorism propaganda, and various forms of abuse and harassment. Anyone with an email could create an anonymous Twitter account, and that ano-nymity empowered people to say some pretty ugly things. Before joining Twitter, Harvey spent years catching child predators. In her twenties, she joined a group called Perverted Justice that posed as young kids online to lure sexual pedophiles into a trap. A few years later, Harvey, who had a petite, slender frame, worked as a decoy to catch bad guys on NBC's *To Catch a Predator*. Harvey wasn't even her real name; she used an alias for fear of retaliation.

When Harvey joined Twitter in 2008, the company subscribed to an "everything goes" mentality around user speech. Former CEO Dick Costolo famously referred to Twitter as the "free speech wing of the free speech party," and the company regularly went to court to protect the identity of users when governments came calling. In 2017, Harvey still mostly subscribed to this mindset, as did her boss, General Coun-sel Vijaya Gadde.

Twitter's reputation as a free speech haven was partly what pushed Gadde to join the company in 2011. Born in India, she spent most of her childhood in East Texas and then New Jersey, where she was almost always the only Indian student in her class. "You feel voiceless," she said years later about her childhood. Twitter, by contrast, "gives you a voice and gives you a community and gives you power." Gadde went to Cor-nell University for undergrad, then New York University Law School before joining the Silicon Valley law firm Wilson Sonsini Goodrich & Rosati where she worked on corporate law. After a decade at the firm, she joined Twitter. By the time Trump was elected, Gadde was Twitter's general counsel, reporting directly to Dorsey, and was arguably the most influential person internally when it came to setting and enforcing the company's speech policies. She was also almost universally in favor of leaving Trump's tweets untouched.

But the factors that went into policing Twitter's users in 2017 were also very different than when either Harvey or Gadde had first joined the company. Twitter was now publicly traded with pressure to grow its user base and entice advertisers, which meant there was a near-constant need to clean up the service. The rulebook had expanded in recent years, and with it so had Twitter's problems. The more it tried to keep the service from devolving into a hell site of racism and harassment, the more it ventured away from its original free speech ideals.

Trump complicated everything. Never before had a legitimate world leader been such a publicly vocal troll, and his fans and supporters followed Trump's lead. He mastered the ability of walking right up to the line without crossing over it—at least as far as Twitter's rulebook was concerned. Twitter left his posts alone, to the dismay of users and critics who wanted the president to show a little more civility. Dorsey was rarely involved in decisions about whether a user crossed the line on Twitter. The CEO didn't like making decisions to begin with, and he generally let Harvey and Gadde handle those calls. Some believed that Dorsey was just passing the buck; Dorsey believed he was deferring to the experts.

As CEO, though, Dorsey and other senior members of Twitter's policy team were routinely pressured to do *something* about Trump. They were denounced both publicly by critics and internally by employees during all-hands discussions and over email. Dorsey was asked for his views on Trump almost every time he appeared in public. Despite his reputation as a woke, lefty tech CEO, Dorsey was stridently uncomfortable with the idea of taking down Trump's tweets. Not only did it bother Dorsey from a free-speech perspective, but the Twitter CEO was a huge proponent of transparency. (He even published notes from his weekly Staff meetings for the whole company to see and shared his performance reviews with employees.)

Hearing from Trump, even if it seemed inappropriate or divisive, was better than not having insight into what the president was thinking, Dorsey argued. "I believe it's really important to have these conversations out in the open, rather than have them behind closed doors," Dorsey said over the summer in 2017. "If we're all to suddenly take these platforms away, where does it go? What happens? It goes in the dark. And I just don't think that's good for anyone."

In September, Twitter faced its first major test when Trump posted a tweet about North Korean dictator Kim Jong-un. "Just heard Foreign Minister of North Korea speak at U.N.," Trump posted. "If he echoes thoughts of Little Rocket Man, they won't be around much longer!" Just one month earlier, Trump had threatened North Korea with "fire and fury" if Kim threatened the U.S., and now he was referring to the country's dictator as "little rocket man" in a tweet to millions of people. North Korea's foreign minister called the post a "clear declaration of war."

Trump's tweet appeared to be a clear-cut rule violation. The Twitter rules forbade tweets that included "threats of violence or promote violence," and it was hard to justify that Trump's tweet was anything but. Yet Twitter did nothing. The outcry to remove the tweet or even suspend Trump got so loud that the company posted a thread explaining its rationale for leaving the tweet up.

"We hold all accounts to the same Rules, and consider a number of factors when assessing whether Tweets violate our Rules," the company wrote from its @GlobalAffairs account. "Among the considerations is 'newsworthiness' and whether a Tweet is of public interest." Twitter added that a tweet's "newsworthiness" had long been a consideration internally when deciding if someone violated a rule, but that factor had never been shared publicly. Nobody outside of Twitter knew a "newsworthiness" policy even existed. "We need to do better on this," the company admitted.

Trump's critics were furious. If newsworthy posts couldn't be a violation, that meant that Trump would likely never be reprimanded for his tweets; everything that he posted was newsworthy by nature of his position. Even using Twitter to threaten another nation with nuclear war wasn't against Twitter's rules. Trump, it seemed, was untouchable.

FOUR

THE ROSE McGOWAN MEETING

J ack Dorsey's office was full. It was Friday the thirteenth of October, and most of Twitter's senior product and policy executives were standing around the conference table in Dorsey's office, nicknamed "Kingfisher." The CEO was leaning against the window, doing what he usually did during meetings: watching silently. For much of the summer and into the early fall, this group had met regularly to try to figure out how to make the service feel safer. They regularly displayed some of the site's most vulgar and offensive tweets onto the projector screen in Dorsey's office—everything from racist or antisemitic rants to clear examples of sexual harassment—and took turns reading them out loud. The tweets were examples of the kinds of things that everyone in the room knew didn't belong on Twitter, but that, for one reason or another, didn't violate the company's rules, which were still poorly defined. The exercise typically made people emotional; sometimes it led to tears.

On this particular Friday, the group was feeling anxious. The actress Rose McGowan had taken to Twitter that week to attack Hollywood producer Harvey Weinstein, whose repugnant and sexually abusive behavior toward women had been outlined in excruciating detail by both *The New York Times* and *The New Yorker* earlier that month. McGowan had received $100,000 from Weinstein years earlier as a settlement for "an episode in a hotel room," and would later claim on Twitter that he'd raped her. McGowan wasn't just going after Weinstein, though. She was also calling out her fellow actors, including Ben Affleck, who she claimed had turned a blind eye to Weinstein's predatory behavior.

Then the tweeting stopped. One of McGowan's posts included a screenshot that showed another person's phone number, which was a violation of Twitter's doxing policy, which forbade people from sharing someone else's private contact info without their consent. McGowan's account was suspended until she deleted the tweet.

McGowan was furious, posting the suspension email she got from Twitter on her Instagram account. "TWITTER HAS SUSPENDED ME," she wrote. "THERE ARE POWERFUL FORCES AT WORK. BE MY VOICE." McGowan wasn't the only one upset.

"Hey @Twitter let us know which of these rules @rosemcgowan broke. Asking for multiple victims of sexual violence," posted actress Jessica Chastain.

"And now THIS?" wrote an exasperated Jamie Lee Curtis. "You allow Twitter freedom to our president but you silence a woman speaking out about sexual harassment?"

Twitter employees were similarly unhappy with the move; it looked like Twitter was simply silencing a sexual assault survivor over a technicality. Overnight, a Twitter boycott started to gain steam with support from several major celebrities, including the model Chrissy Teigen and actors Mark Ruffalo and Alyssa Milano.

Twitter's relationship with celebrity users was incredibly important. Just like the politics team that handled candidates like Trump, Twitter had other teams dedicated to liaising with celebrities. These teams made sure celebs knew the basics about how to tweet, but also gave them better customer support if they were locked out of their account or facing harassment. It was a no-brainer investment for Twitter. Celebrities, known as Very Important Tweeters and referred to internally as "VITs," created a lot of value for the company simply by posting and engaging with fans for free. Outside of Facebook or Instagram, Twitter was one of the few places in the world you could come and hear directly from famous people. A lot of the time, that was great for Twitter. When McGowan or Teigen or Chastain boycotted Twitter publicly, it was a marketing and PR nightmare.

Several months after the McGowan incident, another one of those nightmares played out in front of millions of people. Seth Rogen, the famous actor and Hollywood writer, tweeted about Dorsey on a random Tuesday morning. "I've been DMing with @jack about his bizarre need to verify white supremacists on his platform for the last 8 months or so," he wrote, "and after all the exchanges, I've reached a conclusion: the dude simply does not seem to give a fuck." Rogen had been exchanging direct messages with Dorsey, known as DMs in Twitter parlance, and had complained about the abuse he regularly received on Twitter because he was Jewish. Some of the people who harassed Rogen even had Twitter's blue verification badge, which Twitter gave out to prominent users to help identify them in case someone else tried to impersonate them. While it wasn't the original intention, the blue badges had come to be seen as a sort of Twitter "endorsement" and acknowledgment that a user was someone important to pay attention to.

Dorsey wasn't happy that Rogen called him out publicly and arranged a phone call to discuss the issue privately. According to Rogen, the conversation went something like this:

ROGEN: What would you do if the President told his followers to kill a specific American citizen?

DORSEY: I'd like to think that would be something that would require some action.

ROGEN: You'd like to think?! You haven't talked about it?

DORSEY: Not that specifically.

ROGEN: So, you'd like to think that it would require some action, but you're not SURE that it would? *Maybe* you'd just let him tell his followers to kill someone?

DORSEY: Well . . .

Later in the call, Dorsey told Rogen that Twitter was "merely a mirror of society." Rogen wasn't pleased. "Twitter is a mirror of you," he replied. "When people are saying Twitter is a cesspool—that's you."

Needless to say, Twitter didn't need celebrity users publicly criticizing the company, and it had already been a long summer inside Twitter by the time McGowan's account was suspended. With Trump's constant tweeting and the Unite the Right white supremacist march in Charlottesville also playing out on Twitter, the pressure on Dorsey to finally do something to improve the abuse issues on the service was higher than ever. It was clear that Twitter's rules were insufficient, especially when it came to protecting women and people of color. A study conducted that year by the human rights organization Amnesty International found that more than 7 percent of the tweets sent to female journalists and politicians were "problematic or abusive." For women of color, it was even worse; they were 34 percent more likely to be targeted with abuse than white women. Trump himself played into the problem. In August of 2018, he tweeted that his former White House aide Omarosa Manigault Newman, a black woman, was a "crazed, crying lowlife" and "that dog." To the frustration of many employees inside Twitter, the company did nothing.

The Rose McGowan issue proved to be a breaking point. Dorsey was a staunch believer in leaving up as many tweets as possible, even offensive ones, but the realities of running a for-profit advertising business didn't always align. Absolute free speech wasn't a good strategy if it meant running off other users and advertisers.

The group inside Dorsey's conference room on Friday, October 13, had been discussing ways to make Twitter feel safer for months, but now Dorsey was determined to present something to the company by the end of the day. He even considered livestreaming the entire meeting on Periscope, Twitter's livestreaming video app, to be transparent about the process; thankfully to those in the room, he ultimately decided against broadcasting the messy conversation. Just like Twitter's user base, the group of executives atop Twitter varied on how aggressive they felt the company should be in writing rules that limited the things that people could say. Ed Ho, Twitter's head of product now that Kevin Weil was gone, was in favor of more strict and stringent rules. Other senior leaders, like General Counsel Vijaya Gadde and head of Trust and Safety Del Harvey, were staunch advocates for leaving most everything alone. (Both happened to be absent from the meeting on maternity leave.) Dorsey, perhaps the most ardent free-speech executive left, didn't say much beyond the occasional question.

Late that afternoon, after spending most of the day in discussion, the group stood before Twitter employees at an all-hands meeting and presented a series of anticipated changes. The company planned to crack down on tweets that included hate symbols and would also start to penalize users who were part of violent groups, even if their affiliation with a violent group happened *off* Twitter. "Glorifying violence" was already against the rules, but the types of posts that were considered for punishment were going to be expanded. Purposefully posting nude photos or videos of someone else without their consent, which was commonly referred to as "revenge porn," would now lead to an immediate ban, instead of a temporary suspension. Most of the ideas were half-baked, but the theme was evident: Twitter was going to start removing a lot more tweets.

The group of executives returned to Dorsey's conference room after the presentation to continue hashing out a plan. By now it was early evening, and some executives with flights to New York or Los Angeles canceled them as the daylong meeting dragged on. At 7:35 p.m., Dorsey sent a series of tweets from his iPhone. "We see voices being silenced on Twitter every day," he wrote. "Today we saw voices silencing themselves and voices speaking out because we're *still* not doing enough."

"We decided to take a more aggressive stance in our rules and how we enforce them," he added, pledging more details soon. When someone tweeted back to ask why Dorsey was making such a significant announcement late on a Friday night, he replied that the company "spent the whole day working on it and wanted to announce as soon as we were ready." After years primarily focused on leaving as many tweets up as possible, Twitter was no longer going to be shy about pulling them down.

Late in the afternoon on his last day working at Twitter, Bahtiyar Duysak, a contract worker on the company's Trust and Safety team, opened his computer and deactivated the most closely watched Twitter account in the world. Then Duysak got up from his desk, turned in his laptop and badge, and walked out of Twitter's San Francisco headquarters into the night.

It took only eleven minutes for Twitter executives to realize that President Donald Trump's account had been deactivated and fix the issue. The physical process of switching it back on took just a few clicks of the mouse, though users who visited his account during the outage were greeted with an ominous message: "@realDonaldTrump does not exist." The company tweeted an update a few hours later that the issue had been caused by "a Twitter customer support employee who did this on the employee's last day," an admission that sent the internet into a frenzy.

"Just gonna say it, the employee at Twitter who shut off Trump's account for 11 mins could become a candidate for the Nobel Peace Prize," wrote David Jolly, a former congressman. "How do i tell my parents im marrying the twitter employee?" joked another user. Surely other Twitter employees had dreamed about doing the exact same thing since Trump's election victory, and though no one yet knew who Duysak was, the "rogue" employee was already a folk hero to Trump's most strident critics.

Senior leaders inside Twitter were less enthused. The incident was a massive embarrassment for the company, which scrambled to announce "a full internal review." Not only did it reinforce the idea that Twitter employees were biased against Trump, but it had exposed the company's shoddy security defenses when it came to important accounts. Twitter had some safeguards in place to keep low-level employees from suspending or deleting a prominent account like Trump's, but there was an obvious loophole when it came to deactivating someone's account, which was essentially turning it off without deleting any data or posts. Duysak had exposed that loophole to the world. (Duysak, born and raised in Germany, would later say in an interview that the whole thing had been an accident. "I love America," he added.)

Twitter immediately locked down Trump's account, and shortly after came up with a new system to protect it. The company created a "Top 3" list that included just three prominent users: @realDonaldTrump, @POTUS, and @jack. It put those accounts behind a digital lock and key that was accessible to a very small handful of senior employees. Nobody else at the company could touch the accounts, and even the few people with access could set off various internal alarms if they did something unexpected or without permission. If Trump was angry about the incident, he didn't show it. "My Twitter account was taken down for 11 minutes by a rogue employee," he tweeted the next day. "I guess the word must finally be getting out-and having an impact."

One year into his presidency, it was true that Trump was having a seismic impact on Twitter. Not only had he put the company's speech rules under a microscope and forced Twitter into adopting several new policies, but Trump's emergence as president coincided with a resurgence of Twitter's business. Twitter's push into live video was still a priority in 2017, though the effort had taken a significant hit when the NFL found a new streaming partner after just one season. Amazon paid $50 million in 2017 for the same slate of games Twitter bought the year prior for just $10 million. The company was still streaming hundreds of live events, including Trump's inauguration and red-carpet shows for the Grammys and the American Music Awards, but without the NFL in the mix, the effort was missing its crown jewel.

Twitter's decision to lean into the "it's what's happening" slogan, though, had been prescient. Its role as a breaking-news machine was cemented with Trump in the White House. After all, there was nothing quite so "happening" as watching the sitting U.S. president use his Twitter account to threaten a foreign adversary with nuclear war. Trump wasn't the only thing helping Twitter grow, but he had also made Twitter more relevant and interesting than ever before. Even if people didn't sign up for Twitter, they likely heard about Twitter weekly on the TV or radio, considering how often Trump was using the service to make news.

That relevance paid off. In 2015, when Dorsey first returned, the number of users who logged into the service daily barely budged. With the changes to Twitter's timeline algorithm, the NFL deal, and the presidential election in full swing, Twitter's daily user base grew by 11 percent in 2016; in 2017, Trump's first year as president, daily users were up another 12 percent. Twitter and Dorsey, with an assist from Trump, had done something that seemed almost impossible in the business world: taken a major consumer product that had reached its popularity plateau and jump-started its growth. Over the final three months of 2017, thanks in part to all of the job cuts and other downsizing from the year before, Twitter turned a profit for the first time in company history.

After spending New Year's at his Mar-a-Lago resort in Palm Beach, Florida, to ring in 2018, Trump got back to work creating headaches for Twitter on January 2. "North Korean Leader Kim Jong Un just stated that the 'Nuclear Button is on his desk at all times,'" Trump posted on Twitter. "Will someone from his depleted and food starved regime please inform him that I too have a Nuclear Button, but it is a much bigger & more powerful one than his, and my Button works!" Again, Trump was taunting North Korea about nuclear war.

Twitter published a blog post a few days later titled "World Leaders on Twitter." The post didn't include any policy changes or product updates, and it didn't have an author, though Dorsey was heavily and uncharacteristically involved in the editing. It simply settled a question that Twitter was now getting on a near-daily basis. "There's been a lot of discussion about political figures and world leaders on Twitter, and we want to share our stance," it read. "Blocking a world leader from Twitter or removing their controversial Tweets would hide important information people should be able to see and debate. It would also not silence that leader, but it would certainly hamper necessary discussion around their words and actions."

A simplified version of the post might have read something like this: *We're not removing Trump's tweets, so please stop asking.*

FIVE

#ONETEAM, PT. I

*I*n. *Out. In. Out. In. Out.*

Jack Dorsey sat on the floor with his legs crossed and his back straight, silently meditating on a stage inside one of San Francisco's largest convention halls. High above him, the blue lights inside the Moscone Center had dimmed. Behind him a white Twitter bird sat motionless in the middle of a giant, purple video screen. Had Dorsey opened his eyes, he would have seen nearly all of Twitter's 3,500 employees facing him in their own noiseless trance. From the convention center floor where they all sat looking up at the stage, Dorsey was just a silhouette, like a statue of a skinny Buddha.

It was July 31, 2018, the first day of #OneTeam, Twitter's first-ever company-wide retreat. Dorsey had asked everyone to spend ten minutes meditating together before a full day of presentations from company leadership. Almost all of Twitter's global employees had flown to San Francisco for the three-day event, and the entire morning had been an homage of sorts to Dorsey's unique, personal lifestyle. His mother, Marcia, was the first person onstage to welcome everybody, a nod to the fact that she posted the same "good morning" tweet from her home in St. Louis every day. Besides meditation, Dorsey told people that he started each day with three things—"salt juice," sunshine, and movement—and now Twitter's employees were doing the same. Under their chairs were brown paper sacks with water bottles, pink Himalayan sea salt, and lemon juice, which everyone combined to make Dorsey's "wake-me-up" cocktail. Dorsey pressed a button with his foot and shot flames up from the stage to replicate sunshine, and everyone got some movement when a surprise "flash mob" erupted on stage featuring several of Twitter's senior executives in choreographed dance. The morning even included a brief concert from one of Dorsey's favorite rappers, Jay Rock, who was done and off the stage well before 10 a.m.

For years, Twitter's sales organization had held a popular annual off-site, and other teams at the company were eager to follow suit. Twitter's executives decided it was better and cheaper to roll all these various proposals into one mega-event. What emerged was a full-blown corporate retreat to set a proper vision and rebuild morale. Twitter had been through two rounds of layoffs, a failed sales process, and the first eighteen months of Trump's presidency since Dorsey had returned; it felt like everyone could use a boost.

Dorsey handled much of the vision-setting during his ninety-minute keynote to kick off the week. Twitter, he said, had a mission to "serve the public conversation," corporate-speak for helping people communicate about the things going on around them. This meant keeping Twitter "healthy" and earning people's trust, he said, but also "uniting profit and #purpose" and "being #fast, #free and #fun!" The framing was cheesy, but the idea was simple: Twitter was the place people went to talk about what was happening in the world. One of Dorsey's slides included his belief that Twitter would one day "serve" more than 1 billion people per day. (At the time, Twitter had just 122 million daily users.) Employees spent much of the next couple days in various breakout sessions, where company leaders shared updates and outlined strategy for their respective teams.

To coordinate the event and help create the agenda, Twitter turned to Leslie Berland. As the company's head of people and chief marketing officer, she oversaw Twitter's internal culture and its external reputation. She'd joined Twitter from American Express a few years prior and was both high-energy and vocal about how much she loved working at Twitter. More than anyone in Twitter's upper ranks, she had a knack for coaxing Dorsey out of his shell, and doing so became an important part of the #OneTeam program. The more relatable and accessible Dorsey was to Twitter's growing employee base, the more likely employees would be excited to work at the company.

It wasn't that Dorsey was unapproachable—quite the opposite in fact. He would regularly respond to random emails from rank-and-file staffers and often worked in the Twitter cafeteria or outside on the ninth-floor balcony where anyone could walk up to him with a question. But Dorsey was still an introvert, a billionaire, and a celebrity CEO who wasn't always eager to bask in the limelight. Employees who had meetings with him were surprised at how little he said, and when he did speak, his deep, monotone voice could give off an air of apathy. Dorsey was generally much better at communicating in writing than in person, but he looked surprisingly comfortable and confident on stage at #OneTeam. The event was a chance for people to see Dorsey in a new light, and a chance for Dorsey to win over his employees.

For the most part, the plan to humanize Dorsey worked. He quickly became the star of the three-day show alongside his direct reports, a group simply referred to as "Staff." Employees found his morning routine to be weird, but also endearing and personal. His parents, Marcia and Tim, told childhood stories about their quiet, artsy son and became instant celebrities in their own right, posing for selfies and exchanging tweets with employees well after the conference was over. Dorsey's meditation session had been uncomfortable since most people didn't know what to do with themselves during ten minutes of total silence, and drinking the salt juice was the closest thing to a cult that most employees would ever be a part of. But they also saw more of Dorsey over three days than many of them had in their entire Twitter tenure, and he spent the week chatting with people in the halls and posing for photos. By the end of the week, the catering staff was walking around the conference center with trays of salt juice for people to drink.

On the final night of the off-site, Twitter threw a massive party. Bruce Falck, the man in charge of Twitter's advertising products, breakdanced onstage in front of the entire company. Several other executives who reported to Dorsey competed in a lip-sync battle with choreographed dances and matching costumes. Ned Segal, the CFO, wore glowsticks around his neck and bright orange suspenders; JP Maheu, the head of U.S. ad sales, sported a giant gold chain and a backwards hat. At one point Berland was spotted in the DJ booth high above the throng of dancing employees.

As everyone headed home or to the airport the following morning, it felt like the end of summer camp. Employees swapped inside jokes on Twitter and tweeted about how much they loved their jobs, many adding the hashtag #lovewhereyouwork. Employee attrition at Twitter had always been higher than industry average, but for the next several months, Twitter's HR department noticed that almost nobody left the company. Del Harvey, the head of Trust and Safety who had been at Twitter since 2008, was effusive with praise. "In all my time at @Twitter, I'm not sure I've ever seen folks so energetic, enthusiastic, & ready to collaborate as after #OneTeam," she tweeted. By the time everybody got to work on Monday, offices around the world had salt juice stations set up in the kitchens and cafeterias.

The week did have one major disappointment, though. Rumors had circulated that Dorsey had arranged for a special guest speaker—another famous celebrity and die-hard Twitter user. On the final day of the off-site, before the dance party and lip-sync battle, Dorsey broke the bad news to everyone that the scheduling hadn't worked out.

"So there has been a buzz about an outside speaker that we were going to bring here to speak to us about our service and what we're doing and where we could be better," Dorsey said while pacing the stage. "Unfortunately, he got extremely, extremely busy and isn't able to make it."

It was true that Elon Musk was busy. Earlier in the year, the Tesla CEO had been sleeping on the floor of his car factory to try to increase production of his newest electric car, the Model 3. Most days he didn't even take the time to shower or change his clothes. By early July, things had gotten better, but he still had "one foot in hell" and was mentally drained by the stress. "It's been super-hard. Like there is for sure some permanent mental scar tissue here," he said at the time.

As a consolation, Dorsey read the company his direct-message exchange with Musk from the day that he asked him to come and speak. Musk had replied that he hated speaking events but would make an exception for Twitter. "I do love Twitter and I think it is a force for good," he told Dorsey. The audience cheered when Dorsey read the exchange out loud, and Dorsey himself seemed flattered. "That's pretty amazing," he admitted. He promised Musk would come back some other time. Musk's pep talk to Twitter employees would have to wait.

PART II

FLY

SIX

AFRICA

On a balmy June evening in 2018, Jack Dorsey ducked into a private dining room inside Café Milano in Georgetown, an Italian restaurant not far from the White House with a reputation for attracting the most powerful people in a city that was full of them. Dorsey was there for a secret dinner party. The guest list was rather unusual for a Twitter-sponsored event, but that was also the point. The room was filled with several right-wing conservatives and political operators. Mercedes Schlapp, a communications advisor to President Donald Trump, was there, and so was Guy Benson, a Fox News political commentator and radio host. Grover Norquist, a conservative political activist who built a career fighting tax increases, was in the room, as was the longtime Fox News television host Greta Van Susteren.

Twitter had arranged the dinner so Dorsey could better explain himself. For the past several months, he'd been speaking openly about a need to improve Twitter's "health," a term the company used to encompass all kinds of content issues like hate speech, racism, and spam. Ever since the Rose McGowan meeting the previous fall, health had become a top company priority and was starting to dominate quarterly earnings calls in much the same way "live" did just a few years earlier. In March, Dorsey announced plans to start measuring "the 'health' of conversation" happening on Twitter, and the company was reviewing research proposals to figure out if that idea was even possible. Dorsey thought that to improve something, you needed to be able to measure it, and he wanted to invent new metrics to determine if interactions between Twitter's users were beneficial or abusive. Twitter had also announced it would start hiding some tweets behind a "see more" label if its algorithms determined those tweets included "troll-like behaviors that distort and detract from the public conversation." It was a vague way of saying that Twitter was trying to crack down on tweets that it felt might be abusive or divisive.

Dorsey worried political conservatives would feel threatened by the company's change in focus. His job as CEO was forcing him into an uncomfortable position. Cleaning up Twitter meant less freedom of speech, and conservatives were not happy with the trade-off. With President Trump leading the charge, there was a rapidly growing belief among Republican politicians and conservative media that social media companies, Twitter in particular, were biased against them. Few people in Trump's orbit had forgotten about the #CrookedHillary ad campaign issue, and the following year Twitter had blocked an anti-abortion video ad from Republican Senate candidate Marsha Blackburn because it mentioned "the sale of baby body parts." In late 2017, Twitter suspended Roger Stone, one of Trump's allies, for a series of abusive tweets directed at CNN anchors. Stone threatened to sue.

That Twitter was full of liberal, left-leaning employees was no longer even a debate. It was, and everybody knew it, which made the company's decisions to penalize some conservative politicians even more controversial.

Dorsey's message inside Café Milano was simple: Twitter's health focus was about making people feel safer, not an effort to silence right-wing political ideology. He promised Twitter's changes weren't targeting conservative users, and he spent the night listening to complaints and feedback from his dinner guests who had many opinions about how Twitter should operate. Benson, for one, appreciated the effort, tweeting at Dorsey later that night. "Thank you, @jack, for meeting with a group of conservatives in DC tonight," he wrote. "Much work must be done to build and rebuild trust—as we discussed at length—but step one is actually talking." At one point during the evening, Schlapp stepped out for a phone call and returned, phone in hand, and whispered to one of Twitter's consultants in the room that she had the president on the line. Trump wanted to speak with Dorsey, she said. The Twitter CEO stepped outside to say hello and quickly returned a few minutes later. Nobody appeared to have noticed.

Dorsey was doing a lot more talking than usual that summer. The Café Milano dinner was just one part of the Twitter CEO's political outreach, which included hiring a conservative political strategist, Ron Christie, to help make intros and connections. Dorsey hosted a similar dinner with conservatives in New York the month prior, and had a private meeting at the News Corp. Building in midtown Manhattan with Sean Hannity, the well-known Fox News host and radio personality. He also exchanged private messages with Ali Alexander, a far-right political activist. (Alexander would later go on to help orchestrate the "Stop the Steal" rally on January 6th, 2021, after Trump's election loss.)

In some cases, Dorsey convinced Twitter's critics to come to him. Charlie Kirk and Candace Owens, both from Turning Point USA, a group that promoted conservative ideas to high school and college students, visited Twitter's headquarters in June for a meeting with Dorsey and Chief Marketing Officer Leslie Berland. Owens was a regular critic of Planned Parenthood and the U.S. welfare system, and had been with Kanye West when he made comments to TMZ about slavery being a "choice." She and Kirk were both vocal Trump supporters and had even met with the president in the Oval Office just a few weeks before meeting with Dorsey. The meeting at Twitter took place in a conference room right off the main lobby near the elevators, which was the usual meeting location when Twitter didn't want a guest to be seen walking around the office.

For Dorsey, the conversations weren't just about trying to defend Twitter. He also felt a strong, personal pull toward right-wing politics despite a track record of more liberal and progressive beliefs. Dorsey grew up in a politically divided home. His father was a Republican, his mother was a Democrat, and Dorsey identified "somewhere in the middle." He would later say he valued the dinner table talk that came from having parents who didn't always align.

Some suspected other forces at play. Dorsey could become infatuated with celebrities, especially musicians, and it was common that influences from his personal life would spill over into his work. One time Dorsey tried to get the rapper Jay-Z onto Twitter's board of directors, and even had Chairman Omid Kordestani fly to Los Angeles for a meal with Jay-Z at San Vicente Bungalows, a members-only club in West Hollywood that was so exclusive guests had to cover their phone's camera with a sticker. Kordestani didn't think Jay-Z was a good fit for the board and Twitter passed on an appointment, but Dorsey was undeterred. He found a workaround a few years later when his payments company, Square, bought Jay-Z's struggling music streaming service, Tidal, for $297 million. The deal left a lot of people scratching their heads, but Jay-Z got a board seat after all; it was just at Dorsey's other company.

In the summer of 2018, though, one of Dorsey's major influences was Kanye West, whom the Twitter CEO admired as an artist but also connected with personally. When West rejoined Twitter after a one-year hiatus in April, Dorsey posted a "welcome back" tweet, and shortly after attended the rapper's birthday party in Los Angeles. At the time of Dorsey's conservative outreach, West was a staunch supporter of both Owens and President Trump, posing in pictures wearing the president's red MAGA hat. Some inside Twitter speculated that Dorsey's admiration for West was at least partially fueling his interest in conservative politics. Dorsey had even agitated behind the scenes to get West as a speaker for Twitter's #OneTeam retreat that same summer, and when West's new album, *Ye*, was unveiled, Dorsey tweeted the link with a single-word review—"wow."

Publicly, Dorsey offered a simpler explanation for his conservative outreach. "I personally have not tended to have conversations with many people [on the] more conservative end of the spectrum or right end of the spectrum," Dorsey said. "So goal number one was to say that we're here, be present, and see the folks who I personally haven't talked to, and as an organization, we tend not to naturally lean towards."

Dorsey's efforts were certainly well timed. A few weeks after the Georgetown dinner, the tech news outlet Gizmodo reported that some white nationalists, including Jason Kessler, one of the organizers of the Unite the Right rally in Charlottesville the previous fall, were not appearing in search results on Twitter. That wouldn't seem like much of a problem except for the fact that many of those impacted were Trump supporters, which made the move look political. A few days later, Vice News reported that Twitter was "shadow banning" Republican politicians in search results, essentially hiding them from appearing as a suggested result when people went searching for their name. Twitter blamed the issue on a bug and soon announced that it had been fixed, but not before Trump saw the article and sent a tweet to his now 53 million followers. "Twitter 'SHADOW BANNING' prominent Republicans. Not good. We will look into this discriminatory and illegal practice at once! Many complaints," he wrote.

The term *shadow banning* was not yet widely understood, but it would quickly become a rallying cry for conservatives. The term described an alleged strategy by social networks to secretly hide a user's posts from appearing to anyone else on the service. The user could keep posting, but no one would actually see it. Trump's tweet instantly pushed the term into the mainstream discussion around social networks. "What Is a 'Shadow Ban,' and Is Twitter Doing It to Republican Accounts?" read a headline in *The New York Times*. Twitter published its own blog on the same day as Trump's tweet to try to fight the growing tsunami of complaints. It was titled, "Setting the record straight on shadow banning."

"We do not shadow ban," the company wrote. "And we certainly don't shadow ban based on political viewpoints or ideology."

Republicans weren't buying Twitter's denial, especially with Trump now loudly leading the chorus of accusations. A few weeks later Twitter suspended Alex Jones, the far-right podcaster and radio personality who famously repeated the conspiracy that the Sandy Hook Elementary

School shooting in 2012, which left twenty children dead, was a "hoax." In a video, Jones encouraged his listeners to get their "battle rifles" ready against the media, which violated Twitter's policy against inciting people to violence. Jones was also suspended by Facebook and You-Tube. Trump appeared to take issue with the decision, tweeting a few days later. "Social Media is totally discriminating against Republican/ Conservative voices," he tweeted. "Speaking loudly and clearly for the Trump Administration, we won't let that happen. They are closing down the opinions of many people on the RIGHT."

Whether Twitter's moves were reasonable or not didn't matter. Conservatives felt that Twitter was attacking them. They needed answers, and they wanted Dorsey to provide them.

Congressman Joe Barton didn't know what to make of Jack Dorsey when the executive showed up to testify before Congress on September 5, 2018. In Barton's defense, Dorsey rarely met the expectations that people had when they thought of the CEO of two publicly traded companies. Dorsey showed up on Capitol Hill with his nose ring in, a high collared shirt without a tie, and a long scraggly beard with just a touch of gray. It was an outfit that, by Washington, D.C.'s boring standards, was about as daring and bold as legally allowed. On top of that, Dorsey had read his opening statement before the House Energy and Commerce Committee off his iPhone, and tweeted it out right then and there. The expensive consultants that Twitter had hired to prepare Dorsey for the hearing had been flabbergasted by all of it. *Lose the phone, lose the nose ring, and get a tie*, they'd suggested. Dorsey ignored them.

"I don't know what a Twitter CEO should look like, but you don't look like [what] a CEO of Twitter should look like with that beard," Barton said in his slow, Texas drawl.

"My mom would agree with you," Dorsey replied with a smile, which made Barton and several others laugh.

The rest of the conversation was less funny. Barton, a Republican, spent the next several minutes asking Dorsey why and how Twitter was censoring its conservative users. In his opening statement, Dorsey had already argued that Twitter's internal data showed that there was "no statistically significant difference" between how many views Democrats and Republicans in Congress were getting for their tweets. When Dorsey told Barton that Twitter didn't include political viewpoints or philosophies into the ranking algorithms it used to determine what people see, Barton simply didn't believe him. "That's hard to stomach," he replied. "We wouldn't be having this discussion if there wasn't a general agreement that your company has discriminated against conservatives, most of whom happen to be Republican."

The exchange encapsulated what ended up being a long, grueling day for Dorsey. He was in D.C. after being summoned by Congress to answer questions about Twitter's content moderation practices. The "shadow banning" incident had finally pushed Republicans to act, and Dorsey spent much of his afternoon defending Twitter's policies and algorithms before America's elected officials. Congressman Jeff Duncan from South Carolina complained that when one of his staffers tried to sign up for Twitter, the only accounts that showed up as recommendations for her to follow were liberal politicians. "Donald Trump is the—truly the most successful Twitter user in the history of the site," Duncan added. "President Trump has utilized Twitter in unprecedented ways to get around the traditional news media. I would think that someone in your position would be celebrating that and him rather than trying to undermine him." At one point, the hearing was interrupted by Laura Loomer, the far-right conspiracy theorist who stood up and called Dorsey a liar. "Please help us Mr. President before it is too late!" she yelled before being escorted out of the building. Earlier in the day, Alex Jones had shown up, walking the halls outside the hearing room in an effort to "face my accusers," he told reporters.

Dorsey's day was particularly long since he'd actually flown to D.C. for two separate congressional hearings: a Senate hearing in the morning to talk about Twitter's role in the 2016 U.S. election, and the House hearing in the afternoon to discuss accusations of bias. Facebook's Sheryl Sandberg sat next to Dorsey in the morning session to answer questions about her own social network's role in the election, which worked out well for Dorsey since she took many of the arrows. But Dorsey sat alone during the nearly four-hour-long afternoon hearing, and it was tough to tell if his answers left any impact. The software algorithms that Twitter used to determine what people saw in their feed weren't public, and even if they had been, no one in Congress would have been able to make heads nor tails of them. All the group had to go on was Dorsey's word, and it seemed clear by the end of the day that his word wasn't enough. Running Twitter was becoming an increasingly complicated and exhausting job.

Still, Twitter's team felt good about the ordeal after it was all over. Dorsey had been calm and respectful; just as important, he didn't embarrass himself or get caught in the kind of awkward exchange that could easily go viral online. At the company's D.C. office later that night, more than a dozen employees and advisors who'd helped prepare Dorsey for the marathon day convened to have a few drinks and rehash the hearings. When Dorsey showed up, the group had a toast and congratulated him on surviving his first congressional hearing. Dorsey thanked everyone for their work in prepping him, then went around the room and gave everyone a hug, one by one, before heading to the airport to fly home.

Dorsey spent much of 2018 talking more than usual, but he made up for it in November. The Twitter CEO flew to Myanmar in Southeast Asia and settled into Pyin Oo Lwin, a small town tucked into the hills east of Mandalay, nearly two hours from the nearest international airport and half a world away from Twitter's headquarters. Myanmar was still reeling from a globally recognized genocide when Dorsey arrived. The Rohingya, a predominantly Muslim ethnic minority group, had been largely killed and displaced over years of conflict with the country's majority Buddhist population, including the Myanmar military. A lot of the military's propaganda had been shared and disseminated on Facebook, once again raising serious questions about the role of social networks in politics and culture.

Dorsey, though, was in Myanmar for other reasons. It was his forty-second birthday, and he'd flown all the way to Myanmar to celebrate in the most uncomfortable way imaginable: He signed up for a ten-day, silent meditation retreat. He arrived at a facility on the city's outskirts that taught an ancient form of meditation known as Vipassana. The purpose was, in Dorsey's words, to "hack the deepest layer of the mind and reprogram it" to recognize his own feelings of pain and pleasure more consciously. "Meditation is often thought of as calming, relaxing, and a detox of all the noise in the world," he later tweeted. "That's not vipassana. It's extremely painful and demanding physical and mental work."

For more than a week Dorsey slept on a cot and meditated ten hours per day. There was no reading, no writing, and no music allowed, and there was certainly no Twitter. Students weren't even supposed to make eye contact with each other. One night, the group meditated in a cave, and Dorsey—looking like a hostage in a black beanie, black sweatshirt, black shorts, and a full beard—got 117 mosquito bites before the lights mercifully blew a fuse, plunging everyone into darkness.

It had been more than three years since Dorsey returned to Twitter as permanent CEO, and the lifestyle that he'd adopted to cope with the stresses of having two jobs had evolved significantly. His meditation sessions each morning had grown longer, and he was also meditating in the evenings, typically totaling two hours per day. Dorsey started tinkering with his diet and experimented with fasting, sometimes going a full weekend without a meal. He started taking cold showers and ice baths and used a barrel sauna to rapidly change his body temperature. His intentionally uncomfortable lifestyle was even drawing followers in the form of other tech enthusiasts. *The New York Times* called Dorsey "Gwyneth Paltrow for Silicon Valley."

Unlike Paltrow, though, Dorsey wasn't looking to sell anything. He was simply a human guinea pig enjoying the mental challenge of putting himself into uncomfortable situations. When Dorsey went on a podcast with Ben Greenfield, the fitness guru and author of books with titles like *Boundless* and *Fit Soul*, he talked about how physical suffering made him more confident in other aspects of his life. "I mean, nothing has given me more mental confidence than being able to go straight from room temperature into the cold," he said.

While Dorsey was seeking out ways to experiment on his own body, the Twitter service that everyone used to post tweets was in a noticeable state of stagnation. Twitter was still growing steadily in the spring of 2019, but President Trump's regular shock-tweeting had largely masked the fact that the company rarely shipped new features. When Dorsey first returned as CEO, Twitter made several major changes, like introducing an algorithm to rank tweets and building the live video feature for the NFL.

Since then, though, Twitter had focused primarily on writing new content policies and incrementally improving the Twitter app. Anthony Noto, the CFO who plowed the company headfirst into live video, left Twitter in early 2018 to become the chief executive at the financial services company SoFi; without Noto there to serve as a human bulldozer, Twitter's live video push quickly fizzled. Twitter was still making changes to its algorithms to show people more relevant tweets, for example, or making it easier for users to report someone for racism. But those changes were minor in the world of product development. At times it felt like Twitter wasn't so much building new stuff and going after new users as it was desperately trying to hold on to the people it already had.

Twitter's inertia was particularly noticeable when you looked around the rest of the social media industry. Down south in Los Angeles, Evan Spiegel was routinely cooking up new, bizarre ways for teenagers to share on Snapchat, like photo filters that made your face look like a dog or posts that disappeared after twenty-four hours, called Stories. Facebook had an entire stable of products, including Instagram, WhatsApp, and virtual reality headsets, and CEO Mark Zuckerberg was launching new stand-alone apps every couple of months. Most of those apps flopped, sure, but the point was that Facebook was consistently trying new things—or at least trying to copy things that Snapchat came up with. Even TikTok, a video app owned by a Chinese tech giant called ByteDance, was blowing up in the U.S. thanks to its focus on short, looping videos. Twitter's own version of TikTok, Vine, had been shuttered years earlier.

The product malaise at Twitter was a disappointing reality considering Dorsey's reputation as a product genius. One problem was that Twitter didn't have any consistency atop its product organization, replacing its head of product almost every year. The constant turnover meant projects were always in limbo and priorities changed regularly. When Dorsey finally appointed one of his mentees, Kayvon Beykpour, to the top job in the summer of 2018, he was the sixth person to run Twitter's product group since 2014. Casey Newton, a tech journalist who covered Twitter, likened the job to the role of teaching Defense Against the Dark Arts at Hogwarts in the *Harry Potter* franchise, where each year the professor dealt with some unfortunate accident or scandal that vacated the role. *Vanity Fair* joked that running product at Twitter was "cursed."

An even bigger problem was Dorsey's aversion to making decisions. He rarely forced any kind of product directive or demand that might have expedited Twitter's work. Other famous tech CEOs were much more hands-on. At Facebook, Zuckerberg could become so fanatical about a specific product that he would put the company into a "lockdown" until it was built. At Amazon, Jeff Bezos didn't just come up with the idea for the company's voice-controlled assistant, Alexa, but spent years micromanaging the project and pushing executives on an ever-competitive timeline to get it out into the world.

Dorsey operated differently, asking his direct reports to do most of the execution and decision-making while he served as a counselor along the way. His primary job, he believed, was to ask questions. "If I have to make a decision, I think there is something wrong with the company," Dorsey said in 2019. "If I have to make a decision it means that our folks, our team was not empowered to make a decision." Dorsey put a premium on consensus, often asking his Staff to discuss important decisions and strategy as a collective during Monday morning meetings that would routinely run four hours long. It was an inclusive and diplomatic way of managing that ensured numerous perspectives; it was also incredibly slow and led to a constant stream of second-guessing. Without a dominant CEO pushing for change or demanding new features, Twitter was timid. There was a general fear inside the company of launching new features that might disrupt the company's delicate user growth or incite a riot by users who were ruthless critics anytime Twitter tried something new.

Beykpour was more aggressive. At just twenty-nine years old, he was young, ambitious, opinionated and much more vocal than his boss. When Dorsey made him head of product in 2018, Beykpour had already been reporting to the CEO for a few years, but still had the mindset of an entrepreneur. He'd grown up in the Bay Area, graduated from Stanford, and was looking for new, bigger ideas; there were no "sacred cows" at Twitter that couldn't be changed or reimagined, he told people. Twitter started experimenting with more product changes quickly. In early 2019 it launched a new camera feature in hopes people would tweet more photos and videos. It also rolled out a separate app, called "twttr," specifically so people could prototype new features as the company tested them.

Another big idea came from Mo Al Adham, a product manager on the video team who approached Beykpour with a concern about Twitter's user numbers. Even though the number of people who logged into their accounts every day was growing, the percentage of people who were posting "original" tweets was shrinking. For a variety of reasons, tweeting had become scary. There was always the chance you would post something and get attacked for it, or post something you'd regret years later, or post something and nobody would even see it. As a result, lots of users kept tweets in the "drafts" folder, meaning they typed them out but never hit send and instead saved them for a later date that usually never came.

One solution to this problem was ephemerality—or making sure that posts didn't exist forever. Disappearing posts were already incredibly popular on other social networks like Snapchat and Instagram, which both had Stories so people could post photos and videos with a twenty-four-hour life span. Al Adham wanted to build something ephemeral, too, in hopes of eliminating the "permanence" that came with tweeting. His idea was called Scribbles. It was sort of like Stories in that the posts disappeared after twenty-four hours, but Scribbles were generally for text posts instead of photos and videos. People could use various fonts and colors, and even "co-post" with another user to make it more interactive. Dorsey and Beykpour liked the idea, and by early 2019 Al Adham had the green light to start building something that Twitter could test in the wild.

Later in the year, Beykpour oversaw another major product change. One of the reasons Twitter was so hard to use was that curating a follower list was time-consuming and laborious. Imagine if someone joined Twitter to follow news about their favorite sports team. Getting all that news meant manually finding the players, coaches, and reporters who covered the team and following them one by one. In late 2019, Twitter started letting people follow "topics," including sports teams, bands, and celebrities, to make all that easier. If someone followed the "Seattle Seahawks," for example, Twitter would use software algorithms to find relevant tweets about the team and put them into their feed. "The conversation will come to you," Twitter wrote in a blog post.

At the very least, Beykpour was trying something different: He was actually building new products.

President Donald Trump woke up on Tuesday, April 23, 2019, and did what he often did in the morning: He complained on Twitter. He called *The New York Times* the "Enemy of the People," pointed out how the "Radical Left Democrats . . . have gone totally insane!" and called MSNBC's Joe Scarborough "Angry Dumb and Sick." Then Trump turned his attention to Twitter itself, complaining that the service was "Very discriminatory," and accused the company of removing some of his followers. His follower count, which was around 60 million by this time, would be "much higher than that if Twitter wasn't playing their political games," he wrote. "No wonder Congress wants to get involved - and they should. Must be more, and fairer, companies to get out the WORD!"

Trump's complaints about Twitter were no longer out of the norm, but these particular tweets were conveniently timed. A few hours after Trump posted them, Jack Dorsey was standing in the Oval Office. Trump had invited Dorsey for a visit through Dan Scavino, his advisor and head of social media, and the Twitter CEO arrived with a small entourage, including Vijaya Gadde, Twitter's general counsel, and Colin Crowell, Twitter's vice president of global public policy.

Considering how antagonistic Trump was on Twitter every day, he was unexpectedly friendly in person. Dorsey had met with several world leaders over the years, and they generally ignored the staff that he brought along. Not Trump, who shook everyone's hand and pulled up chairs so the group could sit together around the Resolute desk. Then Trump got to the point: He was upset about his follower count. The president worried that Twitter was intentionally manipulating how many followers he had, either by limiting them or purposefully removing them. Trump had heard from several other Republican politicians with the same concerns, he said.

Dorsey assured him that this wasn't the case, and that Twitter often removes spam accounts in large batches, which can impact users who have millions of followers. He also talked to Trump about the importance of having a civil and healthy dialogue on Twitter. High-profile accounts, like Trump's, have an impact on how other people tweet, he added. Toward the end of the meeting, Vice President Mike Pence walked in to say hello, and Trump introduced him to Dorsey. The president seemed impressed that Dorsey was an entrepreneur who had built two different companies. That afternoon, Trump posted a photo of the meeting to his Twitter account. "Great meeting this afternoon," he posted. "Lots of subjects discussed regarding their platform, and the world of social media in general. Look forward to keeping an open dialogue!"

The truce with Twitter lasted eleven days. "Social Media & Fake News Media, together with their partner, the Democrat Party, have no idea the problems they are causing for themselves," Trump posted on May 4 after Twitter suspended the actor James Woods for posting a violent hashtag. "VERY UNFAIR!"

Jack Dorsey was on the road a lot during the summer and fall of 2019. He was in Paris to visit French president Emmanuel Macron in June and later attended Paris Fashion Week, sitting in the front row at a show for one of his favorite designers, Rick Owens, whom he admired tremendously and whose creations he often wore himself. He visited the Michael Brown memorial in his home state of Missouri, honoring the man whose death had sparked marches in Ferguson years earlier, and he flew to New Zealand to meet with Prime Minister Jacinda Ardern. The two talked about eliminating terrorist content from social media sites after a deadly mass shooting at two mosques in Christchurch was broadcast live on Facebook, and later uploaded to Twitter, earlier in the year.

In mid-September, Dorsey took his senior Staff to Big Sur for an executive retreat along the California coast where he had a house overlooking the Pacific Ocean. Staff had attended a few of these retreats over the years, including in other places like Joshua Tree. At a prior retreat in early 2018, Dorsey had invited Ray Dalio to come speak with the group. Dalio was the billionaire founder of Bridgewater Associates, one of the largest hedge funds in the world. He was also the author of a book called *Principles*, a *New York Times* bestseller about corporate management that included several guiding philosophies, including the concept of "radical transparency," which was right up Dorsey's alley. Dalio tried to convince Twitter leadership to adopt the "Dot Collector," a software program for ranking your colleagues in real-time during meetings. It felt both ridiculous and unnecessary, and the group happily passed on the idea.

In September 2019, though, the team in Big Sur had other things to discuss. Twitter's Staff had become increasingly tight over the years, in part because of previous off-sites like this one, but also because Dorsey's management style had created a tight-knit group. His efforts to reach consensus and his tendency to bring the entire group in on important management decisions meant that Staff worked closely on all kinds of Twitter problems. The strategy was even more prominent thanks to Dorsey's hands-off style and the fact he was still running Square. The group had fights and disagreements, but when Twitter went through drama, which it did often, the group went through the drama together. Some employees inside Twitter thought Staff sometimes operated more like a family than an executive team, which was good for morale and culture, but wasn't the best way to get stuff done or hold people accountable.

Those shortcomings were part of the focus in Big Sur. Staff spent time identifying which executives were responsible for which company decisions, an exercise that seemed relatively elementary for a company of Twitter's size, but also hadn't been fully established and routinely slowed things down. Other parts of the multi-day retreat were more enjoyable. The group meditated together and ate dinner at nearby Big Sur Bakery. Another night, Staff ate dinner at the house while seated on the floor, and Dorsey invited several musicians over to play African drums on the patio, which led to lots of drinking and dancing as the sun slowly dipped over the horizon. By the time everyone went home, there was optimism that Twitter's newfound clarity would make the company faster.

In November, around the time of Dorsey's forty-third birthday, the CEO went on another ten-day silent retreat, this time in South Africa. Optically, the timing was not ideal. Twitter was fresh off a disappointing earnings report that sent the stock falling more than 20 percent in a single day. A glitch in the company's advertising technology had significantly hurt revenue, and even worse, the company said the issues would continue to hurt revenue during the holiday quarter, which was always

Twitter's biggest. Dorsey had also just made a surprise announcement that Twitter was going to stop selling all political ads. There were good reasons for the move. The 2016 election disaster, which included the #CrookedHillary campaign debacle, was still haunting Twitter and other social media companies. President Trump was routinely posting misinformation online, which was putting pressure on Twitter to fact-check his posts. Fact-checking his political ads would be a nightmare scenario for sure. Dorsey thought it was simpler to cut out political ads entirely before the 2020 U.S. election cycle got going. The bad news for Twitter was that the decision meant walking away from millions of dollars in revenue. Twitter stock fell 4 percent on the news.

Dorsey was unbothered by the swirling negativity. A few weeks after the bad earnings report, he was on a plane for Africa to spend most of November touring the continent. He was mostly there to listen. Sub-Saharan Africa had a population of over 1 billion people, which was about the size of the U.S. and Europe combined, and many places in Africa were still bringing people onto the internet for the first time. Dorsey understood the potential, both in terms of getting feedback from eventual Twitter and Square customers, but also in meeting entrepreneurs to better understand the African tech scene.

Dorsey started in Nigeria and met up with several Twitter executives who joined him for a week, including Beykpour, the head of product; Mike Montano, the head of engineering; Parag Agrawal, the chief technology officer; and TJ Adeshola, head of sports partnerships. Dorsey's chief of staff, Sierra Lord, was also on the trip and had arranged much of the itinerary. The group was there to meet with local entrepreneurs, but also to scout Nigeria as a possible location for a new office on the continent. They met with Ngozi Okonjo-Iweala, Nigeria's former finance minister and a Twitter board member, and spoke with students at the African University of Science and Technology in Abuja. At one event, Beykpour was so impressed by an entrepreneur in the audience he offered him a job at Twitter on the spot, and the company ended up hiring him as a contractor. After a few days the group flew to Ghana and visited Cape Coast Castle, an old British fort that was used to hold African prisoners before they were shipped off as slaves some two hundred years earlier. Dorsey then left his Twitter colleagues behind and flew to South Africa for his ten-day silent retreat before continuing solo to Ethiopia for more listening.

The trip was significant for several reasons. During the early parts of the tour with Twitter's executive team, the group talked a lot about Dorsey's vision for a decentralized social networking protocol he wanted to build, called Bluesky, which wouldn't be owned or controlled by any single company. Twitter announced plans to fund a small independent group to start building Bluesky just a few weeks after Dorsey returned from Africa, and Agrawal, who had been on the trip, ended up spearheading the effort internally. But Dorsey also left Africa with a deeper appreciation for Bitcoin. The cryptocurrency was a decade old, but it was still primarily held and used by tech enthusiasts and speculators. Dorsey had been a Bitcoin fan long before his trip, and had been implementing the currency into Square's products for years, but in Africa he met with several entrepreneurs who believed Bitcoin was a solution to many of the continent's banking problems. The biggest draw was that the digital currency wasn't minted or controlled by a specific bank or country. "If you wanna feel it and you wanna feel why it's practical and why it's necessary, spend some time in Africa," Dorsey said of Bitcoin a few months later. "Spend some time in a country and a nation that has to constantly be aware of what their government is trying to do to them, how their government is trying to sell them out, how much control their government has over them through this instrument of currency." The trip stoked a fire inside Dorsey, who went home more excited than ever about cryptocurrencies and blockchain technology that few people in the United States understood and appreciated.

Toward the end of November, as Dorsey waited to take off from Ethiopia's Addis Ababa Bole International Airport, he pulled out his phone and posted a tweet of appreciation for his monthlong adventure. "Sad to be leaving the continent . . . for now," he wrote. "Africa will define the future (especially the bitcoin one!). Not sure where yet, but I'll be living here for 3-6 months mid 2020. Grateful I was able to experience a small part."

The flippant tweet set off an explosion back home in San Francisco. Dorsey was already running two companies at once, and employees were surprised to learn that their CEO also planned to live eight thousand miles away for half the year. They weren't the only ones caught off guard. Twitter's board of directors had no idea about the CEO's plan to live in Africa and many directors were unhappy learning about it from Dorsey's Twitter account. Twitter's shareholders were similarly surprised and displeased. Dorsey boarded his plane to fly home, not realizing that he'd just posted one of the most consequential tweets of his life.

SEVEN

#ONETEAM, PT. II

J ack Dorsey looked like a Times Square street performer when he walked onstage inside the George R. Brown Convention Center in downtown Houston in January 2020. He had on a white space helmet, shiny silver pants, and white platform boots that were all somehow overshadowed by his knee-length, puffy white ski coat. The outfit was a nod to the home of NASA, and Dorsey turned around to reveal a large, black message written on the back of his jacket: #OneTeam.

While it had been only eighteen months since Twitter hosted its first company-wide retreat in San Francisco, the event had been such a massive success for both recruiting and retention that Twitter executives quickly planned another one. Like last time, Twitter flew the entire company—now 4,800 employees—to Houston for the three-day event. Employees spent time in sessions outlining Twitter's priorities and goals, and one morning, everyone spent several hours volunteering around Houston. The agenda was also chock-full of singing and dancing and confetti, and again Bruce Falck breakdanced. Dorsey's parents were there, too, and to the dismay of many, there was more meditation.

As the saying goes, everything is bigger in Texas. If #OneTeam San Francisco had felt like summer camp, #OneTeam Houston was full-blown spring break. There were parties every night with free food, free drinks, and plenty of entertainment. Twitter rented out NASA's Space Center on opening night of the retreat, announcing the party in a video recorded by three astronauts floating inside the International Space Station. The company threw a giant block party on the second night where employees could bop around between restaurants, listen to live music, and ride a Ferris wheel. For the third and final night, Twitter rented out Minute Maid Park, home of Major League Baseball's Houston Astros. Like the first #OneTeam, there was another lip-sync battle, and unlike the first #OneTeam, there was also a fireworks show. On the final morning, a group performed the song "Africa" by Toto, perhaps a tongue-in-cheek nod to Dorsey's controversial tweet from a few months earlier.

Lavish and expensive parties were not uncommon among Silicon Valley tech companies. Several months before Twitter's event, Apple hired Lady Gaga to perform a private concert for employees at its office in Cupertino, California. Facebook had a long history of lavish, corporate holiday parties, including one inside the San Francisco Giants' stadium and another "Winter Wonderland"–themed one at San Francisco's Palace of Fine Arts that featured an ice sculptor wielding a chain saw. In some ways, Twitter was simply keeping up with the Joneses as tech employees had come to expect these kinds of perks when hunting around for a job. Unlike Apple and Facebook, though, Twitter's business wasn't printing money, and #OneTeam Houston came with a price tag of more than $30 million. Some employees questioned whether an expensive corporate off-site made sense just eighteen months after the last one. That is, until they got there.

Executives spent the week talking about Dorsey's vision for Twitter, and the service's impact on the world. At one point Dorsey had a very Dorsey-like moment when he sat on the stage in a white, high-backed chair, spun around so his back was to the entire company, and had a conversation about Twitter's role in the world with a large, rainbow-colored circle that had been projected onto the big screen. It was as if he were talking to God. ("Are we all experiencing delayed side effects of the salt juice?" one employee joked on Twitter.) Throughout the week, the company tried

to remind employees why working at Twitter was so important by bringing in speakers to talk about how the service had impacted their lives.
The mayor of Houston, Sylvester Turner, talked about Twitter's role in
helping search-and-rescue organizations in the aftermath of Hurricane
Harvey. Obiageli "Oby" Ezekwesili, a former Nigerian minister who
was shortlisted for a Nobel Peace Prize a few years earlier, spoke about
using Twitter for a #BringBackOurGirls campaign to raise awareness
about the hundreds of Nigerian schoolgirls who were kidnapped by the
Islamic terrorist group Boko Haram in 2014.

While Twitter's executive team had largely been the stars of the
first #OneTeam, they were replaced in 2020 by actual celebrities. British actress Jameela Jamil spoke, and so did Simone Biles, the gymnast
and Olympic gold medalist.

The two biggest stars of the week were saved for the final night.
Chrissy Teigen, the supermodel and cookbook author who tweeted
religiously, walked onstage to a standing ovation while "Hail to the
Chief" played in the background. Her job title, which was projected
onto the big screen, simply said "Mayor of Twitter." Teigen didn't dis-
appoint, asking Dorsey if he drank his own pee, then joked that if she
had known he'd become so rich she would have tried to date him years
earlier. At one point, Twitter put one of Teigen's tweets up on the screen.
She was a vocal Democrat and even louder Trump antagonist. A few
months earlier, Trump had tweeted about her, referring to her as John
Legend's "filthy mouthed wife," but he didn't include her name. Teigen clapped back: "lol what a pussy ass bitch. tagged everyone but me.
an honor, mister president." Behind the scenes, the White House had
reached out to Twitter asking the company to remove the tweet, which
it didn't. When the tweet flashed up on the screen in front of the whole
company, the crowd went nuts.

Teigen had only one rival for the week's best interview: Elon Musk.
Good on his word, Dorsey had invited Musk back to speak with employees, and the Twitter CEO stood onstage in front of the company and
called Musk on FaceTime from his iPad. Musk answered from his office,

wearing an "Occupy Mars" T-shirt, and his face was projected onto the screen as Twitter's employees cheered wildly.

Musk was already one of Twitter's most popular and controversial users. By January 2020 he had more than 30 million followers, and his tweeting often got him into trouble. In 2018, Musk was sued by a British cave diver after he called the man a "pedo guy" on Twitter for criticizing Musk's suggested plan to save a Thai soccer team from a cave using a mini submarine. That same year, Musk had to give up his role as chairman of Tesla's board of directors as part of a settlement with the Securities and Exchange Commission after he tweeted that he had money to take Tesla private. He didn't have the money, and the SEC sued him, claiming Musk knowingly made "false and misleading statements" that ultimately impacted Tesla's stock.

None of those issues seemed to bother Dorsey, who regularly referred to Musk as his favorite Twitter user. "Elon Musk is incredible," Dorsey said shortly after Musk's appearance at #OneTeam. "He just breaks so many boundaries on our service and I think in a way that allows us all to learn and see and understand."

On FaceTime, while standing before the entire company, Dorsey asked Musk for advice on fixing Twitter. "Give us some direct feedback, critique," Dorsey said. "What are we doing poorly? What could we be doing better? And what's your hope for our potential as a service?"

Before Musk could answer, Dorsey simplified the question. "If you were running Twitter—by the way do you want to run Twitter?—what would you do?"

Musk didn't hesitate. "I think it would be helpful to differentiate between real and [bot users]," he replied, admitting he couldn't always tell who he was interacting with on Twitter. "Is this a real person or is it a botnet or a sort of troll army?" he added. "Sometimes it can be very difficult to [tell]—what's real public opinion and what's not?"

With tens of millions of followers, it was a reasonable issue for Musk, even if most Twitter users never dealt with legions of bots or anonymous trolls. Musk, though, was not a regular Twitter user, and he was frequently trolled by Tesla short sellers on the service, which bothered him a lot. He told Twitter employees that fixing the bot issues would lead to more growth for the entire company. "The more people believe that it's real people talking, the more they'll tune in," he suggested. "The more that they think it's just various groups waging psychological warfare, the more they'll tune out."

The conversation was short but would stick with Twitter employees for years to come. When the time came to say goodbye, employees applauded and Dorsey thanked Musk profusely.

"Elon, we appreciate you so much for everything you're doing around climate change and pushing the boundaries of exploration and human potential," Dorsey said. "So thank you very much, and thank you for using us. We love you."

EIGHT

ELLIOTT

O mid Kordestani was skiing with his kids in Montana when the first phone call came in from an unknown number with a New York City area code. It was late February 2020, and Twitter's executive chairman was enjoying the final days of a weeklong vacation at the Yellowstone Club, the uber-exclusive private ski resort. The club's guest list reportedly included members such as Bill Gates, Justin Timberlake, and Tom Brady. Certainly, the mystery caller could wait. But then the phone rang again. And again.

When Kordestani finally answered, he was greeted by Jesse Cohn, the managing director at Elliott Management. Kordestani didn't know Cohn, but he certainly knew Elliott: The firm was arguably the most dangerous activist investing shop in the world. It was famous for buying large ownership stakes in a company, then using its position as a major shareholder to rapidly force change.

Cohn politely informed Kordestani that Elliott was now one of Twitter's largest shareholders. He'd also sent the Twitter chairman a letter outlining several issues that the firm had with Twitter's operations, and he wanted to set up a meeting to discuss changes Elliott wanted to make. Would Kordestani please read the letter and get back to him as soon as possible?

Vacation over.

The letter outlining Elliott's concerns and demands was technically addressed to the company's board of directors, but it may as well have been addressed to Dorsey personally. It contained several complaints, including that Twitter's stock was undervalued and the company wasn't executing. The firm said it was planning to nominate four new board directors at Twitter's upcoming annual meeting. Most importantly, Elliott took issue with the fact that Dorsey had two jobs; the firm believed strongly that Twitter needed a full-time CEO.

The letter was a standard first salvo for activist investors. At Twitter, though, it landed like a professionally worded hand grenade. Elliott was opening a line of communication to try to negotiate for changes, and Twitter had no choice but to play ball. The company's board and senior management knew that Elliott's sizable ownership stake and strong reputation meant that it had a real chance of taking over enough board seats or corralling enough support from other investors to force Dorsey out of a job. Simply ignoring Elliott, or hoping the firm might go away, wasn't an option.

From the outside, the arrival of activist investors on Twitter's doorstep in February 2020 was somewhat surprising. Twitter's business had been inconsistent for years, oscillating between signs of doom and optimism. However, at this moment in time, there was a lot of optimism. The lingering high from #OneTeam Houston was still felt throughout the company, with Twitter reaping the benefits that usually come with a company-wide retreat, like better retention and higher morale.

Twitter's financials weren't terrible, either. Just a few weeks earlier, at the beginning of February, the company reported better earnings than anyone expected, and the stock soared 15 percent in a single day. Dorsey and Chief Financial Officer Ned Segal told investors that Twitter planned to increase spending by 20 percent in 2020, and a large part of that increase was earmarked for hiring. Plus, Twitter was adding more users, and the company was profitable. Compared to three years earlier, when Twitter was cutting costs and laying off hundreds of employees following its failed sale to Disney, things *appeared* to be going well.

Internally, though, some Twitter executives had spent months bracing for someone like Elliott to show up on their doorstep. Masked by Twitter's positive earnings report was a more concerning reality: Twitter's expenses were growing much faster than its revenue. While the company promised 20 percent expense growth in 2020, its revenue the year before had grown by less than 14 percent, a warning sign that the company's profits might be unsustainable.

Dorsey's tweet about living in Africa for six months had also created a major headache for Twitter's management team and board of directors. He still had two jobs, and the tweet raised all kinds of questions about his commitment to being a CEO. Some investors already worried that Dorsey's part-time arrangement was holding Twitter back. Now he wanted to spend half the year on the other side of the world, a twenty-hour plane ride and eleven-hour time difference from Twitter's San Francisco headquarters.

Dorsey, Segal, and Kordestani spent the weeks after that tweet doing damage control, meeting with several of the company's top investors who wanted to voice their concerns. Some of them were incensed that Dorsey was suddenly planning to pick up and move across the globe. Dorsey's flippant tweet wasn't Elliott's motivation for making an investment, but it certainly helped their case now that the general public was suddenly questioning Dorsey's decision to hold two jobs.

The activist playbook is a simple one: Investors, oftentimes a large hedge fund or private equity fund, look for undervalued companies, then invest heavily in them to acquire voting power. That power allows them to force corporate changes. Sometimes it includes ousting the CEO, or changing the makeup of the board of directors. The whole process is typically short, a few years at most. If things go well, those changes can lead to a quick increase in the company's stock price—and a nice payday for Elliott.

That activist investors would eventually target Twitter had been a foregone conclusion for years, certainly long before Dorsey ever spent time in Africa. Twitter had been considered undervalued for most of its public company life. Facebook, founded just two years before Twitter and operating the same advertising-based business model, had more than twenty times Twitter's revenue in 2019. Its user base was eleven times larger than Twitter's, and that didn't include Instagram or WhatsApp. A lot of investors saw that discrepancy and concluded Twitter was simply mismanaged.

On top of that, Twitter's corporate structure meant the company was an easier target than most. Twitter had just one class of stock, known as "common stock," which any Average Joe could buy with a brokerage account. Rivals like Facebook and Snapchat had common stock, too, but they also had special classes of stock known as "supervoting" shares that were reserved for founders and early investors. At Facebook, supervoting shares owned by just a few people carried ten votes per share instead of the standard one vote per share for common stock, a structure that allowed CEO Mark Zuckerberg to control 58 percent of Facebook's voting power with just 13 percent of its overall stock. Zuckerberg could largely run his business however he wanted without fear of an outside investor coming in to try to pressure him out of a job.

Not so at Twitter, where each share of stock carried just one vote, regardless of who owned it. That meant that anyone with enough money could show up and purchase a sizable stake in the company and there was nothing Twitter management, its founders, or its board of directors could do about it.

A few days after the letter arrived, Twitter's board of directors—folks like Kordestani, Salesforce exec Bret Taylor, and British businesswoman and philanthropist Martha Lane Fox—met for dinner in a conference room inside the company's San Francisco headquarters. The board was in town for a previously scheduled quarterly meeting, but that night over takeout, the discussion inside Twitter's office was all about Elliott. What were Twitter's options? Was there any chance of fending Elliott off? The firm and its founder, Paul Singer, were known to be ruthless and committed. Singer famously won a fifteen-year legal battle with the government of Argentina over an investment deal; he even tried to seize a 338-foot Argentinian naval ship as collateral while it was sitting at a port in Ghana. After Elliott took a stake in Athenahealth in May 2017, then-CEO Jonathan Bush, cousin to President George W. Bush, says he researched Elliott to better understand what he was going up against. The experience was akin to "Googling this thing on your arm and it says, 'You're going to die,'" he told *The New Yorker.*

Twitter and Dorsey were in trouble. By the time everyone headed home for the night, the general consensus was that Elliott was in the driver's seat, and likely had strong support from other shareholders. Still, the board needed more information. More specifically it needed to better understand just how determined Elliott was to kick Dorsey out of his job.

A week after the letter arrived, reps from both Twitter and Elliott met in person for the first time in a conference room at the private jet terminal near the San Francisco airport. On Twitter's side was Kordestani; Gregg Lemkau, Twitter's banking advisor from Goldman Sachs; and Patrick Pichette, an experienced finance executive from Canada who had spent seven years as the chief financial officer at Google before joining Twitter's board in 2017.

On Elliott's side was Marc Steinberg, a Harvard-educated investment banker who joined Elliott in 2015, and Cohn, the firm's thirty-nine-year-old managing partner who led Elliott's U.S. activism business. By the time Cohn approached Twitter, he was a well-known commodity in Silicon Valley. Not only had he been investing as an activist for almost fifteen years—he completed his first deal at age twenty-six —but Cohn was clearly good at it. He purchased a 6,000-square-foot New York City apartment a few years earlier for $30 million, which, according to *The Wall Street Journal*, included "a fireplace clad in rounded marble slabs that extend to the ceiling and an office fit for a master of the universe." Cohn was fresh off other investments in eBay, SAP, and AT&T. If Twitter's board needed a reminder as to Cohn's prowess, the eBay investment had landed him a seat on the company's board. eBay's CEO resigned six months later.

The two sides had a cordial first meeting. Cohn did most of the talking for Elliott and repeated many of the concerns outlined in the letter. Twitter wasn't operating well enough, he said, and the company needed to make some changes to its corporate governance.

Cohn's biggest issue, though, was Twitter needed a full-time CEO. By the end of the ninety-minute discussion, it was clear to Twitter's team that Dorsey's job was in serious jeopardy. Allowing Dorsey to hold two jobs was great for Jack Dorsey, but it wasn't great for Twitter, Cohn argued. It was like letting your five-year-old kid eat candy all day, he continued. The kid would love it, obviously, but that doesn't mean it's good parenting. Cohn tried to get everyone to agree on the simple fact that Dorsey's arrangement was a problem; he also wanted Twitter to announce a formal CEO search to replace Dorsey as soon as the following Monday.

Less than thirty minutes after the meeting ended, as Elliott's private plane took off back to New York, news of the meeting leaked to a journalist at Bloomberg. Up until then, the process had taken place behind closed doors and out of the public eye. Once Elliott's investment became public, speculation about Dorsey's future made headline news in every publication from Deadline to *The New York Times*. "Twitter CEO Jack Dorsey's Job in Peril as Activist Investor Takes Stake," read NPR's headline. CNBC's Jim Cramer, host of the popular *Mad Money* show about Wall Street, said that "the best thing [Dorsey] could do for his shareholders is just retire as CEO of Twitter and focus on running Square full time—or vice versa."

After the Friday meeting, Twitter's top executives and board members spent most of the weekend on the phone discussing what to do. For Dorsey, all the options were terrible. Giving up his job at Square was out of the question. If Twitter fought Elliott, it could lead to a proxy battle down the line where Dorsey's role as CEO could be in the hands of a shareholder vote, a situation that would pose all kinds of distractions. If Dorsey somehow got to keep his job after all that, it would only be because Twitter spent months of time, money, and attention fighting on his behalf. If he lost the proxy battle, Dorsey would be out of a job that he loved. If Twitter settled with Elliott, perhaps giving the activist firm a couple of board seats and promising other changes, Dorsey would keep his job, but Twitter would have a board full of people who wanted him fired.

Bad. Bad. Bad.

As the weekend dragged on and the phone and video calls piled up, Dorsey became despondent. Much of the debate was centered on him personally. Should Dorsey have just one job? Why wasn't Twitter executing well enough? Why did Dorsey send that tweet? Even the idea of settling with Elliott felt like an admission of defeat. At one point over the weekend, an exasperated Dorsey even volunteered to resign if that's what was best for the company.

His mood started to annoy some of the board members and senior Twitter executives who were trying to help him. Dorsey had always been soft-spoken and introverted, and while no one expected him to stand on the table or pound his fist, there was also concern that he didn't seem more committed to fighting for his own job. At another point over the weekend, Pichette delivered a message to Dorsey: If you aren't fully committed to this fight, then the board isn't going to go fight for you. It was a reasonable, if not cold stance to take, but it certainly wasn't the full-throated support that Dorsey was looking for. Colleagues would remember that exchange years later as one of many fissures that surfaced between Dorsey and his board of directors.

Whether it was Pichette's tough love or just a realization that he didn't want to leave Twitter, Dorsey started to come around by the end of the weekend. The board had also come up with a "Hail Mary" plan: If it was going to settle with Elliott and offer Cohn a board seat, it wanted to bring in another investor of its own to try to provide a little balance.

On Saturday afternoon, the day after the airport meeting, Lemkau reached out to Egon Durban, the managing partner and co-CEO of Silver Lake, a well-known private equity firm with several high-profile investments, including the tech company Dell, the vacation rental site Airbnb, and the Chinese tech giant Alibaba. Durban had been at the firm since its founding in 1999 and was friendly with Lemkau from years of Wall Street dealmaking. He also knew Segal from his college days at George-town in the early 1990s. Durban was well respected within tech circles and had built a reputation as a founder-friendly investor, and seemed to try and keep company founders in control when possible. Best of all, he knew and liked Dorsey; the two had met for dinner a few years earlier when Durban was eyeing Twitter for a possible investment.

Twitter's management team wanted Durban to invest and join the board of directors. As part of the deal, Durban would buy a large chunk of Twitter's debt, known as senior convertible notes, which wouldn't come due until 2025. The point was to lock up Silver Lake as a long-term Twitter investor to help protect the company from Elliott's short-term investment strategy. The group also thought adding Durban to the board would mean more protection for Dorsey's job.

By Sunday evening, after a phone call with Dorsey, Durban was ready to invest $1 billion.

Twitter's instinct that Elliott would have broad support with investors turned out to be spot-on. The company's stock price climbed almost 8 percent higher on Monday, a clear sign that investors embraced the fact that one of the world's most successful activist investors was suddenly paying attention to Twitter. Apparently the idea of ousting Jack Dorsey seemed like a good one.

At many tech companies, Twitter included, a lot of employees make a large chunk of their annual compensation in stock awards. Typically, an 8 percent bump in the company's stock price would be cause for cel-ebration. Not inside Twitter. Employees read the news over the week-end that some activist investor many of them had never heard of was suddenly trying to replace their CEO. They woke up Monday morning, booted up their Twitter accounts, and started tweeting about how much they loved Dorsey. The tweets were gushing, the kind of heaping praise you might usually hear during a wedding or birthday toast. Or during a eulogy. Employees all posted using the same hashtag: #WeBackJack.

"I dont say this as often as i should . . . but @Jack is a special leader. He's empathetic, he's transparent, he's decisive, he has a heart for people . . . he's just dope," tweeted TJ Adeshola, Twitter's head of sports partnerships, who had traveled with Dorsey in Africa.

"So proud to work for a company that leads from the front, purpose driven, and values it's Tweeps above all else," tweeted Dalana Brand, an HR exec who led Twitter's diversity and inclusion team. "This is a direct reflection of the values displayed by our amazing leader @jack who serves as a role model for us all."

Dorsey even got support from outside of Twitter's office. "Just want say that I support @Jack as Twitter CEO," tweeted his pal Elon Musk. "He has a good ♥." (When someone replied to Musk that Dorsey should be "working hard" to fix Twitter's bot issues, Musk replied: "This is vital.")

While Musk tweeted support for Dorsey, Dorsey was similarly thinking about Musk. Even though Twitter's board had secured a commitment from Silver Lake's Durban over the weekend, the group was still discussing other potential investors to see if they could find an even better deal. Laurene Powell Jobs, the billionaire philanthropist and investor who had been married to Apple cofounder Steve Jobs for decades, was also seriously considered for the board and explored making an investment, but a deal never materialized. As the week wore on, members of Twitter's executive team and board shuffled in and out of Dorsey's home in San Francisco, making calls and brainstorming potential board candidates. Dorsey's house—with Twitter's corporate security team stationed nearby—offered much more privacy than Twitter's office. Some worried that Elliott might be having Dorsey or other key executives watched.

Dorsey was particularly interested in bringing Musk on board. He had the kind of money that Wall Street guys had, but he wasn't some suit just looking to turn a profit. Plus, Musk actually used Twitter, and seemed to understand what Dorsey was trying to build. But the billionaire tech tycoon was never seriously considered by Twitter's board, a sign, to Dorsey at least, that the board was overly cautious and afraid of rocking the boat. It didn't seem to bother Dorsey that Musk had tweeted himself into multiple lawsuits; the Twitter CEO was disappointed all the same.

That week Dorsey had Durban over to his home in San Francisco for dinner. They discussed the prospect of working together and Twitter's plans and goals, and both sides walked away confident that the deal would work. There was just one remaining hurdle: Nobody had told Elliott.

Jack Dorsey sat in the afternoon sunshine outside the Goldman Sachs office in Menlo Park, about thirty-five miles south of San Francisco. Like almost every major investment bank and venture capital firm, Goldman Sachs had an office on Sand Hill Road, the iconic Silicon Valley thoroughfare near Stanford's campus where the wealthiest and most influential investors in technology all clustered together in tony office parks. It was the kind of place where someone as famous as Dorsey would easily be recognized, but the Twitter CEO didn't care about being inconspicuous; he needed fresh air. He had commuted down to Menlo Park from San Francisco that afternoon in an Uber, picking up Lemkau from an AMPM mini-mart near the San Francisco airport on the way. It was a big day. Dorsey was meeting Jesse Cohn for the first time.

It had been almost a week since Cohn first met with Twitter's board near the San Francisco airport. That same group had since had a second meeting in New York at 200 West Street, Goldman Sachs's global headquarters. Team Twitter had flown to New York and pitched Cohn on the idea of Dorsey keeping his job, arguing that replacing him would kill a lot of momentum that Twitter had been building over the past couple of years. Kordestani, Pichette, and Lemkau asked Cohn to fly to California and meet with Dorsey in person to hear from him directly. Cohn found the pitch disappointing. He'd expected the Twitter group to show up with a plan for a CEO search and perhaps a strategy on how Dorsey might save face on his way out the door. Instead, it seemed like their strategy was to try to impress Elliott with a famous CEO.

Still, Cohn agreed to a meeting and the entire group flew back across the country—in separate jets, of course—to meet at a different Goldman Sachs office, this time with Dorsey in attendance. Most of the conversation again focused on Dorsey's role, a slightly more delicate topic of discussion now that Dorsey was sitting in the room. Cohn challenged Dorsey on whether he would let one of his top executives hold a second job at another company; Dorsey leaned into the fact that he was a founder, attempting to provide a clear and thoughtful vision for what he saw at Twitter. Cohn pointed out Twitter's product stagnation; Dorsey repeated a claim that he'd been using for years, that Twitter was spending lots of time and resources digging itself out of the technical hole that his predecessor, Dick Costolo, had left for him when he returned to the job in 2015. Dorsey was his typical soft-spoken self, but despite the topic of discussion, he was also charming and even funny. "You're a lot more normal than I thought you'd be," Cohn told Dorsey toward the end of the discussion.

"That's the nicest thing anyone has said to me all week," Dorsey replied.

Twitter's group felt the meeting had been a success, and as it ended and Dorsey got up to leave, Lemkau asked Cohn to hold back. There was one more person he wanted Cohn to speak with, an investor who didn't believe that Dorsey should be fired. On cue, and fresh off a round of golf in nearby Monterey, Egon Durban walked into the room. Twitter was throwing its Hail Mary.

Cohn had heard Durban was sniffing around Twitter as well, but didn't expect that the two would suddenly be face-to-face. Not only had Twitter sprung a surprise investor on him at the last minute, but it was one of the tech industry's most successful investors at that. Durban made his case in support of Dorsey, arguing that the CEO had successfully navigated Twitter through "the footsteps of elephants," a nod to the company's much larger competitors like Facebook and Google. Silver Lake was investing, Durban added, and he was taking a board seat. All that was left to discuss was Elliott's role moving forward.

Durban's involvement changed everything. Cohn and Elliott were confident that they could oust Dorsey in a proxy fight if needed, but now they had another option. Even though Twitter considered Durban "friendly," Cohn had also known him for years and felt the same. Investing in Twitter alongside another successful fund might provide a quicker, more lucrative payday than fighting Dorsey for months. A settlement suddenly seemed like a pretty good option to everyone.

As Jack Dorsey was busy battling for his job, the world was quickly shutting down. A newly discovered virus, known as Covid-19, had originated in central China and quickly become a global threat that was suddenly spreading in the United States. An Amazon employee in Seattle got it; so did a contractor who worked for Facebook out of Seattle, prompting the social media company to temporarily close its office. Twitter employees didn't realize it at the time, but many of them later suspected that they'd contracted Covid themselves at #OneTeam. Dozens of employees got sick with flulike symptoms in the weeks after the retreat, and they started posting about it using the hashtag #OneVirus.

On the same Monday morning that Twitter employees were tweeting #WeBackJack, Twitter encouraged its five thousand global employees to work from home, making it one of the first major U.S. companies to do so. For Twitter employees in Hong Kong, Japan, and South Korea, working from home wasn't even an option; it was now mandatory. "Our goal is to lower the probability of the spread of the COVID-19 for us—and the world around us," Twitter wrote in a blog post. "We are operating out of an abundance of caution and the utmost dedication to keeping our Tweeps healthy."

Of course, in early March 2020, operating out of an "abundance of caution" also came with a silver lining: It provided a built-in excuse for Dorsey to walk back the Africa plans that had been the source of so many headaches over the past three months.

On Thursday, March 5, the day after first meeting with Cohn, Dorsey walked into the Palace Hotel in San Francisco for a technology conference hosted by Morgan Stanley. Dorsey hated the idea of spending the morning answering questions for investors, but he always agreed to do one banking conference per year. The timing of this one was both wonderful and terrible. On the one hand, Dorsey's job was under assault by activist investors, and everyone, especially Wall Street, was wondering whether he'd still be employed by the end of the month. On the other hand, Dorsey had a chance to lay out the case for his job in a safe, prepared interview. Dorsey and the Twitter team knew they'd get a question about the CEO's time commitments, and they'd rehearsed the wording they wanted to deliver.

The question didn't come until the very end of the session and was asked by a member of the audience. "There's been reports that you're looking to travel some more," the audience member started. "I'm curious, how are you allocating your time? What are your priorities, and are there any kind of changes to what you're doing in the next few months because of what's going on in the world?"

It was the perfect setup. "Well, I think you're sub-tweeting my Africa tweet a little bit," Dorsey replied. "And I'll be frank, I made a mistake in tweeting that because I did not tweet the 'why' behind it." Africa had a young, growing population, he said, and it was important to understand the continent from a business and technology standpoint. Dorsey also said he was hoping to pressure-test his belief that remote work was possible, even from halfway around the world. "So my intention is not to go over and just hang out or take a sabbatical, but actually, everything I'm doing in San Francisco, doing on another continent," he said.

Dorsey ended his answer with the detail that most investors, especially Elliott, wanted to hear. "However, [with] everything happening in the world, particularly with coronavirus, I have to reconsider what's going on and what that means for me and for our company," he added. Dorsey didn't explicitly say that living in Africa was off the table, but he didn't have to. The unspoken reality was that Dorsey's Africa plans were dead.

The press release hit the news wire before the stock markets even opened on Monday, March 9: "Twitter, Inc. Announces Partnership with Silver Lake and Elliott Management." Silver Lake's Egon Durban was getting a board seat, and so was Elliott's Jesse Cohn. Dorsey got to keep his job. At least for now.

Several other changes were also announced. Kordestani, the executive chairman, was staying on the board but handing over his chairman duties to Pichette, who had been leading the discussions with Elliott throughout the process. Twitter would buy back $2 billion in shares and create a "Management Structure Committee" that would, among other things, review Twitter's CEO succession plan.

Buried further down the press release was a key paragraph that had been hotly contested over the previous couple of days. Twitter announced "ambitions" to improve two key parts of its business. First, it pledged to grow its user base by at least 20 percent in 2020 "and beyond," and second, it promised to increase its revenue growth "and gain share in the digital advertising market."

The word *ambitions* had been negotiated at length before the release was published. Elliott wanted Twitter to describe these new goals as "targets," something Twitter's management group, specifically CFO Segal, was vehemently against. The fear was that formal "targets" were too specific and would apply too much pressure on Twitter, especially heading into an unpredictable global pandemic. "Ambitions" felt more flexible. Of course, it didn't really matter what they were called. Dorsey was essentially on what was known in the industry as a "performance improvement plan." Twitter had agreed to improve user growth and revenue, and it now had Cohn sitting on its board to keep tabs on Dorsey's progress.

After years of speculation about activist investors, Elliott proved in less than a month that anyone with enough money could show up and force changes at Twitter in a matter of weeks.

Dorsey got to keep his job, but emotionally, the whole process had worn him down. The day before the deal was announced, and as all the final details were being ironed out with both Silver Lake and Elliott, Dorsey had gotten cold feet about the arrangement. Suddenly he wanted to fight Elliott instead of settling. The change of heart was too little, too late for Twitter's board. Some of the directors were peeved at Dorsey's sudden change in posture, especially so late in the game and after they'd fought for weeks to negotiate a solution that would save Dorsey's job.

Dorsey, in turn, was peeved that the board was settling with a firm that wanted him fired. Dorsey walked away from the Elliott saga with a new sense of distrust and frustration toward his own board of directors. His hope of bringing Musk onto the board had gone nowhere, and his management style and personal abilities had been questioned both publicly and privately for the better part of a month. Dorsey experienced firsthand the downsides of Twitter's status as a public company, including the constant threat that comes from having a stock structure that allowed anyone with enough money to come in and start throwing their weight around. The reality that Twitter operated a publicly traded company had never been more disappointing.

Elliott was in. Now Dorsey wanted out.

NINE

GO BIG OR GO HOME

"Today you are you, that is truer than true. There is no one alive who is youer than you!"

Jack Dorsey held Dr. Seuss's *Happy Birthday to You!* up to the camera and moved the page back and forth so that everyone on the call could see a birthday cake pop up off the page. "Shout loud," he continued, "I am lucky to be what I am! Thank goodness I'm not just a clam or a ham!"

In April 2020, any kind of social interaction, even over Google Hangouts or Zoom, seemed like a great idea. Twitter had started Storytime to give employees and their children something to do each week while everyone was stuck working from home. With daycares and schools closed because of the growing pandemic, someone had to entertain the kids. Today that someone was Dorsey. A few minutes after Dr. Seuss, he pulled out a second book called *Share My Gift*, a homemade treasure from his childhood that included Dorsey's own colorful illustrations.

A world in which Dorsey served as Twitter's resident librarian had been hard to imagine just a few weeks earlier. Two days after Twitter's board saved Dorsey's job, everything started to shut down. The World Health Organization declared Covid-19 a global pandemic on March 11, and President Donald Trump declared it a nationwide emergency in the United States two days later. California officially shut down on March 19 after Governor Gavin Newsom issued a stay-at-home order for everyone who wasn't working in "critical infrastructure sectors." That meant that Twitter's swanky offices, with free food and arcade games and rosé on tap, were almost completely empty, and Dorsey was reading Dr. Seuss over a video call.

The empty hallways and conference rooms at Twitter's headquarters belied the pressure building inside the company, which was entering the most pivotal stretch in its history. The coronavirus was the biggest global news story since World War II. Every country in the world was impacted, and Twitter's role as a distribution channel for breaking news and updates had never been more important. In the U.S., where Covid-19 restrictions and mandates varied widely by state, governors used the service to update local policies almost every day, and Twitter created a landing page with news and updates about the virus from various health agencies. Trump, in the middle of a reelection campaign, was tweeting dozens of times per day, often about his favorite topic, the "fake news" media, but also increasingly about Covid and its impact on the broader economy.

The convergence of a deadly pandemic, a hotly contested U.S. presidential election, and a sitting president who tweeted everything that popped into his head made Twitter more popular than ever. In the first three months of 2020, Twitter's user base grew 24 percent over the same period one year earlier. In the second quarter, it grew 34 percent. Twitter's servers were under intense stress just to keep the site up and running, a task complicated by the fact many employees were now working from home. "The increased load on our platform has placed unique stresses on our operations," Twitter wrote on its blog, adding that it was working to keep employees "safe and productive under the stress of the new levels of traffic we're seeing on our service." Revenue was down significantly because many advertisers froze spending in the pandemic's early days, but that felt like a short-term problem. Eventually advertisers would come back, and when they did, Twitter would have a much larger audience for them to reach.

As Covid spread and the death toll started to climb, Twitter started fact-checking user posts about the virus to try to keep people safe and minimize the possibility that someone might get sick because of something they read on Twitter. Misinformation was not a new problem for social networks, but with a few exceptions, most misinformation was not against Twitter's rules. The company didn't have a large fact-checking operation like Facebook, which had hired third-party groups to help police certain posts. In fact, fact-checking at Twitter was basically brand-new. In early 2020, the company started to label posts that included "synthetic media," or videos or photos that had been altered to mislead people. For the most part, though, that was it. Before Covid, misinformation had been a relatively minor part of Twitter's total policing efforts.

The pandemic changed that. Twitter's Trust and Safety team, led by Del Harvey, quickly came up with a misinformation policy related to Covid and broadened its definition of "harm" so that it could remove more posts that might put people at risk. The company took its cues from public health officials like the Centers for Disease Control and Prevention, and started demanding users take down tweets that went against expert guidelines about Covid. Users couldn't deny recommendations from global health authorities ("social distancing is not effective") or share alleged cures that were deemed to be dangerous ("drinking bleach and ingesting colloidal silver will cure Covid-19"). A Twitter blog post from March 2020 included nearly a dozen types of posts that were now considered a violation of Twitter's rules.

Not everyone was a fan of Twitter's new policies, including Dorsey. He was very uncomfortable with his company's decision to fact-check tweets about Covid. Dorsey was usually hands-off with Twitter's policies, and externally, he didn't complain. Internally, though, he showed much more interest in Twitter's Covid policies than he did almost any of its other rules or guidelines, requesting to be on email updates when high-profile accounts were flagged for violations. Even though the policies seemed to bother him, the CEO never stepped in to change them.

In early May, as understanding of the virus evolved, Twitter tweaked its policy and started to label posts that included "disputed or misleading" information about the virus but where the "risks of harm associated with a Tweet are less severe." This meant that more tweets could stay up, but they would include a note from Twitter pointing people to more reliable sources of information, like the CDC website. The labels were like a flag, a visible and obvious alert to anyone who saw them that the account holder was sharing dubious or misleading information.

Covid's rise opened up an entirely new world for Twitter. For years, it had operated in a predominantly binary system: Tweets that were a violation were removed, those that were OK stayed up. Now Twitter was trying to find a happy medium, labeling problematic tweets instead of removing them. It began to rely on automated software to apply the labels instead of just the employees working on the company's Trust and Safety team. Eventually Twitter wanted to expand the policy and start labeling misinformation about elections and voting, too, but Covid was taking up a lot of the focus.

They figured they had time to work out those details—the election was still six months away. But then, once again, Trump forced Twitter's hand.

Yoel Roth sat in his Tesla on the corner of Fifteenth and Valencia Streets in San Francisco's Mission District, his computer open on his lap and the traffic buzzing by. Roth wasn't supposed to be working on this Tuesday morning; he had taken the week off to move out of his apartment and across the Bay Bridge to a new house just north of Berkeley. That plan, though, had been derailed by another Donald Trump tweet, and instead of moving, Roth now sat on his computer applying the most notable misinformation label in company history.

Roth had been at Twitter close to five years, initially joining as a twenty-five-year-old intern in need of a break from working on his dissertation.

The son of an electrical engineering professor and a piano teacher, Roth grew up in Boca Raton, Florida, before heading to Pennsylvania to get his undergrad degree at Swarthmore College, working as a "genius" at the nearby Apple Store to make some money along the way. Roth then moved on to get his PhD in communication at the University of Pennsylvania, teaching classes on communication and media studies. He also did research on hate speech for the Berkman Klein Center for Internet & Society at Harvard. He took a short break to intern on Twitter's Trust and Safety team before finishing his PhD in 2015, then came right back to Twitter afterward to work on safety and privacy issues.

A few years later, after the 2016 election debacle, Roth took over as "head of site integrity" at Twitter. The fancy title meant he was in charge of protecting the service from all sorts of election-related issues: spam, information operations, election security, and misinformation. It also meant that he spent more time thinking about Trump's Twitter account than almost everyone else at the company.

By May 2020, Roth's plate was beyond full. Covid had driven several U.S. states to expand their voting policies to let more people vote by mail to minimize in-person interactions. California governor Gavin Newsom signed an executive order in May that guaranteed every registered voter in the state would automatically receive a mail-in ballot ahead of the November general election. Nevada did the same thing for its largest county, which included Las Vegas, ahead of its June primary election, and Michigan was also making it easier for voters to get a ballot in the mail.

Back in Washington, Trump railed against the policies. He spent weeks complaining about mail-in ballots on Twitter, calling them "RIPE for FRAUD" and suggesting that they favored Democrats over Republicans. When Nevada announced its mail-in ballot plan for its primary election, Trump threatened to withhold federal funding from the state. Four days later he tweeted that moving the election to mail-in ballots would lead to the "greatest Rigged Election in history. People grab them from mailboxes, print thousands of forgeries and 'force' people to sign."

Twitter executives watched the tweets closely. The company had rules that forbade people from misleading someone about the logistics of voting; you couldn't claim that an election was on the wrong day, or tweet that people could vote via text, for example. But Trump's tweets weren't an obvious violation on that front. Twitter executives had plans to expand the company's policies regarding voting to include the kinds of things Trump was tweeting, but those plans hadn't been announced. The misinformation labels Twitter was using for Covid weren't even being used for tweets about voting yet.

As they did several times over the years, though, Trump's tweets pushed Twitter into action. On May 26, the president posted two tweets that, for him, appeared routine. "There is NO WAY (ZERO!) that Mail-In Ballots will be anything less than substantially fraudulent," he wrote. California would send ballots to "anyone living in the state, no matter who they are or how they got there," he added, ending with "This will be a Rigged Election. No way!"

Roth and several of Twitter's other top policy and Trust and Safety executives huddled to discuss the tweets. They quickly decided they were inaccurate. California's new policy was to send ballots to every registered voter, not "anyone living in the state," and even though Twitter hadn't been flagging election-related tweets with labels, the company decided that Trump's tweet needed more clarification. For the first time ever, Twitter decided to label one of Trump's posts as misinformation.

The task of applying the label fell to Roth. He was one of the few people inside the company who could even append the label now that Trump's account was on Twitter's "Top 3" list. So Roth sat in his Tesla in San Francisco and added a label to the bottom of both tweets that read, "Get the facts about mail-in ballots." When a user clicked on the label, it took them to a new page that didn't mince words. "Trump falsely claimed that mail-in ballots would lead to 'a Rigged Election,'" it read. "However, fact-checkers say there is no evidence that mail-in ballots are linked to voter fraud."

Twitter was, in essence, calling the president of the United States a liar—and Trump flipped out.

"@Twitter is now interfering in the 2020 Presidential Election," he tweeted that evening before firing off a second tweet: "Twitter is completely stifling FREE SPEECH, and I, as President, will not allow it to happen!" Two days later, Trump issued an executive order in an attempt to roll back some of the legal protections social media companies get when deciding which posts to leave up or take down, a set of protections known as Section 230.

One of Trump's senior advisors, Kellyanne Conway, went on *Fox & Friends* and called out Roth by name for labeling Trump's tweets. While standing in front of the White House, she even spelled out Roth's Twitter username on the air so it would be easier for Fox viewers to find him and harass him. "Somebody in San Francisco go wake him up and tell him he's about to get more followers," she said. A Fox News reporter even combed through Roth's old tweets, and ran a separate story that day highlighting all of the negative things Roth had tweeted about Trump over the years, including one where he called Trump and his team "ACTUAL NAZIS" and another Roth had sent calling Trump a "racist tangerine." (For good measure, they threw in another tweet where Roth called Kentucky senator Mitch McConnell a "personality-free bag of farts.")

The old tweets were embarrassing and certainly didn't look good for Twitter's objectivity. But Conway's attack on Roth was even worse. By the time he woke up on the West Coast his phone was already blowing up, and his Twitter account was full of threatening messages and verbal assaults by Trump's supporters. He received so many death threats that Twitter sent security to his new home to walk through the house and recommend various safety measures, like installing cameras. The attacks picked up even more steam when Trump tweeted at him the following day. "So ridiculous to see Twitter trying to make the case that Mail-In Ballots are not subject to FRAUD. How stupid, there are examples, & cases, all over the place," he wrote. "Our election process will become badly tainted & a laughingstock all over the World. Tell that to your hater @yoyoel." Twitter ended up keeping twenty-four-hour security stationed outside Roth's house for months.

The fact-check labels were just the beginning of Twitter's clash with Trump that week. Across the country, protests had erupted after a white police officer in Minneapolis killed a black man, George Floyd, after pinning him down and kneeling on his neck. Video of Floyd's death was shared on social media, prompting marches and protests across the country as people, many in masks to help prevent the spread of Covid, marched against police brutality. Protests in Minneapolis quickly turned dangerous as protesters vandalized cop cars and storefronts and police fired tear gas and rubber bullets into the crowd. As the protests continued for a second day, and then a third, Minnesota governor Tim Walz activated the National Guard. Eventually, Trump weighed in on Twitter, posting two tweets just before 1 a.m. on May 29, just a few days after Floyd's death.

"These THUGS are dishonoring the memory of George Floyd, and I won't let that happen," he wrote about the protesters. "Just spoke to Governor Tim Walz and told him that the Military is with him all the way. Any difficulty and we will assume control but, when the looting starts, the shooting starts. Thank you!"

Dorsey was awake at his home in San Francisco when the tweet came in, and Twitter's executives scrambled to get online and figure out what to do. Included in the group was Harvey, the head of Trust and Safety, and Sean Edgett, Twitter's general counsel. Their boss, Vijaya Gadde, was out on maternity leave. The group spent a few hours discussing the post on Slack and inside a shared Google Document, which was a common way that teams inside Twitter collaborated since people could edit the document together and share notes in real time.

Just after midnight in California, the decision was made: Trump had violated Twitter's policy against glorifying violence. Since he was a world leader, Twitter wouldn't force Trump to delete the tweet like it would with a regular user. (It was still "newsworthy," after all.) Instead, Twitter hid the tweet behind a warning screen. Other users could no longer like it or comment on it. "This Tweet violated the Twitter Rules about glorifying violence," the warning read. "However, Twitter has determined that it may be in the public's interest for the Tweet to remain accessible."

Twitter had labeled Trump's tweets for misinformation and for violating the company's rules in the same week. There was still almost six more months until the election, but the dam was broken. President Trump's Twitter account was no longer untouchable.

While the Trump relationship quickly deteriorated, Jack Dorsey was thinking about Twitter's long-term future. The settlement with Elliott came with a lot of pressure to improve the company's business and Dorsey needed to convince investors that he should stay on as CEO. As part of the deal, Twitter agreed to host an Analyst Day for investors, offering Dorsey a chance to pitch his vision for Twitter and give Wall Street a sense of what to expect after the Elliott and Silver Lake investments. It was also a chance to reset the company's financial goals now that Twitter had new "ambitions" to grow revenue and users. Analyst Days weren't uncommon among publicly traded companies, but they were uncommon at Twitter; the company hadn't hosted one since 2014.

The good news for Dorsey was that he had more time to get his plan together than originally expected. The Analyst Day was initially scheduled for the fall of 2020 but was pushed until February 2021 because of Covid. The pandemic was making it difficult to judge Dorsey's performance. Twitter's user base was growing quickly, but its revenue was in the gutter. Sales were down 19 percent in the second quarter of 2020 as many marketers cut spending, waiting to see how the pandemic evolved. It certainly wasn't fair to blame Dorsey for that, but it didn't really seem fair to give him full credit for the user growth, either. It seemed like the real test for Dorsey would come once Covid was over, or at least normalized.

In preparation for Analyst Day, Dorsey asked some of his top lieutenants to create a three-year business plan he could share with the
board and investors. The group had been talking for months about a
long-term strategy for Twitter, but now Dorsey wanted something more
concrete that included revenue and user growth targets he could share
with Wall Street. Kayvon Beykpour and Bruce Falck, the guys running consumer and advertising products respectively, spent the spring
and early summer of 2020 pulling numbers together. Parag Agrawal
and Michael Montano, the CTO and head of engineering, were also
involved, brainstorming ways the company's technical teams could
improve the speed of Twitter's product development. Twitter's rise in
popularity was reason to be optimistic, especially since more users
typically led to more revenue down the line. Dorsey wanted to swing
for the fences. "Go big or go home," he told them.

Beykpour had a lot of ideas that he wanted to invest in on the product side. Twitter's decision to let people follow topics instead of just other
users seemed to be working and driving higher engagement. He wanted
to expand the feature so that there would be hundreds of thousands of
topics for people to choose from. Twitter also started work that summer
on an audio feature, called Spaces, so people could broadcast live conversations to anyone who wanted to listen, like having your own radio
studio inside the Twitter app. With everyone stuck at home because of
the pandemic, an audio feature seemed like a good idea, and another
startup called Clubhouse that did the same thing was already blowing
up in the tech community.

Then, of course, there was Scribbles—or what had originally started
as Scribbles. The idea for disappearing text posts had evolved since Mo
Al Adham started working on it in early 2019. Early tests for Scribbles
had been disappointing, and then Twitter had hired a new head of design,
Dantley Davis, who joined after years at Facebook where he had worked
on Stories. When Davis arrived at Twitter, he pushed to transform Scribbles into something that had a proven track record. So in early 2020,
Twitter started testing Fleets, a Stories clone focused on disappearing

photos and videos but with a different name. Fleets, too, was part of Beykpour's long-term product plan.

On the advertising side, Falck wanted to push aggressively into more targeted and personalized ads, known as direct response ads. Twitter had never been very good at direct response ads; the company instead specialized in brand advertising, which was the digital equivalent of running a television commercial or buying a billboard. Brand ads were targeted at a general audience, for example "women who live in California." If a brand ad worked, people might feel more positively toward the advertiser, but they weren't necessarily going to run out and make a purchase right then and there. The vast majority of Twitter's revenue—roughly 85 percent—came from brand advertising.

Direct response ads, though, were more valuable. They were hyper-targeted and designed to drive a specific outcome, like a visit to the advertiser's website or a trip to the App Store to download an app. They could also be creepy. People would often notice them when products that they looked at online would then appear in an ad days or even weeks later. Facebook and Google made most of their money from direct response ads, but Twitter had been slow to adopt them, primarily because the company never built the technology needed to track someone's online behavior, which was necessary to determine if the ads actually worked. Facebook and Google had developed their own versions of this technology over years as Twitter languished behind. Falck's portion of the three-year plan focused on closing that gap.

Falck and Beykpour took Dorsey's *go big or go home* directive to heart and put together an ambitious set of financial and user growth goals to share with Twitter's board. In 2020, Twitter would end up with revenue of $3.7 billion, and a total of 192 million daily users. The company's new three-year plan called for an annual revenue target of more than $9 billion annually and a user base of around 365 million daily users by the end of 2023. That meant annual revenue growth of 35 percent plus almost 58 million new users per year, for three straight years. Agrawal and his infrastructure teams would be necessary, too—he planned to double the pace at which Twitter built new products. To get there, the group thought Twitter needed to hire thousands of new employees to help build the new products and features.

Dorsey authored a document outlining the plan and presented it to Twitter's board of directors. Twitter would come out of the pandemic stronger than before, he told them, not only because the service was proving its value as a news distributor, but because Dorsey had long been an advocate for remote work. Twitter would help prove that people could do their jobs from anywhere. The numbers were ambitious, and Twitter would need to hire aggressively to make them a reality, but Dorsey seemed optimistic, especially considering how upset he'd been just a few months earlier with Elliott's arrival. The three-year plan was approved by the board.

But there was a problem. Twitter's CFO, Ned Segal, wasn't happy with the plan and had fought against it before Dorsey presented it. He wasn't alone. Several members of Twitter's finance team thought the numbers seemed completely unattainable. Twitter hadn't grown annual revenue by more than 25 percent since its first year as a publicly traded company in 2015; the new plan called for 35 percent growth three years in a row. The user numbers were just as aggressive. Twitter would end up having its best user growth year ever in 2020 when it added 40 million new daily users. Now Twitter's product team was targeting 58 million new users per year for three straight years.

Segal was worried that the ambitious numbers would set Twitter up for failure with investors. Plus, the plan was going to be incredibly expensive because it would require so many more employees. His concerns created tensions internally; Beykpour and Falck were on one side trying to go big at Dorsey's request, and Segal and the finance team were on the other trying to keep everybody's feet on the ground. Even after the plan had been approved by Twitter's board, Segal didn't want to share the numbers publicly at Analyst Day. Eventually, the group settled on a compromise. Parts of the aggressive plan were shared internally with employees, but Twitter ended up scaling back the numbers significantly when it finally held its Analyst Day months later.

Publicly, Twitter's revenue goal was cut back to just $7.5 billion from the internal goal of more than $9 billion. The user base goal was pared back from around 365 million to 315 million. Not everyone loved the strategy. Some people on Twitter's Staff worried that having two sets of numbers undermined the internal targets. What did it say about Twitter's goals if the company's executives weren't confident enough to say them out loud?

Wall Street, though, loved the revised numbers and the prospect of Dorsey finally pushing the company more aggressively. Twitter's stock jumped 12 percent when they were eventually revealed at Analyst Day.

Now all Dorsey had to do was deliver Twitter's best year ever.

TEN

BANNING TRUMP

The front cover of the *New York Post* just a few weeks before the presidential election featured a smiling Joe Biden standing next to his son, Hunter, but the accompanying headline was nothing to smile about. "BIDEN SECRET E-MAILS," it read, and an online headline was more damning. "Smoking-gun email reveals how Hunter Biden introduced Ukrainian businessman to VP dad."

The story, published on October 14, 2020, included information gathered off a laptop allegedly belonging to Hunter that had been abandoned at a computer repair shop and turned over to Donald Trump's lawyer, Rudy Giuliani. On the laptop were damaging emails that connected Hunter's dad, the Democratic presidential candidate, to a Ukrainian energy company called Burisma, where Hunter was on the board. The elder Biden had previously claimed he "had never spoken" with Hunter about his overseas business dealings, but the emails suggested that Biden had actually met with Burisma executives at his son's request. Less than a year after the meeting, while Biden was still vice president, he pressured the Ukrainian government to fire a prosecutor who was planning to investigate the company.

On the campaign trail, the story was just what Trump needed. "Congratulations to the @nypost for having exposed the massive corruption surrounding Sleepy Joe Biden and our Country," he tweeted. "He's always been a corrupt politician. Disgraceful!"

Inside Twitter, the story set off all kinds of alarm bells. During the 2016 election, the Russian government had helped orchestrate a hack and leak campaign against Democratic presidential candidate Hillary Clinton, succeeding in getting thousands of emails from her campaign chairman, John Podesta. The emails were later released publicly by WikiLeaks and were incredibly damaging to Clinton's campaign against Trump. Twitter, still scarred by its unintended role in the 2016 election, was on the look-out for a similar hack and leak campaign in the final days before the 2020 election. It even had a policy against sharing or linking to hacked material on Twitter at all.

The *Post* story seemed to fit the bill. Somehow an abandoned laptop from a random computer repair shop that contained damaging emails about a presidential candidate ended up in the hands of Trump's lawyer just weeks before the election. "There was smoke," Yoel Roth, the exec in charge of preventing election interference on Twitter, would explain years later. "Everything about it looked like a hack and leak and smelled like a hack and leak."

The problem, though, was that nobody actually knew if it was a hack and leak. Twitter employees working on policy, Trust and Safety, and public relations all scrambled to figure out what to do, messaging each other on Slack and over email since everyone was still working from home because of Covid. The discussion ended up reaching the highest levels inside Twitter, including Roth, Twitter's top policy exec Vijaya Gadde, and one of Twitter's most senior lawyers, Jim Baker. The group ultimately decided to block the story, which meant preventing people from tweeting the link, or even sharing it in private messages.

"As discussed, this is an emerging situation where the facts remain unclear," Roth admitted in a note to colleagues on the day the story was published. "Given the SEVERE risks here and the lessons of 2016, we're erring on the side of including a warning and preventing this content from being amplified."

Others inside Twitter were skeptical, including several members of Twitter's PR team, which was saddled with explaining the decision to the press. "I'm struggling to understand the policy basis for marking this as unsafe," wrote Trenton Kennedy, a member of the PR team. "Can we truthfully claim that this is part of the policy?" asked Brandon Borrman, Twitter's vice president of communications. Twitter stood strong on its decision to block the story even though it was clear internally that no one truly understood whether it violated Twitter's rules.

That decision, ultimately, was a massive mistake. No one ever confirmed the Biden emails were part of a hack and leak, and years later, they would be verified by security experts as legitimate. Two days after Twitter first blocked the story, and after intense criticism, it reversed its decision, but the damage was already done. Twitter had used its power over the public conversation to belittle a story that was harmful to Biden, and Republican politicians and other Trump supporters were furious. Senators Lindsey Graham and Ted Cruz announced that they wanted to haul Dorsey back to Washington to answer more questions before Congress. Just like four years earlier, Twitter looked like it was intentionally hurting the Trump campaign in the final weeks before a major election. The company's effort to avoid another embarrassing election mishap had resulted in an embarrassing election mishap. Twitter had strayed too far, unintentionally highlighting just how much control the company had over the spread of public information.

Gadde asked for understanding when she tweeted out an updated policy after Twitter reversed the block. "Content moderation is incredibly difficult, especially in the critical context of an election," she wrote. "We are trying to act responsibly & quickly to prevent harms, but we're still learning along the way."

Dorsey, whose hands-off approach meant he wasn't even involved in the decision, was more blunt. "Straight blocking of URLs was wrong," he tweeted, "and we updated our policy and enforcement to fix."

On the day before the election a few weeks later, as the world waited for voters to make their way to the polls in key battleground states like Pennsylvania and Florida, Twitter's board offered up a vote of its own: a vote of confidence in Jack Dorsey.

A new board committee had been formed after the Elliott settlement to review Twitter's corporate structure and evaluate the company's leadership. That analysis was complete, and everyone involved thought Dorsey should keep his job.

"The Committee expressed its confidence in management and recommended that the current structure remain in place," the board wrote in a securities filing, a boilerplate way of saying that the group approved of Dorsey's performance and the three-year plan he'd presented months earlier.

The document also mentioned that the committee had worked with Dorsey to update Twitter's CEO succession plan. All public companies were supposed to have a plan like this, which would kick in during an unlikely emergency scenario, like the CEO getting hit by a bus or suffering some other unexpected accident. What the document didn't say was that Parag Agrawal, the CTO, had been picked as Dorsey's emergency replacement. Behind the scenes, Dorsey had pushed to get Agrawal into the role and Twitter's board had agreed, picking him out of a small group of internal candidates. If anyone was going to take over Twitter, Dorsey wanted it to be Agrawal.

Despite the *New York Post* story, Donald Trump lost his bid for reelection against Democrat Joe Biden. The votes had taken days to count in some states, considering all the mail-in ballots, delaying the official announcement. In the end, though, the race hadn't been that close. Biden won 306 electoral votes compared to Trump's 232; he won the popular vote by more than 7 million total votes. Biden was set to be sworn in as the forty-sixth president of the United States at an inauguration cere-mony at the U.S. Capitol in mid-January. That was, unless Trump could do anything to stop it.

The outgoing president had spent the two months since election night disputing the results to anyone who would listen. On Twitter, his tweets were getting flagged for misinformation on a near-daily basis. Since his election night loss, Twitter had labeled more than three hundred of the president's posts, most of them disputing the election results or calling them "rigged." Twitter's labels pointed people to more accurate infor-mation instead. "Multiple sources call this election differently," some of the labels read. "This claim about election fraud is disputed," others said. Had Trump been a "regular" Twitter user, his account would have been permanently banned after so many repeat violations. As president of the United States, his account remained up thanks to Twitter's "World Leaders" policy.

On the day that Congress was set to certify the election results, Trump stood on a stage on the Ellipse lawn outside the White House and railed against everyone: the media, Congress, and even his favorite social networking site. "Every time I put out a tweet, that's, even if it's totally correct, totally correct, I get a flag," he said. "They don't let the message get out nearly like they should," he added. "I don't care about Twitter. Twitter's bad news."

Around the time Trump wrapped up his speech, Congress convened to certify Biden's electoral win. Trump encouraged his supporters to march to the U.S. Capitol and protest the process. "All of us here today do not want to see our election victory stolen by emboldened radical-left Democrats, which is what they're doing," he said. "We will never give up, we will never concede. It doesn't happen. You don't concede when there's theft involved."

In the hours that followed, some of Trump's supporters did indeed march to the U.S. Capitol, chanting "USA, USA, USA!" along the way. Protesters broke down police barricades and scaled the Capitol walls.

They broke windows to climb inside and unlocked the doors so others could stream in after them. Mike Pence, Trump's vice president, who was overseeing the election certification in the U.S. Senate, was shepherded away by Secret Service agents to a safe location. Other politicians began to shelter in place, and the building was put on lockdown.

Trump did not march to the Capitol, but instead returned to the White House and watched the increasingly violent riot unfold on TV. Images of Trump's supporters breaking windows and walking through the U.S. Capitol were being streamed on every major news outlet in America. As the rioters entered the building and his vice president was whisked away to safety, Trump posted a tweet.

"Mike Pence didn't have the courage to do what should have been done to protect our Country and our Constitution, giving States a chance to certify a corrected set of facts, not the fraudulent or inaccurate ones which they were asked to previously certify," he posted. "USA demands the truth!"

Many of Twitter's employees watched in disbelief from their respective homes as the events played out on television. Trump had already tweeted or retweeted seventeen times that day before posting about Pence, but given the rioters inside the Capitol Building, Trump's attack on Pence was quickly flagged and sent for review by the company's Trust and Safety team.

By this point, Twitter had a reliable system in place for analyzing controversial posts from famous users, including Trump. The tweets were added to a Google Document, where someone from the company's operations team would also paste any relevant Twitter policies the post might violate. Trust and Safety executives could then review the tweet and the policy side by side and make comments in the document for others to see. With everyone working remotely, it had proven to be a relatively quick and reliable way to analyze tweets without the need to get everyone on a phone call or video call. That process typically led to a recommendation on what to do—add a label, perhaps, or put the tweet behind a warning screen—and that recommendation was usually given to Vijaya Gadde, the head of Twitter's legal and policy divisions. After a decision was made, she often looped in Dorsey and gave him a heads-up; he preferred to stay out of the way and let others handle the messy process.

Twitter executives, including Del Harvey and Yoel Roth, reviewed Trump's tweet about Pence in the Google Document and quickly determined that it violated the company's "civic integrity" policy, which forbade people from sharing "misleading information intended to undermine public confidence in an election." At the Capitol, politicians and their staff members were barricading themselves into offices and meeting rooms to avoid the angry mob. A Capitol Police officer shot and killed one of the protesters.

Then Trump tweeted again. This time it was a video message. "I know your pain, I know you're hurt," he spoke into the camera. "We had an election that was stolen from us."

"But you have to go home now," he said, speaking directly to the rioters. "We have to have peace. We have to have law and order." He called the election "fraudulent," then offered his love to the rioters. "Go home, we love you, you're very special," Trump said. That video, too, was flagged by Twitter's internal teams and quickly deemed to be a violation.

At 6:01 p.m. ET, roughly five hours after the riot started, Trump tweeted a third time. "These are the things and events that happen when a sacred landslide election victory is so unceremoniously & viciously stripped away from great patriots who have been badly & unfairly treated for so long," he wrote. "Go home with love & in peace. Remember this day forever!"

Harvey and Roth had seen enough. Trump had spent weeks tweeting about a "rigged" U.S. election, propagating a lie to millions of people and using Twitter's service to do so. Those lies had led to a violent riot at the U.S. Capitol. Multiple people had died. More than 150 police officers were injured in the attack. Roth told colleagues that he felt he had "blood on his hands" given Twitter's role as Trump's megaphone. The group sent a recommendation to Gadde: It was time to ban Trump's account for good.

Gadde, though, disagreed. So did Dorsey.

The Twitter CEO wasn't even in the country. He was at The Brando, an exclusive island resort in French Polynesia that was only accessible via the resort's own private air fleet. Even though he wasn't usually involved in Twitter's enforcement decisions, Gadde had kept him updated throughout the day. The two felt that banning Trump was too steep. Twitter had never even suspended Trump despite all his rule violations. Booting him off Twitter entirely felt much too aggressive.

Instead, they settled on a temporary suspension. Under Twitter's policies, Trump was required to delete the three violating tweets. Once he did, he would start a twelve-hour "time-out" before he could post again. The time-out would hopefully give everyone a chance to catch their breath. Gadde alerted Twitter's Staff, the group of senior executives who reported to Dorsey, and then Trump received an email that his account had been suspended. After years of him pushing the boundaries on Twitter, and hundreds of violations, Twitter had finally cut off the sitting U.S. president.

Twitter announced the decision in a series of tweets from the company's @TwitterSafety account.

"As a result of the unprecedented and ongoing violent situation in Washington, D.C., we have required the removal of three @realDonaldTrump Tweets that were posted earlier today for repeated and severe violations of our Civic Integrity policy," the company posted.

"Future violations of the Twitter Rules," the company continued, "will result in permanent suspension of the @realDonaldTrump account."

The following day, January 7, 2021, a letter decrying Twitter's decision to suspend President Trump started circulating among employees. They weren't worried that Twitter had crossed a line; they worried that Twitter hadn't gone far enough.

The letter was a condemnation of both Trump and Twitter's executives. "For the last four years, we have watched right wing extremists grow on our platform, nurtured by @realDonaldTrump. We have seen Twitter leadership struggle to deal with the violent, hateful rhetoric shared by @realDonaldTrump," the letter read. Trump was no longer a "legitimate democratic actor," it continued; a suspension was not enough.

Employees added three requests: a recap of the company's decision-making process on January 6th; an "investigation into the last several years of corporate actions that led to Twitter's role in today's insurrection"; and a permanent ban of Trump's account. Roughly 350 employees signed the letter.

"We play an unprecedented role in civil society and the world's eyes are upon us," the letter ended. "Our decisions this week will cement our place in history, for better or worse."

After Trump was suspended, he didn't tweet again for another twenty-four hours. When he finally did, on the evening of January 7, Trump condemned the Capitol riot in a formal video address and said that his focus was now on "ensuring a smooth, orderly and seamless transition of power." It was the only tweet he sent all day.

The next morning, January 8, Trump tweeted twice. "The 75,000,000 great American Patriots who voted for me, AMERICA FIRST, and MAKE AMERICA GREAT AGAIN, will have a GIANT VOICE long into the future," he wrote. "They will not be disrespected or treated unfairly in any way, shape or form!!!"

Then he tweeted this: "To all of those who have asked, I will not be going to the Inauguration on January 20th."

Twitter's Trust and Safety team once again reviewed Trump's tweets, and at first the belief was that Trump didn't violate any of the company's rules. "As an fyi, Safety has assessed the DJT Tweet above and determined that there is no violation of our policies at this time," wrote Anika Navaroli, an employee on Twitter's safety policy team, in a Slack message to colleagues about Trump's first tweet. The team also made the same determination for Trump's second tweet about the inauguration.

Gadde, though, wasn't convinced. She worried that Trump's language might be "coded incitement to further violence" depending on how you interpreted his message. Specifically, his use of the term "American Patriots" seemed problematic. If he was referring to ordinary citizens who voted for him, it seemed fine. But if he was referring to the rioters from the U.S. Capitol, then the tweet could have a very different meaning, she suggested.

That afternoon, Twitter held an all-hands meeting with employees, many of them angry that Trump's account was still active. The employee letter that had circulated the day before had been leaked to the press and published in *The Washington Post* earlier that morning. It was clear from the meeting that many employees inside Twitter were unhappy with Trump, but also concerned about Twitter's continued role in providing him a megaphone to invalidate the election.

What employees didn't know was that the wheels to ban Trump were already in motion behind the scenes. The decision was made that Trump's tweets violated the company's "glorification of violence" policy, which forbade people from praising a violent act in a way that "could incite or lead to further violence." His decision to skip the inauguration suggested that he still believed the election had been stolen from him. If you viewed "American Patriots" to mean rioters, then his tweet read like a show of support for those who had vandalized the U.S. Capitol.

Some of Twitter's senior Trust and Safety executives created a document outlining the company's rationale for the decision. When Dorsey asked for the document to be simplified, Harvey started rewriting it, and Roth understood what was about to happen next. "God help us," he wrote to a colleague over Slack, "[it] makes me think he wants to share it publicly."

At 3:21 p.m. PT on January 8, Trump's account officially went dark. Users who went to his Twitter profile no longer saw his tens of thousands of tweets. In their place was a new message from Twitter: "Account suspended."

The blog Twitter posted explaining the decision was almost identical to the internal document Harvey had rewritten at Dorsey's request. "Our determination is that the two Tweets above are likely to inspire others to replicate the violent acts that took place on January 6, 2021," it read, "and that there are multiple indicators that they are being received and understood as encouragement to do so."

After twelve years and more than 56,000 tweets, Twitter finally decided that carrying Trump's messages posed a threat to public safety. @realDonaldTrump's Twitter run was over.

ELEVEN

MAXI JACK

The fear of punishing Donald Trump, which had existed for years among social media companies, evaporated after the Capitol riot on January 6th. With just days left in his presidency, services like Facebook, YouTube, and Snapchat were quick to cut Trump's microphone. They desperately wanted to avoid looking like they condoned the violence from the Capitol, or the president's stolen election claims. Within a matter of days, Trump lost access to hundreds of millions of followers across the world.

Facebook put Trump's account in a two-week time-out. YouTube gave Trump a one-week ban. Both companies soon extended those suspensions indefinitely. Reddit banned one of its popular pro-Trump discussion forums after users there "glorified and incited the violence" from the U.S. Capitol. Snapchat banned him forever.

Trump's supporters in Congress were unsurprisingly quick to condemn the decisions, but so were other world leaders. South Carolina senator Lindsey Graham called it "a serious mistake" and threatened regulation against Twitter. "It's like a censorship court is being created, like the Holy Inquisition, for the management of public opinion," said Mexican president Andrés Manuel López Obrador. German chancellor Angela Merkel called the decisions "problematic," and French president Emmanuel Macron criticized social networks for both helping fuel the violence on January 6th and overstepping their role as speech regulators. "I don't want to live in a democracy where the key decisions . . . *[are]* decided by a private player, a private social network," he said.

Most surprisingly, perhaps, was that CEO Jack Dorsey was similarly bothered by the ban. Unlike Facebook and YouTube, Twitter didn't suspend Trump indefinitely. They'd gone several steps further—a permanent ban—and there was no turning back. Dorsey started receiving death threats, and so did Vijaya Gadde, the Twitter lawyer and policy boss who helped make the decision. Even more troubling for Dorsey was that his parents started receiving threats, too; Twitter had to put security outside their home in St. Louis. For better or worse, Twitter's CEO was used to getting criticism and death threats, but it was rare that his role running the company so directly put his family at risk, too. He spent the first week after the ban reflecting on the decision and what it meant for Twitter long-term.

When he finally tweeted, Dorsey was obviously conflicted. His thread was thirteen tweets long. He wrote:

I do not celebrate or feel pride in our having to ban @realDonaldTrump from Twitter, or how we got here. After a clear warning we'd take this action, we made a decision with the best information we had based on threats to physical safety both on and off Twitter. Was this correct?

I believe this was the right decision for Twitter. We faced an extraordinary and untenable circumstance, forcing us to focus all of our actions on public safety. Offline harm as a result of online speech is demonstrably real, and what drives our policy and enforcement above all.

That said, having to ban an account has real and significant ramifications. While there are clear and obvious exceptions, I feel a

ban is a failure of ours ultimately to promote healthy conversation.
And a time for us to reflect on our operations and the environment
around us.

Having to take these actions fragment the public conversation. They
divide us. They limit the potential for clarification, redemption,
and learning. And sets a precedent I feel is dangerous: the power
an individual or corporation has over a part of the global public
conversation.

The Trump ban had confirmed one of Dorsey's longest-held beliefs:
that internet companies, including his own, had too much power. It was
almost hard to believe given where the service had started. Twitter's
evolution from zippy status updates into a center-stage forum for global
politics meant Dorsey was suddenly responsible for deciding what the
world could and couldn't say. It was a power that he had no desire to
wield, and he never fully embraced his own elevated role in Twitter's
new reality. He used his thread about Trump to pitch Bluesky, his vision
for a social networking system where no one would ever have that kind
of power over speech again.

Bluesky was still in its infancy, and most people either hadn't heard
of it or had no idea how it worked. The easiest way to imagine it was
to think about email, or at least the promise of email. Google, Yahoo,
Microsoft, and numerous other companies all had their own email services, but they were still interoperable, meaning a Google user could
send an email to a Yahoo user even though those products were operated
by competitors. That's because email was built on an open technology
protocol, which was then customized when companies added their own
features and policies.

A social networking protocol would, in theory, work much the same
way. Software developers could use the underlying technology to create
their own networks, with unique designs, policies, and algorithms. People on one network could still interact with those on another, but each

person's experience would be governed by rules for whichever network they signed up for. If you wanted to see every single post, even posts that were racist, sexist, or misinformed, there could be a network for that. If you wanted to filter out a lot of those posts, there would be a network for that, too. There could be an infinite number of networks, each tailored by its individual creator. If you ever wanted to jump from one network to another, that was OK, too; you'd be able to bring all your posts and data with you, which wasn't the case with Twitter or Facebook.

In this alternate universe, Bluesky would make banning a sitting U.S. president much less significant. Trump could simply take his posts and followers with him to another network built on the Bluesky protocol. Companies like Twitter could continue to make content decisions it deemed necessary for business without feeling like they were also infringing on people's freedom of speech.

Unfortunately, Bluesky was still just a dream. In the real world, the fallout from Twitter's Trump ban weighed on Dorsey for months. In March he was hauled back before Congress for yet another hearing on misinformation and Twitter's role in policing user content, this time before the House Energy and Commerce Committee. It was Dorsey's fourth congressional hearing in less than three years.

The Twitter CEO was none too pleased to be summoned. Dorsey had never been a fan of things that required a lot of process, including earnings calls and investor analyst days, and congressional hearings meant days of testimony prep, formalities, and pre-hearing calls with politicians.

Dorsey, who was joined by Facebook CEO Mark Zuckerberg and Google CEO Sundar Pichai, seemed disinterested from the beginning. He joined on video from his kitchen, with cups, plates, and silverware visible in the background behind him. Over his right shoulder sat a Block-clock, which could display the price of Bitcoin. Dorsey had a jacket on but was once again tieless with his nose ring in and a long, graying beard.

He was on Twitter throughout much of the five-hour hearing, at one point mocking some of the questions he was getting from politicians on the panel and liking other tweets that were critical of the hearing while it was still ongoing. He even replied to one of his old Twitter colleagues confirming that, yes, he was barefoot.

Dorsey's tweeting didn't go unnoticed. New York democrat Kathleen Rice called him out for being distracted. "Your multitasking skills are *quite* impressive," she said, sounding thoroughly unimpressed.

Dorsey would end up doing a lot of multitasking in 2021. As the summer wore on, he became obsessed and distracted by another project that had nothing to do with Twitter. And just like during the congressional hearing, he wasn't very good at hiding it.

Jack Dorsey's trip to Miami in June 2021 was the opposite of a ten-day silent meditation retreat. He walked on the beach with a swimsuit model half his age, Flora Carter, and palled around town with David Grutman, the restaurant and nightclub owner who knew seemingly every celebrity to set foot in South Florida. On Friday June 4, Dorsey had dinner at Grutman's steakhouse, Papi Steak, and then stayed out late at LIV, one of Grutman's nightclubs, where a table can cost upwards of $100,000. The next night Dorsey was out at E11EVEN, another Miami club, where the rapper G-Eazy performed followed by the deejay Deadmau5. He finished the weekend with Grutman at Hard Rock Stadium, home of the NFL's Miami Dolphins, to watch boxer Floyd Mayweather fight YouTube star Logan Paul. Dorsey and Grutman hung out with Mayweather before the fight, posing for a photo together in the locker room.

Dorsey was not technically in Miami to party, though he certainly had a good time. The Twitter CEO was in town for Bitcoin 2021, a conference dedicated to the cryptocurrency that had started to consume his life. Dorsey spent much of the weekend talking about Bitcoin with anyone who would listen.

"He's a huge Bitcoin guy. Huge," said Dave Portnoy, the outspoken and controversial founder of Barstool Sports. Portnoy had chatted with

Dorsey and Grutman over dinner one night at one of the Miami mogul's other restaurants, Komodo, and was floored by Dorsey's infatuation with the digital currency. "He actually said if he could, like, get a job where he's just working on Bitcoin full-time, he's so confident in it, he'd like stop everything else and just work on Bitcoin," Portnoy later said on his podcast. "He is as bullish on Bitcoin as anybody I've ever heard . . . this guy is like pro, pro, pro Bitcoin."

Grutman, too, got an earful from Dorsey, who told him that Bitcoin would be worth $100,000 per coin by the end of the year, and $1 million per coin by 2024. At the time, a single coin was worth roughly $35,000. "Buy it," Dorsey advised him.

Bitcoin had already been around for more than a decade by the time Dorsey was pumping up the currency in South Beach. He read the original Bitcoin white paper not long after its release in 2008. "The whole thing was just poetry," he recalled years later. Over the next several years, and with a front-row seat to the world of banking regulation thanks to his role running Square, Dorsey grew enamored with the idea of a global currency that wasn't controlled by any bank or government. It reminded Dorsey of his early days learning to code back in St. Louis before the internet became so commercialized and siloed by various businesses. Bitcoin traded on a public, global ledger called the blockchain, and because it was digital, it could be sent or spent anywhere in the world almost instantly. With Bitcoin, people wouldn't even need banks, Dorsey thought.

Dorsey's trip to Africa a few years earlier had revived his interest in the currency, and Square was suddenly a testing ground for all the CEO's Bitcoin-related ideas. About eight months before Dorsey's Miami trip, Square invested $50 million into Bitcoin to hold on its balance sheet, calling the currency an "instrument of economic empowerment." Square's users could buy and sell Bitcoin just like stocks, and while it wasn't yet public, Square was preparing to build its own Bitcoin wallet for storing the currency offline. Dorsey was even building an entirely new business division within Square to focus exclusively on Bitcoin, which would launch a month after Miami.

In crypto jargon, Dorsey's unwavering commitment to the currency made him a "Bitcoin maxi"—short for "Bitcoin maximalist," and even shorter for "guy who thinks Bitcoin is the one and only true cryptocurrency." To most people outside of crypto, Dorsey just looked like a hardcore Bitcoin hobbyist. He still had two full-time jobs, after all. But then he took the stage in Miami as part of the official Bitcoin 2021 conference.

He walked out for his session titled "Banking the Unbanked" looking more like the owner of a local surf shop than the CEO of two publicly traded companies. Dorsey wore an oversized sunburst tie-dye T-shirt to go along with his shaved head and a long beard. For almost thirty minutes, he preached the gospel of Bitcoin to an audience of believers. Bitcoin would replace banks, he said, and help lead to more renewable energy. It would change the continent of Africa, where he had seen firsthand how many entrepreneurs were working to fix problems related to payments.

"I don't think there's anything more important in my lifetime to work on and I don't think there's anything more enabling for people around the world," Dorsey said.

At one point he was interrupted by Laura Loomer, the conspiracy theorist and activist who had shown up at Dorsey's 2018 congressional hearing and was back to heckle him again. Loomer had long been a wild card for Twitter. Several years earlier she had handcuffed herself to the door of Twitter's New York City office building, and she'd also camped out in front of Dorsey's San Francisco home at one point in protest of the CEO. Twitter executives worried that she would eventually figure out a way to handcuff herself to Dorsey directly. Yet, as she yelled at Dorsey from the audience that "censorship is a human rights violation" and that Dorsey was "interfering in elections," he took her complaints seriously and replied earnestly.

"I recognize the fact that there is an incentive and a corporate incentive and a business incentive that is different than what might be needed for global communication," he replied as Loomer was escorted out of the building. Dorsey was referring to the reality that Twitter had to make difficult speech and policy decisions, like removing certain kinds of posts, because the service was ultimately a business that had to make money and appease advertisers. "My goal in my life in this moment is to remove as much as I can the corporate-ness of our companies," he continued. Dorsey wanted to build more Bitcoin-inspired products at Square, and at Twitter he was focused on Bluesky, which was "inspired entirely by Bitcoin," he said.

"Every single person in the world will benefit and get value from utilizing [Bitcoin]," he said at the end of the interview. "I'm going to do everything in my power to make sure that that happens." The crowd of Bitcoin disciples cheered.

Dorsey's Twitter colleagues were less inspired by the boss's week in Miami. The company policy was still that employees shouldn't be traveling for work because of Covid, which made watching Dorsey hobnob with celebrities and models all week harder to stomach. But mostly they were peeved that he said the quiet part out loud. Twitter had always been considered Dorsey's "favorite child"; even people at Square joked that the CEO loved Twitter more. Now, suddenly, Bitcoin seemed to be his favorite. *I don't think there's anything more important in my lifetime to work on*, he'd said. Apparently, that included Twitter.

As the summer wore on, Dorsey continued to drift away from Twitter. He stopped checking in as frequently with his direct reports, and even though he showed up for video meetings, he started to join without his camera turned on. At monthly all-hands meetings with the whole company, Dorsey started to mail it in, simply reading off his prepared script without as much energy or enthusiasm as people were used to seeing.

In some cases, his lack of interest was becoming excruciatingly obvious. In July of that summer, Twitter shut down Fleets after it became clear that very few people were actually using the feature. It was no secret internally that Dorsey wasn't a fan of Fleets. He'd encouraged Beykpour's team to build Scribbles more than two years earlier, but grew to despise Fleets as it morphed into a rip-off of Instagram and Snapchat's Stories feature. At one point shortly after Fleets was launched, Dorsey was asked during a company all-hands why he never used the product. He simply shrugged and said it wasn't his thing, before handing the meeting over to the Fleets team for an update. When Fleets shut down, Dorsey just tweeted an emoji of a hand waving goodbye. It was a prime example of how Dorsey's hands-off management style could backfire. Even though he thought Fleets was a bad decision, he never stepped in to halt the product or move the team in another direction. When Fleets didn't work out despite more than two years of time and resources, he gave off the impression that he didn't care.

The distance created by Covid seemed to be a factor. Dorsey spent much of 2020 and 2021 living in Hawaii or Costa Rica, and while employees liked to try to guess where he was based on the background of his video calls, it also became clear over time just how much the company missed his physical presence in the office. Bumping into people in the halls and showing up for in-person meetings had been a healthy way of forcing Dorsey out of his shell. Working from home, or from a tropical island, meant it was easier to hide and check out, and colleagues noticed the distance.

When Dorsey did show up in public, it was rarely because of Twitter. In July he joined another Bitcoin conference, this time virtually, where he spoke alongside his pal Elon Musk. Dorsey wore the same sunburst tie-dye T-shirt as he'd worn in Miami and spoke in the same glowing terms about Bitcoin. "My hope is that it creates world peace," he said. When it came to Twitter, Dorsey said that his biggest focus was Bluesky, still a nascent project that wasn't even technically part of the company.

In August, Dorsey visited Musk at Starbase, the SpaceX launch facility in Boca Chica, Texas, along the Gulf of Mexico. He brought along his good friend, the music producer Rick Rubin. Earlier that morning, SpaceX had launched a rocket from Florida on a resupply mission to the International Space Station. "Grateful for @elonmusk & @SpaceX 🖤," Dorsey tweeted. In October, Dorsey was back in Paris for Fashion Week again, attending a party where Diplo deejayed and the club ran out of tequila, forcing employees to scrounge up more bottles from neighboring bars and restaurants in the early hours of the morning.

Members of Staff, Dorsey's direct reports at Twitter, were growing frustrated with his absence. The positive vibes and camaraderie that had been built at #OneTeam and the off-site in Big Sur had evaporated along with Dorsey's time and attention. Some members on Staff were considering new jobs.

Twitter's board of directors was also growing frustrated. The CEO that they'd fought to retain after Elliott arrived was slowly losing interest in the company. Dorsey had even won a symbolic battle in the spring of 2021 when Elliott's Jesse Cohn announced his departure from Twitter's board. Cohn technically resigned, but it was no secret that Dorsey had been agitating for his removal. Still, several members of the board were sad to see Cohn leave. Despite his combative introduction to the company, they considered him helpful and professional during his year as a director. Plus, Twitter's stock had nearly doubled since Elliott's investment became public; Cohn had gotten what he came for.

In early October 2021, Jack Dorsey finally decided to step down as CEO. Given his interest in Bitcoin and his lack of interest in running Twitter, it was a decision that was months overdue. When he told the Twitter board that he was ready to leave, he also told them that he had a successor in mind: Parag Agrawal, Twitter's chief technology officer. As far as Dorsey was concerned, Agrawal was the solution. There was no Plan B.

Agrawal grew up in Mumbai, India, where his father worked at a nuclear research center and his mother was an economics professor. He was geeky in high school, and excelled in chemistry and math, and even won a gold medal as a teenager at an international physics Olympiad competition. He fell in love with stargazing in high school and was awed by the idea of looking at light that may have been emitted hundreds of millions of years earlier. He graduated from the Indian Institute of Technology Bombay, and then moved to the U.S. to get his PhD in computer science from Stanford, earning a reputation along the way for being a top student in a school full of top students. Agrawal joined Twitter as a twenty-seven-year-old software engineer in the fall of 2011 without much professional experience. He worked his way up the ladder internally, first working on the team that built Twitter's advertising technology and later becoming an expert in machine learning algorithms that Twitter eventually used to determine what tweets people saw in their feed. Dorsey promoted him to CTO in 2017, and Agrawal quickly became a thoughtful and reliable member of Staff, earning his boss's trust and respect.

Dorsey's insistence on appointing Agrawal wasn't shocking to the board since he'd already pushed for Agrawal to be the "emergency" CEO replacement a year earlier. Still, some members of the board were reluctant. Agrawal was just thirty-seven years old, which would make him the youngest CEO in the S&P 500. His long tenure inside Twitter also meant that his experience was limited to a single company—not to mention one that was in near-constant turmoil with an inconsistent business. Agrawal was generally well respected by Twitter's Staff group, and while he could be opinionated and even argumentative, he kept a low profile both internally and externally. He certainly wasn't breakdancing on stage at #OneTeam or showing up to meetings with the president. Many employees knew almost nothing about him.

Agrawal, though, seemed to care about a lot of the same stuff as Dorsey. Like his boss, Agrawal was generally uncomfortable with making a lot of rules around what people could and couldn't say on Twitter. More specifically, he preferred to find product solutions to Twitter's speech problems, things like labels or changes to the algorithm instead of more policies. He was also in charge of spearheading Bluesky and was leading the small internal Twitter group that was building products related to cryptocurrencies and the blockchain, areas where Dorsey was incredibly passionate.

Twitter's board debated whether to hire a search firm to look for outside candidates like the company did in 2015 when Dorsey returned.

Some board members, including Robert Zoellick, the former president of the World Bank, were adamant that the group do a formal search, though they were in the minority. During meetings, Twitter's board members tossed around candidates for the job from their respective professional circles, but no one seemed both qualified and, more importantly, interested in running Twitter. Zoellick floated the idea to have Bret Taylor, one of Twitter's other board members and a high-ranking product exec at Salesforce, run the company; the idea never gained traction.

There was a fear that hiring a professional search firm would turn the process into a spectacle like the company had dealt with when Dorsey returned six years earlier. There was just one other board member besides Dorsey left from that 2015 group, but everyone knew how badly things had been bungled. The board had tried to pressure Dorsey into giving up his job at Square, created months of speculation and uncertainty, and ultimately took Dorsey as CEO even though he kept his second job. It wasn't the kind of drama Twitter's board wanted to recreate. Almost nobody inside or outside the company knew Dorsey was stepping down; even some members of Twitter's Staff were still in the dark. So the board ultimately decided to keep things clean and simple. They asked Agrawal to interview for the role.

Agrawal met with everyone on the board individually over several weeks, wrote a long document outlining his vision for the company, and also presented that vision to the entire group. He was an impressive candidate, but also a convenient one. Considering he was Dorsey's first choice, hiring him also came with the bonus of throwing Dorsey a bone on his way out the door. Given the fractured relationship between the CEO and the board ever since the Elliott situation, departing on good terms wasn't necessarily a given. In the end, Twitter didn't seriously consider any other candidates inside or outside the company. Agrawal got the job.

On the Monday morning after Thanksgiving, news finally broke that Dorsey was stepping down. Most Twitter employees weren't even working that day. It was a "day of rest" at Twitter, one of the monthly bonus vacation days the company started giving out after Covid to help people stay sane and motivated. In true Dorsey fashion, he tweeted the email that he sent to the entire company to his millions of followers. The subject line: "Fly."

Dorsey told employees that Agrawal was taking over, and that Taylor had been appointed chairman, taking over for Patrick Pichette. Those changes meant that Dorsey was leaving Twitter with product and engineering executives in charge, an important detail to him since he'd grown to despise Twitter's relationship with Wall Street, especially after the activists. Taylor "understands entrepreneurship, taking risks, companies at massive scale, technology, product, and he's an engineer," Dorsey wrote to employees. "All of the things the board and the company deserve right now."

Dorsey's praise for Agrawal was even more effusive. "Parag has been behind every critical decision that helped turn this company around," he wrote. "He's curious, probing, rational, creative, demanding, self-aware, and humble. He leads with heart and soul, and is someone I learn from daily.

"My trust in him as our CEO is bone deep."

As for his own role at Twitter going forward, Dorsey said that he would stay on the board until the end of his term at the next annual shareholders meeting in May, and then he'd leave the board for good. "I believe it's really important to give Parag the space he needs to lead," Dorsey wrote. People who worked with Dorsey thought he seemed particularly happy to see Pichette stepping down as chairman considering the role he'd played in the Elliott settlement. (Notably, Pichette wasn't mentioned in Dorsey's farewell email.)

Dorsey went out of his way to clarify that he was not being fired. "I want you all to know that this was my decision and I own it," he wrote. "It was a tough one for me, of course. I love this service and company . . . and all of you so much. I'm really sad . . . yet really happy. There aren't many companies that get to this level. And there aren't many founders that choose their company over their own ego. I know we'll prove this was the right move."

What the email lacked was any convincing explanation for *why* Dorsey was leaving. It was true that Dorsey resigned; he'd dictated the timeline for his departure and even handpicked his replacement. But it was also true that running Twitter had become unfun for Dorsey, in part because the board had started to demand real results and accountability that hadn't been expected for years. Elliott's arrival had pushed Twitter to prioritize its business and user growth above all else, a sickening prospect for a man who viewed Twitter more as a public service than a moneymaking machine. Twitter's lofty three-year plan had created a whole new set of expectations, and even with Cohn off the board, Dorsey's job was never going to be safe. He would always be just one or two bad quarters away from another activist gunning for his job.

Elliott was just one factor. Banning President Trump was, in Dorsey's own words, a "failure" of the system that he'd helped build, and a reminder that those kinds of decisions would never go away so long as Twitter had advertisers to please. Covid had pushed Dorsey away from his Staff, first physically and then emotionally, in a way that seemed like it might never recover. And then there was Bitcoin, Dorsey's new passion. At Square, Dorsey could spend as much time on Bitcoin as he wanted. At Twitter, it would always be a distraction.

In the end, the people who knew Dorsey well saw a man who no longer enjoyed a job that had once been his life's calling.

Dorsey's departure was monumental. In almost sixteen years, he'd gone from Twitter cofounder to CEO to board chair to CEO again. No one in history had spent more time thinking about the product or its place in the world. When Dorsey returned as CEO in 2015, Twitter's stagnant user growth meant the company was on the brink of disaster. He'd helped save Twitter and refined its purpose in the world, changing the way that news traveled and people communicated in the process. By the time Dorsey resigned, Twitter was routinely profitable, growing, and more culturally relevant than it had ever been.

Somehow, though, Twitter still underachieved compared to the rest of the tech industry during his tenure. In his six years back as CEO, Twitter's market cap grew by roughly 90 percent. Facebook's value more than tripled in that time; Alphabet, which owned Google and YouTube, saw its value quadruple and then some. Dorsey was never able to fix Twitter's Wall Street woes.

News of Dorsey's departure led to hundreds of replies thanking him and wishing him luck. A few days later, Dorsey's friend Elon Musk tweeted. The post included two pictures side by side. The first was a picture of Soviet dictator Joseph Stalin standing on a boat next to Nikolai Yezhov, an official from Stalin's secret police. Musk had photoshopped Agrawal's face onto Stalin's body, and Dorsey's face onto Yezhov's. In the next picture, Yezhov—or Dorsey—was gone. He'd been pushed overboard by Agrawal. It was a play on Stalin's well-documented propaganda strategy of editing his enemies out of his photographs.

Agrawal had been on the job less than a week and one of Twitter's most prominent users, and Dorsey's favorite tweeter, was already likening him to Joseph Stalin.

Welcome to running Twitter.

PART III

BATTLE FOR TWITTER

TWELVE

IS TWITTER DYING?

Elon Musk was one of Twitter's most prolific users for years, but he officially became a Twitter shareholder on the final day of January in 2022. Musk was antsy. Things at Tesla and SpaceX were going well. Almost too well, in fact. His net worth had ballooned to more than $330 billion during the pandemic after Tesla stock grew more than 700 percent in 2020 alone. When everything in his life was humming along just fine, Musk typically took on a new challenge, or better yet, created a crisis for himself. He started thinking about ways he could spend his massive fortune. "I didn't want to just leave it in the bank," he told his biographer Walter Isaacson. "So I asked myself what product I liked, and that was an easy question. It was Twitter."

On Monday, January 31, Musk spent $23 million on Twitter stock, a relatively small purchase considering the number of zeros visible on his bank account. He added another $20 million to his investment the next day, and then another $31 million on day three. On Thursday, Musk spent more than $125 million on Twitter stock. By the weekend, Musk had acquired more than 6.7 million shares—almost a quarter-billion-dollar investment in just five days. He continued to buy Twitter shares every day for the next two months.

Twitter's new CEO, Parag Agrawal, and the rest of the employees had no idea what Musk was up to as they adjusted to life after Dorsey.

Agrawal tried to leave his mark on the company immediately after getting the job, restructuring Staff to give more power to fewer people in hopes of breaking free from the company's sluggish decision-making process. "My focus has been on improving our execution," he told investors in early February. "I bring a strong amount of urgency to this role."

There were two key beneficiaries of the new structure. Kayvon Beykpour, who was running product under Dorsey, was promoted to general manager, which meant taking over design, research, and engineering for product as well. Bruce Falck, who ran revenue products under Dorsey, now had the same expanded responsibilities on the business side, which included ads and Twitter Blue, the company's subscription service. Agrawal was essentially giving the group that created Twitter's three-year business plan more control over its outcome.

Even without Dorsey in charge, Twitter's financial goals loomed large over the company considering they were now the benchmark every quarter when it delivered its earnings report. The first full year of the three-year plan had been somewhat concerning; Twitter's user growth was already falling well off pace, even compared to the company's smaller, public targets. The boom in usage Twitter had experienced during Covid's initial rise and Trump's bid for reelection slowed the following year, and Twitter added just 25 million new users in 2021—growth of 13 percent. That meant it would need almost 50 million new users for two straight years to hit the goal it shared with investors during its Analyst Day.

Twitter revenue had fared better, but Falck's plan to reorient the company around direct response advertising suddenly looked shaky. Apple had pushed new privacy changes to everyone with an iPhone in the summer of 2021, which meant people had to manually give companies like Twitter and Facebook permission to do the kind of tracking that led to super-personalized advertising. Unsurprisingly, most people were saying "no" to that tracking, and the hypertargeted ads that had turned Facebook into a behemoth were suddenly much less effective. A lot of the projected growth that Falck had built into his plan was expected to come from these kinds of ads. Hitting $7.5 billion in revenue by 2023 looked much more daunting than it had six months earlier.

Compounding the problem was that Twitter spent Dorsey's final year as CEO hiring like crazy to try to meet these new goals. Head count grew around 36 percent in a single year, and Twitter suddenly had more than 7,500 global employees. The company's expenses were up 51 percent in Dorsey's final year, but even with a solid year of business growth, revenue was up just 37 percent. That meant Twitter's spending was significantly outpacing its revenue growth. It was close, but Twitter was no longer profitable.

Shortly after taking over, Agrawal concluded that the company had grown too quickly during the pandemic boom and needed to course correct. He wanted to reset the company's financial goals and weed out low performers. A plan was cooked up to dramatically cut costs, which included a hiring slowdown and a significant round of layoffs that were scheduled for April. Twitter was going to cut more than a thousand jobs.

USA Today's "Women of the Year" list included several household names in 2022. Gymnast Simone Biles was on there and so was philanthropist Melinda Gates and Vice President Kamala Harris. The list also included a relative unknown, Rachel Levine, who was the assistant secretary for health at the U.S. Department of Health and Human Services. Levine was selected for her role as a leader during the global pandemic, but her inclusion on the list got attention for another reason: Levine was the "nation's highest-ranking openly transgender official." Levine, who was married with two kids, had transitioned around 2011 and changed her name from Richard to Rachel. "Moving from one gender to another, especially in your 50s, is a challenge," she later told *The Washington Post*. "But it was very rewarding."

The editors over at the Babylon Bee found Levine's inclusion on the list hilarious. The website, a self-described "Christian news satire" site, routinely mocked transgender people. "Rookie Mistake: Man Becomes Transgender After Holding Wife's Purse for More Than 10 Seconds," read one headline from 2021. "M&Ms Introduces New Trans Character Who Identifies as a Skittle," read another the following year. The *USA Today* list provided low-hanging fruit, and the Babylon Bee came out with its own award a few days later. "The Babylon Bee's Man of the Year Is Rachel Levine," the website proclaimed, and the accompanying story repeatedly referred to Levine as a man. "Who says a dude as accomplished as this can't be named 'Rachel'? This king doesn't care what people think about him!" it read.

When the Babylon Bee tweeted out the story, Twitter froze the publisher's account for violating the company's "hateful conduct" policy. The Bee couldn't unlock the account unless it deleted the tweet, and the site's editors dug in their heels. "They want us to bend the knee and admit that we engaged in hateful conduct," CEO Seth Dillon wrote on the Babylon Bee website. "I can promise you that's not happening."

News of the suspension bothered the actress Talulah Riley, who texted her ex-husband with a request. "Can you buy Twitter and then delete it, please!? xx," she wrote to Elon Musk on March 24. "America is going INSANE." Riley was peeved about Twitter's policies and had been complaining about them earlier that day with her friend Raiyah bint Al-Hussein, Princess of Jordan. "It was a fucking joke," she wrote to Musk about the Babylon Bee. "Why has everyone become so puritanical?"

Riley and Musk had been married and divorced twice—the second divorce came in 2016—but the two were still friendly and Musk was still very rich. Rich enough that buying Twitter and shutting it down was both a joke but also probably possible. Riley texted him an even better idea a few minutes later. "Or can you buy Twitter and make it radically free-speech?" she wrote. "So much stupidity comes from Twitter xx."

Musk texted back a few minutes later. "Maybe buy it and change it to properly support free speech xx," he replied.

In the middle of the night, just about fourteen hours after his text exchange with Riley, Musk posted a poll to his 79 million followers. "Free speech is essential to a functioning democracy," he wrote. "Do you believe Twitter rigorously adheres to this principle?" He included two options, "Yes" or "No," and followed up his tweet with a second, more ominous post. "The consequences of this poll will be important. Please vote carefully."

By this point, Musk had been secretly buying Twitter stock for almost two months and now owned well over 5 percent of the company. He hadn't publicly disclosed his investment even though the Securities and Exchange Commission required investors to submit paperwork once they passed the 5 percent threshold. Musk simply ignored this rule and kept buying Twitter stock anyway. As the votes poured in on his Twitter poll, Musk bought $133 million in Twitter shares, his second-largest single-day purchase.

When the poll closed, more than 70 percent of respondents had voted "no," meaning they thought Twitter did *not* adhere to free speech principles. Musk sent a follow-up tweet. "Given that Twitter serves as the de facto public town square, failing to adhere to free speech principles fundamentally undermines democracy. What should be done?" he asked. "Is a new platform needed?"

This time, the text that appeared on Musk's phone was not from his ex-wife, but from Twitter's ex-CEO. Jack Dorsey had seen Musk's tweet and reached out privately to weigh in on the matter. The two exchanged messages back and forth over the next three and a half hours.

DORSEY: Yes, a new platform is needed. It can't be a company.
     This is why I left.
MUSK: Ok
MUSK: What should it look like?

DORSEY: I believe it must be an open source protocol, funded by a foundation of sorts that doesn't own the protocol, only advances it. A bit like what Signal has done. It can't have an advertising model. Otherwise you have a surface area that governments and advertisers will try to influence and control. If it has a centralized entity behind it, it will be attacked. This isn't complicated work, it just has to be done right so it's resilient to what has happened to twitter.

MUSK: Super interesting idea

DORSEY: I'm off the twitter board mid May and then completely out of the company. I intend to do this work and then fix our mistakes. Twitter started as a protocol. It should have never been a company. That was the original sin.

MUSK: I'd like to help if I am able to.

DORSEY: I wanted to talk with you about it after I was all clear, because you care so much, get it's importance, and could def help in immeasurable ways. Back when we had the activist come in, I tried my hardest to get you on our board, and our board said no. That's about the time I decided I needed to work to leave, as hard as it was for me.

MUSK: Do you have a moment to talk?

DORSEY: Bout to head out to dinner but can for a minute.

About thirteen minutes later, presumably after a short phone call, the text exchange continued. Dorsey blamed Twitter's board for rejecting his idea to bring Musk on as a director after Jesse Cohn and Elliott showed up.

DORSEY: I think the main reason is the board is just super risk averse and saw adding you as more risk, which I thought was completely stupid and backwards, but I only had one vote, and 3% of the company, and no dual class shares. Hard set up. We can discuss more.

MUSK: Let's definitely discuss more

MUSK: I think it's worth both trying to move Twitter in a better
direction and doing something new that's decentralized.

DORSEY: It's likely the best option. I just have doubts. But open

It was one thing for Musk's ex-wife to gas him up on the idea of
buying Twitter. Now, though, Twitter's cofounder was admitting that
the company he created needed major changes. Musk clearly felt Twitter was a threat to democracy; Dorsey appeared to be in agreement,
and had even criticized the company's corporate structure, its board
of directors, and its advertising business. Musk had a sizable investment in the company, which was already much larger than the one
Elliott had amassed when the firm tried to oust Dorsey two years earlier. Elliott's play on Twitter had proven that someone could force a
lot of change at the company with a couple billion dollars and a little
aggression. Musk had both.

That same night, less than an hour after ending his text conversation
with Dorsey, Musk pulled out his phone again and sent another text to
Egon Durban, the Silver Lake investor who was still on Twitter's board
of directors.

The stage was set for Musk to do something big. "This is Elon.
Please call when you have a moment," he wrote. "It is regarding the
Twitter board."

Bret Taylor arrived early at the address provided by his assistant and
looked around at one of the strangest rental houses he'd ever seen. It
was like he'd stumbled onto the set of some kind of postapocalyptic
blockbuster movie. There were several abandoned trucks nearby, not
to mention farm equipment and even animals. The Twitter chairman
pulled out his phone. "This wins for the weirdest place I've had a meeting recently," he typed. "I think they were looking for an airbnb near

the airport and there are tractors and donkeys." He added a shrugging emoji to the message and sent the text to Musk and Parag Agrawal, Twitter's new CEO.

It had been only a few days since Musk first texted Egon Durban, but he had already spoken to several other members of Twitter's board about his investment and unexpected interest in getting involved at the company. Taylor flew home early from a trip to New York so that he could meet Musk in person over dinner while Musk was in the Bay Area for his own set of meetings at Tesla. Agrawal was also coming to dinner, and the Twitter team had scrambled to find somewhere private and convenient, hence the Airbnb.

Twitter's board was eager to work with Musk, not that it had any choice. Musk didn't look like a typical activist investor, but he posed all the same risks that Elliott had presented two years earlier. As Twitter's largest shareholder, he could make everyone's life very pleasant or very miserable depending on how he went public with his investment. After Musk spoke with Durban, he was connected to Taylor, Agrawal, and Martha Lane Fox, the head of the board's nominating and corporate governance committee.

"Elon—everyone excited about prospect of you being involved and on board," Durban wrote to the group when he made the intros. "Next step is for you to chat w three of them so we can move this forward quickly. Maybe we can get this done next few days."

Taylor was new to his role as Twitter's chairman, but dealing with eccentric tech billionaires was old hat for him by the time Musk reached out. Taylor had walked a well-trodden path to the top of the tech industry: undergrad and grad school at Stanford, where he studied computer science, and then an early job building products at Google, including Google Maps. Then he struck out on his own to build a social networking startup called FriendFeed. That business was acquired by Facebook, and Taylor spent three years working for Mark Zuckerberg as the company's chief technology officer back when Facebook was still known as a social network primarily for college kids. Taylor's next startup, a document collaboration business called Quip, was then acquired by Marc Benioff's Salesforce for $750 million. By the time Taylor became Twitter's chairman, he was Salesforce's co-CEO and had mastered the skill of dealing with rich and demanding tech CEOs. Taylor was technical and knew how to build things, which impressed the Zuckerbergs of the world. But he was also low-key, polite, and by-the-book, which made him a helpful complement to people like Benioff, who were loud, brash, and seemed to do whatever the hell they wanted.

All of that made Taylor a good person to meet with Musk. The dinner near the airport was part of a plan to understand more about what Musk wanted, and hopefully build a friendly relationship that would keep him from doing something rash. The Twitter team believed that Musk was considering three options: He wanted to start a competing service, join Twitter's board, or try to buy the company. At dinner, everyone agreed that joining the board was the best (and simplest) option. There was no doubt Musk was qualified. He was an incredibly successful entrepreneur who not only loved using Twitter but seemed to have a lot of ideas for how Twitter could improve. Plus, Dorsey loved him, and Musk owned more Twitter stock than anybody, which meant he was now financially invested in Twitter's success. The three men walked away from their first meeting with a rough outline in place to get Musk onto the board, and it seemed that everyone was excited to work together. "Great dinner :)" Musk texted the group later that night. "Really great," replied Taylor. "The donkeys and dystopian surveillance helicopters added to the ambiance."

Privately, Musk was less enthused than he'd let on. He was particularly worried about Agrawal, who seemed like a nice enough guy, but not the kind of cutthroat leader that Musk felt should be running Twitter. "What Twitter needs is a fire-breathing dragon," he told his biographer Isaacson after the meeting. "Parag is not that." Still, Musk looped in Jared Birchall, who helped manage his wealth as the head of his family office, to start the paperwork that would officially make him a Twitter board member. Later that same evening, Musk got another text from Dorsey: "I heard good things are happening."

Musk's ownership stake in Twitter was made public on April 4 in a securities filing that was published online before the stock market opened. Musk wasn't just a Twitter shareholder; the filing revealed he was Twitter's *largest* shareholder. Musk owned more than 73 million shares, or 9.2 percent of the company. The type of form that he filed, called a 13G, was also surprising. That type of form was typically used for "passive" investments, which suggested that Musk wasn't planning to use his Twitter stake to force any changes at the company.

Twitter investors were thrilled to hear that the world's richest person was suddenly interested in the social network. Twitter stock jumped as much as 27 percent in one day, making a lot of people a lot of money, including Musk himself. His decision to delay his public paperwork was quickly scrutinized by the Securities and Exchange Commission. Since he didn't file the paperwork on time, it was estimated that Musk saved himself well over $150 million by buying shares before the price bump that came with his announcement.

In the moment, though, Musk didn't seem concerned. "Oh hi lol," he cheekily tweeted as the world absorbed the news. Musk's phone was blowing up as friends and acquaintances reached out to congratulate him on the investment and pry about what his endgame might be. Musk got texts from Ken Griffin, the billionaire hedge fund manager at Citadel, and Mathias Döpfner, the CEO of the German media company Axel Springer, who wanted to forge some kind of partnership. Several friends were hopeful that Musk would finally end Twitter "censorship" now that he was a major investor. "Excited to see the stake in Twitter—awesome. 'Back door man' they are saying haha," texted Joe Lonsdale, a venture capitalist and the cofounder of Palantir, the controversial data company known for its counterterrorism work with the U.S. government. "Hope you're able to influence it. I bet you the board doesn't even get full reporting or see any report of the censorship decisions and little cabals going on there but they should—the lefties on the board likely want plausible deniability!"

Joe Rogan, the popular podcast host who'd interviewed Musk a few times on his show, was similarly direct. "Are you going to liberate Twitter from the censorship happy mob?" he texted.

As speculation swirled about what Musk planned to do with his major Twitter stake, Twitter's board scrambled to finish the paperwork needed for him to officially become a director. They wanted to reassure everyone that Musk and his massive investment came in peace, and that he wasn't a threat to Twitter's existence. Fox and Birchall were still swapping paperwork, including a standstill agreement to keep Musk from buying any more stock until things settled down. Agrawal sent Musk a copy of the tweet he wanted to send out to make sure Musk was cool with the language.

The Twitter CEO tweeted the exciting news the next day on Tuesday, April 5, that Musk was joining the board.

"He's both a passionate believer and intense critic of the service which is exactly what we need on @Twitter, and in the boardroom, to make us stronger in the long-term. Welcome Elon!" Agrawal wrote.

Dorsey got emotional when he learned that Musk was joining the board. He was still walking away from the company in a few months, but now he had his protégé in place as CEO and one of his idols in place on the board. His excitement came out in his tweets. "He cares deeply about our world and Twitter's role in it," Dorsey wrote about Musk. "Parag and Elon both lead with their hearts, and they will be an incredible team."

Shortly after Dorsey's tweets, everything went sideways.

Jack Dorsey texted Elon Musk personally to thank him for joining Twitter's board. "Absolutely," Musk replied. "Hope I can be helpful!"

"Immensely," Dorsey assured him. "Parag is an incredible engineer. The board is terrible. Always here to talk through anything you want."

Musk wanted to talk confidentially right away, and the two jumped on a phone call within a couple of hours. Dorsey didn't hold back. *Twitter should not be a publicly traded company*, Dorsey told him, echoing some of the texts that he'd sent to Musk a week earlier that helped kick off the entire board process. Taking Twitter private was not a new idea to Dorsey, who had long despised the public company hamster wheel that meant reporting earnings every three months. Dorsey thought this system made it difficult to make major changes at Twitter since doing so could disrupt user growth or revenue and send the stock tanking. *Fixing Twitter would be easier if the company was private,* he added, *and it could be more focused on execution.*

Musk's attitude about joining Twitter's board appeared to change almost immediately. When one of his Tesla board members, Ira Ehrenpreis, texted Musk later that night to offer advice in case he joined any of Twitter's board committees, Musk seemed disinterested. "I didn't even want to join the Twitter board!" he wrote back. "They pushed really hard to have me join."

Gayle King, the morning show host at CBS, sent Musk a text asking for an interview—and suggesting that Twitter create an "edit" button so people could change tweets after they had been published. "The whole Twitter thing getting blown out of proportion," Musk replied within minutes. "Owning ~9% is not quite control."

As the week went on, Musk sent several messages back and forth with Agrawal. Musk had ideas for changing Twitter, including removing permanent bans and making it easier for regular people to get a blue checkmark by submitting their ID for verification. "I have a ton of ideas, but lmk if I'm pushing too hard," Musk texted the Twitter CEO. "I just want Twitter to be Maximum amazing."

Agrawal, meanwhile, was trying to manage employee morale, which had taken a hit with the news that Musk was joining the board. Investors had loved the move, but some of Twitter's employees were more skeptical. As a guest speaker at #OneTeam, Musk had been fine, but some worried that he was a poor fit for the board considering the company's predominantly liberal and progressive culture. Musk had, after all, famously called another man a "pedo" without any evidence and routinely made weed and sex jokes on Twitter. He also had a history of tweeting inappropriate memes and mocking the concept of gender pronouns, which many people at the company used in meetings and email signatures.

"We know that he has caused harm to workers, the trans community, women, and others with less power in the world," one employee wrote on the company Slack. "How are we going to reconcile this decision with our values? Does innovation trump humanity?" Another who used to work at Musk's car company, Tesla, was also convinced that he was wrong for Twitter. "I'm extremely unnerved right now, because I've seen what he can do firsthand," they wrote.

Some of the comments leaked to *The Washington Post*, and Agrawal was worried that Musk would be bothered by the criticism. He invited Musk to come and speak with employees directly to answer their questions and tried to dismiss the *Post* story as no big deal. "I think there is a large silent majority that is excited about [what] you bring on the board, so this isn't representative," Agrawal texted Musk. "Happy to talk about it – none of this is a surprise."

The two engineers spent the week feeling each other out over text, at one point swapping credentials to show off how technical they were. "I wrote heavy duty software for 20 years," Musk told Agrawal, who replied that he "used to be CTO and have been in our codebase for a long time." Musk didn't like to manage people, he said; he mostly liked to solve technical product problems. "I interface way better with engineers who are able to do hardcore programming than with program manager / MBA types of people," he wrote to Agrawal on Thursday, April 7.

"In our next convo – treat me like an engineer instead of CEO and lets see where we get to," Agrawal replied.

The two never got the chance. Musk was supposed to join Twitter's board on Saturday, April 9, but he'd spent the past week having second thoughts about his decision. The more time he spent with Twitter's board, the less impressed he became. Some of his close friends and family, including his brother Kimbal, were urging him to reconsider his decision. On the morning he was supposed to officially join the board, Musk was in Hawaii staying on Lanai, his friend Larry Ellison's private island. It was three thirty in the morning and Musk was in the midst of an all-nighter when he opened Twitter and decided to torch the company he had agreed to work with.

Musk found a tweet that listed the ten most-followed Twitter accounts on the service—folks like Justin Bieber, Katy Perry, and Taylor Swift. Musk retweeted the list just to point out that many of those accounts "rarely" tweeted.

"Is Twitter dying?" he asked out loud to his 81 million followers. Later he tweeted a poll asking people if Twitter should remove the "w" from its name and start calling the company "Titter" instead. He floated another poll asking if Twitter should convert its San Francisco head-quarters into a homeless shelter, and suggested Twitter should get rid of ads for paying users.

Agrawal was frustrated, and reasonably so. Some of his employees were already upset that Musk was joining the board; now, on the day that board appointment was supposed to become official, Musk was pub-licly embarrassing the company. Agrawal, clearly peeved, sent Musk a text. "You are free to tweet 'is Twitter dying?' or anything else about Twitter – but it's my responsibility to tell you that it's not helping me make Twitter better in the current context," Agrawal wrote, chastising the richest man in the world. "Next time we speak, I'd like to provide you perspective on the level of internal distraction right now and how it hurting our ability to do work."

"I'd like the company to get to a place where we are more resilient and don't get distracted, but we aren't there right now," he continued. Agrawal hoped that getting Musk in front of employees for a Q&A might help alleviate some of their concerns and give them a chance to hear from Musk directly instead of just through his tweets.

Musk, who still hadn't gone to sleep, replied less than a minute later, just after 5 a.m. "What did you get done this week?" he wrote mockingly, snapping back at Agrawal. "I'm not joining the board. This is a waste of time. Will make an offer to take Twitter private."

Agrawal wrote back asking if they could talk. Musk never replied. Then Bret Taylor, Twitter's chairman, texted Musk just minutes later also asking for a call. Musk was about to take off on a flight and couldn't talk, he said, but he sent Taylor a series of texts instead.

MUSK: "Please expect a take private offer"

"Fixing Twitter by chatting with Parag won't work"

"Drastic action is needed"

"This is hard to do as a public company, as purging fake users will make the numbers look terrible, so restructuring should be done as a private company."

"This is Jack's opinion too."

Less than a week after accepting a seat on Twitter's board, Musk was out before it ever became official. Agrawal sent an email to the company the next evening, a Sunday, with the ominous update that Musk had had a change of heart. Agrawal didn't mention that Musk wanted to buy the company—this wasn't the kind of thing you could put in a company-wide email—but employees who read the note could sense that Twitter's relationship with Musk was far from over.

"There will be distractions ahead," Agrawal wrote to his employees. "Let's tune out the noise, and stay focused on the work and what we're building."

THIRTEEN

@ELONMUSK

In some ways, Elon Musk's childhood in South Africa wasn't all that different from that of young boys of his generation. He raced dirt bikes and shot pellet guns with his brother and cousins, and blew stuff up with homemade rockets. In lieu of a lemonade stand, Musk decorated Easter eggs and sold them door-to-door to his wealthy South African neighbors, one of his first forays into entrepreneurship. Musk read every book he could get his hands on, sometimes reading as much as ten hours per day. He had a loving mother who believed, like most mothers, that her son was undeniably brilliant.

She was right. Musk's mind was unique. He loved computers and even wrote code as a twelve-year-old for his own video game, which was covered in a local trade publication. He had a photographic memory and was prone to moments of deep, undisturbed thought that would leave him impervious to anything going on around him. His trances were so routine and so deep that his parents brought him to the doctor to test for hearing issues. If anything, Musk was perhaps *too* smart, often teased for being a brainiac who read encyclopedias for fun and seemed to know the answer to every question thrown his way.

For Musk, though, things were not nearly as idyllic as they seemed, and the happy memories from childhood were few and far between.

Musk was born in South Africa in the summer of 1971, and grew up in a nice house in a nice neighborhood in Pretoria, just outside of Johannesburg. Musk's father, Errol, was a mechanical and electrical engineer who could do all kinds of odd jobs with his hands. His mother, Maye, was a dietician and model who was a finalist in the Miss South Africa pageant just two years before Musk was born. Errol and Maye divorced when Musk was around nine years old, and he eventually moved in with his father, which would prove to be a mistake. Errol was demanding and intense with his kids, sometimes lecturing them for hours at a time. Some of his behavior was apparently so troubling that Musk and his siblings refuse to talk about it. "He's good at making life miserable," Musk said years later, and the rest of his family tends to agree that Errol usually made things unpleasant for everyone who interacted with him. As a result, Musk struggled with his home life all throughout high school, and he grew to despise his father, vowing to keep his own children from ever meeting him. (Years later, Errol would routinely send his son emails full of racist rants and conspiracy theories; he also shockingly had two more kids of his own with his stepdaughter, who was more than forty years his junior.)

Things weren't any better for Musk at school. He was bookish and nerdy, which meant he was often the target of schoolyard bullies who tormented him for years. At one point as an eighth or ninth grader, he got jumped by a gang and pushed down a flight of concrete stairs, a tumble that landed him in the hospital. It was an upbringing that left Musk tougher than most but also less sensitive to some of life's other problems. "People who are worried about words have never been punched in the face," he said in 2022.

Underneath all the misery, Musk adopted a perpetual state of urgency that still permeates almost every facet of his life. When he was around ten years old, Musk got his first computer—a Commodore VIC-20—and quickly opened the workbook that came with it. The book had pages and pages of lessons to teach people the very basics of writing code and it was supposed to take months to complete. Musk was done within seventy-two hours. "I just got super OCD on it and stayed up for three days with no sleep and did the entire thing," he told Ashlee Vance, author of a book about Musk that was released in 2015. "It seemed like the most super-compelling thing I had ever seen." A similar urgency to live in the United States motivated Musk to leave South Africa as a teenager. Around his eighteenth birthday, he moved to Canada, where he had citizenship through his mother. It didn't matter that he didn't have anywhere to live.

Musk eventually found a room with a second cousin and took on a series of odd jobs before enrolling at Queen's University in Ontario in the fall of 1989. The next several years were spent at university: two years at Queen's, where Musk studied business, practiced public speaking, and met his eventual wife, Justine; and then he finally made it to the United States and spent a few years at the University of Pennsylvania, where Musk studied economics and physics. These college years, he would later claim, crystallized his desire to work on projects in technology, space, and renewable energy.

Musk started building things as soon as he finished school, and by the time he started investing in Twitter almost thirty years later, his professional career was a part of Silicon Valley lore. Musk's story was defined by two consistent and prevailing themes: He generally worked longer, harder, and faster than anyone else, and he had an enormous appetite for personal risk.

He founded his first startup, Zip2, in Silicon Valley with his younger brother Kimbal in 1995. The two rented a small office which also served as their apartment for a short time, and built an online business directory, like a Yellow Pages but on the internet. The idea was novel for the mid-1990s, and they quickly raised money from venture capitalists who then changed the business model and pushed Musk out of his CEO role. Zip2 eventually sold to Compaq Computer for more than $300 million a few years later, and Musk made out handsomely: The sale netted him $22 million. One of the first things he bought was a $1 million McLaren sports car, which he drove around San Francisco as if it were a Toyota

Camry. Just as importantly, the Zip2 experience taught him a valuable lesson about corporate control—a similar lesson that Jack Dorsey would also learn the hard way years later at Twitter.

Musk then took more than half of his $22 million and put it into his next business venture, X.com, an online bank that boasted a promotional gimmick that gave all new customers twenty dollars when they signed up for a checking account. Two other entrepreneurs, Peter Thiel and Max Levchin, rented office space from X.com in Palo Alto and were working on a competing company with a clever product that let people send money over email, called PayPal. Eventually, as the two businesses started to compete, they merged, and Musk became CEO and the largest shareholder of the new joint company.

Again, he was pushed out of his job, this time after an employee mutiny. Workers at the newly combined company decided that Musk wasn't properly dealing with a growing list of business issues and went as a group to the X.com board to complain. Musk learned that he'd been ousted while on his honeymoon with Justine; Thiel was appointed CEO, and he quickly changed the name of the company to PayPal. Musk was hurt, but he was about to become even richer. When eBay bought PayPal for $1.5 billion in 2002, Musk made $250 million.

Money provides people with a special kind of freedom to think about the future. In Musk's case, he used that freedom to think about problems that might take years or even decades to complete. After the PayPal sale, now armed with a couple hundred million dollars, Musk truly started to dream big. He grew obsessed with exploring space and eventually sending humans to Mars. It was an idea inspired (in part) by the fear that something, someday might happen to Earth that would force humans to live on another planet. So Musk moved to Los Angeles, and around the same time that PayPal sold to eBay, he started Space Exploration Technologies, known as "SpaceX," with his own money. He hoped the commercial space venture would not only build rockets, but eventually colonize Mars.

Two years later Musk invested another $6.5 million of his money into another company called Tesla, which was working on an electric car to help solve a different but similarly grandiose problem: that humanity was too dependent on fossil fuels. Musk was immediately the company's largest shareholder, became its chairman, and by 2008 was also the CEO.

He wasn't just a rich guy sitting in the boardroom. In both cases, Musk spent considerable amounts of time and personal financing to keep things going. He garnered a reputation as a difficult boss who worked long days, rarely took a vacation, and demanded the impossible from his employees. Musk had a habit of setting audacious and completely unrealistic goals at both companies. He originally thought that SpaceX's first rocket would take off just fifteen months after the company's founding, and that the first flight to Mars would take place by the end of the decade. SpaceX's first launch, which was unsuccessful, didn't happen for almost four years; its first *successful* launch took six years. As of December 2023, SpaceX still hadn't sent a rocket to Mars.

At Tesla, Musk and his team thought they would deliver their first car, a shiny red sports car called the Tesla Roadster, to the general public by early 2006; it didn't arrive until mid-2008. The delays and elongated timelines meant that both companies were routinely strapped for cash in their early days, and Musk spent most of his own money to keep the businesses running. In early 2008 he sold the McLaren to help pay the bills. By the end of 2008, both companies were dangerously low on cash. Musk closed a round of funding for Tesla on Christmas Eve just hours before the company would have otherwise gone bankrupt.

The pain and stress and drama would all be worth it. SpaceX had its first successful rocket launch in 2008 and quickly became the global leader in the commercial space industry. By early 2022, SpaceX not only sent rockets carrying satellites and other payloads into outer space regularly, but the company mastered technology that allowed those rockets to return to Earth in one piece so that they could be reused, which was previously unheard-of. Tesla, meanwhile, didn't just become the world's most successful electric car company; it became arguably the most successful car company, period. In October 2021, Tesla's market value surpassed $1 trillion, making it the most valuable car manufacturer in the world. At one point Tesla was worth more than its top five competitors combined. A year later, in 2022, Tesla delivered more than 1.3 million electric vehicles.

As Musk's net worth expanded, so did his empire, and it seemed there was no problem too complex to try to tackle. In 2016 he founded Neuralink, a company building "brain-computer interfaces"—implantable brain chips that use brain activity to control the output on a computer or a phone. He also launched The Boring Company, a business that was "sort of a hobby company" focused on building tunnels underground for high-speed travel. He continued to speak regularly about colonizing Mars, and unironically threw out the idea of creating artificial suns by constantly setting off thermonuclear explosions in outer space.

Musk was even doing his part to save the world from another looming crisis: population collapse. "If people don't have more children, civilization is going to crumble. Mark my words," he said during a 2021 interview. By April 2022, Musk had at least nine kids of his own, with three different women. His net worth was $270 billion, making him the richest person in the world. And now he was ready to add another complex challenge to his to-do list: restore free speech to the world.

It was time to buy Twitter.

Part of what made Elon Musk's initial bid for Twitter so hard to understand was that Musk, despite his oodles of money and fame and success, had the sense of humor of a twelve-year-old boy. At The Boring Company, Musk once created and sold a flamethrower to the general public after a joke he saw in one of his favorite movies, *Spaceballs*. A joke from another comedy, *The Dictator*, featuring Sacha Baron Cohen, was inspiration for Musk's decision to make SpaceX's Starship rocket "more pointy." He loved making sex jokes (69!) and weed jokes (420!) and spent a decent amount of time each day posting memes on Twitter considering he was also running several businesses at once.

Sometimes Musk's antics got him into trouble. After he smoked weed with the podcaster Joe Rogan during a taping in 2018, Musk and most of his SpaceX employees were rewarded with a year of random drug tests by the U.S. government since SpaceX had federal contracts. The situation was both hilarious and terrible. "The consequences for me and for SpaceX were actually not good," Musk later admitted, though he still laughed about it.

Musk's favorite place to get in trouble, though, seemed to be on Twitter, where he tweeted a steady stream of consciousness, oftentimes while sitting on the toilet. There was the time Musk was sued for calling a cave diver a "pedo" in a 2018 tweet. Musk had also been sued after tweeting that he had "funding secured" to take Tesla private at $420 per share in 2018, which was both a weed joke and, as far as the Securities and Exchange Commission was concerned, a lie. The agency sued Musk and settled with him, forcing him to give up his role as Tesla's chairman.

Musk's relationship with Twitter the company had also been complicated over the years, though he'd never technically run afoul of Twitter's rules. Quite the opposite, in fact. Dorsey's infatuation with Musk meant he often referred to the billionaire as his "favorite tweeter," and when Twitter expanded its "Top 3" list to a "Top X" list that gave special account protections to dozens of world leaders, Dorsey made sure Musk's account was added. But Musk also loved to complain about Twitter, and privately did so for years, first to Dorsey, and later to Agrawal. He didn't love that Twitter allowed an account called @ElonJet that tracked the location of his private plane, and had even complained to Agrawal about @ElonJet as recently as January 2022, right around the same time that he started buying Twitter stock. Musk also didn't like that there were so many bots that sent him messages about spam and cryptocurrencies, and he hated that Twitter was full of Tesla short sellers who seemed determined to attack his company and its stock price. Musk's complaints would often funnel from Dorsey or Agrawal to Twitter's top lawyer, Vijaya Gadde, who would then pass them on to her team. On several occasions, employees had to drop what they were doing to man-ually remove bots from Musk's feed. Musk even had his personal law-yer, Alex Spiro, get on the phone with Dorsey and Gadde multiple times over the years to hammer home his frustration over the bots and shorts, which he felt were manipulating Tesla's stock price.

So when Musk submitted a formal bid to buy Twitter for $54.20 per share on the evening of April 13, it was easy to understand why some of the board members were hesitant. It had been less than two weeks since Musk had agreed to join the board. He then changed his mind, leaving Twitter looking like a clown show. Then there was the fact that Musk had filed paperwork with the SEC that suggested his Twitter investment was passive. Even the offer price raised questions. Was he just making another weed joke? Did he actually have the money lined up to make a deal? Was this all just one big troll?

Musk's offer letter certainly sounded serious. "I invested in Twitter as I believe in its potential to be the platform for free speech around the globe, and I believe free speech is a societal imperative for a functioning democracy," he wrote to Twitter's board. "However, since making my investment I now realize the company will neither thrive nor serve this societal imperative in its current form. Twitter needs to be transformed as a private company."

The letter also included a threat. "My offer is my best and final offer and if it is not accepted, I would need to reconsider my position as a shareholder," he wrote.

Musk didn't want to negotiate, and if Twitter declined his deal, he'd most likely sell his shares at a sizable profit and watch Twitter's stock tank from the sidelines. Twitter's board had no option but to take Musk seriously. They just hoped Musk was planning to do the same.

Musk's formal bid for Twitter made him even more popular and inter-esting than usual. Joe Lonsdale, the investor who called Musk "back

door man," was back in his inbox, this time with an invitation to meet
Florida governor Ron DeSantis, who was apparently "outraged" at
Twitter's board and rooting hard for Musk. Gayle King was also back
with another interview request. "This is as the kids of today say a
'gangsta move,'" she messaged him. Marc Merrill, the cofounder of
Riot Games, wrote Musk that he was "the hero Gotham needs," and
even Sam Bankman-Fried, the CEO of the cryptocurrency exchange
FTX, reached out to try to set up a meeting. (Within eighteen months,
FTX would crash and Bankman-Fried would be convicted on seven
counts of fraud, conspiracy, and money laundering.)

No one was more excited than Musk's friend Jason Calacanis. They
had met years earlier when Calacanis was a tech journalist and later
bought the very first Tesla Model S from Musk after its release in 2012.
The two exchanged dozens of messages in the two weeks after Musk's
offer, and Calacanis had no shortage of ideas. Twitter should share more
revenue with video creators like YouTube does, he wrote. The company
should move to Texas and require remote workers back to the office
within sixty days, he added. He laid out the case for Musk to cut more
than half of the company's employees. "Hard Reboot the organization,"
he wrote in a private message. When Musk finally asked him to be a
strategic advisor once the deal closed, Calacanis accepted less than a
minute later. "Board member, advisor, whatever," he wrote. "You have
my sword." Then, just in case, he added: "Twitter CEO is my dream job."

Even if Musk wanted to make Calacanis's dreams come true, he
needed to figure out how to get his hands on about $46 billion to buy
the 91 percent of shares he didn't already own and pay for other closing
costs and legal fees. As the richest person in the world, Musk had the
money, at least on paper. The problem was that most of it was tied up
in his other companies, namely Tesla. Selling $40 billion in Tesla stock
wasn't really an option since it would send the stock price tumbling and
send a message to investors that Musk was more interested in Twitter
than running his $1 trillion car company. A more logical solution was
to borrow the money or entice other investors to join his bid. As soon as

he sent his offer letter, Musk's bankers at Morgan Stanley were hard at work calling other banks and investors to line up the funding.

Musk, too, was hustling for the money and joined calls with potential banking partners to share his rough business plan. He promised to make dramatic cost cuts at Twitter, including layoffs, if the deal went through, and discussed the idea of expanding Twitter's business to focus more on subscriptions. Billionaires typically know a lot of other billionaires, and Musk's Rolodex also proved handy. In some cases, like with Oracle founder and Tesla board member Larry Ellison, a billion-dollar commitment came together as quickly as if Musk was asking to borrow five dollars for a cup of coffee. Musk texted Ellison on April 20, one week after sending the offer letter to Twitter's board:

MUSK: Any interest in participating in the Twitter deal?

ELLISON: Yes . . . of course 👍

MUSK: Cool

MUSK: Roughly what dollar size? Not holding you to anything, but the deal is oversubscribed, so I have to reduce or kick out some participants.

ELLISON: A billion . . . or whatever you recommend

MUSK: Whatever works for you. I'd recommend maybe $2B or more. This has very high potential and I'd rather have you than anyone else.

ELLISON: I agree that it has huge potential . . . and it would be lots of fun

MUSK: Absolutely :)

Ellison, whose net worth was around $100 billion, invested $1 billion.

Even with folks like Ellison on board, no one was sure if the deal would come together. Twitter's board couldn't even tell if Musk was a serious buyer, and he'd eroded a lot of trust when he agreed to join Twitter's board but then decided to trash the company instead. In a public interview at the TED conference the day his bid became public, Musk said he didn't even care about Twitter's finances. "This is not a way to sort of make money," he said. "My strong intuitive sense is that having a public platform that is maximally trusted and broadly inclusive is extremely important to the future of civilization. I don't care about the economics at all." Skeptics weren't sure what to make of his reasoning. Who spends $46 billion without any concern for getting it back?

Musk, though, was serious and was also working on a backup plan in case his Twitter bid was rejected. At the TED conference, he'd also been asked about a "Plan B" onstage but refused to share details. Privately, though, he was messaging with confidants about an idea for a blockchain-based social network that let users post messages on the blockchain's public ledger. Musk was even meeting with engineers to discuss building the blockchain idea just in case his Twitter deal failed to materialize.

Twitter's board started anxiously waiting to see if Musk could pull the financing together for his bid. Jack Dorsey, though, started tweeting as if the deal was already done. Typically during a takeover discussion, everyone involved stays quiet to avoid disrupting the process. Dorsey didn't seem to care about the formal process and sent several tweets that didn't do Twitter's board any favors. Dorsey argued that Twitter's status as a publicly traded company was a major problem. "As a public company, twitter has always been 'for sale,'" he tweeted. "That's the real issue." Then he took a swipe at Twitter's board, saying that the group had "consistently been the dysfunction of the company." It was a weird self-own. Not only had Dorsey been directly involved in picking the entire board, but he'd been a member himself since Twitter's founding. In fact, he was *still* a board member. In the heat of a hostile takeover negotiation, Dorsey's tweets landed poorly with some of his colleagues. The fractured relationships got worse. Several board members were ready for Dorsey to move on no matter what happened with the deal.

On April 20, Musk's team submitted a series of letters and paperwork to the Securities and Exchange Commission: Musk had his financing in order. The arrangement outlined $46.5 billion in funding from several different sources. Musk would borrow $12.5 billion as a personal loan, using his Tesla shares as collateral. Twitter, the company he was purchasing, would borrow $13 billion from banks as well; given interest rates, the loan would lead to about $1 billion per year in interest payments. Musk would personally provide the remaining $21 billion on his own, either by selling his Tesla stock or finding other equity investors, like Ellison, to help him out.

The filing included another new piece of information: Musk's offer was "no longer subject to business due diligence." He didn't even want to look under the hood before driving Twitter off the lot. Musk had the money in place, and he wanted the company bad.

Twitter's board no longer wondered whether Musk was serious about buying the social network. Now they just had to decide if his offer price of $54.20 per share was a good deal, and the group spent the weekend huddled with their bankers and lawyers to decide. Typically, an offer like this might inspire other potential buyers and set off an auction. Not this time. Not only was Musk moving quickly, but many of the largest possible suitors had already looked at Twitter's business a few years earlier when Disney and Salesforce passed on a deal. Regulators in the U.S. had also cracked down on tech acquisitions in the years since. The Federal Trade Commission was already suing Facebook over claims of "illegal monopolization." The Justice Department was preparing to sue Google over similar claims. Even if they could get a deal approved by regulators, there were no other relevant or interested buyers for Twitter.

Twitter's finance team started using internal models to project where the business would be on its own without Musk as the owner. The team came up with multiple scenarios to present to the Twitter board, essentially low-, mid-, and high-performing outcomes. It quickly became clear that Twitter was unlikely to hit its internal revenue target no matter which outcome they relied on. In one projection, Twitter management estimated the company's revenue would be $7.2 billion in 2023, below both Twitter's public and private goals. It was hard to imagine Twitter hitting its user growth goals, either. Twitter's bankers, Goldman Sachs and JP Morgan, also created financial projections for Twitter's business, and both banks concluded that Musk's offer was "fair."

As the board frantically discussed its options, Musk, who does everything in his life at a million miles per hour, started getting impatient. On Sunday, April 24, just ten days after his offer became public, Musk sent Twitter another letter that arrived while the board was deliberating. "As we discussed, $54.20 has been and will remain my best and final offer, period," the letter included. The attached merger agreement that Musk's lawyers sent along was "seller friendly," he added, and it was clear that Musk was ready to walk away from Twitter entirely if the board rejected his offer. This was all "intended to make this easy on all to get to a deal asap," Musk's lawyers told Twitter when they sent everything over.

The two sides spent Sunday evening and into Monday morning negotiating. (Musk also stayed up all night, but not because he was working on the deal; instead he'd been at a party with friends and had too much Red Bull.) Twitter's lawyers worked in a handful of other small changes to the agreement, including keeping the company's right to hire and fire employees without Musk's approval until the deal closed. They also added another clause known as "specific performance" to the contract, which meant that Musk couldn't simply walk away from the deal and pay monetary damages. As long as Twitter upheld its end of the bargain, a court could order Musk to follow through on the agreement, even if he changed his mind. Of course, none of that would likely matter; Musk very clearly wanted to buy Twitter.

Around 2:48 p.m. on Monday, April 25, the New York Stock Exchange halted trading of Twitter's stock. Two minutes later, a press release hit the newswire: "Elon Musk to Acquire Twitter."

Musk would pay $44 billion to take Twitter private. All existing shareholders would get $54.20 per share when the deal closed later that year. Twitter's board had voted unanimously to sell the company to Musk.

The announcement formalized what had seemed completely unbelievable just a few weeks earlier. It had been just thirty-two days since Musk received the text from his ex-wife complaining about the Babylon Bee, a text that prompted him to ask his followers if the world needed an alternative to Twitter. At that point, no one even knew Musk owned Twitter stock. Now, suddenly and incredibly, he was committed to buying the entire company. Twitter hadn't even been a public company for nine years, and now Dorsey was getting his wish. Twitter would no longer be beholden to Wall Street investors who cared solely about its business and user growth. Musk didn't care about the economics—he'd said so himself—which meant Twitter was free from the pressures of needing to grow a big business to justify its existence. For the first time in history, Twitter could simply focus on what it did best: offering the world a place to converse and argue and opine. Its role as the world's global consciousness might finally be enough.

That night, Dorsey tweeted. Twitter should never have been a public company, he wrote. "It has been owned by Wall Street and the ad model. Taking it back from Wall Street is the correct first step." Dorsey was ecstatic about the outcome, and was ready to hand over the company that he'd founded to a man that he admired greatly. If anyone could fix Twitter's problems, it was Musk. "Elon is the singular solution I trust," Dorsey tweeted. "I trust his mission to extend the light of consciousness."

Earlier in the day, four minutes after the press release was published, Dorsey had messaged Musk privately to share those sentiments personally.

DORSEY: "Thank you" 🖤
MUSK: "I basically followed your advice!"
DORSEY: "I know and I appreciate you. This is the right and only path. I'll continue to do whatever it takes to make it work."

FOURTEEN

DEAL ON HOLD

Parag Agrawal's unofficial audition to keep his job as CEO was over almost as soon as it started.

The day after the Twitter-Musk deal was announced, Jack Dorsey messaged Elon Musk to set up a call with Agrawal. "I want to make sure Parag is doing everything possible to build towards your goals until close," Dorsey wrote to Musk. "He is really great at getting things done when tasked with specific direction."

Dorsey drew up a document for the meeting with a list of things he wanted to go over, including problems Twitter was working on, short-term action items, and long-term priorities. He sent it to Musk for review. "Getting this nailed will increase velocity," Dorsey wrote, and he even sent Musk the Google Meet link for the call. He was clearly hoping that his new pick for owner would like his old pick for CEO.

The call was a disaster. Whatever Agrawal said about Twitter's product direction fell flat with his soon-to-be boss. There had also been an uncomfortable moment when Musk demanded that Agrawal fire Vijaya Gadde, Twitter's top lawyer and policy exec, who had been deeply involved in making the final decision to ban Donald Trump and block the Hunter Biden laptop story. Even if he'd wanted to, it was unclear if Agrawal could fire Gadde given the pending deal. Musk wasn't technically the owner yet and wasn't supposed to be making demands. Agrawal told Musk he wouldn't fire Gadde; Dorsey, who had worked with Gadde for the better part of a decade, didn't jump in to defend her.

"You and I are in complete agreement," Musk wrote to Dorsey after the call ended. "Parag is just moving far too slowly and trying to please people who will not be happy no matter what he does."

"At least it became clear that you can't work together," Dorsey replied. "That was clarifying."

Musk couldn't fire Gadde, so instead he decided to criticize her publicly. The same day as the phone call, Musk sent a tweet about Gadde's role in the Hunter Biden laptop story. "Suspending the Twitter account of a major news organization for publishing a truthful story was obviously incredibly inappropriate," Musk wrote to his 84 million followers. Within twenty-four hours he posted a second tweet criticizing Gadde, this one a meme claiming that Twitter had "left wing bias" and mocked an appearance she'd made on Joe Rogan's podcast a few years before.

The tweets worked like a dog whistle for people who had long disliked Twitter's policies and felt the company was censoring conservatives. Gadde gave them an outlet for their frustration, and her account was quickly flooded with criticism. People posted derogatory messages about her Indian heritage, using the term "curry" or referencing India's caste system. Many tweets called on her to be fired, and several of the posts violated Twitter's rules and had to be removed.

Some Twitter executives rushed to Gadde's defense, including two of the company's previous CEOs. "Bullying is not leadership . . . What's going on?" Dick Costolo tweeted at Musk. "You're making an executive at the company you just bought the target of harassment and threats."

"Just to say, there are many defensible _nuanced_ perspectives on content moderation and, also, @vijaya is one of the most thoughtful, principled people I know," wrote Ev Williams.

Employees were quick to note that one former CEO was initially silent. Dorsey didn't tweet about the incident for three days. When he finally did, he didn't mention Gadde by name, but took responsibility for the Biden laptop decision. Sort of.

"Every decision we made was ultimately my responsibility*," he wrote, adding a literal asterisk to the tweet. "*it's also crazy and wrong that individuals or companies bear this responsibility," he continued. Dorsey's effort to claim responsibility was undercut by another subsequent tweet where he said Twitter reversed the decision on the laptop story as soon as he found out about it, the implication being that Gadde made the call without his knowledge.

The Musk deal wasn't even a week old, but employees were already starting to sour on their old boss. Dorsey had long been a favorite among Twitter employees, not necessarily because he was a strong business leader, but because he made working at Twitter feel special and important. He'd been approachable and sensitive to employee issues. Twitter's senior Staff had always appeared tight, and at the very least, Dorsey seemed to genuinely care about Twitter employees, often saying how much he loved them and appreciated them. This was the man whose parents showed up at company-wide retreats, and who spent part of his workday reading Dr. Seuss to employees' kids.

Over the past month, though, Dorsey had seemed like a different person. He'd publicly complained about Twitter's board, and bemoaned the company's very existence as a for-profit company. Some Twitter employees were disappointed that Dorsey had so openly defended Musk and championed his purchase of the company, considering the new owner was a terrible culture fit for the generally left-leaning Twitter. Musk loved to make vulgar sex jokes, had fought against unions at Tesla, and openly mocked people who put their pronouns in their Twitter bios. Dorsey seemed happy to ignore all that; he'd even called Musk the "light of consciousness." Now Dorsey was pushing one of the company's biggest mistakes—the Hunter Biden laptop call—onto one of his direct reports, a woman he'd tasked with making those kinds of difficult decisions for years so that he didn't have to. Dorsey wasn't CEO anymore, but employees were starting to feel betrayed nonetheless.

Agrawal was struggling to maintain employee morale, which seemed to be deteriorating by the day. Some people were excited about Musk when the deal was initially announced. Musk had so much money that he could do virtually anything he wanted. This was a man trying to put humans on Mars and rid the world of gas-guzzling cars, after all. Now what he wanted was to work on Twitter. That was both exciting and validating to some Twitter employees who were ready to see what the company would look like under Musk's watchful eye.

Many employees, though, seemed to fall somewhere on the spectrum between generally worried and predominantly furious. Several voiced their concerns about Musk on the company's internal Slack, with messages leaking to the press. "We're all going through the five stages of grief in cycles and everyone's nerves are frazzled," one employee wrote in a message published by the *New York Post*. "Not the place to say it perhaps, but I will not work for this company after the takeover," wrote another. Agrawal was getting lots of questions about *why* Twitter sold the company. As a board member, he'd been directly involved in the decision to sell to Musk but couldn't seem to come up with a good reason for the deal besides the fact that it made money for investors. It seemed as if Agrawal was constantly channeling *The Godfather*'s Michael Corleone: *It's not personal, it's strictly business.* In multiple company-wide meetings after the deal was announced, Agrawal repeatedly used the word *fiduciary* to explain the decision. Twitter's board had to think about shareholder value above all else, he said. Musk's offer was simply too good to pass up.

It was an unsatisfying answer for employees who had spent years working for a company that often preached its purpose and value to the world. Making the decision to sell for Wall Street investors didn't sit right with people who felt like they'd signed up for something more meaningful. Even worse was that Agrawal suggested that the whole thing could have been avoided if Twitter had simply performed better as a company.

"I could have done things differently. I think about this a lot," he told employees a few days after the deal closed. "I feel accountable for my actions I've taken over the last decade. I've only been in this job for four months, but I've been at the company for a decade. And yes, we could have done better. Should have done better."

Ten days after the deal was signed, Twitter held yet another all-company meeting, its third since the deal was announced. Executives had prepared a slide deck to try to motivate people who were feeling downtrodden and demoralized since many employees assumed Musk would come in and dismantle the company. The title slide read "Why Bother?" and did little to inspire. Agrawal, who had Covid and was home sick, made a brief appearance and passed the presentation over to Jay Sullivan, one of Twitter's senior product leaders. He tried to rally the troops by reminding employees that they had a responsibility to each other and were still working on a product used by hundreds of millions of people. Twitter is still a vital vehicle for some of the world's most important conversations, he added. *We're all in this together.*

Another exec soon got up to remind everyone that it was officially May, which meant it was "mental health awareness month." *Be sure to take care of yourselves*, she said.

Elon Musk stood on the red carpet just outside the Metropolitan Museum of Art in New York City and started making faces as dozens of cameras flashed around him. He oohed and aahed. He cringed. He struck a serious pose, like he was deep in thought or had just smelled something questionable. Musk had arrived for the annual Met Gala in a black tuxedo and a white bow tie, his mother, Maye, on his arm. The event served as a fundraiser for the museum but doubled as a place for the world's rich and famous to be seen, usually in a glamorous outfit by a famous designer. Actress Blake Lively wore a Versace dress with a train that looked to be about fifteen feet long. A very slim Kim Kardashian was in attendance after losing sixteen pounds in just three weeks so that she could fit into the actual dress worn by Marilyn Monroe in 1962 when she sang "Happy Birthday" to President John F. Kennedy. The year before at the Met Gala, Congresswoman Alexandria Ocasio-Cortez wore a white dress with the words "Tax the Rich" written in bright red on the back.

Compared to the rest of the attendees, Musk looked both sharp and rather boring, "like I'm from *Downton Abbey* or something," he said. As the new owner of Twitter, though, there was arguably no one in attendance more intriguing. It had been exactly one week since his $44 billion deal was announced, and Musk held court alongside Maye with a gaggle of red-carpet reporters. "I admire good style so we're just going to walk around and sort of see the great outfits," he said. That wasn't all he was going to do. "I'm going to ask people in there, 'Please! Please! Please help me buy Twitter!'" he joked.

Buried beneath the funny faces and lighthearted pleas for help was a real conundrum: Musk needed to come up with a lot of money. A few days before the Met Gala, Musk sold $8.5 billion in Tesla stock to help chip away at the $21 billion he'd promised Twitter and his banking partners that he'd personally deliver. "No further TSLA sales planned after today," he tweeted, a pledge that meant he'd need to find the rest of the money elsewhere.

Musk's bankers at Morgan Stanley were working to find investors. They had initially lined up Puerto Rican billionaire and private equity bigwig Orlando Bravo, but he'd unexpectedly backed out, creating even more urgency to find money. Michael Grimes, the head of global technology banking at Morgan Stanley and one of the industry's most well-connected money guys, sent Musk a message about meeting with Sam Bankman-Fried, who was running the crypto exchange FTX. He's an "Ultra Genius and doer builder," Grimes claimed, and more importantly, he was very interested in working with Musk. "It could get us 5bn equity in an hour," Grimes added. Musk agreed to get together. "So long as I don't have to have a laborious blockchain debate," he replied.

Musk, meanwhile, was working his own network. He'd already hooked his pal Larry Ellison, and now he turned to other tech heavyweights. He exchanged texts with Reid Hoffman, the venture capitalist and cofounder of LinkedIn, suggesting his firm put in $2 billion. Musk asked his friend David Sacks, another VC and a former executive at PayPal, if he was open to an investment. Jason Calacanis offered to fundraise on Musk's behalf. Musk even convinced Dorsey to roll over his ownership stake in Twitter, valued at just under $1 billion. (Later on, to ease his anxiety, Musk would promise Dorsey that if he ever wanted to cash out he could do so at $54.20 per share no matter how much the company was worth.)

Finding the money to buy Twitter hadn't seemed like much of an issue five weeks earlier when Musk first approached the company's board. His net worth at the time had been around $270 billion after Tesla stock had climbed almost 25 percent in the month of March. Tesla's stock then promptly fell 20 percent, including 13 percent in a single week. Musk's net worth shrank by about $40 billion over a five-week stretch. He still had plenty of money, but the economy was looking sketchier and sketchier. Russia was at war with Ukraine, creating issues for the European economy that were impacting the rest of the world. Inflation was also up significantly. In May, the Consumer Price Index, which broadly tracks the cost of goods in the U.S., had its largest one-year jump since 1981.

A few days after the Met Gala, Musk restructured his plan to buy Twitter. He had originally signed up for a $12.5 billion personal loan backed by his Tesla shares; with Tesla's stock dropping, he cut that loan in half to avoid having to pledge even more shares to satisfy the loan requirements. That meant Musk needed to find another $6.25 billion on his own. He was now personally responsible for coming up with $27.25 billion.

The good news was that Musk's effort to find help had been fruitful. On the same day he restructured his loan, he submitted a list of investment partners with the Securities and Exchange Commission. Ellison had indeed chipped in $1 billion after his text exchange with Musk a few weeks earlier. Sequoia Capital, one of the tech industry's most illustrious venture capital firms, was in for $800 million; the firm had already invested in several of Musk's other ventures, including X.com, SpaceX, and even The Boring Company. Andreessen Horowitz, another prominent

VC firm, was in for $400 million. Musk had rounded up a total of $7.1 billion in pledges. He was chipping away.

Musk visited Twitter's San Francisco office for the first time on a Friday evening, May 6, to meet with some of the company's management team and start the due diligence process that he'd initially waived in his rush to buy the company. Musk arrived late, and sat in the middle of a large conference room table on the second floor of Twitter's office across from Ned Segal, the company's chief financial officer. Twitter CEO Parag Agrawal was in attendance, too, but had to join via video since he still had Covid. The rest of the room was filled with various bankers, lawyers, and corporate development people.

The group rushed through as many topics as they could for more than two hours. Twitter offered some projections for its finances; Musk was worried about Twitter's spending, encouraged the company to cut costs and head count. Musk was also concerned about the size of Twitter's user base. Twitter had long had a clause in its quarterly earnings reports that less than 5 percent of its total user base might be spam or bot accounts, meaning they weren't real people. Musk wanted to know how that number was calculated. Based on his experience on Twitter, the bot number had to be much, much higher, he thought. The Twitter team promised to get back to him.

When the two sides adjourned, there was a disconnect about how the meeting went. The Twitter group seemed pleased. It was clear Musk didn't really understand the company's advertising business, but everyone had seemed cordial and polite, and that part of the company was certainly learnable.

Musk, though, walked away with a very different mindset. He thought Twitter had been ill-prepared and he was particularly peeved that there hadn't been a clear answer to his question about bots. The company had instead promised to get back to him. He would later complain privately that the Twitter team had seemed like a bunch of "fucking idiots." Most importantly, Musk walked away convinced that he had overpaid for Twitter. "It was the worst diligence meeting I have ever witnessed in my life," he later said.

The bot issue lingered with Musk for the next several days. On May 8, Grimes sent Musk a message about appointing a temporary CFO to help close the deal. Musk needed someone he could trust to help handle his debt deals with the banks. Grimes wanted to ensure they could keep things moving at "ludicrous speed," which meant picking a CFO quickly to start handling those banking partners. He mentioned two candidates for the job, both of whom Musk had already met. He didn't like either of them. "Neither were great," he wrote back. "They asked no good questions and had no good comments."

In fact, Musk wasn't happy with much of anything at the moment. He wanted to take a beat. "Let's slow down just a few days," he wrote back to Grimes. He wanted to wait until the world heard from Russian president Vladimir Putin, who was supposed to give a speech the next day and talk about his war with Ukraine. "It won't make sense to buy Twitter if we're headed into WW3," Musk added.

The delay would also give him more time to hear back from Twitter about the bot issue. The company's inability to explain how it calculated the number of bot accounts at his meeting a few days earlier was still gnawing at him. "They couldn't answer that on Friday, which was insane," Musk wrote to Grimes. "If that number is more like 50% or lower, which is what I would guess based on my feed, then they have been fundamentally misrepresenting the value of Twitter to advertisers and investors." He still wanted to do the deal, he said, but he needed to make sure that Twitter wasn't lying.

Musk spent a few more days ruminating while lawyers and bankers on both sides continued to work toward closing the deal. Twitter had sent Musk some updated material about the bots, which both sides were expected to discuss in a follow-up meeting the next Friday, May 13.

Twitter never got the chance to go deep on the issue with Musk. The billionaire woke up the morning of the follow-up meeting and, without any warning to his lawyers or bankers, posted a tweet.

"Twitter deal temporarily on hold pending details supporting calculation that spam/fake accounts do indeed represent less than 5% of users," he wrote. Musk had spent weeks pulling every lever at his disposal to buy Twitter as quickly as possible. This was a company he simply *had* to have. Now with his net worth shrinking, Europe at war, and his sudden suspicion that Twitter was lying about the size of its user base, he wasn't so sure.

The meeting that afternoon was a complete disaster. Musk followed up his tweet about putting the deal "on hold" with a second post two hours later that said he was "Still committed to acquisition," though it felt like a halfhearted commitment. He only sent the tweet after his lawyer, Alex Spiro, and his business manager, Jared Birchall, pleaded with him to walk back his comments. Musk never showed up to the meeting, sending some of his advisors instead.

It's probably good that Musk was absent. The Twitter team's explanation for how the company counted bots had been uninspiring. Twitter said human reviewers combed through a list of 100 accounts per day, or roughly 9,000 per quarter, that the company counted as active users. Reviewers used internal data like an account's IP address or whether there was a phone number attached to try to determine if the account holder was a real person. Through this process, they found that less than 5 percent of the accounts they listed as active users were bots. Musk's advisors repeatedly challenged the Twitter executives on the methodology, peppering them with questions throughout the two-hour meeting, seemingly skeptical that Twitter was telling the truth. This time, nobody left the meeting feeling optimistic.

Even though Musk missed the meeting, he was briefed shortly afterward. That afternoon, he tweeted publicly about Twitter's bot-counting methods, saying he was planning to replicate them himself. "My team will do a random sample of 100 followers of @twitter," he wrote. "I invite others to repeat the same process and see what they discover. . . ." After Twitter's lawyers called to complain that Musk was breaking his nondisclosure agreement by sharing the methodology publicly, Musk was in disbelief. "Twitter legal just called to complain that I violated their NDA by revealing the bot check sample size is 100!" he tweeted. "This actually happened."

In the weeks that followed, Musk started hammering Twitter about the bot issue any chance he could get. He suggested Twitter's executives had been lying for years, sometimes throwing out accusations that appeared to be based on nothing more than his own speculation. "There is some chance [bots] might be over 90% of daily active users," he tweeted the day after the disaster meeting. A few days later, Musk appeared virtually at a conference in Miami run by some of his friends, including Sacks and Calacanis, who cohosted a popular podcast called *All-In*. "Currently what I'm being told is that there's just no way to know the number of bots [on Twitter]," Musk told attendees, who had paid $7,500 per ticket for the exclusive event. "It's like, as unknowable as the human soul." Musk repeated his claim that bots could be as high as 90 percent of Twitter's user base, or at least 20 percent on the conservative side, he said. Unsurprisingly, Musk added that *sure*, he would also be open to renegotiating his Twitter deal at a lower price if possible. It wasn't "out of the question," he said.

Agrawal made the mistake of trying to confront Musk's attacks head-on with a thoughtful, nuanced reply. The Twitter CEO posted a public thread that was fifteen tweets long explaining how Twitter counted bots, including the fact that Twitter used internal data that was visible only to the company to finalize its estimates. He admitted that the process was difficult to get right. "The hard challenge is that many accounts which look fake superficially – are actually real people," he wrote. "And some of the spam accounts which are actually the most dangerous – and cause the most harm to our users – can look totally legitimate on the surface."

Musk replied to Agrawal by posting a poop emoji.

No one knew for certain what game Musk was playing. It seemed likely that he wanted to walk away from the deal after catching a strong case of buyer's remorse. His comments at the *All-In* conference suggested that maybe he was simply looking for a better deal. Musk's net worth was still falling, now down to around $210 billion, or tens of billions less than it had been just two weeks earlier at the Met Gala. It was incomprehensible that Musk was truly surprised that there were bots on Twitter. He'd been complaining about bots for years and made fixing Twitter's bot problem one of his core priorities when buying the company. The fact that less than 5 percent of Twitter's active users were bots had also been disclosed in public filings for years. No one needed due diligence to find that out. Musk, it seemed, just didn't believe Twitter was telling the truth.

No matter his endgame, Musk's dramatic change of heart had quickly erased any excitement that had materialized after the deal was first announced. Also gone was any trust that had remained between the two sides. Twitter executives, in particular, were suddenly worried that anything they shared with Musk or his advisors might show up publicly on his Twitter feed. Musk and Twitter, two groups tied together with a binding merger agreement, were suddenly at war.

Despite the rapidly increasing tension, Agrawal seemed determined to keep running Twitter as if the deal didn't exist. In the spring of 2022, as Elon was trying to buy the company, Agrawal spun up a major internal project to change the way Twitter made decisions about content violations. The effort was given a code name, Project Saturn, and was driven by the reality that almost nobody was happy with Twitter's role in policing content. Many people, Musk included, thought Twitter strayed too far into censorship; others thought Twitter gave people too much leeway to post hate and misinformation. Project Saturn was an overhaul of the entire system, a way to give users more control over their experience and increase transparency for times when Twitter did need to step in and dole out a punishment.

The plan included multiple phases, called "horizons," to be implemented over several years. The most urgent changes, known as Horizon 1, were set for later in 2022 and included a plan to eliminate permanent bans as a form of punishment for most rule violators. Instead, Twitter would hand out longer suspensions, like thirty-day, ninety-day and one-year time-outs. People who had already been banned from Twitter, like Donald Trump, would have a chance to earn their way back. Project Saturn also included plans for a points system so people could track their violations and understand whether they were on the cusp of a more severe punishment.

Eventually, in Horizons 2 and 3, users would get the chance to pick which algorithm was used to display tweets in their feed. One day, if all went according to plan, Twitter would even introduce a "reputation score" that would influence the kinds of features users would get access to, or how widely their tweets were distributed.

As Musk was trashing Twitter, executives internally were working on condensing these massive changes into a white paper they hoped to present later in the year. Agrawal and Gadde were both involved in its development, but so were other senior leaders from Twitter's Trust and Safety, product, and design teams. Many of the changes seemed to align with things that Musk had talked about himself, including eliminating permanent bans. At the very least, the company would have something meaningful to show him when the deal closed.

Like Musk, Agrawal was also worried about Twitter's expenses. The company had been planning a series of major cost cuts in April that included company-wide layoffs to eliminate more than 1,200 jobs, but those plans were quietly set aside once Musk made an offer to buy the company. The worsening economy was not just impacting Musk's net worth, though. It was also making Twitter's three-year plan look worse and worse by the week. In mid-May, Agrawal carried out as much of his cost-cutting plan as he could. He emailed the company on a Thursday morning to announce that Twitter was suddenly in a hiring freeze, and in some cases might be rescinding job offers that had already been extended. Everyone was told to spend less on marketing, travel, and events. "Please continue to treat Twitter's resources as you would your own," Agrawal wrote, "and manage tightly to your budgets, prioritizing what matters most."

The biggest shock, though, was that Agrawal also fired two key executives: head of consumer products, Kayvon Beykpour, and head of revenue products, Bruce Falck, both of whom had been promoted when Agrawal took over as CEO just a few months earlier. Falck found out he'd been fired just days before it was announced; Beykpour found out while on paternity leave with his infant daughter.

The timing caused a lot of head-scratching internally, mostly because it seemed odd to fire two very senior executives while the Musk deal was still in limbo. Agrawal's email didn't provide a reason for the firings, but it did hint at Twitter's business shortcomings. "At the beginning of the pandemic in 2020, the decision was made to invest aggressively to deliver big growth in audience and revenue," Agrawal wrote. "As a company we did not hit intermediate milestones that enable confidence in these goals." It was, of course, a reference to the three-year plan that Beykpour and Falck had helped architect, and it was clear that Agrawal was hoping to reset the entire business strategy.

The month of May kept getting weirder for Twitter employees. On May 19, Business Insider published a story detailing sexual harassment allegations against Musk. In 2018, SpaceX had paid $250,000 to settle a sexual misconduct claim after a former flight attendant was allegedly sexually harassed by Musk on the company's corporate jet. Among the allegations was that Musk had exposed himself and propositioned the woman in a private room while receiving a massage, and that he even "offered to buy her a horse" in exchange for an erotic massage.

Musk quickly called the allegations "utterly untrue" and accused Business Insider of writing a hit piece "to interfere with the Twitter acquisition." The story was certainly unflattering, and offered more validation for Twitter employees who were already upset that Musk was buying the company. Then, somehow, the situation got even worse. A week later at Twitter's annual shareholder meeting, Dorsey officially stepped down from the board for good. He had not been nominated for reelection, which meant that his sixteen years as a formal employee or director at the company were officially over.

Musk celebrated by making a sex joke. "Jack off the board!" he posted on Twitter. Then Dorsey replied with a tweet of his own that only included one character: a horse emoji.

Inside Twitter, employees were horrified. Whether or not the accusations were true, their former CEO and future CEO were publicly joking about Musk's sexual harassment allegations. A crude joke wasn't out of the ordinary from Musk, but Dorsey's post stung. The former CEO had long been a champion of women and minorities at Twitter, and once again his tweet felt completely out of character. It had been a week since the harassment allegations were first published, and Twitter's management hadn't addressed them at all. Dorsey's tweet pushed people over the edge.

"As a woman working at Twitter, I find this radio silence extremely disheartening," one employee wrote on Slack.

"I'm so ashamed and embarrassed," wrote another. "The silence is deafening."

Dorsey, who had once been a beloved figure inside Twitter and who was responsible for much of Twitter's touchy-feely corporate culture, had quickly fallen out of favor with his old employees. Everyone inside Twitter knew Dorsey admired Musk, but no one would have pegged him as a guy who would make jokes about sexual harassment.

A third employee had seen enough. "Elon and Jack," he wrote, "are both a disgrace at this point."

Musk's first real chance to win over skeptical employees came on June 16 when he joined a company-wide video call for a Q&A session to talk about his vision for Twitter. Musk's timing was terrible. For weeks he'd been bashing Twitter's user numbers, essentially accusing the company and its executives of lying. The sexual harassment allegations had made Musk even less appealing, and now federal regulators from the SEC were investigating his Twitter stock purchases, which hadn't been disclosed appropriately. Twitter employees weren't even sure if Musk still wanted to buy the company. His tweet about putting the deal "on hold" had forced Twitter executives to meet with the entire company to explain that putting a deal on hold wasn't actually something that Musk could do. Winning over the hearts and minds of Twitter workers would be an uphill battle.

Plus, Musk was running late. Twitter employees sat in their kitchens and bedrooms and home offices waiting on Musk to join the call, a sense of frustration growing before he'd even said a word. Twitter executives had fretted over the meeting given the increasing animosity that Twitter employees seemed to feel toward Musk, not to mention the fact that the deal seemed to be imploding. Chief Marketing Officer Leslie Berland was tasked with moderating the Q&A since she normally emceed the company's all-hands meetings; she had spoken with Musk earlier in the week to try to prepare. Everything felt fragile and tense. Agrawal had learned first-hand that challenging Musk could push him even further away from the deal. So Berland had to be respectful and polite, but still had to be tough enough that employees wouldn't mutiny. When Musk finally joined the call in a white button-down shirt splayed open at the collar, he appeared to be on his phone in his kitchen, his hair poofed up in a way that gave the impression he'd either been up all night or just rolled out of bed.

Berland started off with a softball. "You love Twitter," she stated matter-of-factly. "Why do you love Twitter? And also why did you and do you want to buy Twitter?"

Musk said he learned so much from people on Twitter, and it gave him a direct and clear way to express himself to the public. "Some people use their hair to express themselves," he joked. "I use Twitter."

But the conversation went sideways almost immediately as Musk spoke for almost eight minutes straight, his thoughts ping-ponging all over the place. He criticized the media ("It's obviously overwhelmingly negative") and then got into his views on content moderation ("people should be allowed to say pretty outrageous things"). He talked about the need to add more users, turning Twitter into an "everything" app like WeChat in China, and lamented the fact that Twitter sent so much traffic to YouTube.

Musk really started to lose his audience about fifteen minutes in when he got a question about remote work. Twitter employees had been working remotely for over two years, since the beginning of the pandemic, and many had relocated to different cities or states. Musk, though, was not a fan of remote work, which wasn't a possibility at his other companies. You can't build cars or rockets when everyone is working from their living rooms. "The bias definitely needs to be strongly towards working in-person," Musk said, though exceptions would be made for all-star talent. "If somebody is exceptional then remote work can be OK."

Then Musk got to potential layoffs, and everyone on the call felt even worse. "The company does need to get healthy. Right now the costs exceed the revenue so that's not a great situation to be in," he said. "So there would have to be some rationalization of head count and expenses to have revenue be greater than costs otherwise Twitter is simply not viable or can't grow." Musk was right about Twitter's business, but it didn't mean it was fun to hear. Again, there would be exceptions made for all-stars. "Anyone who is like obviously a significant contributor should have nothing to worry about."

At one point, Musk started talking about his political views, which he described as "moderate" and "pretty close to the center." He'd voted Democrat his whole life, he said, until the most recent elections in Texas, where he voted for a Republican for Congress, Mayra Flores. Musk ended the call by talking about his general life mission to "extend the scope, scale and lifespan of consciousness." Whether it was putting people on Mars, ridding the world of fossil fuels, or saving free speech from the woke-happy mob, Musk's goal was always to protect humanity from disaster. "Civilization will come to an end at some point but let's try to make it last as long as possible," he said, which led him to one final thought about aliens and traveling to other star systems. (Musk had never seen "actual evidence for aliens," he confirmed.)

Twitter employees were almost universally disappointed. Their first interaction with Musk had gone about as poorly as anyone could have imagined. Musk's off-the-cuff style came across as ill-prepared and aloof. Remote work was on the way out. Layoffs were coming, too. Even

Musk's identity as a political moderate didn't sit right with employees. Flores had reportedly spread claims on social media that the January 6th riot was caused by the political left and repeatedly used a hashtag of the far-right conspiracy theory QAnon.

Twitter's internal Slack channels had been blowing up in real time throughout the entire conversation. The discussion had been particularly polarizing, as some employees were bothered by Musk's decision to vote for Flores and others felt that discussing Musk's personal voting choices was inappropriate for a corporate meeting. Generally, though, employees used Slack to mock Musk personally:

"y'all told me this man was a genius"

"why do I feel like he was not prepared for this meeting?"

"So I now need to worry about becoming unemployed depending on whether I'm considered 'exceptional.'"

"is it too early to get a DRINK?"

It didn't matter whether ending remote work or cutting the company's bloated head count were reasonable business decisions. The meeting had given Twitter employees an hourlong, unfiltered look into Musk's frame of mind, which turned him into an even scarier boogeyman. Amir Shevat, the head of Twitter's developer products, watched the interview live from his home office in Austin, Texas, with Twitter's Slack channels open on a second screen as the angry employee messages poured in. After the call was over, Shevat got several anxious phone calls from people on his team who were suddenly worried about their jobs, or even ready to quit. The Musk Q&A was supposed to make people feel better about the pending acquisition. It largely did the opposite. Shevat later summed it up darkly: "It was probably the most cringe-worthy experience in my career."

FIFTEEN

TWITTER V. ELON R. MUSK

Elon Musk made the two-hour-and-eighteen-minute flight from Austin, Texas, to Sun Valley, Idaho, and quietly slipped in the back door at the Sun Valley Lodge, avoiding the gaggle of reporters stationed out front. Musk was in town to speak at Allen & Company's annual retreat, commonly referred to as "summer camp for billionaires." Musk made the flight on his Gulfstream Thursday afternoon but wasn't slated to speak until the conference's final day, Saturday, July 9, where he had a coveted finale time slot. All the guests at Sun Valley that week were rich and famous, though no one more so than Musk.

The conference was as glamorous as its unofficial title made it sound. Allen & Company, a boutique investment bank, compiled an exclusive invite list each year of the world's most powerful business leaders. Facebook's Mark Zuckerberg, Fox chairman Rupert Murdoch, and legendary investor Warren Buffett were already on property by the time Musk arrived, and the local airport was littered with private jets. The resort had the expected amenities, including a pool, tennis courts, and a 20,000-square-foot spa. There was also a bowling alley, an outdoor amphitheater, and most importantly, lots of dealmaking. Sun Valley had given birth to some of the biggest media and technology deals of all time. Comcast mapped out a deal to acquire NBCUniversal from General Electric at a condo along the ninth hole of a golf course in Sun

Valley in 2009, and it was also where the seed was planted for Disney's $19 billion acquisition of ABC in 1995. Amazon's Jeff Bezos met secretly at Sun Valley with Donald Graham, the CEO of *The Washington Post*, before inking a deal to buy the newspaper in 2013.

In 2022, though, Sun Valley would be remembered instead for a deal that fell apart.

Musk didn't wait until Saturday to take center stage at the conference. On Friday, his lawyers sent a letter to Vijaya Gadde, Twitter's top lawyer, terminating his $44 billion deal to buy the company. Musk's lawyers argued that Twitter had repeatedly withheld information from him that was relevant to the deal, most notably, data he needed to make his own calculation about how many "false and spam" accounts were included in Twitter's user base. "While Twitter has provided some information, that information has come with strings attached, use limitations or other artificial formatting features," the lawyers argued. It was a fancy way of saying that Twitter wasn't being helpful to close the deal like the company had promised.

Having an accurate sense of Twitter's total audience was important for the company's advertising business. If Twitter was showing ads to a bunch of bots instead of real people, as Musk suspected, it could greatly impact Twitter's value. Musk believed the spam issue might even amount to a "material adverse effect," a subjective term that meant Twitter's alleged misrepresentations were dramatically altering the business Musk believed he was buying. At the end of the letter, and for good measure, Musk also complained about the business changes CEO Parag Agrawal made a few months earlier, including firing two of his top lieutenants. Twitter had failed to "conduct its business in the ordinary course" as it had promised, Musk argued.

The letter, which was submitted to the Securities and Exchange Commission, brought to life a nightmare scenario for Twitter: that Musk would walk away from the deal, sell his stake, tank the stock, and leave Twitter standing alone as an independent company with significantly poorer investors, employees, and executives. Twitter's stock fell 7 percent when Musk's letter became public. It was trading around $34 per share, well below Musk's $54.20 offer price, a sign investors were highly skeptical that a deal would get done.

Bailing on a $44 billion deal made Musk's scheduled Sun Valley appearance even more intriguing. Adding to the tension was that Twitter had three of its own staying at the resort that week. Agrawal, CFO Ned Segal, and Twitter chairman Bret Taylor were all in attendance and suddenly very popular, though not for the reasons they might have hoped.

During Musk's highly anticipated interview the following day, he spoke briefly about Twitter, but primarily dodged any questions about the deal. Twitter needed to be more transparent about user data, he said, and he still disagreed with the decision to ban Donald Trump. At one point he even polled the audience, asking them to raise their hands if they *actually* believed spam bots were less than 5 percent of Twitter's user base. Mostly, though, Musk spoke about SpaceX and his eventual hope to put humans on Mars, which he referred to as a "civilian life insurance."

While he spoke, Agrawal, Segal, and Taylor sat silently in the audience alongside their wives, watching the man who had spent the last several months treating Twitter like a yo-yo. First the board seat debacle, now the sale. In an alternate universe, perhaps they would have shared a celebratory drink with Musk to commemorate the merger. Instead, everyone kept their distance. The lawyers would do the talking from here on out.

Twitter sued Elon Musk in the Delaware Court of Chancery three days later, demanding that the court force Musk to follow through on his deal to buy the company. Twitter couldn't afford to let the deal collapse. Not only would it be generally embarrassing and devastating to employee morale, but the Twitter board would likely be exposed to all kinds of shareholder lawsuits from people who wanted to get their $54.20 per share.

The argument made in Twitter's sixty-two-page lawsuit was rather simple: Musk had agreed to buy Twitter, and he didn't have a legitimate reason to walk away. Twitter's lawyers painted Musk as a disingenuous hypocrite who was trying to save his own wallet now that the economy had taken a turn. Musk had certainly known that Twitter had spam and bot accounts on the service, the lawsuit continued. Musk had even mentioned "defeating the spam bots" as a top priority in the joint press release announcing the $44 billion deal. His timing had simply been terrible.

"Having mounted a public spectacle to put Twitter in play, and having proposed and then signed a seller-friendly merger agreement, Musk apparently believes that he—unlike every other party subject to Delaware contract law—is free to change his mind, trash the company, disrupt its operations, destroy stockholder value, and walk away," the lawsuit read. Every day that went by led to more damage to Twitter's business, the company's lawyers argued, especially since Musk was loudly and publicly arguing that Twitter's user numbers were bogus. Twitter also filed a motion to expedite the dispute, asking for the judge to schedule a trial in September to minimize any ongoing damage to its business.

As for Agrawal's decision to fire his top executives and freeze hiring: "Musk's counsel was notified of those decisions at the time and raised no objection," the suit claimed, adding, "These decisions aligned with Musk's own stated priorities" to cut costs.

Twitter hired the well-respected New York law firm Wachtell, Lipton, Rosen & Katz to represent the company in Delaware, where Twitter was incorporated. The firm's co-chair of litigation, Bill Savitt, had been working on mergers-and-acquisitions cases for decades, and immediately took the helm of Twitter's fight against Musk. Savitt had once driven a cab in New York to pay the bills and dreamed of life as a musician before becoming one of the best corporate lawyers in the business. He had all the credentials: degrees from Brown University and Columbia Law School, where he was editor in chief of the *Columbia Law Review* before taking a clerkship with Supreme Court justice Ruth Bader Ginsburg. Over the years, Savitt had worked with the private equity firm KKR, real estate giant Sotheby's, and Charter Communications, which faced litigation after its merger with Time Warner in 2015. If a legal dispute arose around a merger or acquisition, Savitt was usually involved. "If you read the *Wall Street Journal*, you might as well be looking at Bill Savitt's daily calendar," read one profile of Savitt in the legal publication Lawdragon. Things went well enough that when Savitt and his wife bought a $5.4 million condo on New York's Upper West Side in 2016, they were featured in *The New York Times* real estate section.

Agrawal emailed employees about the lawsuit a few hours after it was filed. He didn't mention Musk by name, saying instead that "we plan to hold the buyer fully accountable to fulfill his contractual obligations." Agrawal's email also came with a warning about distractions and increased media attention. The company would need to be focused and resilient. Ultimately, Agrawal was optimistic. "We will prove our position in court and we believe we will prevail."

When Lauren Pringle first realized that Twitter was going to sue Elon Musk in the Delaware Court of Chancery, she was ecstatic. As the editor in chief of The Chancery Daily, a small trade publication that focused exclusively on the court's daily comings and goings, Pringle had been waiting years for a high-profile case like this one to sweep through Delaware. She'd only worked at The Chancery Daily for a few months but had been the publication's first subscriber some ten years earlier when her close friend and former colleague, Kyle Wagner Compton, started writing a newsletter for the small universe of lawyers and judges who were deeply entrenched in the court's activity. Pringle's love for corporate law developed during her time at the University of Pennsylvania law school in the mid-2000s. The general public, she thought, didn't fully appreciate just how impactful corporate law was on everyday life.

Musk could change all that. The richest person in the world had just prompted the highest-profile case the court had seen in years. It was a gold mine for writers and journalists, particularly someone like Pringle who actually understood how the Court of Chancery worked. *Here's an opportunity to share corporate law with the world in a way that's really going to resonate with people*, she thought.

There was just one problem: Pringle couldn't find the Twitter password for The Chancery Daily's account. It only had four hundred followers and was (clearly) gathering dust, but Pringle already knew that a case involving Twitter and Musk would be huge on Twitter itself. If The Chancery Daily was going to reach the new audience she envisioned, publishing their work directly to Twitter was a must. So Pringle created a new account in early July, adding an underscore to the old name to differentiate it, and started tweeting out her analysis of the lawsuit. Whenever new motions were filed, or the judge offered an opinion, Pringle was tweeting from @chancery_daily. Within three months, @chancery_daily had more than thirteen thousand followers and Pringle had a full-time job translating the biggest trial of the year for every major news outlet in the country. Friends and Twitter followers even gave her a new nickname: "Chance."

Pringle's instincts were spot-on. The Delaware Court of Chancery had never seen anything quite like *Twitter, Inc. v. Elon R. Musk*. Nearly everything about the lawsuit created a spectacle for the court system, which wasn't used to getting so much attention. The looming trial drew media interest from all over the world, and the court's phones were ringing off the hook. The court's press office was planning to issue as many as two hundred media credentials, and held weeks of meetings to talk about logistics like security and crowd control for the looming trial. The high-profile dispute suddenly made working in Delaware look like a great idea to law students up and down the country; in late 2022, the Delaware Court of Chancery received a huge influx of clerkship applications.

Everything about the lawsuit was intriguing, even for people who had no idea where Delaware was on a map. The court's chancellor, Kathaleen McCormick, a soft-spoken and no-nonsense judge who grew up in the state, was profiled in *The New York Times*, *The Wall Street Journal*, and *The Observer* as the legal battle rolled on.

Elon Musk's lawyer, Alex Spiro, was already a celebrity in his own right and brought an added element of bravado to the case. Spiro had cemented his role as Musk's legal muscle when he successfully defended his billionaire client after Musk was sued for defamation by the British cave diver he'd called a "pedo" on Twitter. When Spiro wasn't billing Musk, he was working for other A-listers like Jay-Z or billionaire Robert Kraft, who owned the NFL's New England Patriots. Spiro was at his best in front of a jury, where his confidence and showmanship could shine, but even in the humdrum business of Chancery Court he generated interest in the Twitter-Musk tie-up.

All the excitement around the case distracted somewhat from a stark reality: that Musk's chances of winning seemed very, very slim. Abandoning the merger agreement he'd signed would most likely hinge on whether Musk could prove not only that Twitter had lied about its user base, but that those lies were significant enough to cause a "material adverse effect" to its business. Musk had signed a seller-friendly deal, after all, and Twitter had added language that would keep Musk from simply paying a financial penalty to walk away. Most legal experts seemed to be in agreement that Musk was a significant underdog.

Twitter struck its first win just a week after filing its lawsuit when McCormick sided with Twitter's request for an expedited trial. She set the trial for a week in October instead of February, which had been Musk's preference. "The reality is, continued delays threaten imminent harm" to the company, she said, echoing Twitter's arguments.

The expedited trial was good news for Twitter, which was indeed starting to struggle. In mid-July, Twitter reported disappointing earnings, including a year-over-year revenue decline and a net loss of $270 million for the quarter. A week later, it closed or cut down office space in several key markets to help reduce costs, including San Francisco and New York.

Each day that went by without a resolution was also crushing morale and productivity. Inside Twitter, the case had become a tremendous distraction. Not much was getting done since nobody wanted to spend a bunch of time and energy building things that Musk might dismantle anyway. The lingering trial was also making things miserable for some of Twitter's senior leaders. Project Veritas, the right-wing undercover media organization known for using hidden cameras and microphones to record people without their knowledge, had already showed up unannounced at Chairman Bret Taylor's neighborhood in the East Bay. Chief Marketing Officer Leslie Berland had it even worse after someone from Project Veritas called her pretending to be a florist with a delivery of flowers. After finding out when she'd be home, they surprised her outside her building in New York. Executives and employees alike spent the summer of 2022 in limbo, waiting for some kind of clarity. By mid-August, with the hiring freeze still in full effect, attrition at Twitter was up to 18 percent.

Lawyers for Elon Musk and Twitter spent most of the summer doing all kinds of lawyerly things like filing motions and writing letters to the judge to complain about the other side's lawyers. Musk filed counterclaims to Twitter's initial lawsuit in late July, essentially his denial of all Twitter's allegations, and argued that the company had knowingly withheld important information he needed to do his own bot calculation. Twitter had provided "only buzzwords and high-level descriptions" of its own bot methodology, Musk argued. Musk's lawyers acknowledged that their client had been difficult to pin down for meetings, a claim that Twitter made in its own suit, but that was only because he "saw these meetings for what they were—distractions from the important requests his team was making about user data."

Both sides started to subpoena anyone and everyone who seemed relevant to the deal. Jack Dorsey was subpoenaed, of course, and so were Kayvon Beykpour and Bruce Falck. Twitter subpoenaed virtually every bank or investment group that might have had a conversation with Musk, plus several of his friends and business partners. Larry Ellison received a subpoena, as did Marc Andreessen, whose venture capital firm had given

Musk $400 million for the deal. When David Sacks, the former PayPal exec who was friends with Musk, received his subpoena, he held up the massive stack of paperwork during an interview on Bloomberg Television, calling it an "overly broad fishing expedition." "I've been a vocal critic of Twitter's management, maybe they don't want me talking about these issues," he added. Musk's lawyers agreed with Sacks, arguing in a letter to the judge that Twitter's subpoena requests were overly broad.

The only sign that a deal might eventually get done was when Musk sold another $6.9 billion of Tesla stock in early August, which was notable in part because he'd already promised Tesla investors he was done selling shares. He framed the sale as a precaution, and once again promised investors that he was done. "In the (hopefully unlikely) event that Twitter forces this deal to close *and* some equity partners don't come through, it is important to avoid an emergency sale of Tesla stock," he tweeted as an explanation.

A few weeks later, Musk appeared to get the big break he was hoping for when a former Twitter executive, Peiter "Mudge" Zatko, filed a whistleblower complaint against Twitter with U.S. regulators, including the Department of Justice. Mudge had worked at Twitter for just fourteen months but held one of the top jobs at the company, leading all of Twitter's security efforts and reporting directly to Dorsey. In the world of online hacking, Mudge was a legend, having carved out a long career in both tech and government jobs, including time running cyber programs for the research-and-development agency for the U.S. Department of Defense, known as DARPA. Dorsey had hired Mudge in late 2020 after an embarrassing incident earlier that summer when a seventeen-year-old hacker from Florida gained access to some of Twitter's most important accounts, including Joe Biden's and Musk's, and posted tweets promoting a Bitcoin scam. Dorsey, who had always fashioned himself a hacker, admired Mudge and recruited him to secure Twitter's systems. There was hope that the hire might also help Twitter save face with a security industry that suddenly viewed the company as a bit of a joke.

The short-lived relationship was doomed from the beginning. Dorsey was checking out from Twitter almost as soon as Mudge arrived, and the two barely spoke even though Dorsey had recruited him aggressively. Mudge estimated that Dorsey said just fifty words to him over half a dozen phone calls during his first twelve months on the job. Twitter employees were similarly unimpressed with Mudge, who was a decorated hacker but not necessarily a great manager. Agrawal fired Mudge shortly after he replaced Dorsey as CEO, and now Mudge was publicly airing Twitter's dirty laundry in the middle of its $44 billion legal fight with Musk.

Mudge's accusations were damning. Twitter's security systems were outdated and inefficient, he claimed, and most troubling was that Mudge believed Twitter was violating a privacy promise it had made to the Federal Trade Commission in 2011. At the time, Twitter had pledged to do a better job of protecting user data after a separate incident gave hackers access to private user information. Twitter had signed a "consent decree" promising to improve its security, with the expectation that the FTC could come calling at any time to review its systems and issue fines if Twitter wasn't in compliance. Mudge alleged that his colleagues told him "unequivocally that Twitter had never been in compliance with the 2011 FTC Consent Order, and was not on track to ever achieve full compliance."

Musk and his lawyers didn't start salivating until page 9 of the whistleblower complaint, though, where there was a section titled "Lying about Bots to Elon Musk." Mudge claimed that Agrawal's explanation for calculating Twitter's user base was misleading. Even worse, Mudge said that Twitter executives didn't actually know how many bots there were on the service.

The complaint spurred everybody into action. Both sides subpoenaed Mudge, and Musk's lawyers asked to delay the trial so they could include his accusations in their counterclaims and spend more time mining Mudge for information. "It all comes down to weighing speed versus finding the truth," Spiro, Musk's lawyer, told Judge McCormick during a hearing in early September. "Finding that truth is going to take more time. It will take a few more weeks."

Twitter's lawyers argued that Mudge had nothing to do with spam and bot accounts while he worked at Twitter, and had never complained or raised concerns about the company's methods while he worked there. They called the timing of the allegations "very, very strange," a poorly disguised suggestion that Mudge was trying to aid Musk by coming forward.

Mudge's attacks on Twitter ended up being less damning than they first appeared. His claim that Twitter had no idea how many bots there were was probably true, but that wasn't what was up for debate. There could be a billion bots on Twitter, but so long as Twitter didn't count those bots as active users, then the company wasn't lying in its quarterly earnings reports as Musk had suggested. In fact, Mudge acknowledged that Twitter actually did a good job of weeding out bots from that more formal user count. "Twitter is already doing a decent job excluding spam bots and other worthless accounts from its calculation" of active users, the complaint said. Twitter's security flaws were indeed a concern, though. In fact, Twitter had been fined $150 million just a few months earlier for violating the same FTC consent decree Mudge referenced in his complaint. But Twitter's shoddy security wasn't the reason Musk was trying to walk away from his deal.

In the end, McCormick let Musk add details from Mudge's allegations to his counterclaims but refused to push back the date of the trial. "I am convinced that even four weeks' delay would risk further harm to Twitter too great to justify," she wrote in her decision. It was another win for Twitter, and a good indication that McCormick didn't view Mudge's accusations as a game changer for the trial.

By the end of September, it felt like almost everything about the lawsuit was going Twitter's way. McCormick slammed Musk for failing to hand over his personal text messages that were relevant to the trial, claiming that some of them had shown up from other people, raising questions about why he hadn't supplied them himself. Mudge's whistleblower complaint had turned out to be a bust, at least as far as Musk was concerned, and in mid-September, Twitter shareholders voted to approve the Twitter-Musk merger. The vote was a formality, but it had also been one of Musk's final escape hatches. Had shareholders voted the deal down, Musk could have walked away without penalty. Instead, 98.6 percent of votes cast were in favor of the deal. Everyone wanted their $54.20 per share.

Then on September 29, the court published dozens of documents that had been collected and uncovered during the trial's discovery process. Among them were forty pages of Musk's private text messages with friends, bankers, and even his ex-wife. The document dump had everything. His messages to Larry Ellison and Gayle King were in there, and so were his private correspondences with Joe Rogan, Jason Calacanis, and his banker, Michael Grimes.

The document dump gave the world a peek behind the curtain at how one of the most intriguing business deals of all time came together. It was shocking to see how spontaneous and haphazard a $44 billion business decision could be, and while Musk emerged looking both powerful and uber-connected, the messages also gave the impression that his decision to buy Twitter had been just as spontaneous as it seemed from the outside. The messages were also embarrassing for some of Musk's friends; many seemed to fawn over every decision that Musk made. "What is so illuminating about the Musk messages is just how unimpressive, unimaginative, and sycophantic the powerful men in Musk's contacts appear to be," wrote columnist Charlie Warzel in *The Atlantic*. "Whoever said there are no bad ideas in brainstorming never had access to Elon Musk's phone."

No one, though, emerged from the document dump looking worse than Dorsey. The former Twitter CEO spent much of his summer in Paris, watching from afar as Twitter and Musk did battle over his former company's future. He'd largely stayed quiet about Twitter since the deal was signed, instead tweeting about his personal interests like Bitcoin and his favorite rapper, Kendrick Lamar, who had released a new album that Dorsey couldn't stop playing. He seemed to be enjoying life now that he'd left Twitter in the rearview mirror. At Paris Fashion Week in June, Dorsey sat just a few seats away from Lamar as he performed live at a Louis Vuitton show where male models strutted down a bright yellow runway inside a courtyard at the Louvre. Dorsey even made a brief cameo in one of Lamar's music videos, the two clinking glasses together in a dimly lit lounge.

The text messages immediately brought Dorsey back to the very heart of Twitter's summer from hell. They showed how Dorsey encouraged Musk to join the board, and then encouraged him to change course and buy Twitter instead. They showed how Dorsey had tried to facilitate a relationship between Musk and Agrawal, only to dismiss his successor after a bad phone call. The decision to sell Twitter wasn't Dorsey's to make alone; the Twitter board unanimously approved the sale. But no one fully realized just how involved Dorsey had been in Twitter's sale until the messages came out. Employees who had loved and defended Dorsey for years felt betrayed and angry. The former CEO's reputation among Twitter employees would never be the same.

Perhaps seeing his personal text messages splashed all over the internet pushed Musk over the edge. Or maybe he was worried about what might come out during his own deposition, which was scheduled for early October. Musk's lawyers had delayed as long as possible, but with the trial less than a month away, Musk was running out of time and would eventually need to answer questions under oath for several days. Whatever the reason, Musk had a change of heart. On Monday, October 3, just hours after Agrawal finished his own deposition, Musk's lawyers sent Twitter a letter. Their client wanted to revive the original deal—the same price and the same terms that were agreed upon way back in April. After months of fighting in the press and in courtrooms, Musk was done.

For the second time in six months, Musk agreed to buy Twitter.

PART IV

TWITTER 2.0

SIXTEEN

LET THAT SINK IN

O n the morning of Wednesday, October 26, 2022, Elon Musk picked up a white porcelain sink and carried it into the lobby of Twitter's San Francisco headquarters.

"Entering Twitter HQ—let that sink in!" Musk tweeted, posting a video of himself carrying the sink and giggling at his own joke, a wide smile on his face as his voice echoed off the lobby walls. In typical Musk fashion, the stunt was a nod to an internet meme where people take the popular phrase literally by replying to anyone who says it online by posting a picture of a sink standing in an open doorway. *Let that sink in. No seriously, it's cold out here!*

After months of contentious and expensive legal fighting, Musk's frivolous dad joke marked the unofficial end of *Twitter, Inc. v. Elon R. Musk*, though many Twitter employees failed to see the humor. The man who planned to fire them, the man who had just spent six months criticizing their bosses and questioning their business, the man who had tried everything he could to *not* buy Twitter, was suddenly walking through the front door to turn the company inside out.

The new boss's appearance in San Francisco was a surprise to almost everyone and had been cobbled together at the last minute. The deal hadn't officially closed and the formal deadline was still two days away. Most employees weren't even in the office. Leslie Berland, Twitter's CMO who had interviewed Musk during the uninspiring employee all-hands earlier that summer, only found out about Musk's scheduled visit the previous afternoon when it was mentioned by Twitter's security team. After realizing Musk had no plan or agenda for the visit, Berland scrambled to organize a slate of meetings so that he wouldn't just be aimlessly wandering the halls. She then hopped on a private jet that same morning in New York, flew across the country, and raced to Twitter's office to serve as Musk's chaperone. She shot off a hasty email that landed in employees' inboxes as many of them were still having their morning coffee and booting up their computers.

> Subject: Elon office visit
> Hi Team,
>
> As you'll soon see or hear, Elon is in the SF office this week meeting with folks, walking the halls, and continuing to dive in on the important work you all do. If you're in SF and see him around, say hi! For everyone else, this is just the beginning of many meetings and conversations with Elon, and you'll all hear directly from him on Friday.
>
> I'll be in the SF office shortly too, excited to see all of you!
>
>
>
> LB

By midmorning, the Twitter gossip mill was humming. Musk, wearing a black T-shirt, black jeans, and holding his toddler son, X, on his hip, walked through the office with Berland, flanked by his security detail and his biographer Walter Isaacson. As the group made its way through Twitter's cafeteria, starstruck employees at first kept their distance. Standing almost six-foot-two with a broad chest and shoulders, Musk was both physically intimidating on top of the whole *richest man in the world* thing. The employees who did make it into work that day took photos and videos on their phones, gawking at the new boss like he was a Hollywood celebrity. Word of Musk's whereabouts traveled fast among employees, some eager to catch a glimpse of the new boss, others now aware of which sections of the office to avoid.

Manu Cornet, a software engineer who also served as the company's resident cartoonist, was gutsier than most. He'd spent much of the past six months tweeting out sketches criticizing Twitter management and Musk over the chaotic deal, so when Cornet heard that Musk was in the office, he printed off one of his cartoons at a nearby coworking space and headed into the building. At one point during the day, Musk walked by Cornet's desk and the engineer handed his new boss the cartoon. It was a picture of Musk out shopping, browsing shelves laden with various tech company logos. Musk had accidentally knocked the Twitter bird off the shelf, smashing it into pieces on the ground, while the shop owner calls out, "You break it, you buy it!" Cornet signed the cartoon and added an inscription: "For Elon Musk, I hope you don't mind a 'court jester' at Twitter or you'll have to get me fired." Musk took the comic and gave it a glance. "Well, I bought it anyway," he replied, and walked off. Cornet wasn't fired—at least not right away.

As the tour progressed, Musk made his way to Twitter's in-house coffee shop, The Perch, where he leaned against the counter and was finally approached by a scrum of curious employees eager to pick his brain. Some asked Musk questions about his plans for Twitter's product, or shared their own ideas for new features. Musk talked about his own experience using Twitter. At one point he got serious, telling employees that sometimes reading the tweets and replies from critics on Twitter actually made him sad. Apparently, no level of money or fame can spare you from the Twitter trolls.

Despite the mess of the prior six months, several people who met Musk during his first few days inside Twitter's headquarters walked away surprisingly optimistic. Musk had a way of charming people, even those who were determined not to like him. He was more inquisitive and thoughtful than people expected, earnestly asking lots of questions. Most importantly, he had a skill for saying the things that people wanted to hear. Standing at The Perch, surrounded by anxious employees, someone finally brought up layoffs. Employees had spent months dreading Musk's arrival, in part because they knew it would most certainly mean dramatic cost cuts. A few days earlier, *The Washington Post* had reported that Musk was planning to fire 75 percent of Twitter's workforce. Was it true?

No, Musk replied. He didn't even know where that number came from. Perhaps the new boss wouldn't be so bad after all.

Musk changed his Twitter bio on that first day to "Chief Twit." He set up camp with a group of advisors on the second floor of 1 Tenth Street, a second office building directly behind the company's more prominent Market Street headquarters. Twitter had leased several floors of the back building for years and even commissioned a glass skybridge connecting the two buildings so employees could easily get from one to the other without having to ride the elevators. But the office space on 1 Tenth had recently been deserted. Twitter's "work from anywhere" policy meant that far fewer people were coming into the San Francisco office, and the company largely stopped using those floors to cut down on cleaning costs.

The vacancy meant Musk had plenty of room to spread out. He quickly adopted the entire second floor as his unofficial command center. There were several conference rooms in rotation for meetings, security guards stationed at the elevators, and plenty of room for his two-year-old son, X, to run around. Since Musk was constantly running late, a large open space right off the elevator served as a holding pen for employees who had to kill time waiting for their turn to meet the boss. The delays were impossible to avoid given Musk's jam-packed schedule. Except for his brief office tour, he spent his first few days at Twitter in nonstop meetings, largely conducting the due diligence that he had neglected to do before buying the company.

A handful of trusted advisors and loyalists joined him during those first few days. There were several venture capitalists, including David Sacks, who was hosting Musk at his house in San Francisco; Jason

Calacanis, another friend and angel investor; and Sriram Krishnan, a former Twitter product executive who had recently joined the venture capital firm Andreessen Horowitz, which invested $400 million in Musk's Twitter deal.

He also called in loyalists from his other companies and business ventures. Jared Birchall, the head of his family office, was there, and so was Alex Spiro, his lawyer who had just spent months fighting Twitter in court. Antonio Gracias, another venture capitalist who'd been on the board of directors at both Tesla and SpaceX, quickly became a powerful presence. Dozens of SpaceX and Tesla engineers, led by Musk's cousins James and Andrew, also showed up to meet with Twitter engineers and review the company's code. Steve Davis, the president of Musk's tunnel company, The Boring Company, would draw eyerolls from Twitter employees when news eventually circulated that he wasn't just helping out but actually living in the office with his partner and newborn child. Employees immediately started referring to Musk's group of advisors as "the goons."

The group quickly fanned out, embedding themselves into the various pockets of Twitter's business. Spiro met with the legal and policy groups, Birchall and Gracias with sales and marketing. Sacks met with most of Twitter's top product people. The group served as both translators and cheerleaders for their boss, conveying Musk's ideas and trying to keep Twitter employees from freaking out. "He's here to win," Gracias told a group of Twitter's sales leaders. "He's a winner. He wins everywhere." Spiro tried to explain Musk's vision to Twitter's skeptical lawyers and Trust and Safety employees. He also tried to quell concerns that Musk and his advisors were suddenly going to turn Twitter into some kind of Trump-obsessed, right-wing social network. "I'm more liberal than you might expect," he told them.

Musk seemingly met with everyone, including a brief meeting with Agrawal, but he was primarily focused on one group above all else: engineers. Part of Musk's plan to "fix" Twitter was to expedite the company's ability to make new products and features, and that would mean prioritizing engineers. "Software engineering, server operations & design will rule the roost," he tweeted a few weeks before taking over. Musk wasn't unique in his assessment. In Silicon Valley, software engineers are often prioritized over other workers given their rare skill set and the fact that they actually build the products that other groups like sales and marketing try to promote. As a result, software engineers often attract the highest salaries in tech and benefit from near-constant job security since most tech companies are in perpetual need of more warm bodies to write code. As an engineer himself, Musk was primarily interested in spending time with the people he best understood.

It was with this in mind that Musk's first meeting on his first day was with several of the company's top engineers and product executives, an effort by Berland and the rest of Twitter's management to try to impress the new CEO right off the bat. The meeting was framed to attendees as a "casual conversation" meant for Musk to ask questions, and while the Twitter group had hoped to talk about machine learning and plans to better personalize the service and improve its feed algorithm, the conversation ping-ponged all over the place. Musk wanted to talk about various coding languages and seemed particularly intrigued with Twitter Blue, the company's nascent subscription product. He asked the group to point him to whoever was in charge of coding Twitter Blue; this was someone he needed to meet, he said. At one point early in the meeting Musk pulled out his phone and announced that he had to tweet something; attendees learned after the ninety-minute meeting was over that Musk had briefly paused the discussion to tweet the sink video.

Despite his inquisitive nature, it quickly became clear to employees who shuffled in and out of meetings with Musk that the new boss knew almost nothing about Twitter's product or advertising business. Even worse, Musk didn't seem to have much of a plan for fixing things. Almost all of Musk's product ideas were things the company had previously considered and either disbanded or shelved, sometimes years earlier. He talked about bringing back Vine, for instance, the short video app that Twitter had shut down almost six years prior. In his meeting with the group running Twitter Blue, the discussion included the idea of offering different types of verification badges for different types of accounts, again a concept that had been kicked around for years.

One of the biggest issues, employees noticed, was that Musk's understanding of Twitter was colored almost entirely by his own experience as a user, which was far from normal considering he was a billionaire with more than 110 million followers. Musk was great at using Twitter and understood the power of the service as well as anybody. For years he didn't pay to advertise his car company, Tesla, in part because Musk himself served as a living, breathing billboard. He could do more to attract attention with a single tweet (for free!) than any thirty-second television spot. Much like another famous tweeter, President Donald Trump, Musk understood that being both authentic and controversial was the ideal recipe for getting attention on Twitter, and he had a knack for mixing the two to perfection.

But employees also found Musk was out of touch with the "average" Twitter experience. He quickly gravitated toward products and features that would fit his own specific needs regardless of whether they would be good for the broader service. In a meeting with Twitter designers, for example, employees showed Musk a prototype the company was testing internally that displayed how many "views" a tweet got alongside other metrics like retweets or likes. Twitter was considering including this view-count metric as a perk for paying Twitter Blue subscribers, but the group was also skeptical about displaying view counts publicly. They thought about making the numbers visible only for the person who sent the tweet, if at all. For most people, knowing that a lot of other users saw their tweet but didn't "like" their tweet could be demoralizing. View counts also posed a potential problem for new users, who got very few views on their tweets to begin with. Since most people had no followers when they first joined, and since the main timeline was focused on showing popular tweets, posts from new users were the digital equivalent of yelling into the void. Twitter even had an internal name for the issue: the "lonely birds" problem. View counts would just remind these new users that no one was seeing their posts.

None of this mattered to Musk, who latched on to the view counts idea instantly and spent most of the group's short meeting focused on it. He thought the idea of public view counts would be perfect for exposing whether Twitter was secretly shadow banning someone. Of course, some Twitter employees felt there might be another motivation, too: Public view counts would let Musk and everyone else see just how popular *his* tweets were.

The morning after Musk walked through the front door with a sink, Vijaya Gadde met over video call with some three hundred people who worked on the policy and legal teams under her jurisdiction. Almost nobody knew that Musk had already tried to get Gadde fired during his phone call with Agrawal months earlier, but it was largely assumed that her days at Twitter were numbered. Not only had she spent the summer suing Musk over the deal, but the new owner had openly criticized Gadde's decisions on the Hunter Biden laptop story and the Trump ban. He just didn't seem to like her very much.

On that Thursday morning, though, Gadde was still there, and her team was greeted with some surprising news: She'd met with Musk one-on-one for the first time the night before. Despite the inevitable tension from meeting someone she'd just spent months fighting in court, the roughly thirty-minute interaction had been cordial, though Musk kept saying he was "fried." The two spoke about Project Saturn, Agrawal's plan to revamp Twitter's content policies, and Gadde asked Musk about using his satellite internet service, Starlink, to help Twitter users circumvent government censorship. She even asked Musk if he'd thought about his potential conflicts in China, where Tesla had a factory in Shanghai. It seemed possible the Chinese government might use Tesla's business there to apply pressure on Musk at Twitter. Some members of Gadde's team took the Musk meeting as a positive sign. Perhaps, at the very least, she would stick around to help with the transition, they thought.

At around 4 p.m. PT that afternoon, Musk officially closed on his $44 billion deal to buy Twitter. Gadde was fired immediately. CEO Parag Agrawal and CFO Ned Segal were also terminated; both had left the office earlier that day in anticipation of the axe. Sean Edgett, Twitter's general counsel who'd been deeply involved in the lawsuit, was also fired and escorted out of Twitter's headquarters by security. Half of Twitter's senior leadership team had been ousted less than thirty seconds after Musk took control.

Twitter's executives had prepared accordingly, and arranged for other people to take over their jobs in case they were immediately fired. This was the group, after all, that had just successfully sued Musk, forcing him to buy the company. When Musk was originally negotiating with the board, he told Chairman Bret Taylor that he was trying to buy the company in part because he had zero confidence in Twitter's management. None of them expected to keep their jobs.

As part of Musk's purchase agreement, all four executives were set up with a "golden parachute" that would kick in if they were laid off within the first year after the deal closed. The arrangement meant that some or all of their stock awards, worth millions of dollars, would vest immediately. Those types of payouts were common in mergers to encourage everyone to work toward getting the deal done. Agrawal and Gadde knew they'd likely lose their job by selling to Musk, for example, but at least they'd get paid out ahead of schedule. Agrawal alone was set to make roughly $50 million just by being laid off.

At least, that's what was supposed to happen. When the Twitter executives got an email confirming they'd been terminated, Musk added one more "fuck you" for each of them. He didn't lay them off. Instead, he fired them all "for cause," thus eliminating their golden parachutes. If Agrawal and Gadde wanted to collect their millions, they would need to fight Musk in court. Again.

Eliminating the golden parachutes wasn't enough for Musk. A few days after the deal closed, several members of Twitter's legal team received letters from Musk requesting that they set up time for an interview with his lawyers. "The company is investigating certain conduct of its directors, officers, and advisors," the letter read, and employees were asked to retain all communication and documents related to the merger deal, Twitter's financial reporting, and even its handling of Peiter "Mudge" Zatko, the whistleblower.

"Please immediately start to retain all documents and communications relating to your employment at Twitter, including email, text, or instant messages on any platform." Musk wasn't just withholding golden parachutes; he was also hunting for dirt on the executives who'd fought him in court in hopes of suing them back. Musk wanted revenge.

Around 9 p.m. the night that the deal closed, after a day full of meetings and firings, Musk sent out a tweet: "the bird," he wrote, "is freed."

Yoel Roth started crying when he first learned that his boss, Gadde, had been fired, but he didn't have much time to grieve. Shortly after he got the news, he quickly received a separate text from an unfamiliar Tesla engineer summoning him to Musk's second-floor office area. Now that Musk was officially the owner, he wanted to know more about the internal systems that Twitter used to police user accounts. As the head of Trust and Safety, Roth was the resident expert. He made the trek down to Musk's command center, walking past the company's Halloween party on his way as kids in costumes ran around the office blissfully unaware of all the corporate drama unfolding around them.

Roth made it through various levels of security to reach Musk's floor, which was bustling with activity, his son X running around with a nanny. Roth had never met with Musk before, but the new boss seemed eager to understand the technology Twitter used to enforce rules violations, add misinformation labels to tweets, and even suspend users for infractions. Roth gave Musk a demo by pulling up the billionaire's own account and showing him how it worked. There was concern from Musk's team that a rogue Twitter employee might try to suspend or alter Musk's account without permission, a reasonable concern considering that a few years earlier a Twitter employee had deactivated Donald Trump's account on his last day at the company.

Roth made a series of recommendations on the spot. His first was that Musk continue to work with Twitter's external content moderators—contractors who handled the bulk of Twitter's policing and took down spam or abuse but otherwise had limited access to user accounts. Brazil was in the midst of an important election, Roth explained, and there was fear that Twitter could be abused to spread misinformation or stoke violence. To Roth's pleasant surprise, Musk agreed that the third-party contractors shouldn't be touched.

The second recommendation was that Twitter *should* restrict many of its internal Trust and Safety employees from accessing these tools, primarily because their access was much broader than the third-party contractors'. Many of them had the ability to suspend accounts, for example. It was best to minimize the threat of some grumpy employee going rogue, Roth explained. Again, Musk agreed, and Twitter cut this broad access down to just a dozen people.

The last recommendation was that Twitter should restrict almost everyone internally from accessing its most important accounts, known as the "Top X" list, which included most heads of state and other high-profile users, like Jack Dorsey and Musk himself. The two decided that the only person internally who should have access to alter those accounts should be Roth.

Done. Done. Done.

Roth walked away from his first exchange with Musk pleasantly surprised, and cautiously optimistic. He had expected Musk to dismantle Twitter's content moderation machine on day one, especially after learning of Gadde's firing. Instead Musk had listened to him, and even agreed with all his recommendations. It was a very positive start.

The following day—Musk's first *official* day as Twitter's new owner—was nothing short of pandemonium. Even though the deal had closed the night before, Musk hadn't made any formal announcement to employees about the milestone. He also didn't acknowledge that he had just fired the CEO, CFO, general counsel, and the head of policy. Employees instead discovered that information from their coworkers or by reading the news.

Adding to the confusion was that two pranksters walked out of Twitter's San Francisco office on that Friday morning carrying cardboard boxes and claiming they'd just been fired. National news organizations camped outside, including CNBC and the *Daily Mail*, quickly interviewed the "employees" and ran stories saying that layoffs had begun. Actual Twitter employees briefly panicked before realizing that no one recognized either guy. The two had used fictitious names, "Rahul Ligma" and "Daniel Johnson," that when combined (Ligma Johnson, as in "lick my johnson") formed the kind of crude joke that would have killed on the middle school playground. By the time the media realized they'd been duped, it was too late. Musk, of course, found it all hilarious and later posed for a picture with the two "employees." "Important to admit when I'm wrong & firing them was truly one of my biggest mistakes," he tweeted.

Things were just as chaotic inside Twitter. Musk and "the goons" were still holding meetings, and more and more Tesla engineers were arriving to review Twitter's code. Kayvon Beykpour, the head of product who had been fired just months earlier, was seen walking around the office and had a private meeting with Musk, raising questions about a possible return. Ideas for new Twitter products and features were being tossed around by everybody. During one product meeting, Sacks casually suggested that Twitter add a paywall to the entire website as a new way to make money, an idea that would have dramatically altered the entire service.

By midday, engineers received the bizarre direction to physically print copies of their software code. "Please print out 50 pages of code you've done in the last 30 days," an executive assistant wrote in one of Twitter's

Slack channels. "Recency of code is important but also use a code that shows complexity of our code." In some cases, employees were told that Musk himself would review the code directly, so engineers started hovering around the printers with stacks and stacks of paper. Shortly after, they received another instruction on Slack. "UPDATE: Stop printing," it said. Someone, somewhere had realized that physically printing Twitter's entire code base was unnecessary, and that reviewing code on a laptop would work just fine. "If you have already printed, please shred in the bins on SF-Tenth. Thank you!" The code reviews never ended up happening anyway.

Musk, meanwhile, tweeted his way through the day. "Let the good times roll," he wrote just after 5 a.m., a mere thirty minutes after promising an account with the username @catturd2 that he would investigate whether it was being shadow banned. Around 11 a.m. local time he pledged to form a "content moderation council with widely diverse viewpoints" to review all of Twitter's major content policy decisions, including bringing back accounts like Trump's that had been banned under previous management. Just three hours later he sent another tweet promising that "anyone suspended for minor & dubious reasons will be freed from Twitter jail." Just after lunch, around the time that engineers were printing off their code, Musk declared that "Comedy is now legal on Twitter."

Not everyone was having as much fun as Musk. That same day the new boss saddled two of Twitter's top business executives, Jon Chen and Julianna Hayes, with the miserable task of overseeing company-wide layoffs. Twitter had come close to a major round of layoffs the prior April but postponed the cuts since Musk was planning to buy the company. But Chen and Hayes still had the original layoff plan and suggested that Twitter update and repurpose it. It would mean cutting roughly 20 percent of the company. Musk signed off on the idea, giving them just twenty-four hours to finalize everything. They left the meeting with Musk, and Hayes floated a scenario in which they both resigned and walked out of the building. They ultimately decided that leaving the task to Musk and his advisors would be even worse for employees, and instead called Twitter's head of HR, Kathleen Pacini. The trio huddled together to discuss a plan and soon relayed the dreaded instruction to Twitter's managers to start ranking employees on their teams in preparation for cuts.

Complicating the process was that, unbeknownst to them, Musk had also asked the Tesla and SpaceX engineers, led by his cousins James and Andrew, to oversee a similar ranking exercise with Twitter's engineering teams. They had spent the first twenty-four hours after Musk closed his deal combing through Twitter's code base and reviewing employee contributions to try to identify low performers. Musk told them that he wanted to cut Twitter's engineering teams by more than 90 percent.

The Twitter group had asked for ranked lists to be turned in that same evening, setting off a mad scramble, especially for large teams with hundreds or even thousands of people. It wasn't clear how Musk wanted the company to look when all was said and done, so there was no formal guidance as to what types of employees managers should try to keep.

On the engineering side of the company, the Tesla engineers started recommending that managers rank people by whether they had written at least one hundred lines of code in the past month, a relatively unhelpful standard considering many employees in the product org, including most managers, didn't actually write code. On bigger teams with dozens or even hundreds of employees, stack ranking became almost impossible considering the lack of context. Should managers prioritize employees based on seniority? What about physical location? It was largely believed that Musk would reverse Twitter's "work from anywhere" policy—was it worth putting remote workers high on the list to try to save their job if they didn't live near an office? Managers were also getting additional direction from Musk's advisors. Gracias told leaders on the sales team that Twitter should just keep anyone who was "excellent" or "exceptional."

The result was that managers turned in dozens of inconsistent lists. Some had identified the top 30 percent and the bottom 30 percent of employees in their organization. Leaders from the team that handled sales and worked with advertisers, which had some 1,400 employees, thought the layoffs would only impact 20 percent of their group.

Other managers, like Amir Shevat, the exec handling developer products from Austin, didn't receive any parameters at all. When he asked the Twitter team leading the process what his ranking criteria should be, the response he got back was "we don't know." Shevat was told to rank his team at around 6 p.m. that night and submitted the list as a Google Doc just four hours later; his access to the document was immediately cut off without any further explanation.

Day one was officially over.

Working for Elon Musk typically means moving so fast that everything else, including showers, meals, and most definitely sleep, is considered secondary and dispensable. Working nights and weekends is the norm, and all-nighters are not uncommon. As a young twentysomething entrepreneur in San Francisco, long before he was the world's richest man, Musk developed a reputation for practically living at the office. When he founded Zip2, the yellow pages directory for the internet, Musk would often sleep on a beanbag by his desk, waking each morning once employees trickled in and gave him a kick to get up and start his day. During busy production stretches at Tesla in 2018, Musk was known to sleep out on the factory floor, too busy to go home or even to take a shower. "I wanted my circumstance to be worse than anyone else at the company on purpose," he explained later. "Like whatever pain they felt, I wanted mine to be worse." Musk was willing to live in the trenches if necessary, but he expected his employees to join him. "He preferred a scrappy, hard-driven environment where rabid warriors felt psychological danger rather than comfort," wrote Isaacson, his biographer.

It was a new kind of mindset for Twitter, and it quickly caught on with some of the company's engineers. Manu Cornet, the cartoonist, slept on a couch at the office for the first time on Friday, Musk's first full day as Twitter's owner. The new CEO had quickly identified a few projects that were of absolute priority, among them a revamped version

of Twitter Blue, the company's subscription offering. The group building it was scrambling to impress Musk and match his urgency. Cornet
wasn't technically part of the Twitter Blue team, but he had heard rum-
blings that employees working on the feature would be fired if they didn't
get a new demo of the product in Musk's hands in a matter of days. So
he volunteered to help out, and stayed late enough working at the office
that sleeping on a couch sounded like a reasonable idea.

Musk had incredibly lofty and unrealistic ambitions for Twitter Blue.
In meetings with the team over those first few days, he announced that
he expected subscription revenue to grow from almost nothing to 50
percent of the company's total business—a jump that would equate to
several billions of dollars per year. Musk believed Twitter was too reliant on advertising revenue to survive and it needed a second business
line. Subscriptions seemed like a good option, in part because Twitter already sold a subscription product, but also because subscriptions
seemed to work at more traditional media properties, like Netflix and
The New York Times.

Before Musk's arrival, though, Twitter's subscription efforts had been
nascent and focused almost entirely on power users. Building a subscription product had been kicked around internally at Twitter for years before
Dorsey finally green-lit the project in late 2020 after Elliott showed up.
The team working on it considered several names—Twitter One, Twitter
Plus, Twitter Premium—but Dorsey had come up with Twitter Blue, and
to the dismay of the company's marketing team, the name stuck. At just
$4.99 per month, Blue offered subscribers small perks like the option to
change the color of the app icon on their phone or upload longer videos.
Eventually, the team wanted to sell an ad-free version of Twitter as part
of the subscription, but that hadn't happened yet.

At the time of Musk's arrival, Blue was a nonmaterial part of the
company's business, and Musk thought it was "an insane piece of shit."
He wanted to overhaul the set of features people received when they subscribed. To make serious money, Musk needed to entice normal, everyday
Twitter users to hand over their credit cards, not just Twitter power users.

One way to do this, he thought, was to include Twitter's "blue check" verification badges as part of the subscription package. For years Twitter had added these badges, which were technically a white check mark inside a blue circular badge, to users' profile pages to identify notable accounts, like those belonging to celebrities, politicians, and journalists. In practice, the checkmarks were meant to help other people on Twitter understand which accounts were official or authentic since anyone could create an imposter account using a random email address. But the checkmarks also carried a sort of social cachet. A blue check was like a badge of honor confirming that you were *somebody* on Twitter even if no one knew who you actually were.

Musk understood that the blue checks had value, and that Twitter had spent years handing them out for free. At first he wanted to charge $20 per month for a Twitter Blue subscription, but once the price leaked to the press, users freaked out. "$20 a month to keep my blue check? Fuck that, they should pay me," tweeted the author Stephen King, who had 7 million followers. "If that gets instituted, I'm gone like Enron." Musk took notice. "We need to pay the bills somehow!" he replied. "How about $8?" Just like that, Twitter settled on a new monthly price for Twitter Blue: $7.99.

Musk's belief wasn't only that blue checkmarks were valuable; he also saw selling them as a solution to the bot problem he'd been complaining about for months. A bot account wouldn't spend $8 per month, Musk reckoned, which meant selling verification badges would help separate the real people from the bots. (Of course, this logic assumed that all real people on Twitter *would* pay $8 per month, yet another example of how out of touch Musk was with the average Twitter user.) Musk also took issue with the way that the badges had previously been awarded. Oftentimes getting a blue check was more about knowing someone who worked at Twitter than actually being notable. He seemed to take considerable issue with the fact that many journalists had badges, giving them a higher status and more authority on Twitter than he thought they deserved. Musk called Twitter's verification program a "lords &

peasants system." For all these reasons, he was hell-bent on changing it as soon as possible.

To get Twitter Blue over the line, he turned to Esther Crawford, a manager on the product team who had been involved in many of Twitter's more experimental product ideas, including new features meant to lure content creators to the app. Crawford wasn't the most senior product person at Twitter, nor was she even the second or third most senior. But she was a startup founder who had joined Twitter when the company bought her social media app, Squad, just a few years earlier and was used to the grind and hustle that Musk expected. Most importantly, she was eager to work for Musk, a reality that made her a bit of an outlier among many of her colleagues. Musk gave Crawford a little over a week to revamp and relaunch Twitter Blue, which would now include a verification badge for paying subscribers. It was an absurdly fast turnaround in normal times, but one that felt particularly rushed given all the other chaos of the takeover. The tech news site The Verge reported that if the team didn't meet a November 7 deadline, the day before the U.S. midterms, everyone would be fired.

A few days after the deadline was set, Crawford too was sleeping at the office. A colleague posted a photo of her lying on the floor of a conference room in a silver sleeping bag, a black eye mask covering her eyes. Crawford retweeted the image and added her own caption: "When your team is pushing round the clock to make deadlines sometimes you #SleepWhereYouWork."

Many of Crawford's colleagues were unimpressed. Twitter wasn't known as the kind of workplace that required employees to sleep at work under any circumstance. Far from it, in fact. Work-life balance had always been an important recruiting tool for tech companies like Twitter. During Covid, Twitter even started giving employees an extra day off every month to help with mental burnout. Crawford's post wasn't just considered an endorsement of Musk's unhealthy work expectations, but it was also seen as a bit of performative ass-kissing. Crawford was undeterred by the complaints. "Since some people are losing their minds

I'll explain: doing hard things requires sacrifice," she wrote in a series of tweets a few hours later. "I love my family and I'm grateful they understand that there are times where I need to go into overdrive to grind and push in order to deliver." Several months later, Crawford would elaborate even more. "I think of life as a game," she wrote on Twitter, "and being at Twitter after the acquisition was like playing life at Level 10 on Hard Mode."

No matter how her colleagues felt about it, the image of Crawford curled up in her sleeping bag confirmed at least one thing: Twitter's comfortable, employee-friendly corporate culture was now a thing of the past.

Layoffs weren't the only way that Musk planned to cut costs. Within days of buying Twitter, he assigned Steve Davis, The Boring Company president, the task of figuring out other ways to save money. In a meeting with several Twitter leaders over that first weekend, Davis told them that they needed to come up with $500 million in annual savings. One obvious opportunity was to reduce Twitter's office space, especially since layoffs were already in the works.

One of the executives in that meeting was Tracy Hawkins, the company's vice president of real estate. She scrambled to put together a spreadsheet detailing all the company's various leases, some fifty contracts in total. Included on the list were several contracts she thought the company could try to cancel, although doing so would require termination fees, of course. When Hawkins presented the list and set of fees to Davis a few days later, he waved them off. "We just won't pay those," he allegedly told her, according to a lawsuit filed against the company. "We just won't pay rent."

SEVENTEEN

THERMONUCLEAR

E lon Musk's Gulfstream touched down at Teterboro Airport in New Jersey, not far from Manhattan, at around 2 a.m. on Halloween morning. Musk had spent much of his first weekend as Twitter's owner holed up in the company's San Francisco headquarters, then made the 4.5-hour flight from California to start the week at Twitter's New York office. He was in town to convince the world's largest advertisers that the company he just bought was still a safe place to spend their money.

Twitter's sales executives spent the weekend arranging meetings for Musk with some of the company's most important advertising partners, and the hope was that the new boss could relieve concerns that had cropped up over the previous seventy-two hours. Unfortunately, there were a lot of them. As soon as Musk's deal closed there was an immediate resurgence of tweets containing racist slurs and Covid-19 misinformation. There was a 1,300 percent increase in users tweeting the N-word on Twitter across several languages; at its peak, the N-word was tweeted 170 times every five minutes, up from less than a dozen times every five minutes before Musk's takeover. The Anti-Defamation League saw 1,200 tweets and retweets posting antisemitic memes in the first twenty-four hours after Musk's deal closed. The group claimed that people were "explicitly drawing inspiration from @elonmusk's takeover of the company." Controversial Twitter users like Georgia congresswoman Marjorie Taylor Greene saw an immediate spike in followers. Some of the problematic tweets were posted by automated accounts, but not all of them; presumably, people who believed Musk would be more lenient about enforcing Twitter's rules came to test the waters right away.

Worst of all was that Musk himself was tweeting out conspiracy theories. The new CEO posted a link that weekend to a story touting a conspiracy theory about a recent attack on Paul Pelosi, who was married to the U.S. Speaker of the House, Nancy Pelosi. The story claimed the attack was not carried out by a right-wing nut job as had been reported, but instead was the result of a dispute Paul Pelosi had with a male escort. Musk deleted the tweet, but not before it garnered widespread attention— and criticism from people who viewed it as both harmful and offensive.

The spike in offensive tweets was concerning to advertisers. The very last thing big brands like Pepsi or Apple wanted was to spend money on a Twitter ad that showed up in a feed full of racist posts. After major news outlets started reporting on the racist tweets, sales leaders at Twitter scrambled to soothe anxious marketers, jumping on calls with major brands like Kellogg's, Adidas, Apple, and Microsoft to try to ease their concerns. Musk may have felt Twitter's rules were too stringent, but marketers still thought they were important.

Musk had already acknowledged their anxiety. "Twitter obviously cannot become a free-for-all hellscape," he wrote in a message to advertisers the day the deal closed. "Our platform must be warm and welcoming to all." But the spike in racist content still legitimized fears that Musk would turn Twitter loose in all the wrong ways. Suddenly the company's advertising business, which accounted for roughly 90 percent of Twitter's annual revenue, looked vulnerable. There was no dancing around it: The meetings in New York needed to go well.

The good news was that Musk didn't show up late, though he did cut it close. He arrived at the New York office that Monday morning just ten minutes before his first meeting with Mark Read, the CEO of WPP, the world's largest media agency. Twitter executives breathed a sigh of relief to see Musk on time but were startled by his entourage. Not only did Musk have his two-year-old son, X, with him, but he also brought his mother, Maye Musk, to the office. Twitter's employees assumed she was there to babysit X, but instead Maye intended to join the meetings. Jason Calacanis, the venture capitalist who was also Musk's friend, joined as well.

Musk met with Read, who was in London, over video call. WPP controlled billions of advertising dollars for clients like Unilever, Mars, and IBM, making it a high-stakes first discussion. Read and Musk hit it off. He asked Musk to meet with some of WPP's clients directly to answer their questions. Musk, of course, said yes. Read, clearly a salesman himself, told Musk he'd love to help with Tesla's advertising someday if the electric carmaker ever decided to start marketing itself. Maye, a longtime model, was charming, and asked a few insightful questions of her own. By the end of the meeting, Read and Musk had swapped phone numbers and confirmed the mutual benefits of working together. That Twitter needed WPP was obvious. But WPP *wanted* to keep working with Twitter, too, in part because it offered an alternative to larger platforms like Facebook and Google. Marketers never like to have too much of their budget tied up in any single service. The meeting was a good start.

Musk's next meeting was with Bill Koenigsberg, the CEO of Horizon Media. He represented brands including Capital One and Burger King. Again Musk was charming and engaging. But he also previewed the kind of self-destructive tendencies that would get him and Twitter into trouble repeatedly in the weeks and months to follow. Musk would often say the things that his partners wanted to hear, and then do the things that would make them shake their head in disbelief. More often than not, these transgressions seemed to happen publicly on Twitter. The new Twitter owner was incredibly adept at tweeting himself into trouble.

During the meeting with Horizon, Koenigsberg mentioned that many of his clients had been asking whether Twitter would let former president Donald Trump back onto the service. Musk told Koenigsberg that he, too, was getting that same question from people. Musk had already pledged to bring Trump back, but given that the former president was one of the most polarizing and controversial users Twitter had ever had, any plan to restore his account would typically be handled delicately, with ample communication to advertisers about how Twitter planned to moderate a man known for aggressively attacking his rivals and trying to undercut democracy. Given the general anxiety that advertisers were already feeling about Twitter, it was a moment for a thoughtful and measured response.

Instead, Musk pulled out his phone and tapped out a tweet: "If I had a dollar for every time someone asked me if Trump is coming back on this platform, Twitter would be minting money!" he wrote. He read it aloud to the room, and asked if he should post it to his 112 million followers. Only Twitter's head of sales, JP Maheu, objected to the idea, knowing it would create a flurry of unanswerable questions. Musk just laughed and posted it anyway, inevitably creating more anxiety among advertisers. Maheu would learn soon enough that Musk did not like to be challenged.

On top of saving face with advertisers, Musk also met with some of the company's most high-profile content partners, including NFL commissioner Roger Goodell. The league had signed contracts to put some of its valuable, professionally produced videos onto the service. The NFL posted loads of highlights to Twitter, as did the NBA. Twitter then ran quick video ads before the highlights started, splitting the revenue with the leagues. Twitter usually guaranteed these partners a certain return, meaning the NFL would get paid whether Twitter sold the ads or not. Goodell visited Musk at Twitter's New York office, a chance for Musk to make the same type of pitch he'd made to Read and Koenigsberg: that Twitter was safe, and he was eager to work with partners to prove it and alleviate their concerns. Just like any other advertiser who put content on Twitter, the NFL didn't want its touchdown celebrations appearing alongside tweets from Nazis.

Musk's lawyer, Alex Spiro, was also in New York, joining several of his boss's meetings, shaking hands and trying to calm partners. Spiro's A-list roster of clients meant he had worked with many of the major sports leagues and media companies before, and Twitter hoped having him on hand might offer another familiar face.

Later that night, Twitter's top sales executives—minus Maheu, who wasn't invited—jumped on a phone call with Musk. The meetings that day had gone well enough, but the company was not in the clear; many advertisers were still worried about Musk's plans for Twitter. Then the group got more bad news: Sarah Personette, Twitter's chief customer officer and most senior business leader, had resigned and was officially gone. Personette had been a visible and comforting face for Twitter's advertisers the last few years. Her departure would undoubtedly create even more concern once word got out. Maheu was officially the top sales executive left.

The next morning, Personette's departure was made public. Robin Wheeler, Twitter's head of U.S. sales, held a video call with her team to try to instill a sense of calm. *Take a deep breath*, she told them. *Everything is going to be OK*. In the middle of the meeting, Wheeler was interrupted by someone on the call. Maheu was being escorted out of the New York office by security, the employee announced. Leslie Berland, the company's CMO and cultural leader who had been Musk's chaperone in San Francisco the previous week, was also walked out that same day. Wheeler, completely caught off guard, didn't know what to say; the meeting ended abruptly as everyone tried to make sense of what in the hell was going on. Maheu was fired less than twenty-four hours after pushing back on Musk's tweet.

The whole purpose of Musk's visit to New York was to convince advertisers that all was under control and that Twitter was a stable and safe place to continue spending money. Now Twitter's top two sales leaders were gone, and overnight the company had become the one thing that advertisers hated the most: It was completely unpredictable.

Twitter's layoffs were taking longer to orchestrate than Musk had initially planned. It turns out coordinating job cuts for thousands of people in twenty-four hours wasn't really feasible, especially when the process was being run by multiple groups. Other obstacles were also slowing things down. Musk and some of his advisors were worried Twitter might be paying people who didn't actually work there. Apparently this was an issue at other large tech companies with tens of thousands of global workers. So Chief Accounting Officer Robert Kaiden spent the weekend with the laborious task of trying to verify that every employee at the company was a real human. Musk was also adamant that managers defend the people they wanted to keep, meaning some managers spent the weekend adding notes to their lists to explain why remaining employees were "exceptional."

When managers first submitted their employee lists late on Friday, most had assumed that layoffs were coming over the weekend, or on Monday morning at the latest. That date was key: Many of Twitter's roughly 7,500 employees were scheduled to vest some of their stock awards the following day, on Tuesday, November 1. Executives at Twitter believed that Musk was trying to cut people before they vested, which would save the company millions. In some cases, employees made the majority of their salary via stock awards that vested just four times per year. Now that Twitter was private, any vested stock was supposed to be paid out to employees in cash at $54.20 per share. The November 1 vest was going to cost Twitter and Musk just over $200 million in payouts.

But Monday came and went without major job cuts, and employees breathed a collective sigh of relief. Musk formally approved the stock payouts on Halloween, though he waited until late that night, causing undue stress for members of Twitter's finance team who were anxiously awaiting the green light. At the very least, people who were about to be fired would get one final bonus payment to take with them.

The delays ended up benefiting a lot more people than initially planned. Each time the Twitter group running the layoff process met with David Sacks and Antonio Gracias that week, Musk's advisors pushed for more and more cuts. The original plan to cut 20 percent of staff had been pushed closer to 50 percent of the company just a few days later.

Musk was also desperate to save money in other ways. Steve Davis, who was working to shed $500 million in other expenses at the same time, told Twitter employees to go out and renegotiate every contract the company had. Twitter immediately cut corporate credit cards for employees and, as Davis had promised, stopped paying rent at its offices.

Musk spent the week working hard to win back skeptics. As promised, he met with some of WPP's clients alongside Mark Read. He also met with civil rights groups, which had become vocal critics of social networking companies and their content policies. Unlike conservative politicians, though, organizations like the NAACP, Color of Change, and the Anti-Defamation League didn't think social networks did enough policing. They had essentially become industry watchdogs, challenging companies to improve their hate speech policies and pressuring advertisers to withhold spending if they didn't. A few years earlier, civil rights groups organized a Facebook advertising boycott that included dozens of household brands, including Adidas, Coca-Cola, and Ford. Musk clearly understood their influence and held a phone call with several of the groups, promising to uphold Twitter's misinformation policies ahead of the upcoming election. He also repeated plans to create a content moderation council to review whether banned accounts like Trump's should be restored.

Despite his efforts, advertisers were still spooked. Musk's words meant little considering the tornado swirling around him. The spike in hate speech simply couldn't be ignored, and neither could the fact that several of his top sales executives quit or were fired just days into his takeover. Now brands were wondering about a possible Trump return, too. Major advertisers continued to call Twitter seeking answers that the company's sales team didn't have. In the first week after Musk's takeover, hundreds of top advertisers stopped buying Twitter ads. IPG, one of the largest advertising agencies in the world, advised all its clients, including brands like Nintendo and CVS, to pause their advertising campaigns. Musk quickly got frustrated that his promises to advertisers weren't working, and started needling those who were pulling back. He posted a poll to his Twitter followers asking people which option Twitter's advertisers should support: "Freedom of speech" or "Political 'correctness.'"

Wheeler was tapped as the new head of global sales and marketing after Maheu and Berland were escorted out of the office. A Twitter veteran, Wheeler had risen through the ranks internally after starting in sales from Twitter's small Atlanta office more than ten years earlier. She took the top job under one condition: Musk had to speak with Twitter's Influence Council, a group of senior media and advertising executives who often gave the company advice and offered outside perspective. The new CEO had been solid in one-on-one meetings with advertisers so far, and this was a chance for several influential industry executives to hear from him at once.

The Influence Council call happened on Thursday, November 3, one week after the Twitter deal officially closed. Musk and Wheeler sat side by side on the video call from a conference room on the second floor of Twitter's San Francisco office. Yoel Roth, the head of Twitter's Trust and Safety group, joined from a nearby conference room to answer any policy questions that cropped up. Many of the biggest brands in the world—all of them incredibly risk-averse—had executives dial in, including household names General Electric, Mastercard, NBC, and Ford.

Musk, as was becoming routine, *said* all the right things. Twitter would be a service for "freedom of speech, not freedom of reach," he said, meaning that even if the company relaxed some of its rules, tweets with questionable content wouldn't be shown to many people. He talked again about the content moderation council he was planning to create and its role in deciding whether Trump or others would be reinstated. Musk fielded difficult questions, including one from the Ford executive about whether he'd use his role at Twitter to give Tesla a competitive advantage against other automakers. Presumably Musk would have data and insights into what Ford and other car companies were doing around marketing and product launches. Most if not all of the automakers had paused spending on Twitter once Musk took over for fear he'd abuse his new role. Musk, of course, told the Ford exec she had nothing to worry about.

The roughly ninety-minute meeting was seen both internally and externally as a positive step for Twitter. Perhaps this was the turning point at the end of a very long week. Maybe it had all been a brief misunderstanding between image-conscious brands and Twitter's new, eccentric owner. Wheeler and Musk high-fived after the meeting ended. "See?" he told her. "I can sell ads."

But then Musk tweeted. The very next day, less than forty-eight hours after meeting with civil rights groups, Musk blamed "activist groups" for a "massive drop in revenue" that he was seeing at Twitter. These groups were pressuring advertisers to halt their ad campaigns even though "nothing has changed with content moderation and we did everything we could to appease the activists," he wrote.

"Extremely messed up!" Musk continued. "They're trying to destroy free speech in America."

Someone replied to Musk's tweet saying that he should "name and shame" advertisers that were cutting down on their spending. Musk couldn't help but take the bait.

"A thermonuclear name & shame is exactly what will happen if this continues," Musk wrote.

Twitter's sales executives couldn't believe their eyes. All their efforts from the past week, including meetings with Read, Goodell, and the Influence Council, were suddenly undone by another one of the new CEO's self-destructive tweets. More phone calls were now pouring in asking what Musk meant by his threat. If there was anything at risk of a thermonuclear explosion, it was suddenly Twitter's advertising business.

Erik Berlin was sitting in a lounge area on the fifth floor of Twitter's office with several colleagues, some of them already with drinks in their hands, when the email announcing layoffs finally arrived. The message from Twitter's human resources team carried the subject line "Update regarding our Workforce" and told employees to prepare for a second email sometime in the next fifteen hours. If the email was delivered to an employee's work account, then their job was safe; emails sent to their personal inbox meant they had been fired. The announcement included a generic note thanking people for their contributions and patience, and employees quickly noticed it wasn't signed by an actual person, but rather just "Twitter."

Berlin, an engineering manager who'd joined Twitter a few years earlier when the company acquired his podcasting startup, read the email alongside colleagues who were all getting the update at the same time. It was just after 5 p.m. in San Francisco, and almost exactly one week to the hour after Musk closed his deal to become Twitter's new owner. A security guard walked over to usher Berlin and others out of the office. For safety reasons, Twitter was closing its headquarters and revoking everybody's badge access until the layoffs were over; the company didn't want laid-off workers still getting into the office. The group migrated to a watering hole called the Beer Hall, across the street from the office, to keep drinking as they waited to see if they still had a job.

The first week under Elon Musk had done little to quell concerns for the large group of employees who were already worried about his arrival. Many of them hadn't even heard from the new CEO. Musk hadn't sent an email to the company or hosted a meeting to answer questions. Instead employees were following their new boss's moves in the press and from his Twitter account, two places where it was quickly becoming clear that Twitter's business was teetering dangerously. As managers compiled layoff lists, some employees secretly jockeyed to be included; getting laid off seemed like a better option than working for Elon Musk.

As the evening wore on, employees started to learn that they'd been fired, but not from a separate email as they'd been promised. Instead most found out that they'd lost their job when they suddenly lost access to their work emails and Twitter's Slack channels. Twitter had never cut this many people at once before, so the team running the layoffs built a special tool that was supposed to cut a person's access as soon as the email was sent. But the quick turnaround meant the tool was never tested until it went live, and it mistakenly booted people from Twitter's internal systems before the follow-up emails were delivered.

Berlin made it home from the bar before he realized he'd been cut. Amir Shevat, the developer product executive who had to submit his own layoff list the week before, was apparently on somebody else's list; his access was cut just after midnight local time as he sat staring at his computer screen in Texas. One employee had their access revoked in the middle of a late-night product meeting with Esther Crawford, the exec racing to finish Twitter's revamped subscription service. The employee was booted from the call without warning. As the night wore on, one of Twitter's main internal Slack channels turned into one giant stream of blue heart emojis, employees' way of saying goodbye.

Typically corporate layoffs happen behind closed doors, but Twitter employees openly grieved for their jobs, and for the company they were leaving. Twitter was full of people who were very comfortable posting publicly, after all. Feeds quickly filled up with blue heart emojis and salute emojis as people announced they had been cut. Private message groups on Signal and iMessage were blowing up as employees reacted to the news and shared updates and gossip about who may or may not still be employed. Alphonzo Terrell, who led Twitter's social media team, was hosting a video call with his group as everything unfolded that night. He decided to start a live audio room using Twitter Spaces so people could speak with one another and share stories about their time at Twitter. Terrell called it "Tweep Therapy," and the Space lasted well past midnight as thousands of people tuned in to listen and share stories. It felt like a memorial service.

Musk ended up firing half of Twitter's roughly 7,500 employees. Those who woke up anxious and bleary-eyed on Friday morning to find that they still had a job started messaging on Signal and Slack to figure out who else was still employed. The rushed process and haphazard rollout meant that many employees who were saved quickly realized that their managers were no longer there, but they didn't have clarity around who they now reported to.

The cuts hit all corners of the business. Twitter's marketing team, which had been around four hundred people, was decimated, with just a couple dozen employees remaining. The roughly one-hundred-person public relations team was cut down to two, both of whom would leave within the next week. (Musk, of course, thought that he could simply handle all the marketing and PR for Twitter himself.) The "People Team" that handled HR, recruiting, and diversity efforts cut more than two hundred people, or 60 percent of staff. Twitter's product and engineering groups were hit particularly hard; well over 50 percent of people across both groups were eliminated, including tons of engineers focused on critical infrastructure projects responsible for keeping the service up and running. The steep cuts led to a range of issues as people were laid off before passing off projects or critical information to colleagues who remained.

The cuts to Twitter's engineering teams also led to rampant speculation that the entire website might come crashing down at any minute. Some users started encouraging others to download the data associated with their tweets and accounts so that they'd have it once the site disappeared. Twitter had implemented a "code freeze" a few days prior to layoffs, part of an effort to keep the site stable and prevent outgoing employees from going rogue and pushing changes on their way out the door. But the company suddenly had so many holes that remaining workers feared a feature might break that no one in the building would know how to fix. Still others worried about the company's ability to fight misinformation ahead of the upcoming U.S. midterm elections, which were less than a week away.

A few teams fared better than others. Wheeler's sales team was largely saved thanks to Twitter's urgent need to make money and win back advertisers. She only lost about 25 percent of her org, and still had more than 1,000 employees who handled sales and worked with advertisers. Musk had also spared most of Twitter's Trust and Safety group, at first a surprise given his previous comments about Twitter's policy decisions, but also a clear effort to convince advertisers that Twitter still cared about keeping the site safe. Roth, who was also safe, tweeted that just 15 percent of his group was laid off.

On Friday afternoon, Musk finally addressed the layoffs in a tweet but offered no signs of sympathy. "Regarding Twitter's reduction in force, unfortunately there was no choice when the company is losing over $4M/day," he wrote, adding that everyone would be offered "3 months of severance." This wasn't technically true. The U.S. Department of Labor required employers with more than one hundred workers to give people sixty days of notice before a "mass layoff." As a result, the employees that Twitter laid off stayed on the company's payroll for two months—this counted as the sixty-day notice period and the employees didn't have to do any work. Then those employees were officially terminated and offered one month of severance. So, while it was true that employees would get three months of pay, they were offered just one month of severance. That distinction mattered. Twitter and Musk would face multiple class-action lawsuits from employees after the layoffs, which claimed Musk didn't pay employees what they were contractually owed.

The day after the layoffs happened, Dorsey finally tweeted. "Folks at Twitter past and present are strong and resilient. They will always find a way no matter how difficult the moment," he wrote. "I realize many are angry with me. I own the responsibility for why everyone is in this situation: I grew the company size too quickly. I apologize for that."

It was true, of course. Many employees were livid with their former boss. For months they'd watched in shock and frustration as Dorsey continually supported Musk, Twitter's true "light of consciousness," while the new owner attacked the company and its executives. After years of preaching to them about Twitter's role in society, and how Twitter was more than just a corporation created to make money for shareholders, Dorsey had helped orchestrate a deal that put Twitter in the hands of a man that many of them could never align with. Going big and growing the company too quickly during the Covid boom was forgivable. Many felt differently about Dorsey's relentless support for Musk.

Employees who had once defended Dorsey with #WeBackJack and bought into his Twitter mission suddenly turned on him. "You threw Twitter's investors, employees, and users under a bus in a fit of pique. GTFO," one former employee replied to Dorsey. Another employee was even more blunt. "Fuck you," he wrote. "Yo sneaker game weak. Bitcoin ass bitch."

Dorsey didn't clap back, but instead ended his message with a touch of sorrow. "I am grateful for, and love, everyone who has ever worked on Twitter," he wrote. "I don't expect that to be mutual in this moment . . . or ever . . . and I understand. ♥"

"How bad is it?"

It was Friday evening, the same day as Twitter's layoffs and just hours after Musk threatened to go "thermonuclear" on Twitter's advertisers. He was on the phone with Robin Wheeler, his head of sales, trying to figure out what the hell was going on with Twitter's business. The list of advertisers who had paused their Twitter ads was still growing, and now included United Airlines, REI, and Volkswagen. Musk couldn't understand what the problem was, and he was growing irritable. He had not yet changed any of Twitter's speech policies, and while the spike in racist tweets was a problem, the team had worked quickly to get the situation under control and remove many of the offending accounts. Musk still didn't seem to understand that his own behavior remained an issue.

Wheeler started with the obvious, telling Musk that his "thermonuclear" tweet had been a problem. "You don't want to go to war with advertisers," she warned.

"Oh, I will go to war," he replied. "And I win wars."

Another reason, Wheeler offered, was that some advertisers who *were* still running ads on Twitter were getting harassed by users for doing so. Apparently, employees weren't the only ones upset by Musk's Twitter takeover. Even regular users were starting to troll brands that were spending money on the service, trying to pressure them to stop.

Musk was incensed. He sent a text message to both Wheeler and Yoel Roth, Twitter's head of Trust and Safety. "Yoel, please suspend all Twitter accounts that are engaged in harassment of our advertisers to get them to stop advertising on Twitter," he wrote. "That is not OK."

Roth was confused. Pressuring an advertiser to stop spending money—even trolling an advertiser—was certainly not against Twitter's rules. People pressure brands about how they spend their money all the time, both on and off Twitter. Suspending users for trolling brands would be impossible to justify under Twitter's rules. It certainly wasn't aligned with Musk's stated pledge to uphold free speech.

But Musk wasn't just upset that rando Twitter trolls might be getting in the way of his business. It was deeper than that. Musk believed Twitter was good for society, which meant that anyone standing in the way of Twitter's success was committing some kind of moral turpitude. If Twitter didn't have rules to block this kind of behavior, he would simply create them. Musk called Roth and spent the brief conversation ranting and raving that trolling Twitter's advertisers was akin to people "blackmailing" the company. "Blackmail is against our rules now," he declared.

Roth hung up and contemplated quitting right then and there. Instead, he called Wheeler and asked her to talk Musk off the ledge. Up until now, Roth had been cautiously optimistic about Musk's takeover. Despite an expectation that Musk would come in and shred Twitter's rulebook on day one, he had let Roth largely operate as he wanted. For the first time, Musk was making the kind of demand that crossed all sorts of lines around user speech.

Wheeler succeeded in talking Musk down, but the incident was a reminder that Musk's "free speech" pledge could be tossed out the window on a whim. It was the first time that Musk had tried to silence people who caused issues for him as Twitter's new boss, but it wouldn't be the last.

EIGHTEEN

TWITTER BLUES

The aftershocks from Friday's layoffs were felt over the weekend as the remaining Twitter employees tried to pick themselves up and keep the company operating. Embarrassingly, Twitter managers realized the company had accidentally fired too many people and was now short-staffed. There was an "opportunity to ask folks that were left off if they will come back," one manager posted in Slack, saying the company needed help with some key infrastructure teams and maybe the iOS and Android apps. Any nominations were due within twenty-four hours. "If any of you have been in contact with folks who might come back and who we think will help us, please nominate tomorrow before 4."

New leadership roles were also starting to solidify, given that the entire C-suite was now gone. Robin Wheeler was running sales and marketing. Roth was still leading Trust and Safety, which included enforcing the rules around speech. Behnam Rezaei, a senior engineering manager, was now running engineering for the entire company, a high-profile job given Musk's belief that engineers were the most important employees in the building. Musk had a general rule: Engineers should never report to someone who was not also an engineer.

Any hope inside Twitter that Musk had spent the weekend reflecting on his own role in the company's business demise was quickly shattered Monday morning. He woke up and tweeted two jokes about masturbation. "What do you call someone who is a master at baiting?" he posted, presumably drawing giggles from any teenage boys who followed his account. In another tweet he included a screenshot of Mastodon, a new competing social network that was having some technical issues, and wrote, "If you don't like Twitter anymore, there is awesome site called Masterbatedon."

Either Musk didn't see his own behavior as having any effect on the company's advertising malaise, or he simply didn't care. For Musk, shock-tweeting and pushing out controversy to his 115 million followers (the number was growing by the day) had long been the norm, but now he seemed to realize that his tweets were also driving considerable attention to Twitter. Outside of Donald Trump, Musk was the best in the world at making news with his Twitter account. Tweeting jokes about masturbation was perhaps part of the show—a spectacle created to encourage people to show up and watch Twitter's new ringleader in action.

Musk spent that Monday posting about the upcoming U.S. midterms, encouraging people to vote for a Republican Congress to help balance out the Democratic president Joe Biden. Musk had been a Democrat at one point, he confessed, but not anymore. He posted a joke about the ridiculous conspiracy theory that birds aren't real. That evening he acknowledged that Twitter usage was thriving despite the chaos surrounding his takeover. "Twitter usage is at an all-time high lol," he tweeted. "I just hope the servers don't melt!" Nothing keeps people captivated quite like watching a disaster unfold before their very eyes.

For an advertising business like Twitter's, "all-time high" usage would typically be great news. More users meant more attention, which meant more advertising money. But this obvious reality made it even more frustrating to Musk that Twitter's advertisers were keeping their distance. The Twitter Influence Council meeting had been undone by Musk's "thermonuclear" threat and there were still dozens of advertisers asking questions and anxiously awaiting more information about Musk's plans to police the service. So Twitter's executives decided to parade Musk around again; only this time they wanted to do it publicly. Up until now, all of Musk's advertiser meetings had been behind closed doors, and while many of the details were leaking to the press anyway, speaking publicly would eliminate the middleman and hopefully get Musk's message out far and wide.

On Wednesday, November 9, Musk went live on Twitter Spaces in what was billed as an "advertiser Town Hall." Wheeler moderated the conversation again and Roth also joined to answer policy questions. More than 114,000 people tuned in live to hear Musk speak in what was believed to be the largest Twitter Space ever, a sign of just how captivating Musk and the Twitter takeover story had become. The CEO repeated all the high notes that he'd been delivering privately for the past week. Twitter was creating a content moderation council to review suspended accounts, he said, and the company was still removing bad content as quickly as possible. The rules haven't changed, he assured people, and just because people will have freedom of speech doesn't mean they will get freedom of reach. "At the end of the day, I am the Chief Twit here, so the responsibility is mine," he added. "If things go wrong, it's my fault."

Musk even floated a far-fetched idea that people would eventually connect their bank accounts to Twitter, and the company could then offer an "extremely high yield" on a user's balance before offering other banking services like debit cards and checks. It was all part of a broader plan to make Twitter "as useful as possible," he said. He ended the call by earnestly encouraging people who had feedback or questions for him to simply reply to one of his Twitter posts, a completely unrealistic approach to customer service considering his massive following. Apparently, Musk wasn't just the "Chief Twit," but was also Twitter's top customer service agent.

A few times during the Space, Musk referred to Twitter Blue, the revamped subscription product that Twitter had been scrambling to launch. In fact, the new version of Twitter Blue that allowed people to buy blue checkmarks had been unveiled that very morning. To Musk, Twitter Blue was yet another example of why advertisers should spend money at the company. Charging $8 for a blue verification badge would help eliminate the bots on Twitter, he argued, making it easier for brands to know they are reaching real people. Each person who pays for a blue badge will need a credit card associated with their account, which would theoretically make it both expensive and difficult for people to run bot or spam armies. "They start to need a lot of credit cards and a lot of phones," he added. "And eventually they will stop trying." Musk seemed completely convinced that any real human on Twitter would gladly pay $8 per month, leaving only those bot accounts without a verification check. "This will work out extremely well," he concluded.

The major flaw in Musk's subscription system, though, wasn't just the incorrect assumption that everyone would happily pay Twitter every month. It was that paying for a blue badge didn't require identity verification; users just needed to put a credit card on file and they could set up their account to look like any famous person or brand that they wanted. Since blue checks had always been used as a sign of legitimacy on Twitter, impersonators could presumably trick people into thinking they were someone else for the price of a Subway sandwich.

Twitter had originally hatched a plan to avoid this by unveiling an "official" badge for some big accounts in addition to the blue checks. So while anyone who paid $8 would get a blue check, only major brands or celebrities would get an "official" label. In practice, this system worked the same way that the original blue check system worked. Unsurprisingly, that meant Musk hated it. He killed off the "official" badges that very morning, saying they were an "aesthetic nightmare" that created a "two class system."

Wheeler asked Musk about the risk of impersonators. "This is definitely a concern from our partners," she added.

It was clearly not a concern for Musk. "If someone tries to impersonate a brand, that account will be suspended and we will keep their

$8," he replied. "They can keep doing that and we'll just keep their $8 again."

"Do it all day long," he challenged. "They will stop."

In the middle of the night, while most Twitter employees were sleeping, Musk emailed the company for the first time since he'd taken over as CEO. It had been two weeks since he walked into the San Francisco office carrying a sink and most employees had not heard anything directly from Musk since he started. His first formal communication to the entire company was ominous.

Subject: Difficult Times Ahead

Sorry that this is my first email to the whole company, but there is no way to sugarcoat the message.

Frankly, the economic picture ahead is dire, especially for a company like ours that is so dependent on advertising in a challenging economic climate. Moreover, 70% of our advertising is brand, rather than specific performance, which makes us doubly vulnerable!

That is why the priority over the past ten days has been to develop and launch Twitter Blue Verified subscriptions (huge props to the team!). Without significant subscription revenue, there is a good chance Twitter will not survive the upcoming economic downturn. We need roughly half of our revenue to be subscription.

Of course, we will still then be significantly reliant on advertising, so I am spending time with our sales & partnerships teams to ensure that Twitter continues to be appealing to advertisers. This is the Spaces discussion that Robin, Yoel and I hosted today: [link]

The road ahead is arduous and will require intense work to succeed. We are also changing Twitter policy such that remote work is no longer allowed, unless you have a specific exception. Managers will send the exception lists to me for review and approval.

Starting tomorrow (Thursday), everyone is required to be in the office for a minimum of 40 hours per week. Obviously, if you are physically unable to travel to an office or have a critical personal obligation, then your absence is understandable.

I look forward to working with you to take Twitter to a whole new level. The potential is truly incredible!

Thanks,

Elon

The email greeted employees like a gut punch. Musk's message made it sound like Twitter's business was circling the drain. On top of that, everyone was suddenly expected in the office that very morning. Twitter employees had been able to work remotely for almost three years; many of them had relocated to take advantage of the flexibility. Some people didn't even live in the same state as one of Twitter's offices. Anyone naïve enough to think that Twitter's employee-friendly corporate culture would survive under Musk was quickly corrected.

Perhaps Musk was already seeing problems arise with Twitter Blue, or maybe he just wanted to make good on his promise to Twitter's advertisers, but in either instance, he quickly sent a second email to the entire company. It was much shorter.

Subject: Top Priority

Over the next few days, the absolute top priority is finding and suspending any verified bots/trolls/spam.

Thanks,

Elon

It turns out Wheeler had good reason to be nervous about brand imper-sonators. Buying a blue checkmark for $8 made for a fun, cheap way to troll people online, and impersonators arrived en masse the day after Twitter Blue relaunched. Every major brand, including Musk and his own companies, was seemingly a target. Some of the imposters were just there for laughs, posting crude humor. An account with the username @TeslaReal, which had the same profile photo and blue checkmark as the real @Tesla account, posted that all Teslas would be "inoperable effective immediately" due to an issue with the car's navigation systems. Most people figured out quickly that the account was an imposter, but it still sent off several other posts before it was finally suspended. One showed a picture of Musk next to the sex offender Ghislaine Maxwell with the caption "appreciation post for our amazing founders." Another post went viral with more than 22,000 likes: "BREAKING: A second Tesla has hit the World Trade Center."

As embarrassing as it was for Musk, at least he was able to do some-thing about it as Twitter's owner. Other brands and celebrities were left paralyzed as they watched random people pony up $8 for the joy of mocking them online. One user posing as Nintendo of America with the same profile image coupled with a blue badge posted a picture of Mario giving everyone the middle finger. A parody account for former presi-dent George W. Bush, now boasting an official-looking blue checkmark, posted that he "missed killing Iraqis." A verified parody account for for-mer British prime minister Tony Blair replied, "Same tbh."

Twitter advertisers were furious. One particularly damaging tweet was sent by a user impersonating the pharmaceutical giant Eli Lilly. The account, which included a blue verification badge and the same profile photo as the real Eli Lilly account, posted, "We are excited to announce insulin is free now." The tweet was up for more than six hours before

Twitter suspended the account, and executives inside Eli Lilly panicked as they watched the tweet go viral. When all was said and done, the pharmaceutical company decided to pause all ad spending on Twitter. "We apologize to those who have been served a misleading message from a fake Lilly account," the company's real account posted later that day. It's unclear how much the fake tweet resonated with investors, but Eli Lilly's stock fell almost 4 percent the following day.

Inside Twitter, employees were similarly frantic. The Trust and Safety team, which had spent the previous few days monitoring tweets around the U.S. midterms, suddenly shifted focus to try to suspend all brand imposters. There were so many pranksters that the group had to prioritize the highest profile incidents, ignoring many of the smaller perpetrators. Twitter had been full of impersonator accounts for years, some of them quite funny or popular, but they had never been verified before, which made it less likely that anyone would take them seriously. Now Musk tried to adjust Twitter's policies on the fly, tweeting that impersonator accounts would need to include the word "parody" in both the account's username and bio if they wanted a blue checkmark.

The rollout was a complete disaster. Musk had hoped for a grand unveil that would eliminate bots, impress advertisers, and, most importantly, make Twitter money. Instead, the grand unveil made Twitter look mismanaged, and pushed advertisers even further away. Omnicom Group, another major media agency that worked with brands like McDonald's and Apple, sent a letter to clients the following day recommending that they pause spending on Twitter.

Musk's bungling of the Twitter Blue rollout was particularly infuriating for Yoel Roth and Twitter's Trust and Safety group. Not only were they forced to scramble to try to suspend imposter accounts as they cropped up, but the team had predicted these impersonation issues and even warned Musk about them. In an internal report compiled the week before, the Trust and Safety team laid out a series of risks to launching the Twitter Blue project. Among them: "Impersonation of world leaders, advertisers, brand partners, election officials, and other high

profile individuals." Included on the group's list of concerns was that
there would be no way for regular users to report impersonators to the
company. "Legacy Verification provides a critical signal in enforcing
impersonation rules, the loss of which is likely to lead to an increase in
impersonation of high-profile accounts on Twitter," it said. The report
was ultimately ignored.

At least one person at Twitter found humor in the whole thing. "Quite
the day!" Musk tweeted close to midnight that evening. "Some epically
funny tweets. 😂 😂 " The next morning, Twitter suspended the subscription offering until further notice.

Elon Musk's first all-hands meeting as Chief Twit happened on the same
day that brand imposters were running wild, and employees were alerted
less than an hour before the meeting was scheduled to begin. Musk wanted
everyone to show up to the "Aviary," a conference area on the tenth floor
of Twitter's San Francisco office, for a hastily organized Q&A session.
After almost two weeks of silence, employees were about to hear from
Musk for the third time in a twelve-hour stretch.

Given the short notice and the fact that employees learned they
had to start coming back to the office that very morning, only a couple
dozen Twitter employees made it into the room to see Musk speak; most
watched via video. Musk, in his standard black pants and black T-shirt,
stood before a large "living wall" adorned with green plants and flanked
by two projector screens. Per usual, he was fifteen minutes late.

"Hello," he said. "Nice to meet you all." Musk started by explaining why Twitter was such an important service to the world, calling it
a "public town square" where people can have civilized debates. It will
be a "battleground of ideas that can hopefully take the place of the violence in a lot of cases. So people can just be talking instead of physically fighting," he said. "I think there's a tremendous amount of good
that Twitter can achieve for humanity."

As with most of Musk's long chats (this one lasted an hour), his mind seemed to wander, seemingly driven by a never-ending stream of consciousness that was full of half-baked product ideas and lofty ambitions. Musk wanted to get into payments, which he called a "transformative opportunity," repeating his goals from the previous day about giving users high-yield bank accounts. He wanted Twitter to help video creators make money just like they did on YouTube, acknowledging that Twitter was nowhere close; it didn't even allow people to post long videos or make money from the shorter videos that they did upload. Twitter needed to help people find the best content, something TikTok was particularly good at, Musk added. Maybe that would mean reviving Vine, the short-form video service Twitter shuttered years earlier. Maybe it would mean something else. Generally, nothing was off the table with Musk. In private meetings with employees, he was similarly telling people that Twitter shouldn't worry about copying competitors, or the cost of new products. If it might make the company money, it was worth trying.

Most of Musk's product ideas were unrealistic, at least right away. Banking was a highly regulated industry for a reason. Simply spinning up high-yield savings accounts or offering payment services was the kind of thing that often took years to figure out. There were also many reasons that YouTube was the biggest video service in the world. Twitter, which was primarily built around text posts and links, wasn't anywhere close to providing competition for the most successful video business on the internet.

But the fact that Musk wanted to take on YouTube or give people savings accounts was also exactly why some people had initially been optimistic about his arrival. Musk was bold and ambitious to a fault. This was the same man who was building self-driving cars and routinely promised that humans would construct a colony on Mars. It was clear Musk didn't have a concrete plan for Twitter, but the things he cooked up certainly sounded exciting to employees who had spent years moving too slowly and taking small swings. "Just try weird stuff," he told employees that day. "It's nothing ventured, nothing gained. If we're too cautious, then how do we make revolutionary improvements? Revolutions are not done with caution."

To a certain type of employee, Musk's boldfaced optimism about Twitter's product potential might have been a turning point if he hadn't been as equally pessimistic about the state of Twitter's business. Musk warned employees repeatedly that the world was barreling toward a recession, and recessions require tough decisions. Part of Musk's anxiety around cost cutting was that he'd survived multiple recessions before, navigating them while working at both PayPal in 2000 and Tesla in 2009. "I have recession PTSD," he admitted. If Twitter didn't get its spending under control, there was a possibility the company wouldn't survive. "We just definitely need to bring in more cash than we spend," he told employees. "If we don't do that and there's a massive negative cash flow, then bankruptcy is not out of the question."

If the possibility of bankruptcy spooked Twitter employees, it was nothing new to Musk. He'd been dangerously close to bankruptcy at both Tesla and SpaceX over the years, hustling to make payroll and keep the companies alive by any means necessary. Openly discussing bankruptcy had become part of Musk's management style, presumably a strategy to motivate employees and inspire a sense of urgency. A few days earlier, Musk had sold $4 billion worth of Tesla stock, a move he now told employees was intended specifically to "save Twitter."

"It was excruciatingly difficult to keep us alive in 2009," Musk said about Tesla, once again leaning on examples from his other companies, which he did often. "And the reason we were able to keep alive is partly by just being paranoid. It's like Andy Grove's famous statement: 'Only the paranoid survive.' Well then, we are going to be paranoid, and we're going to survive."

Musk was finally asked about his demand via email that everyone show up to the office, a huge point of contention for employees who had become accustomed to the remote work lifestyle. Musk was unflinching in his expectations. "Basically, if you can show up in an office and you do not show up at the office, resignation accepted," he said. "End of story."

What the group didn't yet realize was that Musk had already received a series of resignations that morning. As Musk stood talking to employees on the tenth floor, Roth and Wheeler stood together inside Roth's office one floor below and hit send on their resignation emails together; they were sick of running behind Musk with a fire extinguisher. And they weren't alone.

Within weeks of Musk's takeover, several Twitter executives started to fret about the potential legal ramifications of working for their new boss. Way back in 2011, Twitter was penalized by the Federal Trade Commission for a series of privacy missteps that enabled hackers to gain access to some private user information. As part of its settlement with the FTC, Twitter signed a "consent decree" with a twenty-year jurisdiction, meaning that Twitter was officially on notice and at risk of further fines and penalties if it didn't do a better job protecting user privacy going forward. Several years later, Twitter violated the decree; the company was using phone numbers that people had submitted for privacy reasons, like two-factor authentication, to target them with advertising. The FTC fined Twitter $150 million in 2022, an embarrassing misstep that put Twitter back in the regulator's crosshairs. As part of the settlement, Twitter was required to beef up its privacy programs and participate in third-party audits. It created a five-person Data Governance Committee of senior executives who were responsible for making sure the company stayed compliant. Building product features at Twitter now required jumping through several extra hoops to ensure nothing would violate the decree.

Given the severity of the layoffs, and the fact that Musk was suddenly pushing everyone to work a million miles per hour, some executives started to worry. The five-person compliance group was quickly whittled down to three members following a couple of resignations. It seemed possible that Twitter either couldn't, or wouldn't, follow the

the new executive team. The turmoil inside Twitter, which had always been one of the newsiest companies in the world, was reaching impressive new heights.

On Sunday morning, November 13, Musk opened Twitter and posted an apology. "Btw, I'd like to apologize for Twitter being super slow in many countries," he wrote, blaming the issue on some of the software code in Twitter's app.

The criticism bothered Eric Frohnhoefer, a Twitter engineer who'd been at the company for eight years. Twitter was indeed slow, but not for the reasons Musk was claiming, he thought. Twitter had long given employees full range to criticize executives internally, and many employees took advantage of the freedom. It was common practice for employees to use Slack channels or even public tweets to complain about decisions made by Twitter's leaders, including former CEO Jack Dorsey. So Frohnhoefer didn't think twice before replying to Musk's tweet. "I have spent ~6yrs working on Twitter for Android and can say this is wrong," he posted, publicly refuting his new boss.

A few hours later, Musk saw the criticism. "Then please correct me," he wrote back. "Twitter is super slow on Android. What have you done to fix that?" Frohnhoefer sent a series of technical tweets back explaining his thinking on the issue, but the damage was done. Musk replied to a separate user shortly thereafter saying Frohnhoefer had been fired; Frohnhoefer didn't even realize it until a friend sent him Musk's post. He was later booted from Twitter's email and Slack systems. Another Twitter software engineer, Ben Leib, also commented on Musk's apology post. "I can confidently say that this man has no idea wtf he's talking about," he wrote. Leib was also fired for the criticism.

"It sucked," Frohnhoefer later wrote in an op-ed in *Newsweek*. "One of the core values of Twitter was to 'communicate fearlessly to build trust.' If you thought something wasn't right or if you thought a product decision was wrong, you were encouraged to talk to that person. Under Old Twitter, I think I would still have a job."

What Frohnhoefer and others quickly learned that week was that old Twitter was dead. Frohnhoefer and Leib were just the beginning. Over the next few days Musk fired dozens of Twitter employees for either criticizing him publicly or pushing back against him on internal Slack channels. A small group of loyal engineers, including Musk's cousins, scoured the company's internal systems to find people who weren't devoted to the new owner, and therefore not trustworthy. The emails from Twitter HR said that employees' "recent behavior violated company policy."

Sasha Solomon, another engineer who worked remotely from Portland, Oregon, had been needling Musk on Twitter for weeks. "We will be scheduling multiple all-hands every day until morale improves," she tweeted mockingly after Musk's first all-company meeting. When he then tweeted about Twitter's Android app being slow, she was peeved, since it was related to the work she and her team handled. She let fly on Twitter, assuming that Musk was mentioned in so many tweets that he wouldn't ever see it anyway. "You don't get to shit on our infra if you don't know what the fuck it does while you're also scrambling to rehire folks you laid off," she wrote on Twitter. Solomon soon found out she was fired when she tried to log into her computer for a work call and realized she'd been locked out. Her husband, who also worked at Twitter but hadn't posted anything, was also let go the next day without explanation. "I said it before and I'll say it again," Solomon later tweeted. "Kiss my ass elon."

As Twitter employees watched Musk publicly duel with his own workers, many couldn't help but shake their heads at what the company had become. Twitter's corporate culture had been turned inside out in just a few short weeks. "Twitter has always been about open expression," Solomon said later. "Internally, we've always been very vocal. If you have something to say, you never had to worry about repercussions." Not so under Musk. Not only were people suddenly scared to challenge the new boss, but executives were quitting left and right. Many of those who remained had no desire to be there. Employees were mocking the CEO, and he was mocking them right back. Twitter was in a sad state.

One person hadn't given up hope: Jack Dorsey. Twitter's old CEO was still convinced that the Musk experiment would eventually work. "Twitter will survive and thrive but it will take some time," he posted on Twitter the day after Musk mocked the employees he fired, calling them "geniuses." When another user asked Dorsey why he didn't save Twitter, he replied promptly: "I did."

On Wednesday, November 16, Twitter employees received another email from Elon Musk.

Subject: A Fork in the Road
Going forward, to build a breakthrough Twitter 2.0 and succeed in an increasingly competitive world, we will need to be extremely hardcore. This will mean working long hours at high intensity. Only exceptional performance will constitute a passing grade.

Twitter will also be much more engineering-driven. Design and product management will still be very important and report to me, but those writing great code will constitute the majority of our team and have the greatest sway. At its heart, Twitter is a software and servers company, so I think this makes sense.

If you are sure that you want to be part of the new Twitter, please click yes on the link below.

Anyone who has not done so by 5pm ET tomorrow (Thursday) will receive three months of severance.

Whatever decision you make, thank you for your efforts to make Twitter successful.

Elon

Despite Twitter's 50 percent layoffs, the company was still too big, especially the sales team. With more and more advertisers pausing, the sales group suddenly looked bloated and less useful than it had a few weeks earlier. Plus, it seemed clear that many of the employees who survived the first round of cuts didn't want to work for Musk anyway. He'd already weeded out some workers by scouring Slack, but the cuts needed to be deeper. The easiest way forward was to let people decide for themselves if they still wanted to stick around.

Employees were baffled by the email. Some thought it was a hoax and refused to click the link. Others thought it was a test of loyalty and clicked the link immediately. Still others immediately contacted employment lawyers. They wanted to be sure that refusing to sign the document wouldn't preclude them from receiving severance; no one really trusted the new boss. Some started jokingly referring to the decision as a "red pill, blue pill" choice, a nod to the popular sci-fi movie *The Matrix*. Employees now had to decide: Were they hard-core? Or was Twitter better left as somebody else's problem?

Many employees were leaning toward the latter. As the deadline loomed, Musk and his cadre of Tesla and SpaceX engineers scrambled to meet with some of Twitter's most talented engineers to try to convince them to stay at Twitter 2.0. (The Tesla engineers claimed that working for Musk would make you very rich.) Musk sent another email just hours before the 5 p.m. deadline slightly softening his stance on remote work. "Regarding remote work, all that is required for approval is that your manager takes responsibility for ensuring that you are making an excellent contribution," he wrote. In total, nearly 1,200 employees took the buyout, including entire teams that were critical for keeping the site operational. Two-thirds of the roughly 7,500 employees who worked at Twitter on the day Musk walked in with the sink were now gone.

Twitter emailed staff to announce that offices would be closed on Friday after the deadline, part of a plan to give the security team time to sort out which employees still worked at the company. But Musk immediately tossed that plan aside and sent an email asking engineers to report to the tenth floor of Twitter's San Francisco office that day at 2 p.m. for a meeting to review code. "Only those who cannot physically get to Twitter HQ or have a family emergency are excused," he wrote.

If anyone was wondering what the new, hard-core version of Twitter would look like, they were getting a glimpse. Musk had even started sleeping on a couch at the office. Just as he did with his other companies, Musk was demonstrating his commitment to Twitter's employees and expected a similar level of commitment in return. Four and a half hours before the meeting was scheduled to start, he sent employees another email. "If possible," he wrote, "I would appreciate it if you could fly to SF to be present in person."

NINETEEN

VOX POPULI, VOX DEI

E ven for a billionaire, Elon Musk spent a lot of time on his private jet. He was constantly flying on his Gulfstream to meetings and rocket launches and other "rich guy stuff," like visiting the pope or attending the Super Bowl. It wasn't uncommon for Musk to make multiple trips between SpaceX's headquarters near Los Angeles, and Tesla's Gigafactory in Texas in the same week. Musk was routinely in the Bay Area, too, since Tesla had a major manufacturing facility in Fremont, just south of Oakland. In 2020, a Florida teenager even set up an account, @Elonjet, solely for the purpose of tracking Musk's plane. After the takeover, many Twitter employees started following the account so they'd know whether the new boss was in the office.

With Twitter in the rotation, Musk was flying more than ever. In early December he flew three hours from Oakland to New Orleans for a surprise meeting with French president Emmanuel Macron. At a private room inside the New Orleans Museum of Art, the two had what Macron later called a "clear and honest discussion" about Twitter's content policies and European regulations. Musk then hopped right back on the plane and flew back to the Bay Area. The next day, December 3, he was sitting on his Gulfstream again preparing for a cross-country flight to the East Coast, and Musk had time to kill. Instead of kicking back with a book or taking a nap, he opened the Twitter app on his phone and

VOX POPULI, VOX DEI

joined a live audio Spaces chat that was already in progress. The chat room was hosted by several of Musk's most vocal supporters, including Mario Nawfal, an entrepreneur and crypto-enthusiast, and Kim Dotcom, an early internet hacker who was living in New Zealand to avoid extradition to the U.S. for alleged internet crimes. Musk joined them and spoke for well over two hours, his voice cutting in and out as the plane took off and flew across the western United States; nearly 100,000 people tuned in live to listen to him speak. In the wake of the Macron meeting, it quickly became clear that Twitter's policies and its role in policing internet speech were heavy on his mind.

Musk had plenty to discuss. After spending his first few weeks in charge cutting head count, wooing advertisers, and trying to relaunch Twitter Blue, Musk had only recently turned his attention to Twitter's content moderation rules. The weekend before Thanksgiving, Musk made the drastic decision to reinstate Donald Trump's account based on the results of an impromptu poll. The "Chief Twit" asked his 117 million followers if Trump should be reinstated, letting them vote either yes or no. More than 15 million votes were cast, and 52 percent voted in favor of reinstatement. Musk himself noted that many of the votes may have come from bots, which was ironic, of course, considering his years-long crusade against Twitter bots, but that didn't seem to matter when it came to Trump. He reinstated Trump the next day. "The people have spoken," he wrote, adding the Latin phrase "Vox Populi, Vox Dei"—*the voice of the people is the voice of God.*

Musk had spent weeks promising advertisers that reversing account bans and suspensions wouldn't happen without first consulting a yet-to-be-formed content advisory council. It turns out those promises were meaningless, and the Trump reinstatement was just the beginning. Musk quickly started wielding power as Twitter's owner and final decision-maker. A few days after reinstating Trump, he eliminated Twitter's rule banning misinformation about Covid-19. Then he ran another poll asking if Twitter should offer "general amnesty to suspended accounts," which was also endorsed by voters. "Vox Populi, Vox Dei," Musk tweeted again. Then things got complicated. Musk sent a tweet to the rapper Ye, aka Kanye West, welcoming him back to Twitter. West hadn't posted for weeks because the prior Twitter regime had blocked his account after he shared an antisemitic tweet. With Musk in charge, West felt comfortable posting again. Within days he tweeted a picture of a swastika inside the Star of David. Even Musk couldn't justify something that egregious. "I tried my best," Musk tweeted before he suspended West again.

The West suspension was one of the first topics of conversation as Musk sat on his Gulfstream. "It's important that people know that was my decision," Musk said. "Posting swastikas in what is obviously not a good way is an incitement to violence," he added. "I personally wanted to punch Kanye, so that was definitely inciting me to violence. So that's not cool."

"At the end of the day, I think we all just want to have a future where we're not oppressed, and where speech is not suppressed and we can say what we want to say without fear of reprisals," Musk added. For months Musk had explained his content moderation approach in simple terms: If it was legal, it was allowed. "As long as you're not like really causing harm to somebody else you should be able to say what you want."

Musk's views on policing content were different than what Twitter was used to, and he took a much more hands-on approach than his predecessor. Former CEO Jack Dorsey almost never made decisions about whether an account should be banned or suspended, instead outsourcing that task to a group of people reporting to him. That process meant that decisions about policies could be slow, messy affairs, with Twitter executives holding grueling meetings to discuss the nuances of free speech. Twitter almost never attributed the decision to ban or suspend a user to a specific employee, instead crediting those decisions to the company or team.

Musk, by contrast, seemed completely comfortable making major decisions all by himself. Suspending West, for example, was Musk's call, and so was reinstating Trump based on the results of a hasty user poll.

The Chief Twit was making decisions on the fly and wasn't hiding from the fact that those decisions were his. Everyone knew who was in charge.

All of these changes weren't just a reflection of Musk's personality; they were also part of his sales pitch. Musk wanted Twitter 2.0 to look and feel different than the old regime, part of a strategy to win back conservative users who, like him, believed Twitter had overstepped in its censorship of online speech. Bringing back Trump was an easy win. So was supporting West (at least initially). But simply changing things moving forward wasn't enough. Musk also seemed hell-bent on obliterating Twitter 1.0 and all the executives who had fought him in court and forced him to buy the company.

To do this, Musk decided to air Twitter's dirty laundry. He brought in a handful of journalists to comb through all of Twitter's internal messages, including emails and private Slack and Google messages, and write stories about Twitter's major content decisions. It was part of a plan to expose years of Twitter's perceived biases. "Sunshine is a great disinfectant," Musk explained. He'd granted the handpicked journalists "unfettered access" to any internal documents they wanted. "This is not like a North Korean tour guide situation," he joked from his plane. The journalists could "go anywhere you want, whenever you want, wherever you want, however you want."

The project became known as the "Twitter Files," and Musk billed it as an embarrassing but important way for Twitter to win back trust. He believed that being more "truthful" than other networks might serve as a differentiator to help Twitter grow its user base in the long run.

The first Twitter Files dump was less than twenty-four hours old when Musk held court on his Gulfstream. It had been widely anticipated, with Musk hyping it up to his followers and retweeting the journalist Matt Taibbi as he shared updates. Musk had personally invited the journalists to Twitter's offices to review the files, though it appeared that he was more involved than simply sending out the invitations. "We're double checking some facts," Musk tweeted right before the Twitter Files debuted.

The first dump looked at Twitter's handling of the Hunter Biden laptop incident from just before the 2020 U.S. election. Future Twitter Files dumps covered other events, like internal conversations related to Trump's suspension, and messages between Twitter employees and U.S. law enforcement agencies about suspending accounts or removing tweets. The purpose of the exercise was to make Twitter look corrupt and biased against conservatives, and for many people it worked. The Twitter Files showed that company executives often back-channeled with government agencies or removed accounts that were flagged to them by the FBI or a presidential campaign. It also showed that Twitter cut down the reach for some controversial users, keeping their accounts from trending on the service without telling them. It wasn't exactly shadow banning, but Twitter had still impacted the distribution of some people's tweets without their knowledge.

Still, the Twitter Files mostly fell flat for much of the mainstream media, which eagerly awaited the first installment but pretty much stopped paying attention by Twitter Files #3. To those who had followed Twitter's policy decisions closely, the files confirmed a lot of things that people already knew: Making content moderation decisions was messy, complicated, and often imperfect. The emails showed employees disagreeing over what to do, or questioning whether a suspension was actually within the rules. Few people would dispute that Twitter had made a mistake in censoring the Hunter Biden laptop story. Twitter executives even apologized publicly for the move shortly after it happened. Policing speech for the world was a terrible job and Twitter executives had certainly struggled at times with the responsibility.

Musk, though, seemed dedicated to making sure that Twitter's old executives were punished publicly for their mistakes. When much of the media downplayed the explosiveness of the Twitter Files, Musk lashed out. "They're trying to turn it into a nothing-burger because they were complicit in deceiving the American public," Musk said of the media. "Shame on them."

While most of the news about Musk's first few weeks as Twitter's owner had focused on his business decisions, it was becoming clear that Musk wanted to be remembered for his impact on Twitter's content decisions as much as anything else. At one point during the conversation from his Gulfstream, Musk was asked why he bought Twitter to begin with. It wasn't just the Babylon Bee, Musk said, but more of a feeling that had been growing for some time. "We are traveling the path more and more of suppression of free speech. And this was just getting me concerned," he said. Perhaps unsurprisingly, his motivation was similar to why he also wanted to colonize Mars. "My biological neural net concluded that it was important to buy Twitter, and that if Twitter was not bought and steered in a good direction that it would be a danger for the future of civilization."

Musk acknowledged that bringing free speech back to the masses didn't come without consequences, and he suggested that doing so could even get him killed. "The risk of something bad happening to me or even literally being shot is quite significant," he said. "I'm definitely not going to be doing any open-air car parades, let me put it that way. It's not that hard to kill me if somebody wanted to. So hopefully they don't."

Whether or not Musk was *actually* in any real danger wasn't clear. Ironically, though, Musk's own tweets started creating serious safety issues for other people. On December 10, someone on Twitter dug up another old tweet from Yoel Roth, the former Trust and Safety executive. In the newly resurfaced tweet, which was from 2010, Roth had posed a question: "Can high school students ever meaningfully consent to sex with their teachers?" His tweet linked to an article in the publication Salon that was asking the same question.

Musk, though, took the old tweet out of context. He then tweeted an excerpt from Roth's college dissertation in which Roth argued that gay dating apps like Grindr should adopt safety policies for teenagers who were already using the services anyway despite age restrictions. "Looks like Yoel is arguing in favor of children being able to access adult Internet services in his PhD thesis," Musk wrote to his 121 million followers. Twitter's CEO, without any actual evidence, was suggesting that Roth was a pedophile.

Roth was suddenly the target of intense harassment and abuse as Musk's followers piled on. It was eerily similar to the time Kellyanne Conway had spelled his name out loud on Fox News after labeling Donald Trump's tweet, but somehow worse because Roth was no longer working at Twitter or had the company's protection. Even his friends and family were getting harassed. The threats got so bad that Roth and his husband were forced to leave their home and hide out somewhere secret for their own safety. They never moved back. A few months later, Roth sold his house and relocated permanently.

The Twitter Files caught the attention of Jack Dorsey. The former Twitter CEO had been in charge for almost all the decisions that the Twitter Files were now dissecting, and a few days after the first installment was published, Dorsey published a blog post of his own.

He wrote about some of Twitter's failures, including the reality that outside pressures, including a reliance on advertising, had pushed the company to make certain content decisions that he didn't necessarily agree with. Being an advertising business meant creating a safe place for paying customers. (Musk, of course, was learning this the hard way.) It also meant being overprotective at times about what kind of content to remove. "I generally think companies have become far too powerful, and that became completely clear to me with our suspension of Trump's account," Dorsey wrote. "As I've said before, we did the right thing for the public company business at the time, but the wrong thing for the internet and society."

Dorsey pushed back on the notion that Twitter had acted in favor of any political party while he was in charge. "There was no ill intent or hidden agendas," he wrote, but he also admitted that "mistakes were made." Dorsey once again pushed the idea of a decentralized social network. He wrote:

> Of course governments want to shape and control the public conversation, and will use every method at their disposal to do so, including the media. And the power a corporation wields to do the same is only growing. It's critical that the people have tools to resist this, and that those tools are ultimately owned by the people. Allowing a government or a few corporations to own the public conversation is a path towards centralized control.

Dorsey also admitted something that everyone who worked with him already knew: that he had largely checked out after Elliott Management arrived on Twitter's doorstep roughly twenty months before his resignation. Dorsey had stopped fighting for many of the principles he believed in. "I completely gave up pushing for them when an activist entered our stock in 2020," he wrote, saying that his vision for content moderation didn't work at a public company. "I planned my exit at that moment knowing I was no longer right for the company."

Dave Chappelle, one of the most successful comedians in the world, ended his show on Sunday, December 11, by inviting a surprise guest onto the stage. "Ladies and gentlemen," Chappelle said, a drink in hand, "make some noise for the richest man in the world."

By the time Elon Musk walked onstage, arms outstretched to acknowledge the sold-out arena, the boos were already raining down hard. Musk was inside the Chase Center, home of the NBA's Golden State Warriors and just two miles from Twitter's San Francisco headquarters, but he was greeted with the opposite of a hometown welcome. Like most billionaires, Musk was typically treated like a hero whenever he showed up in public. Presumably, he was expecting more of the same alongside Chappelle. Instead he was treated to what must have been one of the most uncomfortable five-minute stretches of his professional career.

Once the boos started, they never stopped. Chappelle tried to make light of the situation. "It sounds like some of the people you fired are in the audience," he joked, calling out the boo birds for being in the cheap seats. Two minutes went by, then three, the crowd still booing. Chappelle made a joke about opening the first comedy club on Mars, to try to cut through the awkwardness. At the three-and-a-half-minute mark, Musk, who hadn't said more than a few words, finally asked Chappelle what he should say. The audience booed even louder. "Don't say nothing," Chappelle quipped. "It will only spoil the moment." Eventually Chappelle coaxed Musk into yelling the comedian's famous tagline—"I'm rich, bitch!"—which felt as unnatural as it was accurate. The cameo was a total disaster.

After a Twitter user called Musk out for the embarrassing appearance, claiming 80 percent of the audience was booing, Musk pushed back. "Technically, it was 90% cheers & 10% boos," he wrote in a tweet he would later delete. "But, still, that's a lot of boos, which is a first for me in real life (frequent on Twitter). It's almost as if I've offended SF's unhinged leftists . . . but nahhh."

It was the beginning of a terrible week for Musk. Two days later, at a gas station in South Pasadena, near Los Angeles, one of Musk's security guards got into an altercation with an alleged stalker who had an interest in both Musk and his ex-partner, the singer Grimes. Musk would later tweet that the "crazy stalker" had followed his Tesla thinking that Musk was inside, but instead the car was carrying his two-year-old son, X. Musk tweeted that the stalker "later blocked car from moving & climbed onto hood," though he never filed a formal report. The alleged stalker later claimed to *The Washington Post* that he was driving for Uber Eats, but that story fell apart when he also admitted that he believed Grimes was sending him coded messages in her Instagram posts and that Musk was tracking his whereabouts.

The interaction clearly spooked Musk. The day after it happened, he made a swift policy change at Twitter, banning "any account doxxing real-time location info of anyone," which he called "a physical safety violation." In a second tweet, Musk made it clear that this included @ElonJet, the account that tracked his private plane. Musk was suggesting that the alleged stalker had only known the location of the car because of the private jet account. In reality, the gas station incident happened almost twenty-four hours after @ElonJet posted that Musk had landed in Los Angeles. Plus, the gas station itself was twenty-six miles from the airport. No matter. Musk was suspending @ElonJet, and said that he would take legal action against Jack Sweeney, the account's twenty-year-old owner.

The incident got considerable press attention, and several journalists covering Musk pointed out that people could still get info on the billionaire's private jet from other services, like Instagram or Mastodon. This pushed Musk even further over the edge, and he started suspending journalists on Twitter for tweeting links to @ElonJet's other social media pages. Reporters from *The New York Times*, *The Washington Post*, and CNN were all suspended, and so was the sports commentator Keith Olbermann. "They posted my exact real-time location, basically assassination coordinates," Musk tweeted in defense of the suspensions, saying that a link to his plane's information, even if it wasn't on Twitter, was cause for being banned under the new policy that he'd created the day before.

The irony was impossible to ignore. For months Musk had argued that his entire reason for buying Twitter was to uphold free speech. *As long as it wasn't illegal, it was OK on Twitter*, he'd said over and over again. Musk had even used Sweeney's account as an example of how committed he was to the idea that people on Twitter could say whatever they wanted. "My commitment to free speech extends even to not banning the account following my plane, even though that is a direct personal safety risk," he wrote on November 6, just over a month earlier. Suspending @ElonJet, and then doubling down by suspending several legitimate journalists, made Musk look like a hypocrite. He'd hated that Twitter was heavy-handed by suspending or banning accounts before he took over, and now he was suspending accounts for posting publicly available information about his plane. The rules, it seemed, applied to everyone—save for Twitter's new owner.

A few days later, Musk was back on his private jet headed east across the Atlantic Ocean. After a quick pit stop in London to refuel, Musk's jet turned southeast toward Doha, the capital of Qatar. By the time he landed, nearly seventeen hours after first taking off from San Jose, the World Cup final was just a few hours from kickoff.

The World Cup had always been a major moment for Twitter. Alongside the Olympics, it was one of the very few truly global events, and the World Cup was always a good boost to Twitter's user growth and advertising revenue as people flocked to the service to watch highlights and keep up on match commentary. Musk was aware of the significance, and emailed the company a month earlier when the tournament started to make sure everyone else was aware, too.

> Subject: Top priority this weekend
> . . . is ensuring that Twitter does an awesome job supporting the World Cup. Please do whatever it takes to ensure that this is the best possible experience for users.
> Thanks,
> Elon

Now Musk had flown to Doha to watch Argentina face off against France in the World Cup final. He sat in a private box near one of the goals, joined by several other prominent investors and business associates, including Mansoor Bin Ebrahim Al-Mahmoud, CEO of Qatar Investment Authority, which had invested $375 million into Musk's Twitter deal.

(Musk had agreed to attend the match as part of the investment.) Jared Kushner, former president Trump's son-in-law, was also in the box, and Musk met briefly with Turkey's president, Recep Tayyip Erdogan, and took a selfie with the celebrity chef known as "Salt Bae." Musk tweeted throughout the match, doing his best to generate as much hype and attention for the final as possible. "Goal by Argentina!" he wrote alongside a video of the soccer star Lionel Messi. "Evenly matched game!!" he added to another video of French forward Kylian Mbappé. Musk replied to other users talking about the match, like Kim Dotcom and Lex Fridman, the computer scientist and popular podcaster, and tweeted about how many other people were tweeting. Users mockingly pointed out that tweeting from the stadium meant he was inadvertently sharing his own "assassination coordinates."

As the match moved into extra time and eventually a shoot-out, one of Twitter's main corporate accounts posted a series of tweets outlining another new policy: It was now against Twitter's rules to post links to other social media sites, including Facebook, Instagram, Mastodon, and even Trump's Truth Social. "We recognize that many of our users are active on other social media platforms," read one of the tweets that was later deleted. "However, we will no longer allow free promotion of certain social media platforms on Twitter."

The uproar from Twitter users was both instantaneous and incredulous. "This is just sad," wrote Aaron Levie, the CEO of the enterprise software company Box, and an avid Tweeter. Paul Graham, a well-known Silicon Valley investor who tweeted often at Musk, called it the "last straw" and posted a link for people to follow him on Mastodon. (His Twitter account was then temporarily suspended.) Even Edward Snowden chimed in. "This is a bad policy and should be reversed," he wrote.

To Musk, the policy seemed obvious, and at first he tried to defend it by saying that "traditional" publishing companies would never let competing outlets advertise for free. Of course, Twitter wasn't a traditional media company and forbidding people from linking to other websites felt like the furthest thing from free speech. Fresh on the heels of the journalist suspensions, it was yet another misstep for Musk, who was making up the rules at Twitter as if he were running his own private kingdom. A few hours later Musk budged, though not entirely. "Policy will be adjusted to suspending accounts only when that account's *primary* purpose is promotion of competitors, which essentially falls under the no spam rule," he wrote on Twitter. Walking back the policy was the right move, but Musk still looked like a tyrant, and Twitter still looked weak; apparently posting a link to your Instagram account was suddenly a serious threat to Twitter's business. Between the World Cup final and the botched links policy, Musk spent a considerable amount of his day on Twitter, posting more than thirty times in a twenty-four-hour period.

At 2:20 a.m. in Doha, long after the match was over, Musk was still awake and thinking about the bad policy. "Going forward, there will be a vote for major policy changes," he tweeted. "My apologies. Won't happen again."

Then three minutes later, Musk did what he did best: started controversy with one of his tweets. "Should I step down as head of Twitter?" he asked, tweeting a poll to his followers. Just like the Trump poll from the month before, Musk gave people just two options: "Yes" or "No." "I will abide by the results of this poll," he added, later tweeting, "As the saying goes, be careful what you wish, as you might get it."

It had already been assumed that Musk would eventually hand over the reins at Twitter. He was, after all, still running both Tesla and SpaceX, companies significantly more valuable than Twitter had ever been. But no one thought Musk would step aside this soon, and certainly not based on the whims of Twitter's user base. As the votes started to multiply, Musk continued tweeting into the early morning, his posts becoming more and more demoralizing.

"The question is not finding a CEO, the question is finding a CEO who can keep Twitter alive," he wrote to one follower. "No one wants the job who can actually keep Twitter alive. There is no successor," he wrote to another. Fridman, the podcaster, replied to Musk and volunteered for the job. "You must like pain a lot," Musk replied. "One catch:

you have to invest your life savings in Twitter and it has been in the fast lane to bankruptcy since May. Still want the job?"

Around 4:30 a.m. in Doha, Musk sent another message. "Those who want power are the ones who least deserve it," he wrote. Six hours later, with the poll still open and the votes pouring in, Musk's jet took off for the United States.

More than 17.5 million users voted, and most of them—57.5 percent— were in favor of Musk stepping down. He didn't publicly acknowledge the poll's results for a full two days, but eventually pledged to step aside. "I will resign as CEO as soon as I find someone foolish enough to take the job!" he finally tweeted. "After that, I will just run the software & servers teams."

If Musk was surprised by the results, he didn't say so publicly, though he shouldn't have been shocked. Things at Twitter were going horribly. The company's revenue was down 40 percent in December 2022, a troubling sign since the holiday quarter was typically the biggest of the year. The decline was extra disappointing considering Twitter had the added benefit of the World Cup that month, an event that usually attracted major advertisers. The ad struggles also meant Twitter needed more money, and Musk's first debt interest payment, which was estimated at $300 million, was due at the end of January. Musk sold another $3.6 billion worth of Tesla stock in mid-December, his third multi-billion-dollar sale since promising he was done selling way back in April. He also started looking around for other investors, hoping that people would buy into Twitter at the same $54.20 per share price that he'd paid to acquire the company months earlier. It was a tough sell: On December 30, Fidelity cut the value of its Twitter holdings in half, meaning that the bank thought Twitter was worth significantly less than what Musk had paid for it just two months earlier.

So Musk kept shedding costs. Two days before Christmas, he made an impromptu flight north to Sacramento to personally oversee the removal of hundreds of server racks from one of the company's three data centers as part of a cost-cutting expedition. (Musk would later say he regretted the haphazard decision, which created issues for months and led to several major Twitter outages.) Back in San Francisco, he turned the eighth floor of Twitter's headquarters into a makeshift hotel. With fewer people working at the company, Twitter had excess space, so it converted several conference rooms into bedrooms. This way visitors from Musk's other companies could sleep at the office instead of expensive hotel rooms when they flew in to help.

Mainly, though, Musk stopped paying the bills, daring business partners and landlords to come and collect. Twitter was no longer paying rent globally; its office leases were estimated at $130 million annually. Twitter was sued in December by one of its San Francisco landlords for failing to pay $136,000 in rent. It was later sued by the landlord for its San Francisco headquarters for almost $7 million in late rent payments. Two separate consulting firms Twitter had hired during its lawsuit with Musk also claimed the company owed them $2.2 million and $1.9 million, respectively. Twitter even stiffed the private jet company it hired to fly CMO Leslie Berland to San Francisco the day that Musk walked into Twitter's office with the sink.

On top of everything, Musk had caught the attention of regulators. The city of San Francisco sent a letter seeking more info about the eighth-floor bedrooms; apparently turning office space into "hotel" rooms without permits was against the law. What regulators didn't know was that Musk planned to go even further. He wanted to build more bathrooms onto the newly created "hotel" rooms, including a separate bathroom next to his own office so he wouldn't need to wake his security team to walk across the building when he needed to pee in the middle of the night. When Joseph Killian, the employee in charge of design and construction for Twitter's offices, expressed concern about violating San Francisco building codes, he was admonished for putting his concerns in writing over email, according to a lawsuit Killian and colleagues later filed against Twitter. Steve Davis, The Boring Company president whom

Musk had tapped to slash costs, allegedly told Killian that Twitter didn't need to follow those rules.

Musk and his team also demanded that Killian install new locks and space heaters in the rooms even though they weren't up to code, the lawsuit claims. Killian resigned in protest.

Twitter had also attracted renewed attention from the Federal Trade Commission, which quickly noticed that the executives who were supposed to ensure Twitter was adhering to the privacy agreement it had signed a few months earlier had all quit. At least two of them, Chief Privacy Officer Damien Kieran and Chief Information Security Officer Lea Kissner, were subpoenaed and interviewed by the FTC shortly after they resigned.

Given all the issues piling up, the idea that Twitter might face another massive fine, or even bankruptcy, didn't seem out of the question. Worst of all was that almost all of Twitter's issues had been self-inflicted. It was as if Musk had shot his own patient and was now standing over the operating table trying desperately to revive him. His antics at Twitter were so bad that even Tesla's board of directors complained to Musk during a December meeting that Twitter's missteps were hurting the carmaker's brand. Kimbal, Musk's brother and staunch supporter, found the whole thing hard to watch; he stopped following Musk on Twitter because the CEO's tweets were too nerve-racking to read. "The giant elephant in the room was that he was acting like a fucking idiot," Kimbal told Musk's biographer, Walter Isaacson.

Under normal circumstances, this confluence of missteps might spell doom for a company and its CEO. But Twitter, of course, was far from normal. Not only did its CEO have no board or public shareholders to answer to, but he had a seemingly endless amount of money to help keep the lights on if absolutely necessary. Plus, Musk had a strong stomach. He'd been close to bankruptcy before at both SpaceX and Tesla and had a track record of riding a company to the brink of disaster before somehow reversing course. Musk once said that there was a time he thought that both SpaceX and Tesla had less than a 10 percent chance of survival;

both companies not only survived, but far exceeded everybody's expectations. As 2022 came to an end, Twitter was now the company on the
brink of disaster.

In late December, a few days before Christmas, Musk made a special
appearance with several of his advisors, including David Sacks and Jason
Calacanis, for a taping of their popular podcast, *All In*. Sacks joined the
podcast on video from Twitter's office, sitting near the in-office coffee
shop, The Perch, where Musk had held court with employees two months
earlier after walking in holding the sink. As Sacks turned his camera
around to show the rest of the group the nearly empty office, one of the
other hosts, investor and entrepreneur David Friedberg, jokingly asked,
"Where are the people that work there?" The group laughed. "Too soon,"
Calacanis said.

Musk joined an hour into the podcast, looking tired yet surprisingly
undeterred by the walls that seemed to be caving in around him. "Twitter customer support at your service," he joked as he sat next to Sacks
in front of the camera. Musk acknowledged that running Twitter had
been a challenging experience. "It's been quite a roller coaster," he said.
"I mean it's exciting, but I think it sort of has its highs and lows to say
the least." Twitter's expenses were under control, he continued. "The
company's not, like, in the fast lane to bankruptcy anymore," he added.

For a man who had shown shockingly little self-awareness for much
of the prior two months, Musk acknowledged what many people already
knew: that Twitter's success—or failure—was now solely on his shoulders. He still didn't have a board of directors. There were no public shareholders. He had fired or run off almost all the senior Twitter executives
who had been there for years. Whatever Twitter was going to become
next, be it a YouTube competitor, a bank, or an "everything" app, it would
become because of Elon Musk.

"I can just go and take actions that are drastic," he said. "Obviously,
if I make a bunch of mistakes then Twitter won't succeed, and that will
be pretty embarrassing and sad."

CONCLUSION

Elon Musk officially killed Twitter in late July 2023. Twitter's iconic bird logo was removed from the App Store and scrubbed from the walls inside the company's San Francisco office. Musk needed just one letter in its place: *X*.

Musk had always loved the letter *X*. It was his son's name, after all, and X.com was also the name of one of his first startups. Now X was the name of his favorite social network, too. So on July 23, almost nine months after he took over, he started erasing the Twitter brand that had existed for more than seventeen years. The Twitter app, which had always been blue with a white bird in the middle, was suddenly black with a white *X*. Musk had the letter *X* projected onto the outside of Twitter's headquarters in San Francisco and arranged for a giant metal *X* to be constructed on the roof of the building high above Market Street downtown. (Of course, Musk never got the appropriate permits, and the sign was removed just three days later after city officials received dozens of complaints and notified the company it was violating safety codes.)

Musk's decision to abandon a brand that was both globally recognized and synonymous with breaking news was a questionable decision. To many people, it was also just a formality. Musk had been dismantling the things that made Twitter *Twitter*—its culture, its employees, and its news value—since the moment he and his sink walked through the door.

Musk had a vision to turn Twitter into something new and was happy to see the old bird go.

Exactly *what* that new thing was still wasn't clear nine months into his tenure. In many ways, the product itself looked pretty much the same as it did during Twitter 1.0, though Musk was making other changes that were harder to see. He applied for money transfer licenses so X could get into payments, part of his hope to transform the service into an "everything app." He also started sharing advertising revenue with some popular users, a way of encouraging them to use the service even more. Most notably, Musk leaned into his pledge to make X more free-speech. He eliminated the service's Covid-19 misinformation policies and rolled back suspensions for several conservative users. Ali Alexander, the Trump supporter who helped orchestrate the "Stop the Steal" rally on January 6th, returned. So did Nick Fuentes, a known white national-ist. (Both were promptly suspended again.) After Fox News surprisingly parted ways with one of its biggest stars, Tucker Carlson, in April 2023, Musk cheered on Carlson as he brought his popular talk show onto X instead. President Donald Trump returned, too, albeit briefly. In August 2023, he tweeted his mug shot after being booked in Fulton County jail on charges he tried to overturn the presidential election results in Geor-gia. Trump used the tweet to try and garner campaign donations, and Musk retweeted the post to all of his followers. "Next-level," he wrote.

It was almost understandable why Musk wanted to leave "Twitter" behind. X represented a fresh start and a departure from all the things about Twitter that made Musk fume. It was also a chance to distract every-one from the fact that Musk's first nine months in charge had been an unmitigated business disaster. Many of the advertisers Musk had spooked during the first few weeks following the takeover still hadn't returned, or if they did, they spent much less. Musk remained his own worst enemy. In November of 2023, he posted a tweet of support when another user wrote that "Jewish communities have been pushing the exact kind of dia-lectical hatred against whites that they claim to want people to stop using

against them." "You have said the actual truth," Musk replied, prompting widespread backlash from users and advertisers. Apple, IBM, Disney, and several other major brands paused advertising on X in protest.
Shortly after, Musk took the stage at *The New York Times* DealBook
Summit and said he didn't care if advertisers boycotted his service. "If
somebody's going to try and blackmail me with advertising, blackmail
me with money—go fuck yourself," he proudly announced.

All of Musk's antics meant that X's business got crushed. Musk said
in July 2023 that advertising revenue was down 50 percent. By September, U.S. ad revenue was down 60 percent. X was still cash-flow negative
and had massive interest payments on the debt Musk took out to finance
his deal. On top of that, his plan to diversify X's revenue by building
a major subscription business never materialized. It turns out very few
people wanted to pay $8 per month for a blue checkmark.

By the time Musk rebranded to X, the company was worth just $20
billion, or less than half the $44 billion he'd paid the previous fall. At
least Musk had a sense of humor about it. "Say what you want about
me, but I acquired the world's largest non-profit for $44B lol," he joked
to his followers.

Most of X's issues stemmed from Musk himself, who continued to
run the company as if his decisions carried zero consequences. In April,
he finally painted over the *w* on the Twitter sign outside the company's
headquarters, turning "Twitter" into "Titter." The next day he changed
his username on the service to "Harry Bolz." Musk had fired the entire
PR team, so anytime someone in the press sent an email to the company's press relations address, they received an auto-reply that included a
poop emoji. The antics were familiar to anyone who had followed Musk's
career, and may have been more or less harmless if not for the fact that
X relied on brand-conscious advertisers for almost all of its revenue.

Other decisions carried even more significance. Musk removed the
blue checkmarks from all users who didn't pay for a Twitter Blue subscription, meaning thousands of journalists, celebrities, and news organizations

were no longer verified. It quickly ate away at Twitter's reputation as a global news source. The effort eliminated the "dual class" system that had bothered Musk for so long; now anyone with $8 could get a blue check. But the decision also eroded Twitter's most valuable use case: its role as a fast, mostly reliable source for breaking news. A blue check no longer verified a person's identity, which made it virtually impossible to know who was tweeting from any given account. It also meant professional journalists and news organizations were no longer distinguished from the masses, making it harder to quickly find trustworthy information. Major publications such as *The New York Times*, *Politico*, and *The Washington Post* declined to pay for the checkmarks or let their reporters expense them. "It's evident that verified checkmarks no longer represent authority and expertise," the *Post* said in a statement. Twitter's reputation as the fastest place to learn what was happening in the world had largely evaporated. Months later, when Israel went to war against the terrorist group Hamas, X was littered with false and misleading posts. Musk himself encouraged people to follow accounts known for spreading false information. (He later deleted the tweet.)

Musk eroded trust in other ways, too. After attending the Super Bowl in Phoenix in February 2023, Musk returned to California infuriated that a tweet he posted about the Philadelphia Eagles had gotten fewer views than President Joe Biden's tweet about the Eagles. What followed was a mad dash by employees to tweak Twitter's algorithms so that Musk's tweets got preferential treatment. The group accidentally overdid it, flooding everyone's Twitter feed with Musk's posts. Musk laughed it off, and blamed the issue on a software bug—but the incident simply reminded everyone Musk can and will tailor the service to his own benefit whenever he feels like it.

On the heels of Twitter's struggles, other companies smelled blood in the water. Several tried to build Twitter clones in the first half of 2023, an effort to fill a perceived void and try to catch disgruntled users who were leaving Twitter behind. Among the new competitors was "Threads," a Twitter lookalike from Mark Zuckerberg and Instagram. "I think there should be a public conversations app with 1 billion+ people on it," Zuckerberg wrote at launch. "Twitter has had the opportunity to do this but hasn't nailed it."

Zuckerberg and Musk had feuded for years before Threads entered the picture. They openly disagreed about the future risks of artificial intelligence; Musk thought AI was dangerous, and Zuckerberg thought Musk was being alarmist. But Musk also had a disdain for Zuckerberg's social networking products and thought that Instagram made people depressed and sad. The two had never competed head-to-head before Threads, but it quickly became clear that a simple business rivalry wasn't enough. Musk challenged Zuckerberg to a cage fight, and Zuckerberg, who was obsessed with MMA, accepted. What followed were several days of performative online theater that ended when Musk did what he did best: tweeted something ridiculous. "Zuck is a cuck," he wrote on X shortly after Threads launched. "I propose a literal dick measuring contest." Zuckerberg called off the fight a few days later. "I think we can all agree Elon isn't serious and it's time to move on," he wrote.

When Musk first acquired Twitter, he set out with a goal to make the app "maximally trusted and broadly inclusive." One year into Twitter 2.0, Musk has failed to do both. Twitter, now X, has lost its hold as the most important social network for news; instead, its role as a shock-and-awe service, with Musk playing the pied piper, has been magnified. It's sometimes hard to tell if Musk is being serious, or if he understands his own power. He still uses his vast following in dangerous ways. Almost ten months after suggesting that Yoel Roth was a pedophile, forcing him to sell his home, Musk again tweeted about his former employee after Roth appeared as a speaker at a tech conference. "I have rarely seen evil in as pure a form as Yoel Roth," Musk wrote to his nearly 160 million followers. This time Roth didn't see all the abuse directed his way; he was no longer using Twitter.

It's possible that Musk will still turn everything around. He did it at Tesla, he did it at SpaceX, and he certainly has the money to do it again at X. Year one was a disaster, but Musk doesn't operate on one-year time horizons. Perhaps this is just the beginning of his next great turnaround story. On most days, though, it seems that the only person standing in the way of such an outcome is Musk himself. "I learned a ton from watching Elon up close—the good, the bad and the ugly," wrote Esther Crawford, the product exec who slept on the floor in a sleeping bag to try to meet one of Musk's early deadlines. (She was fired several months later in yet another round of cost cuts.) "His boldness, passion and storytelling is inspiring, but his lack of process and empathy is painful."

"Elon has an exceptional talent for tackling hard physics-based problems," she continued, "but products that facilitate human connection and communication require a different type of social-emotional intelligence."

It's hard to know exactly how Jack Dorsey feels about Twitter's demise. He rarely tweets anymore. Dorsey has largely stayed out of the spotlight since stepping down from Twitter's board of directors in mid-2022. It's tough to imagine, though, that *this* is what Dorsey envisioned when he encouraged Musk to buy and save the company that he'd founded. Musk seems to be learning the hard way that having power and control over global speech is a much greater burden than most people realize.

There is an irony in what has happened. One of Dorsey's biggest issues with Twitter was that it had too much power and control over global speech. Now X still has that power, but it is controlled by a single person: the richest man in the world, with no board of directors, no public shareholders, and seemingly no concerns about creating globally significant speech policies on a whim. The power that Dorsey so worried about has only been further centralized.

Dorsey is at least partly disappointed in how everything played out. In April 2023, six months after Musk closed the deal, Dorsey shared a few introspective posts about Twitter on Bluesky. The decentralized social network that he had envisioned for years before stepping down as CEO had finally launched in early 2023, and ironically, quickly became one of the many Twitter lookalikes to crop up in the wake of Musk's stumbles. In his posts, Dorsey was unapologetic about what had happened to Twitter. Instead he once again lamented Twitter's existence as a public company, arguing that the sale was inevitable thanks to Twitter's corporate structure and the demands of Wall Street.

"We had zero protection from activists. More were in the wings," Dorsey wrote, a reference to investors like Elliott Management. "The market [downturn] and the collapse of the ad business would have opened a significant opportunity for them to come in again, and I doubt it could survive another attack."

"If Elon or anyone wanted to buy the company, all they had to do was name a price that the board felt was better than what the company could do independently. This is true for every public company," he continued.

Jason Goldman, an early Twitter board member, responded to one of Dorsey's posts with a simple but loaded question: "Do you think Elon has proven to be the best possible steward for the platform?"

Dorsey, as he tends to do, answered earnestly.

"No," he wrote back. "Nor do I think he acted right after realizing his timing was bad. Nor do I think the board should have forced the sale. It all went south."

"But it happened," he continued, "and all we can do now is build something to avoid that ever happening again."

ACKNOWLEDGMENTS

The opportunity to write this book and tell this story has truly been a privilege. I initially thought this project would look very different, and in late 2021 I set out to write a book about Twitter and its then-CEO Jack Dorsey. When Dorsey unexpectedly resigned at the end of that year, I assumed I had my ending. A few months later, just as I was submitting my book proposal and meeting with publishers, Elon Musk entered the picture. The rest, as they say, is history. I've always been a believer that timing is indeed everything, and this book certainly proved that.

I owe a tremendous debt to all the sources and Twitter employees who trusted me to tell this story. Journalists are particularly adept at pestering people and constantly asking for things—time, attention, introductions, information. I've spent much of the past two years asking others for help, and I'm so grateful to those who were willing to provide it. Many of them spoke with me for hours, sometimes on several different occasions, in order to help me understand this story. Without those people, this book and this version of Twitter's history simply wouldn't exist.

The first two people I called when I decided that a book sounded like a fun idea were my Bloomberg editors, Brad Stone and Sarah Frier. From the very first conversation and without hesitation, they were standing in my corner encouraging me to pursue this project. Not only are they both incredible journalists and writers, but they're also fantastic mentors and leaders. I'm forever grateful for their support and consider myself lucky I get to call them colleagues.

My agent, Pilar Queen from UTA, believed in this story from the beginning and did what all great agents do: kept me from losing my mind and encouraged me to stay focused on the things that mattered most. I am thankful to have her on my team.

I'm also grateful to Amar Deol and the wonderful team at Atria for taking a chance on a first-time author. Amar saw potential in this book—and saw potential in me as a writer—from the outset, and I'm fortunate that he gave me a shot. Stephanie Hitchcock is a saint, and joined this project just as it was reaching its most critical stage to help get everything over the finish line. She was calm, determined, and resourceful, and I'm grateful to her for putting up with all of my late-night emails and relentless questions as the pieces fell into place. Hannah Frankel and Erica Siudzinski were both reliable and supportive allies, and their ability to keep all the trains running on time was truly impressive.

One of the best parts about working at Bloomberg is that I am surrounded by colleagues who are the very best at what they do. The summer of 2022 was an all-hands-on-deck situation in our newsroom as Musk bought Twitter, then didn't buy Twitter, then decided to buy Twitter again. Any success I had covering that story, both as it unfolded and in the weeks and months that followed, was thanks to a tremendous team of colleagues. Ed Ludlow is without a doubt the hardest working man at Bloomberg, and his hustle and willingness to collaborate are inspiring. Dana Hull and Max Chafkin helped me better understand Musk and the world where he operates. Jef Feeley spent countless hours talking with me about the Delaware Court of Chancery, a topic I never expected I'd be interested in. Emily Chang helped bring this story to life with her strong interviews and reporting and was always willing to collaborate and offer guidance. My editors Tom Giles and Jillian Ward kept us all focused and motivated to keep pushing as the story twisted and turned, sometimes several different times in the same day.

I'm thankful to Alex Barinka and Aisha Counts, my partners on the social media beat, who not only provided support during my reporting, but covered for me while I took time away from the always hectic news cycle to write this book. I owe them both several cocktails. Other colleagues like Mark Bergen, Brody Ford, Davey Alba and Max Adler made covering Twitter an easier and more enjoyable experience because of their own strong reporting and camaraderie.

I read several books during this process, but I relied heavily on three books in particular. Ashlee Vance's *Elon Musk* was a bible for me, and provided a tremendous foundation as I started covering Musk for the first time. Ashlee was a reliable sounding board and source of encouragement throughout this process, and I'm so happy he works at Bloomberg. Nick Bilton's *Hatching Twitter* was similarly instrumental. I think I read it three times over the past year alone, and routinely referenced the book and Nick's stellar reporting as I tried to make sense of Twitter's messy and important early years. Lastly, Walter Isaacson's biography of Elon Musk provided lots of color and insight into the CEO's world as the Twitter deal was unfolding. I learned a lot from Walter's reporting, and *Battle for the Bird* is a stronger story because of it.

Covering social media is both a rewarding and frustrating job; rewarding because you get to cover the most important stories and businesses in the world, and frustrating because the beat is littered with talented and well-sourced journalists who are always looking to ruin your day with a great scoop of their own. As you'll see in my Notes, I relied heavily on the work of many other great journalists to tell this story. While I wish they'd all take more vacations, I'm also grateful that they continue to push me personally and work tirelessly to hold these companies accountable.

I have such an incredible support system outside of my day job. Several of my friends and family members read this book before it came out, offering advice and feedback that were instrumental during my editing process. Thank you to Derek, Ty, Lizzy, Kasey, Spencer, and Jason for your time and feedback. I also have the biggest cheerleaders you could ever imagine: my parents. I'm fortunate enough to have six parents who care about me and my career, and they offered unconditional love and support as I pursued this project.

And lastly, to my wonderful wife, Jessica: This story would not exist without you. You are such a steady rock for our family, and I'm so grateful to have you as a partner. Writing a book is a roller coaster of emotions—some days it felt like the best job in the world, and other times, it had me questioning every decision I'd ever made. (Writing a book while having two kids was a fun idea, wasn't it?!) You were there for all of it, and you constantly sacrificed so that I could prioritize this project and give it my all. I love you.

NOTES

INTRODUCTION

1 **dialed up Radiohead's "Everything In Its Right Place":** Jack Dorsey (@jack), "[Tidal Link]," Twitter, April 25, 2022, 6:41 p.m., https://twitter.com/jack/status /1518767238081171456.

2 **It was his biggest regret:** Jack Dorsey (@jack), "The idea and service is all that matters to me, and I will do whatever it takes to protect both. Twitter as a company has always been my sole issue and my biggest regret. It has been owned by Wall Street and the ad model. Taking it back from Wall Street is the correct first step." Twitter, April 25, 2022, 7:03 p.m., https://twitter.com/jack/status/1518772754782187520.

2 **"Civilizational risk is decreased . . . Twitter as a public platform":** TED, "Elon Musk Talks Twitter, Tesla and How His Brain Works—Live at TED2022," YouTube, 2022, https://www.youtube.com/watch?v=cdZZpaB2kDM.

3 **"I don't believe anyone . . . extend the light of consciousness":** Jack Dorsey (@jack), "In principle, I don't believe anyone should own or run Twitter. It wants to be a public good at a protocol level, not a company. Solving for the problem of it being a company however, Elon is the singular solution I trust. I trust his mission to extend the light of consciousness." Twitter, April 25, 2022, 7:03 p.m., https://twitter.com/jack/status /1518772756069773313.

3 **"I know . . . whatever it takes to make it work":** Twitter Inc. v. Elon R. Musk, X Holdings I Inc., and X Holdings II Inc. (Court of Chancery of the State of Delaware, July 12, 2022), Exhibit H, 27.

5 **"one of the worst-aged tweets of all time":** Bloomberg, "Twitter Founders on Musk's Tumultuous Takeover | The Circuit," YouTube, 2023, https://www.youtube.com/watch?v= SKia5QUiGkE.

5 **"It all went South":** Jack Dorsey (@jack.bsky.social), "No. Nor do I think he acted right after realizing his timing was bad. Nor do I think the board should have forced the sale. It all went south. But it happened and all we can do now is build something to avoid that ever happening again. So I'm happy Jay and team and nostr devs exist and building it." Bluesky, April 28, 2023, 6:13 p.m., https://bsky.app/profile/jack.bsky.social/post /3juhx7ctgsk2k.

6 **"I think so . . . differently and better":** Casey Newton, "Inside Twitter's Emotional Friday All-Hands," Platformer, April 29, 2022, https://www.platformer.news/p/inside -twitters-emotional-friday?s=w.

CHAPTER 1: JACK IS BACK

9 **He even auditioned twice for *Saturday Night Live*:** "Dick Costolo: How Twitter's CEO Jumpstarted a Social Media Revolution," Bessemer Venture Partners, March 2, 2023, https://www.bvp.com/wish-i-knew/dick-costolo.

10 **was promoted to CEO just one year later:** Michael Arrington, "Oh, RSS Is Definitely Dead Now: Feedburner CEO Dick Costolo to Become Twitter COO," TechCrunch,

September 2, 2009, https://techcrunch.com/2009/09/02/oh-rss-is-definitely-dead-now
-feedburner-ceo-dick-costolo-to-become-twitter-coo/.

10 **joining regular CrossFit classes:** Emily Jane Fox, "Former Twitter C.E.O. Dick Costolo
Has Dreams of Being a Fitness Guru," *Vanity Fair*, September 29, 2016, https://www
.vanityfair.com/news/2016/09/dick-costolo-fitness-chorus.

10 **play a key role in helping protesters organize:** Catherine O'Donnell, "New Study
Quantifies Use of Social Media in Arab Spring," UW News, September 12, 2011, https://
www.washington.edu/news/2011/09/12/new-study-quantifies-use-of-social-media-in
-arab-spring/.

10 **Facebook added 43 million new users:** Facebook Inc., Annual Report Form 10-K
for the Fiscal Year Ended December 31, 2014 (filed January 29, 2015), 35, from Meta
Investor Relations, https://s21.q4cdn.com/399680738/files/doc_financials/annual
_reports/FB2014AR.pdf.

10 **Twitter added just 4 million:** Ben Popper, "Twitter's User Growth Has Stalled, but Its
Business Keeps Improving," The Verge, February 5, 2015, https://www.theverge.com
/2015/2/5/7987501/twitter-q4-2014-earnings.

11 **"Hey Dad . . . who are ahead of you":** "Dick Costolo: How Twitter's CEO Jumpstarted
a Social Media Revolution."

11 **"Running Twitter . . . a wacky company to run":** Kara Swisher, "Twitter's Former
C.E.O. Has a 'Too Bad, So Sad' Approach to Content Moderation," *New York Times*,
January 3, 2022, https://www.nytimes.com/2022/01/03/opinion/sway-dick-costolo-kara
-swisher.html?showTranscript=1.

12 **sailing around the world by himself:** Stanford Graduate School of Business, "Jack
Dorsey: The Future Has Already Arrived," YouTube, 2013, https://www.youtube.com
/watch?v=AckvbL5Tfic.

12 **got so severe he stopped speaking:** Mella TV, "Mella Special featuring Jack Dorsey:
Founder and CEO of Twitter," YouTube, 2020, https://www.youtube.com/watch?v=
nN3aTTHL1c4.

13 **an IBM PC Junior in the mid-1980s:** David Kirkpatrick, "Twitter Was Act One,"
Vanity Fair, March 3, 2011, https://www.vanityfair.com/news/2011/04/jack-dorsey
-201104.

14 **"other outcasts . . . wall street district after 8":** Jack Dorsey, "The Orange Moon of
New Amsterdam," Gu.st, http://gu.st/writ/orange_moon_of_york.

14 **"real-time, up-to-date, from the road":** Jack Dorsey, *twttr sketch*, photograph, July 5,
2006, Flickr, https://www.flickr.com/photos/jackdorsey/182613360/in/photostream/.

14 **"I'm at the bison paddock":** D. T. Max, "Two-Hit Wonder," *New Yorker*, October 14,
2013, https://www.newyorker.com/magazine/2013/10/21/two-hit-wonder.

15 **At one point Dorsey got a tattoo:** Nick Bilton, "@Jack," in *Hatching Twitter: A True
Story of Money, Power, Friendship, and Betrayal* (New York: Portfolio Penguin, 2013),
34.

15 **Dorsey enrolled in the Healing Arts Center in St. Louis:** Berkeley Engineering,
"View from the Top: Jack Dorsey, Square & Twitter," YouTube, 2013, https://www
.youtube.com/watch?v=rn9lTpD-yKc.

15 **including a job writing ticketing system software:** Berkeley Engineering.

16 **sent him a copy of his resume, which only included his first name:** Bilton, "@Jack," 31.

16 **accidentally ran it aground:** Tony Stubblebine, "What Was It Like to Work with Jack
Dorsey on the Early Versions of Twitter?" Quora, https://quorasessionwithcoachtony
.quora.com/Tony-Stubblebine-What-was-it-like-to-work-with-Jack-Dorsey-on-the-early
-versions-of-Twitter.

16   **Apple launched an update:** "Apple Takes Podcasting Mainstream," Apple Newsroom,
     June 28, 2005, https://www.apple.com/newsroom/2005/06/28Apple-Takes-Podcasting
     -Mainstream/.

17   **Dorsey brought up the status concept:** Nick Bilton, "Status," in *Hatching Twitter*,
     56–59.

17   **"having some coffee. heading home. sleep":** Nick Bilton, "Just Setting Up My Twttr,"
     in *Hatching Twitter*, 69.

17   **Twitter had fewer than five thousand users:** Max, "Two-Hit Wonder."

18   **it was fewer than 140 characters:** Dan Fost, "Austin's SXSW Festival Atwitter over
     Twitter / Conference-Goers Use It, Give It 'Best Blog' Award," SFGATE, January 16,
     2012, https://www.sfgate.com/business/article/Austin-s-SXSW-festival-atwitter-over
     -Twitter-2569138.php.

18   **more than 100,000 people had signed up for Twitter:** Nick Bilton, "The First CEO," in
     Hatching Twitter, 102.

18   **He wasn't even convinced that Twitter should be a real company:** Bloomberg,
     "Twitter Founders on Musk's Tumultuous Takeover | The Circuit," YouTube, 2023,
     https://www.youtube.com/watch?v=SKia5QUiGkE.

19   **"You can either . . . but you can't be both":** Nick Bilton, "The Dressmaker," in
     Hatching Twitter, 120.

19   **He also felt furious and betrayed:** Lara Logan, CBS News, "The Innovator: Jack
     Dorsey," YouTube, 2013, https://www.youtube.com/watch?v=eKHoTOYTFH8.

20   **to explore "high-tech business ventures":** Mark Kukis, "Is Iraq Ready for Twitter?
     New Media in a War Zone," *Time*, April 23, 2009, https://content.time.com/time/world
     /article/0,8599,1893244,00.html.

20   **he sat next to Secretary of State Hillary Clinton:** Jackson West, "Twitter Cofounder
     Hangs with Hillary," NBC Bay Area, January 8, 2010, https://www.nbcbayarea.com
     /news/local/twitter-cofounder-hangs-with-hillary-jw/1884420/.

20   **Dorsey joined a panel with famed Chinese artist and activist Ai Weiwei:** Joab
     Jackson, "Twitter in China? In Due Time, Twitter Founder Promises," Computerworld,
     March 16, 2010, https://www.computerworld.com/article/2756197/twitter-in-china--in
     -due-time--twitter-founder-promises.html.

20   **"Ensuring that the right . . . Ev had no idea he was playing":** Nick Bilton, "Secret
     Meetings," in *Hatching Twitter*, 245.

20   **Williams was fired and replaced by Dick Costolo:** Claire Cain Miller, "Shift at the
     Top of Twitter as a Founder Steps Aside," *New York Times*, October 4, 2010, https://www
     .nytimes.com/2010/10/05/technology/05twitter.html.

21   **put the glossy brochures they typically handed out at conferences onto CD-ROMS:**
     Jim McKelvey, "Bob and the Pyramids," in *The Innovation Stack: Building an
     Unbeatable Business One Crazy Idea at a Time* (New York: Portfolio Penguin, 2020),
     11.

21   **"I felt like someone had beaten up my younger brother, and I was furious":**
     McKelvey, 16.

21   **McKelvey couldn't accept her American Express card:** McKelvey, 17.

21   **They called the company Square, short for "square up":** McKelvey, 53.

22   **The company had almost 1,200 employees:** Square Inc., Form S-1 (filed October 14,
     2015), 148, https://www.sec.gov/Archives/edgar/data/1512673/000119312515343733
     /d937622ds1.htm.

22   **was valued at $6 billion:** Laura Lorenzetti, "Square Worth $6 Billion after Latest $150
     Million Fundraising Round," *Fortune*, October 6, 2014, https://fortune.com/2014/10/06
     /square-worth-6-billion-after-latest-150-million-fundraising-round/.

22   **he was also Square's largest shareholder:** Square Inc., Form S-1.

22 **"As I said last week . . . that won't change":** Jason Del Rey, "Jack Dorsey Says He Will Not Leave His Role as Square CEO," Recode, June 16, 2015, https://www.vox.com /2015/6/16/11563620/jack-dorsey-says-he-will-not-leave-his-role-as-square-ceo.

23 **Twitter's revenue grew 58 percent:** Twitter, Inc., Annual Report Form 10-K for the Fiscal Year Ended December 31, 2015 (filed February 29, 2016), 43–47, https://www.sec .gov/Archives/edgar/data/1418091/000156459016013646/twtr-10k_20151231.htm.

24 **working long hours and requiring his teams to do the same:** Matt Day, "'Absolutely a Sprint': How Andy Jassy Raced to the Top of Amazon," Bloomberg, July 2, 2021, https:// www.bloomberg.com/news/articles/2021-07-02/after-bezos-new-ceo-inherits-amazon-on -a-roll-but-roiled-by-labor-unrest?sref=dZ65CIng.

24 **on pace to reach $10 billion in sales faster than Amazon's commerce business:** Amazon.com Inc., Annual Report Form 10-K for Fiscal Year Ended December 31, 2015 (filed January 28, 2016), 2, from Amazon Investor Relations, https://s2.q4cdn.com /299287126/files/doc_financials/annual/2015-Annual-Report.pdf.

25 **the board told Dorsey on a conference call that the job was his:** Nick Bilton, "Twitter Is Betting Everything on Jack Dorsey. Will It Work?" *Vanity Fair*, June 1, 2016, https:// www.vanityfair.com/news/2016/06/twitter-is-betting-everything-on-jack-dorsey.

25 **"We assumed we would . . . while also running Square":** Abhirup Roy and Yasmeen Abutaleb, "Twitter Appoints Jack Dorsey CEO, Seeks New Chairman," Reuters, October 5, 2015, https://www.reuters.com/article/uk-twitter-ceo-dorsey -idUKKCN0RZ16720151005.

25 **attending a VIP dinner at Bar Tartine in San Francisco with celebrities:** Ian Mohr, "Power Crowd Fêtes New Twitter CEO Jack Dorsey," PageSix.com, October 8, 2015, https://pagesix.com/2015/10/07/power-crowd-fete-new-twitter-ceo-jack-dorsey/.

CHAPTER 2: #ITSJUSTFUCKINGUS

26 **Jack Dorsey's day . . . would make coffee:** "Jack Dorsey Live Chat on Product Hunt," Product Hunt, December 22, 2015, https://www.producthunt.com/live/jack-dorsey #comment-201387.

27 **Square's advisors even floated the idea of postponing the deal altogether:** Mike Isaac and Leslie Picker, "Shares of Square Soar by 45% After Public Offering," *New York Times*, November 19, 2015, https://www.nytimes.com/2015/11/20/business/dealbook /square-ipo.html.

27 **arranged for the bell to ring when his mom, Marcia, used her Apple Watch to buy a bouquet of flowers:** CNN Business, "Dorsey Unfazed by Square's Lower IPO Price," YouTube, 2015.

27 **"tough but necessary":** Jack Dorsey (@jack), "Made some tough but necessary decisions that enable Twitter to move with greater focus and reinvest in our growth." Twitter, October 13, 2015, 5:35 a.m., https://twitter.com/jack/status /653912031997751296.

27 **Dorsey decided to give back $200 million of his Twitter stock:** Kurt Wagner, "Project Morale Boost! Jack Dorsey Is Giving Away Nearly $200 Million of His Twitter Stock to Employees," Recode, October 22, 2015, https://www.vox.com/2015/10/22/11619968 /project-morale-boost-jack-dorsey-is-giving-away-nearly-200-million-of.

28 **Twitter's user base didn't grow at all:** Twitter, Inc., Annual Report Form 10-K for the Fiscal Year Ended December 31, 2015 (filed February 29, 2016), 43, https://www.sec.gov /Archives/edgar/data/1418091/000156459016013646/twtr-10k_20151231.htm.

28 **Twitter's stock was trading near an all-time low:** Jen Wieczner, "Twitter's Stock Has Fallen to Its Lowest Point Ever," *Fortune*, February 8, 2016, https://www.fortune.com /2016/01/08/twitter-stock-low/.

28 **The company was secretly working on several new features, including longer tweets so people could post more than 140 characters at a time:** Kurt Wagner, "Twitter

Considering 10,000-Character Limit for Tweets," Recode, January 5, 2016, https://www
.vox.com/2016/1/5/11588480/twitter-considering-10000-character-limit-for-tweets.

28 **Dorsey even bought everyone a book:** Kurt Wagner, "Jack Dorsey Returned to Twitter
Two Years Ago—but He Still Hasn't Saved the Company," Recode, October 4, 2017,
https://www.vox.com/2017/10/4/16382954/jack-dorsey-twitter-ceo-progress-stock-tweets
-140-video-live-users.

30 **some speculated that he might one day make a good commissioner:** Alexei
Oreskovic, "Twitter's Anthony Noto Was Reportedly on the Shortlist to Be the Next
Commissioner of the NFL," Business Insider, June 15, 2015, https://www.businessinsider
.com/fired-twitter-cfo-elon-musk-deal-period-pulled-mental-muscles-2022-10.

30 **and in the elevators:** Niketa Patel (@Niketa), "Love that this is in the elevator at @
TwitterNYC today!!!#itsjustfuckingus #oneteam." Twitter, February 1, 2016, 9:02 a.m.,
https://twitter.com/Niketa/status/694204212796866561?s=20.

31 **"It's staying . . . it allows for of-the-moment brevity":** "140 Characters 'Is Staying,'
CEO Says While Looking at Twitter's History," Today, NBC, 2016, https://www.today
.com/video/140-characters-is-staying-ceo-says-while-looking-at-twitter-s-history
-647319107566.

31 **Dorsey had gotten cold feet:** Wagner, "Jack Dorsey Returned."

32 **Users were so upset that the hashtag #RIPTwitter started trending on the service:**
Alex Hern, "Jack Dorsey Calms #RIPTwitter with Carefully Worded Non-Denial,"
Guardian, February 8, 2016, https://www.theguardian.com/technology/2016/feb/08/jack
-dorsey-riptwitter-timeline-twitter.

32 **"Live commentary, live connections, live conversations":** "Twitter Q4 2015 Quarterly
Results Transcript," Twitter Investor Relations, February 10, 2016, https://s22.q4cdn.com
/826641620/files/doc_financials/2022/q1/Final-Q1%E2%80%9922-earnings-release.pdf.

32 **executives used the word *live* 36 times in just 54 minutes:** Felix Gillette and Sarah
Frier, "#GrowthStall: Twitter's Moment of Solemn Reflection," Bloomberg, March 21,
2016, https://www.bloomberg.com/features/2016-twitter-turns-ten/?sref=dZ65CIng.

33 **Broadcast networks CBS and NBC had paid $450 million apiece:** Richard Sandomir,
"CBS and NBC Will Split a Bigger Deal for Thursday N.F.L. Games," New York Times,
February 1, 2016, https://www.nytimes.com/2016/02/02/sports/football/nfl-thursday-cbs
-nbc-networks.html.

33 **Twitter beat out Facebook and Amazon to win the streaming rights for a paltry $10
million:** Scott Soshnick, Sarah Frier, and Scott Moritz, "Twitter Gets NFL Thursday
Night Games for a Bargain Price," Bloomberg, April 5, 2016, https://www.bloomberg
.com/news/articles/2016-04-05/twitter-said-to-win-nfl-deal-for-thursday-night-streaming
-rights?sref=dZ65CIng.

33 **other programs with partners like CBS, Bloomberg, and the NBA:** Kurt Wagner,
"Twitter Will Livestream Some MLB and NHL Games Starting This Fall," Recode, July
25, 2016, https://www.vox.com/2016/7/25/12260820/twitter-livestream-mlb-nhl-games
-mlbam.

33 **Twitter's $10 million deal with the NFL led to more than $50 million in revenue:**
Kurt Wagner, "Twitter Wants to Sell Its NFL Ad Spots for More than $50 Million,"
Recode, June 22, 2016, https://www.vox.com/2016/6/22/12006468/twitter-nfl-ad-deal-50
-million-dollars.

34 **"What's everyone talking about?... When will it end?":** Twitter, "Twitter: See What's
Happening," YouTube, 2016, https://www.youtube.com/watch?v=kIe5CHbOZVE.

35 **He owned a five-acre estate on the Big Island in Hawaii:** Michael Keany, "The 25
Most Expensive Homes in Hawai'i," Honolulu Magazine, September 19, 2010, https://
www.honolulumagazine.com/the-25-most-expensive-homes-in-hawaii/.

35 ***Fortune* readers selected Benioff as the magazine's "Businessperson of the
Year":** J. P. Mangalindan, "Vote: Businessperson of the Year 2014, Reader's Choice |

Tech Edition," *Fortune*, November 6, 2014, https://fortune.com/2014/11/06/vote
-businessperson-year-tech/.

35 **Benioff was furious:** Nico Grant, "Salesforce's Success Rides on One Man's Gut,"
Bloomberg, May 23, 2019, https://www.bloomberg.com/news/articles/2019-05-23/this
-software-giant-runs-on-one-man-s-gut?sref=dZ65CIng.

35 **bidding up the price repeatedly:** Mark Bergen, "The Tick-Tock Story of How LinkedIn
Shopped Itself to Microsoft, Salesforce and Google," Recode, July 2, 2016, https://www
.vox.com/2016/7/2/12085428/linkedin-microsoft-salesforce-google-deal-timeline.

36 **"Plus, Twitter was struggling . . . beneficial for us both":** Marc Benioff and Monica
Langley, "Trust," in *Trailblazer: The Power of Business as the Greatest Platform for
Change* (New York: Currency, 2019), 55.

36 **considered building his own streaming platform . . . expedite that timeline
significantly:** Robert Iger, "If You Don't Innovate, You Die," in *The Ride of a Lifetime*
(New York: Random House, 2019), 190.

37 **he controlled just over 3 percent of Twitter's voting power:** Twitter Inc., Proxy
Statement: Notice of 2016 Annual Stockholders' Meeting (filed May 25, 2016), 62,
Securities and Exchange Commission, https://d1lge852tjjqow.cloudfront.net/CIK
-0001418091/dbfc1c62-2b4d-4d75-b39c-f95e3fa2ed2e.pdf.

38 **"The nastiness," Iger confessed, "is extraordinary":** Maureen Dowd, "The Slow-
Burning Success of Disney's Bob Iger," *New York Times*, September 22, 2019, https://
www.nytimes.com/2019/09/22/style/disney-bob-iger-book.html.

39 **Twitter laid off roughly 350 employees, or 9 percent of the staff, and closed several
international offices:** Kurt Wagner, "Twitter will cut 9 percent of its workforce, or
roughly 350 people," Recode, October 27, 2016, https://www.vox.com/2016/10/27
/13399872/twitter-layoffs-q3-earnings.

CHAPTER 3: @REALDONALDTRUMP

42 **He was polling well:** Jennifer Agiesta, "Poll: Donald Trump Surges to 32% Support,"
CNN, September 10, 2015, https://www.cnn.com/2015/09/10/politics/donald-trump-ben
-carson-cnn-poll/index.html.

42 **including folks like Secretary of State Hillary Clinton and Senator John McCain:**
Kurt Wagner, "Jack Dorsey's Stand Against Trump Marks a Long-Debated Red Line,"
Bloomberg, June 10, 2020, https://www.bloomberg.com/news/features/2020-06-10
/inside-twitter-and-jack-dorsey-s-stand-against-donald-trump?sref=dZ65CIng.

43 **"I will totally protect Israel . . . Very pro–Second Amendment":** Nick Gass, "Trump,
in Twitter Q&A, Promises to Solve America's Problems," *Politico*, September 21, 2015,
https://www.politico.com/story/2015/09/donald-trump-twitter-q-and-a-213884.

44 **to help promote . . . or one of his many golf courses:** Michael Barbaro, "Pithy, Mean
and Powerful: How Donald Trump Mastered Twitter for 2016," *New York Times*, October
5, 2015, https://www.nytimes.com/2015/10/06/us/politics/donald-trump-twitter-use
-campaign-2016.html.

45 **Trump was being retweeted 28 times more often than he was one year earlier:**
Oren Tsur, Katherine Ognyanova, and David Lazer, "The Data Behind Trump's
Twitter Takeover," *Politico*, April 29, 2016, https://www.politico.com/magazine/story
/2016/04/donald-trump-2016-twitter-takeover-213861/.

45 **the ability to measure his growing popularity in real time:** Barbaro, "Pithy, Mean and
Powerful."

45 **Former Florida governor . . . "develop a massive headache":** Kevin Quealy, "The
Complete List of Trump's Twitter Insults (2015–2021)," *New York Times*, January 19,
2021, https://www.nytimes.com/interactive/2021/01/19/upshot/trump-complete-insult
-list.html.

45 **He once tweeted that Arianna Huffington:** Donald Trump (@realDonaldTrump), ".@ariannahuff is unattractive both inside and out. I fully understand why her former husband left her for a man- he made a good decision." Twitter, August 28, 2012, 7:54 a.m., https://twitter.com/realDonaldTrump/status/240462265680289792.

45 **"sue her plastic surgeon!":** Donald Trump (@realDonaldTrump), "I'm having a real hard time watching the Academy Awards (so far). The last song was terrible! Kim should sue her plastic surgeon! #Oscars." Twitter, March 2, 2014, 6:30 p.m., https://twitter.com /realDonaldTrump/status/440313189062823937.

45 **The retort cut Novak so deeply she didn't leave her house for days:** Barbaro, "Pithy, Mean and Powerful."

45 **almost 93 percent of employee political donations went to Democratic candidates in 2016:** "Twitter Profile: Recipients," OpenSecrets, https://www.opensecrets.org/orgs /twitter/recipients?toprecipscycle=2022&id=D000067113&candscycle=2016.

45 **set public hiring goals to diversify the company's workforce:** Jeffrey Siminoff, "Building a More Inclusive Twitter in 2016," *Twitter Blog*, Twitter, January 19, 2017, https://blog.twitter.com/en_us/topics/company/2017/building-a-more-inclusive-twitter-in -2016.

46 **"I'm [for] traditional marriage":** "Donald Trump on CNN's State of the Union," *CNN Pressroom* (blog), June 28, 2015, https://cnnpressroom.blogs.cnn.com/2015/06/28/donald -trump-on-cnns-state-of-the-union-im-in-it-to-win-it-i-will-make-our-country-great-again/.

46 **"Freedom of expression . . . are afraid to speak up":** Vijaya Gadde, "Twitter Executive: Here's How We're Trying to Stop Abuse While Preserving Free Speech," *Washington Post*, April 16, 2015, https://www.washingtonpost.com/posteverything/wp /2015/04/16/twitter-executive-heres-how-were-trying-to-stop-abuse-while-preserving -free-speech/.

47 **began selling them for over $1 million to major advertisers:** Lauren Johnson, "Twitter's Branded Emojis Come with a Million-Dollar Commitment," *Adweek*, February 2, 2016, https://www.adweek.com/performance-marketing/twitters-branded -emojis-come-million-dollar-commitment-169327/.

48 **"Sure, it was more aggressive . . . but that was the goal":** Gary Coby, "A Call with Jack: How Twitter CEO, Jack Dorsey, Restricted Advertising for Trump's Campaign," Medium, November 18, 2016, https://medium.com/@garycoby/twitter-restricts-trump -eb7e48ccf5ff.

48 **According to Coby . . . pulled the ad campaign entirely:** Coby.

49 **"We told them it was BS . . . was just insulting":** Coby.

51 **"The conference table," he said, "was only so big":** Nancy Scola, "Source: Twitter Cut Out of Trump Tech Meeting over Failed Emoji Deal," *Politico*, December 14, 2016, https://www.politico.com/story/2016/12/donald-trump-twitter-emoji-crooked-hillary -232647.

51 **Trump entered the White House as the most politically polarizing president in decades:** "How America Changed During Donald Trump's Presidency," Pew Research Center, January 29, 2021, https://www.pewresearch.org/2021/01/29/how-america -changed-during-donald-trumps-presidency/.

51 **Trump said there were "very fine people on both sides" of the incident:** Glenn Thrush and Maggie Haberman, "Trump Gives White Supremacists an Unequivocal Boost," *New York Times*, August 15, 2017, https://www.nytimes.com/2017/08/15/us /politics/trump-charlottesville-white-nationalists.html.

51 **earned a tweet of praise from David Duke:** David Duke (@DrDavidDuke), "Thank you President Trump for your honesty & courage to tell the truth about #Charlottesville & condemn the leftist terrorists in BLM/Antifa." Twitter, August 15, 2017, 1:45 p.m., https://twitter.com/DrDavidDuke/status/897559892164304896.

51 **He tweeted that mainstream media outlets like *The New York Times* and *CNN* were "the enemy of the American People!"** Donald Trump (@realDonaldTrump), "The FAKE NEWS media (failing @nytimes, @NBCNews, @ABC, @CBS, @CNN) is not my enemy, it is the enemy of the American People!" Twitter, February 17, 2017, 1:48 p.m., https://twitter.com/realDonaldTrump/status/832708293516632065.

51 **claiming that they would be a "burden":** Donald Trump (@realDonaldTrump), ". . . victory and cannot be burdened with the tremendous medical costs and disruption that transgender in the military would entail. Thank you." Twitter, July 26, 2017, 6:08 a.m., https://twitter.com/realDonaldTrump/status/890197095151546369.

51 **Russian propaganda firm . . . Trump's sons and other members of his campaign staff:** Robert S. Mueller, *Report on the Investigation into Russian Interference in the 2016 Presidential Election*, U.S. Department of Justice, March 2019, https://www.justice .gov/archives/sco/file/1373816/download.

52 **Warner was none too pleased . . . "how serious this issue is":** Tony Romm, "A Top Democratic Senator Briefed by Twitter on Russia and the 2016 Election Called the Company's Explanation 'Frankly Inadequate,'" Recode, September 28, 2017, https:// www.vox.com/2017/9/28/16381296/senate-congress-warner-twitter-russia-fake-news -2016-election.

52 **"predicting and designing for catastrophes":** Kashmir Hill, "Meet Del Harvey, Twitter's Troll Patrol," *Forbes*, July 20, 2014, https://www.forbes.com/sites/kashmirhill /2014/07/02/meet-del-harvey-twitters-troll-patrol/?sh=2de93d1232da.

53 **"free speech wing of the free speech party":** Amir Efrati, "Twitter CEO Costolo on Apple, Privacy, Free Speech and Google; Far from IPO," *Wall Street Journal*, October 18, 2011, https://www.wsj.com/articles/BL-DGB-23367.

53 **"gives you a voice and gives you a community and gives you power":** Kurt Wagner, "Twitter's Top Lawyer Is Final Word on Blocking Tweets—Even Donald Trump's," Bloomberg, January 15, 2020, https://www.bloomberg.com/news/articles/2020-01-15 /twitter-s-gadde-is-final-word-on-blocking-tweets-even-trump-s?sref=dZ65CIng.

54 **"I believe it's really important . . . don't think that's good for anyone":** Kurt Wagner, "Twitter CEO Jack Dorsey Wants Donald Trump to Keep Tweeting," Recode, May 11, 2017, https://www.vox.com/2017/5/11/15624874/president-donald-trump-twitter-jack -dorsey-tweet.

54 **"Just heard Foreign Minister . . . they won't be around much longer!":** Donald Trump (@realDonaldTrump), "Just heard Foreign Minister of North Korea speak at U.N. If he echoes thoughts of Little Rocket Man, they won't be around much longer!" Twitter, September 23, 2017, 8:08 p.m., https://twitter.com/realDonaldTrump/status /911789314169823232.

55 **Trump had threatened North Korea with "fire and fury":** Peter Baker and Choe Sang-Hun, "Trump Threatens 'Fire and Fury' Against North Korea If It Endangers U.S.," *New York Times*, August 8, 2017, https://www.nytimes.com/2017/08/08/world/asia /north-korea-un-sanctions-nuclear-missile-united-nations.html.

55 **North Korea's foreign minister called the post a "clear declaration of war":** Bill Chappell, "'Declaration of War' Means North Korea Can Shoot Down U.S. Bombers, Minister Says," NPR, September 25, 2017, https://www.npr.org/sections/thetwo-way/2017 /09/25/553475174/declaration-of-war-means-north-korea-can-shoot-down-u-s-bombers -minister-says.

CHAPTER 4: THE ROSE McGOWAN MEETING

56 **would later claim on Twitter that he'd raped her:** Ryan Parker and Chris Gardner, "Rose McGowan: Harvey Weinstein Raped Me," *Hollywood Reporter*, October 12, 2017, https://www.hollywoodreporter.com/news/general-news/rose-mcgowan-confirms-claim -harvey-weinstein-raped-me-1048343/.

57 **"TWITTER HAS SUSPENDED ME . . . BE MY VOICE":** Rose McGowan (@rosemcgowan), "TWITTER HAS SUSPENDED ME," Instagram, October 11, 2017, https://www.instagram.com/p/BaImG1Mle7b/.

57 **"Hey @Twitter . . . victims of sexual violence":** Jessica Chastain (@jes_chastain), "Hey @Twitter let us know which of these rules @rosemcgowan broke. Asking for multiple victims of sexual violence, https://support.twitter.com/articles/18311." Twitter, October 12, 2017, 5:21 a.m., https://twitter.com/jes_chastain/status/918451606030618624.

57 **"And now THIS . . . about sexual harassment":** Jamie Lee Curtis (jamieleecurtis), "And now THIS? You allow Twitter freedom to our president but you silence a woman speaking out about sexual harassment? @rosemcgowan." Twitter, October 12, 2017, 7:09 a.m., https://twitter.com/jamieleecurtis/status/918478792498208770.

57 **including the model Chrissy Teigen and actors Mark Ruffalo and Alyssa Milano:** Anna Codrea-Rado and Amie Tsang, "Twitter Users Split on Boycott over Platform's Move Against Rose McGowan," *New York Times*, October 13, 2017, https://www.nytimes.com/2017/10/13/technology/twitter-boycott-rose-mcgowan.html.

58 **"I've been DMing with @jack . . . does not seem to give a fuck":** Seth Rogen (@Sethrogen), "I've been DMing with @jack about his bizarre need to verify white supremacists on his platform for the last 8 months or so, and after all the exchanges, I've reached a conclusion: the dude simply does not seem to give a fuck." Twitter, July 3, 2018, 8:28 a.m., https://twitter.com/Sethrogen/status/1014168992376766470.

58 **According to Rogen . . . "When people are saying Twitter is a cesspool—that's you":** Seth Rogen, "Verification," in *Yearbook* (New York: Crown, 2021), 206–15.

59 **A study conducted that year . . . twice as many abusive tweets as white women:** "Troll Patrol Findings," Troll Patrol Report, 2018, https://decoders.amnesty.org/projects/troll-patrol/findings.

59 **"crazed, crying lowlife" and "that dog":** Donald Trump (@realDonaldTrump), "When you give a crazed, crying lowlife a break, and give her a job at the White House, I guess it just didn't work out. Good work by General Kelly for quickly firing that dog!" Twitter, August 14, 2018, 4:31 a.m., https://twitter.com/realDonaldTrump/status/1029329583672307712.

60 **the company planned to crack down . . . instead of a temporary suspension:** Erin Griffith, "Here Are Twitter's Latest Rules for Fighting Hate and Abuse," Wired, October 17, 2017, https://www.wired.com/story/here-are-twitters-latest-rules-for-fighting-hate-and-abuse/.

60 **"We see voices being silenced on Twitter every day":** Jack Dorsey (@jack), "1/ We see voices being silenced on Twitter every day. We've been working to counteract this for the past 2 years." Twitter, October 13, 2017, 7:35 p.m., https://twitter.com/jack/status/919028949434241024.

60 **"Today we saw voices silencing themselves and voices speaking out because we're *still* not doing enough":** Jack Dorsey (@jack), "4/ Today we saw voices silencing themselves and voices speaking out because we're *still* not doing enough." Twitter, October 13, 2017, 7:35 p.m., https://twitter.com/jack/status/919028953284673536.

60 **"We decided to take a more aggressive stance in our rules and how we enforce them":** Jack Dorsey (@jack), "6/ We decided to take a more aggressive stance in our rules and how we enforce them." Twitter, October 13, 2017, 7:35 p.m., https://twitter.com/jack/status/919028955226636288.

60 **"spent the whole day working on it and wanted to announce as soon as we were ready":** Jack Dorsey (@jack), "Because we spent the whole day working on it and wanted to announce as soon as we were ready." Twitter, October 13, 2017, 9:50 p.m., https://twitter.com/jack/status/919062878103023618?s=20.

61 **"a Twitter customer support employee who did this on the employee's last day":** TwitterGov (@TwitterGov), "Through our investigation we have learned that this was

done by a Twitter customer support employee who did this on the employee's last day. We are conducting a full internal review." Twitter, November 2, 2017, 7:00 p.m., https://twitter.com/TwitterGov/status/926267806261407744.

61 **"Just gonna say it . . . the Nobel Peace Prize":** David Jolly (@DavidJollyFL), "Just gonna say it, the employee at Twitter who shut off Trump's account for 11 mins could become a candidate for the Nobel Peace Prize." Twitter, November 2, 2017, 6:19 p.m., https://twitter.com/DavidJollyFL/status/926257441817415685.

61 **"How do i tell my parents im marrying the twitter employee":** Sarah Hagi (@geekylonglegs), "how do i tell my parents im marrying the twitter employee?" Twitter, November 2, 2017, 7:36 p.m., https://twitter.com/geekylonglegs/status/926276751323430913.

62 **"I love America":** Ingrid Lunden and Khaled "Tito" Hamze, "Meet the Man Who Deactivated Trump's Twitter Account," TechCrunch, November 29, 2017, https://techcrunch.com/2017/11/29/meet-the-man-who-deactivated-trumps-twitter-account/.

62 **"My Twitter account . . . having an impact":** Donald Trump (@realDonaldTrump), "My Twitter account was taken down for 11 minutes by a rogue employee. I guess the word must finally be getting out-and having an impact." Twitter, November 3, 2017, 3:51 a.m., https://twitter.com/realDonaldTrump/status/926401530013642765.

62 **Amazon paid $50 million:** Nick Wingfield, "Amazon Will Stream N.F.L.'s Thursday Night Games," *New York Times*, April 4, 2017, https://www.nytimes.com/2017/04/04/business/media/amazon-stream-nfl-thursday-night-football.html.

63 **"North Korean Leader . . . and my Button works!":** Donald Trump (@realDonaldTrump), "North Korean Leader Kim Jong Un just stated that the 'Nuclear Button is on his desk at all times,' Will someone from his depleted and food starved regime please inform him that I too have a Nuclear Button, but it is a much bigger & more powerful one than his, and my Button works!" Twitter, January 2, 2018, 4:49 p.m., https://twitter.com/realDonaldTrump/status/948355557022420992.

63 **"There's been a lot . . . around their words and actions":** "World Leaders on Twitter," *Twitter Blog*, Twitter, January 5, 2018, https://blog.twitter.com/en_us/topics/company/2018/world-leaders-and-twitter.

CHAPTER 5: #ONETEAM, PT. I

64 **Jack Dorsey sat on the floor with his legs crossed and his back straight:** Leslie Berland (@leslieberland), "@jack #oneteam." Twitter, July 31, 2018, 11:18 a.m., https://twitter.com/leslieberland/status/1024358637999779840.

64 **"salt juice," sunshine, and movement:** Candi Castleberry (@candi), "10 min meditation with @Jack In the first 30 min of the day . . .1) Water w/lemon and salt 2) Sunshine 3) Get moving 4) Gratitude and 3) a WIN. #PrettyAwesome CEO #OneTeam." Twitter, July 31, 2018, 9:59 p.m., https://twitter.com/Candi/status/1024519975195697152.

65 **off the stage well before 10 a.m.:** Victoria Najjar (@victorianajjar), "Thank you @jayrock for opening up the day! @jack was really hoping you'd sing along! #OneTeam." Twitter, July 31, 2018, 9:32 a.m., https://twitter.com/victorianajjar/status/1024332091641585664.

67 **"In all my time . . . after #OneTeam":** Del Harvey (@delbius), "In all my time at @Twitter, I'm not sure I've ever seen folks so energetic, enthusiastic, & ready to collaborate as after #OneTeam. Also glad I was able to finally meet some tweeps I've worked with for years in person! Safe travels to all heading home. [GT]." Twitter, August 3, 2018, 3:17 p.m., https://twitter.com/delbius/status/1025505873215479808.

68 **"It's been super-hard . . . mental scar tissue here":** Tom Randall, "'The Last Bet-the-Company Situation': Q&A With Elon Musk," Bloomberg, July 13, 2018, https://www.bloomberg.com/news/features/2018-07-13/-the-last-bet-the-company-situation-q-amp-a-with-elon-musk?sref=dZ65CIng.

68   **He promised Musk would come back some other time:** Jon Carmichael, "Jack Dorsey
     Commentary on Jon Carmichael Eclipse Photograph—Full Version," YouTube, 2021,
     https://www.youtube.com/watch?v=2SfPogWOu9k.

CHAPTER 6: AFRICA

71   **Grover Norquist . . . Greta Van Susteren:** Tony Romm, "Inside Facebook and Twitter's
     Secret Meetings with Trump Aides and Conservative Leaders Who Say Tech Is Biased,"
     Washington Post, June 27, 2018, https://www.washingtonpost.com/technology/2018/06
     /27/inside-facebook-twitters-secret-meetings-with-trump-aides-conservative-leaders
     -who-say-tech-is-biased/.

71   **reviewing research proposals to figure out if that idea was even possible:** Jack
     Dorsey (@jack), "Recently we were asked a simple question: could we measure the
     'health' of conversation on Twitter? This felt immediately tangible as it spoke to
     understanding a holistic system rather than just the problematic parts." Twitter, March 1,
     2018, 7:33 a.m., https://twitter.com/jack/status/969234282706169856.

72   **"troll-like behaviors that distort and detract from the public conversation":** Del
     Harvey and David Gasca, "Serving Healthy Conversation," *Twitter Blog*, Twitter,
     May 15, 2018, https://blog.twitter.com/en_us/topics/product/2018/Serving_Healthy
     _Conversation.

72   **Twitter had blocked an anti-abortion video ad from Republican Senate candidate
     Marsha Blackburn:** Hayley Tsukayama, "Twitter Blocked a Congresswoman's
     Antiabortion Ad over 'Baby Body Parts.' But It Allowed an Identical Tweet,"
     Washington Post, October 10, 2017, https://www.washingtonpost.com/news/the-switch
     /wp/2017/10/10/twitter-blocked-a-congresswomans-antiabortion-ad-over-baby-body
     -parts-but-it-allowed-an-identical-tweet/.

72   **Stone threatened to sue:** Jon Levine, "Roger Stone Says He Will Sue Twitter Over
     Account Suspension (Exclusive)," TheWrap, October 29, 2017, https://www.thewrap.com
     /exclusive-roger-stone-says-he-will-sue-twitter/.

72   **"Thank you, @jack . . . step one is actually talking":** Guy Benson (@guypbenson),
     "Thank you, @jack, for meeting with a group of conservatives in DC tonight. Much
     work must be done to build and rebuild trust — as we discussed at length — but step
     one is actually talking. Appreciate it, sir." Twitter, June 19, 2018, 6:40 p.m. https://
     twitter.com/guypbenson/status/1009249487511080961.

73   **He also exchanged private messages with Ali Alexander:** Kirsten Grind and
     John D. McKinnon, "Facebook, Twitter Turn to Right-Leaning Groups to Help Referee
     Political Speech," *Wall Street Journal*, January 8, 2019, https://www.wsj.com/articles
     /facebook-twitter-solicit-outside-groups-often-on-the-right-to-referee-political-speech
     -11546966779?mod=hp_lead_pos5.

73   **had been with Kanye West when he made comments to TMZ about slavery being
     a "choice":** Sean Rossman, "Candace Owens' Rapid Rise Defending Two of America's
     Most Complicated Men: Trump and Kanye," *USA Today*, October 19, 2018, https://www
     .usatoday.com/story/news/investigations/2018/10/19/candace-owens-found-her-place
     -conservative-politics-age-donald-trump-alongside-kanye/1521771002/.

73   **had even met with the president in the Oval Office just a few weeks before meeting
     with Dorsey:** Jonathan Swan, "Trump Huddles with Charlie Kirk and Candace Owens,"
     Axios, May 25, 2018, https://www.axios.com/2018/05/25/trump-huddles-with-charlie
     -kirk-and-candace-owens.

73   **His father was a Republican, his mother was a Democrat, and Dorsey identified
     "somewhere in the middle":** Joe Rogan, interview with Jack Dorsey, *The Joe Rogan
     Experience*, #1236, podcast audio, February 2, 2019, https://www.jrepodcast.com
     /episode/joe-rogan-experience-1236-jack-dorsey/.

74 **guests had to cover their phone's camera with a sticker:** Guy Trebay, "The San Vicente Bungalows: Hollywood's New Clubhouse," *New York Times*, February 23, 2019, https://www.nytimes.com/2019/02/23/style/san-vicente-bungalows-jeff-klein.html.

74 **bought Jay-Z's struggling music streaming service, Tidal, for $297 million:** Kurt Wagner and Lucas Shaw, "Square to Buy Jay-Z's Music Service Tidal, Appoint Him to Board," Bloomberg, March 4, 2021, https://www.bloomberg.com/news/articles/2021-03-04/square-to-buy-music-service-tidal-make-jay-z-a-board-member?sref=dZ65CIng.

74 **attended the rapper's birthday party in Los Angeles:** Emma Stefansky, "Rick and Morty, a Mountain Cake, and Jack Dorsey: Inside Kanye West's 41st Birthday Party," *Vanity Fair*, June 10, 2018, https://www.vanityfair.com/style/2018/06/kanye-west-41-birthday-party-kim-kardashian.

74 **tweeted the link with a single-word review—"wow":** Jack Dorsey (@jack), "Wow." Twitter, June 1, 2018, 10:45 p.m., https://twitter.com/jack/status/1002788214518657024.

74 **"I personally have not . . . to naturally lean towards":** Peter Kafka, "Twitter CEO Jack Dorsey Talked to NYU's Jay Rosen for an Hour, on the Record," Recode, September 14, 2018, https://www.vox.com/2018/9/14/17857486/twitter-jack-dorsey-nyu-jay-rosen-bias-neutrality-presence-politics-recode-media-podcast.

75 **were not appearing in search results on Twitter:** Bryan Menegus and Tom McKay, "Twitter May Be Demoting Controversial Accounts in Search Results," Gizmodo, July 22, 2018, https://gizmodo.com/twitter-may-be-demoting-controversial-accounts-in-searc-1827788070.

75 **Twitter was "shadow banning" Republican politicians:** Alex Thompson, "Twitter Appears to Have Fixed 'Shadow Ban' of Prominent Republicans like the RNC Chair and Trump Jr.'s Spokesman," VICE, July 25, 2018, https://www.vice.com/en/article/43paqq/twitter-is-shadow-banning-prominent-republicans-like-the-rnc-chair-and-trump-jrs-spokesman.

75 **"Twitter 'SHADOW BANNING' . . . Many complaints":** Donald Trump (@realDonaldTrump), "Twitter 'SHADOW BANNING' prominent Republicans. Not good. We will look into this discriminatory and illegal practice at once! Many complaints." Twitter, July 26, 2018, 4:46 a.m., https://twitter.com/realDonaldTrump/status/1022447980408983552.

75 **"What Is a 'Shadow Ban,' and Is Twitter Doing It to Republican Accounts?":** Liam Stack, "What Is a 'Shadow Ban,' and Is Twitter Doing It to Republican Accounts?" *New York Times*, July 26, 2018, https://www.nytimes.com/2018/07/26/us/politics/twitter-shadowbanning.html.

75 **"We do not shadow ban . . . viewpoints or ideology":** Vijaya Gadde and Kayvon Beykpour, "Setting the Record Straight on Shadow Banning," *Twitter Blog*, Twitter, July 26, 2018, https://blog.twitter.com/en_us/topics/company/2018/Setting-the-record-straight-on-shadow-banning.

76 **violated Twitter's policy against inciting people to violence:** Cecilia Kang and Kate Conger, "Twitter Suspends Alex Jones and Infowars for Seven Days," *New York Times*, August 14, 2018, https://www.nytimes.com/2018/08/14/technology/twitter-alex-jones-suspension.html.

76 **"Social Media is totally discriminating . . . many people on the RIGHT":** Donald Trump (@realDonaldTrump), "Social Media is totally discriminating against Republican/Conservative voices. Speaking loudly and clearly for the Trump Administration, we won't let that happen. They are closing down the opinions of many people on the RIGHT, while at the same time doing nothing to others. . . ." Twitter, August 18, 2018, 4:23 a.m., https://twitter.com/realDonaldTrump/status/1030777074959757313.

76 **tweeted it out right then and there:** Jack Dorsey (@jack), "Thank you Chairman Walden, Ranking Member Pallone, and the committee, for the opportunity to speak on behalf of Twitter to the American people. I look forward to our conversation about our

commitment to impartiality, transparency, and accountability." Twitter, September 5, 2018,10:56 a.m., https://twitter.com/jack/status/1037399063447121922.

78   **had been largely killed and displaced over years of conflict with the country's majority Buddhist population, including the Myanmar military:** Megan Specia, "The Rohingya in Myanmar: How Years of Strife Grew Into a Crisis," *New York Times*, September 13, 2017, https://www.nytimes.com/2017/09/13/world/asia/myanmar-rohingya-muslim.html.

79   **"Meditation is often . . . physical and mental work":** Jack Dorsey (@jack), "Meditation is often thought of as calming, relaxing, and a detox of all the noise in the world. That's not vipassana. It's extremely painful and demanding physical and mental work. I wasn't expecting any of that my first time last year. Even tougher this year as I went deeper." Twitter, December 8, 2018, 5:19 p.m., https://twitter.com/jack/status/1071575105065500672.

79   **Students weren't even supposed to make eye contact with each other:** Jack Dorsey (@jack), "I did my meditation at Dhamma Mahimā in Pyin Oo Lwin. This is my room. Basic. During the 10 days: no devices, reading, writing, physical exercise, music, intoxicants, meat, talking, or even eye contact with others. It's free: everything is given to meditators by charity." Twitter, December 8, 2018, 5:19 p.m., https://twitter.com/jack/status/1071575116796973056.

79   **got 117 mosquito bites before the lights mercifully blew a fuse:** Jack Dorsey (@jack), "We also meditated in a cave in Mandalay one evening. In the first 10 minutes I got bit 117 times by mosquitoes. They left me alone when the light blew a fuse, which you can see in my heart rate lowering." Twitter, December 8, 2018, 5:21 p.m., https://twitter.com/jack/status/1071575413804064768.

79   *The New York Times* **called Dorsey "Gwyneth Paltrow for Silicon Valley":** Nellie Bowles, "Jack Dorsey Is Gwyneth Paltrow for Silicon Valley," *New York Times*, May 2, 2019, https://www.nytimes.com/2019/05/02/fashion/jack-dorsey-influencer.html?smid=tw-nytstyles&smtyp=cur.

80   **"I mean, nothing has given me more mental confidence than being able to go straight from room temperature into the cold":** Ben Greenfield and Jack Dorsey, "The Jack Dorsey Podcast: Advanced Stress Mitigation Tactics, Extreme Time-Saving Workouts, DIY Cold Tubs, Hormesis, One-Meal-A-Day & More," Ben Greenfield Life, March 16, 2019, https://bengreenfieldlife.com/podcast/time-saving-workouts/.

81   *Vanity Fair* **joked that running product at Twitter was "cursed":** Abigail Tracy, "Twitter's Cursed Head-of-Product Role Claims Another Victim," *Vanity Fair*, June 7, 2016, https://www.vanityfair.com/news/2016/06/twitter-head-of-product-jeff-seibert.

81   **spent years micromanaging the project and pushing executives on an ever-competitive timeline:** Brad Stone, "The Secret Origins of Amazon's Alexa," *Wired*, May 11, 2021, https://www.wired.com/story/how-amazon-made-alexa-smarter/.

81   **"If I have to make a decision . . . empowered to make a decision":** Mella TV, *Mella Special featuring Jack Dorsey: founder and CEO of Twitter*, YouTube, 2020, https://www.youtube.com/watch?v=nN3aTTHL1c4.

82   **launched a new camera feature:** Edgar Alvarez, "Twitter's Revamped Camera Is Its Answer to Stories," Engadget, March 13, 2019, https://www.engadget.com/2019-03-13-twitter-camera-redesign-snapchat-instagram-stories.html.

82   **It also rolled out a separate app, called "twttr":** Sarah Perez, "Twitter's New Prototype App 'TWTTR' Launches Today," TechCrunch, March 11, 2019, https://techcrunch.com/2019/03/11/twitters-new-prototype-app-twttr-launches-today/.

83   **"The conversation will come to you":** "Product Introducing Topics," *Twitter Blog*, Twitter, November 11, 2019, https://blog.twitter.com/en_us/topics/product/2019/introducing-topics.

84 **either by limiting them or purposefully removing them:** Tony Romm, "Trump Met with Twitter CEO Jack Dorsey—and Complained about His Follower Count," *Washington Post*, April 23, 2019, https://www.washingtonpost.com /technology/2019/04/23/trump-meets-with-twitter-ceo-jack-dorsey-white-house/.

84 **"Great meeting this afternoon . . . keeping an open dialogue!":** Donald Trump (@ realDonaldTrump), "Great meeting this afternoon at the @WhiteHouse with @Jack from @Twitter. Lots of subjects discussed regarding their platform, and the world of social media in general. Look forward to keeping an open dialogue!" Twitter, April 23, 2019, 1:54 p.m., https://twitter.com/realDonaldTrump/status/1120793199650463747.

85 **"Social Media & Fake News Media . . . VERY UNFAIR!":** Donald Trump (@ realDonaldTrump), "How can it be possible that James Woods (and many others), a strong but responsible Conservative Voice, is banned from Twitter? Social Media & Fake News Media, together with their partner, the Democrat Party, have no idea the problems they are causing for themselves. VERY UNFAIR!" Twitter, May 4, 2019, 11:31 a.m., https://twitter.com/realDonaldTrump/status/1124743267873116160.

85 **attended Paris Fashion Week, sitting in the front row at a show for one of his favorite designers:** Rachel Tashjian, "What Was Jack Dorsey Doing at Paris Fashion Week?" *GQ*, June 28, 2019, https://www.gq.com/story/fashion-news-6-28-19.

85 **two talked about eliminating terrorist content from social media:** Derek Cheng, "Twitter Boss Jack Dorsey Meets Jacinda Ardern at the Beehive," NZ Herald, September 8, 2019, https://www.nzherald.co.nz/nz/twitter-boss-jack-dorsey-meets-jacinda-ardern-at -the-beehive/CGMBFTCY2O3QKS2WC2HBKVIYHE/.

86 **the issues would continue to hurt revenue during the holiday quarter:** Sara Salinas, "Twitter Stock Plunges as Company Blames Ad Targeting Problems for Earnings Miss," CNBC, October 24, 2019, https://www.cnbc.com/2019/10/24/twitter-twtr-earnings-q3 -2019.html.

87 **Twitter stock fell 4 percent on the news:** Kurt Wagner and Ben Brody, "Twitter CEO Dorsey Bans Political Ads in Swipe at Facebook," Bloomberg, October 30, 2019, https:// www.bloomberg.com/news/articles/2019-10-30/twitter-to-ban-political-advertising -globally-ceo-dorsey-says?sref=dZ65CIng.

87 **Sub-Saharan Africa had a population of over 1 billion people, which was about the size of the U.S. and Europe combined:** Population Facts, United Nations Department of Economic and Social Affairs, December 2019, https://www.un.org/en/development /desa/population/publications/pdf/popfacts/PopFacts_2019-6.pdf.

87 **They met with Ngozi Okonjo-Iweala:** Ngozi Okonjo-Iweala, "Great to welcome Jack Dorsey and the fantastic Twitter team Parag, Kayvon, TJ, Michael, Sierra, to Nigeria and Africa for their first visit to discuss entrepreneurship and how the Twitter platform can help young people create digital jobs." Facebook, November 11, 2019, https://www .facebook.com/NgoziOkonjoIweala/posts/2730637583653155/.

88 **Twitter announced plans to fund a small independent group:** Jack Dorsey (@jack), "Twitter is funding a small independent team of up to five open source architects, engineers, and designers to develop an open and decentralized standard for social media. The goal is for Twitter to ultimately be a client of this standard." Twitter, December 11, 2019, 6:13 a.m., https://twitter.com/jack/status/1204766078468911106.

88 **"If you wanna feel it . . . instrument of currency":** "Twitter CEO Jack Dorsey Reacts to GOT7 & Meditating with Spiders," YouTube, *The CouRage and Nadeshot Show*, 2020, https://www.youtube.com/watch?v=A12wAWyaR1s.

88 **"Sad to be leaving the continent . . . experience a small part":** Jack Dorsey (@jack), "Sad to be leaving the continent . . . for now. Africa will define the future (especially the bitcoin one!). Not sure where yet, but I'll be living here for 3-6 months mid 2020. Grateful I was able to experience a small part." Twitter, November 27, 2019, 11:39 a.m., https://twitter.com/jack/status/1199774792917929984.

CHAPTER 7: #ONETEAM, PT. II

91 **announcing the party in a video recorded by three astronauts floating inside the International Space Station:** Shefali Shah Mirakhur (@shahsr), "Best party invite. Ever. @TwitterOneTeam." Twitter, January 14, 2020, 3:11 p.m., https://twitter.com/shahsr/status/1217222720972378112.

91 **Apple hired Lady Gaga:** Raymond Wong, "Lady Gaga Performed Private Apple Concert as a Tribute to Steve Jobs," Mashable SE Asia, May 19, 2019, https://sea.mashable.com/tech/3879/lady-gaga-performed-private-apple-concert-as-a-tribute-to-steve-jobs.

91 **that featured an ice sculptor wielding a chain saw:** Arielle Pardes and Annie Goldsmith, "The Buzz Is Gone: Tech Companies (with a Few Exceptions) Are Reining in Once-Legendary Holiday Parties," The Information, December 16, 2022, https://www.theinformation.com/articles/the-buzz-is-gone-tech-companies-with-a-few-exceptions-are-reining-in-once-legendary-holiday-parties.

91 **"Are we all experiencing delayed side effects of the salt juice?":** Andy (@andysaurusrex), "Are we all experiencing delayed side effects of the salt juice? #OneTeam." Twitter, January 14, 2020, 8:38 a.m., https://twitter.com/andysaurusrex/status/1217123748098297856.

92 **kidnapped by the Islamic terrorist group Boko Haram in 2014:** Aanu Adeoye and Bukola Adebayo, "Bring Back Our Girls Activist Oby Ezekwesili Vows to Disrupt 'Nigeria's Politics of Failure,'" CNN, November 22, 2018, https://www.cnn.com/2018/11/22/africa/nigeria-oby-ezekwesili-politics/index.html.

92 **John Legend's "filthy mouthed wife":** Donald Trump (@realDonaldTrump), ". . . musician @johnlegend, and his filthy mouthed wife, are talking now about how great it is - but I didn't see them around when we needed help getting it passed. 'Anchor' @LesterHoltNBC doesn't even bring up the subject of President Trump or the Republicans when talking about . . ." Twitter, September 8, 2019, 8:11 p.m., https://twitter.com/realDonaldTrump/status/1170897586364006405.

92 **"lol what a pussy ass bitch. tagged everyone but me. an honor, mister president":** Chrissy Teigen (@chrissyteigen), "lol what a pussy ass bitch. tagged everyone but me. an honor, mister president." Twitter, September 8, 2019, 9:17 p.m., https://twitter.com/chrissyteigen/status/1170914148919590914.

92 **the White House had reached out to Twitter asking the company to remove the tweet:** Bess Levin, "Yes, the Trump White House Demanded Twitter Remove Chrissy Teigen's Tweet Calling Trump a 'Pussy Ass Bitch,'" Vanity Fair, February 8, 2023, https://www.vanityfair.com/news/2023/02/chrissy-teigen-donald-trump-tweet-removed.

93 **Musk was sued by a British cave diver:** Edvard Pettersson and Dana Hull, "Musk Says 'Pedo Guy' Tweet Was Response to Unprovoked Attack," Bloomberg, December 3, 2019, https://www.bloomberg.com/news/articles/2019-12-03/elon-musk-was-hurt-by-caver-s-p-r-stunt-insult-lawyer-says?sref=dZ65CIng.

93 **the SEC sued him, claiming Musk knowingly made "false and misleading statements":** Dana Hull and Benjamin Bain, "Elon Musk Can Stay Tesla CEO, but Not Chairman, Under SEC Settlement," Bloomberg, September 29, 2018, https://www.bloomberg.com/news/articles/2018-09-29/elon-musk-and-sec-reach-settlement-on-fraud-charges?sref=dZ65CIng.

93 **"Elon Musk is incredible . . . and see and understand":** "Twitter CEO Jack Dorsey Reacts to GOT7 & Meditating with Spiders," YouTube, The CouRage and Nadeshot Show, 2020, https://www.youtube.com/watch?v=A12wAWyaR1s.

93 **he was frequently trolled by Tesla short sellers on Twitter:** Dana Hull, "The Tesla Skeptics Who Bet Against Elon Musk," Bloomberg, January 22, 2020, https://www.bloomberg.com/news/features/2020-01-22/the-tesla-tslaq-skeptics-who-bet-against-elon-musk?sref=dZ65CIng.

111 **Governor Gavin Newsom issued a stay-at-home order:** Governor Gavin Newsom, Executive Order N-33-20, March 4, 2020, https://www.gov.ca.gov/wp-content/uploads /2020/03/EO-N-33-20-COVID-19-HEALTH-ORDER-03.19.2020-002.pdf.

111 **"The increased load . . . we're seeing on our service":** Vijaya Gadde and Matt Derella, "An Update on Our Continuity Strategy during COVID-19," *Twitter Blog*, Twitter, March 16, 2020, https://blog.twitter.com/en_us/topics/company/2020/An-update-on-our -continuity-strategy-during-COVID-19.

112 **which had hired third-party groups to help police certain posts:** Sara Fischer, "Exclusive: Facebook Adding Part-Time Fact-Checking Contractors," Axios, December 17, 2019, https://www.axios.com/2019/12/17/facebook-fact-checking-contractors.

112 **Twitter's Trust and Safety team . . . now considered a violation of Twitter's rules:** Gadde and Derella, "An Update on Our Continuity Strategy."

113 **"risks of harm associated with a Tweet are less severe":** Yoel Roth and Nick Pickles, "Updating Our Approach to Misleading Information," *Twitter Blog*, Twitter, May 11, 2020, https://blog.twitter.com/en_us/topics/product/2020/updating-our-approach-to -misleading-information.

114 **every registered voter in the state would automatically receive a mail-in ballot:** Musadiq Bidar, "Newsom Signs Executive Order Declaring California a Vote-by- Mail State," CBS News, May 9, 2020, https://www.cbsnews.com/news/newsom-signs -executive-order-declaring-california-a-vote-by-mail-state-2020-05-08/.

114 **Nevada did the same thing for its largest county, which included Las Vegas, ahead of its June primary election:** Elise Viebeck, "Mailing of Ballots to All Voters in Las Vegas Area Puts Sharp Focus on Election Safeguards," *Washington Post*, May 29, 2020, https://www.washingtonpost.com/politics/mailing-of-ballots-to-all-voters-in-las-vegas -area-puts-sharp-focus-on-election-safeguards/2020/05/28/912c099a-9f63-11ea-b5c9 -570a91917d8d_story.html.

114 **Michigan was also making it easier for voters to get a ballot in the mail:** Daniel Dale, Ryan Nobles, and Abby Phillip, "Fact Check: Trump Falsely Claims Michigan Sent Out Absentee Ballots and Broke the Law," CNN, May 20, 2020, https://www.cnn.com/2020 /05/20/politics/fact-check-trump-michigan-nevada-ballots-voting/index.html.

114 **"RIPE for FRAUD":** Donald Trump (@realDonaldTrump), "Absentee Ballots are a great way to vote for the many senior citizens, military, and others who can't get to the polls on Election Day. These ballots are very different from 100% Mail-In Voting, which is 'RIPE for FRAUD,' and shouldn't be allowed!" Twitter, April 8, 2020, 4:34 p.m., https://twitter.com/realDonaldTrump/status/1248031484532928514.

114 **suggesting that they favored Democrats over Republicans:** Donald Trump (@ realDonaldTrump), "Republicans should fight very hard when it comes to state wide mail-in voting. Democrats are clamoring for it. Tremendous potential for voter fraud, and for whatever reason, doesn't work out well for Republicans. @foxandfriends." Twitter, April 8, 2020, 5:20 a.m., https://twitter.com/realDonaldTrump/status /1247861952736526336.

114 **Trump threatened to withhold federal funding from the state:** Donald Trump (@ realDonaldTrump), "State of Nevada 'thinks' that they can send out illegal vote by mail ballots, creating a great Voter Fraud scenario for the State and the U.S. They can't! If they do, 'I think' I can hold up funds to the State. Sorry, but you must not cheat in elections. @RussVought45 @USTreasury." Twitter, May 20, 2020, 6:11 a.m., https:// twitter.com/realDonaldTrump/status/1263094958417985538.

114 **"greatest Rigged Election in history. People grab them from mailboxes, print thousands of forgeries and 'force' people to sign":** Donald Trump (@ realDonaldTrump), "The United States cannot have all Mail In Ballots. It will be the greatest Rigged Election in history. People grab them from mailboxes, print thousands of forgeries and 'force' people to sign. Also, forge names. Some absentee OK, when

necessary. Trying to use Covid for this Scam!" Twitter, May 24, 2020, 7:08 a.m., https://twitter.com/realDonaldTrump/status/1264558926021959680.

115 **The company had rules that forbade people from misleading someone about the logistics of voting:** Twitter Safety, "Strengthening Our Approach to Deliberate Attempts to Mislead Voters," *Twitter Blog*, Twitter, April 24, 2019, https://blog.twitter.com/en_us/topics/company/2019/strengthening-our-approach-to-deliberate-attempts-to-mislead-vot.

115 **"There is NO WAY . . . No way!":** Donald Trump (@realDonaldTrump), ". . . living in the state, no matter who they are or how they got there, will get one. That will be followed up with professionals telling all of these people, many of whom have never even thought of voting before, how, and for whom, to vote. This will be a Rigged Election. No way!" Twitter, May 26, 2020, 5:17 a.m., https://twitter.com/realDonaldTrump/status/1265255845358645254.

115 **California's new policy was to send ballots to every registered voter, not "anyone living in the state":** Ben Christopher, "California's (Mostly) All-Mail 2020 Election, Explained," CalMatters, June 25, 2020, https://calmatters.org/explainers/california-all-mail-election-explained-november-2020/.

115 **"Trump falsely claimed . . . linked to voter fraud":** Kurt Wagner and Alex Wayne, "Twitter Adds Fact-Check Label to Trump Tweets for First Time," Bloomberg, May 26, 2020, https://www.bloomberg.com/news/articles/2020-05-26/trump-s-tweets-on-mail-in-voting-fact-checked-by-twitter?sref=dZ65CIng.

116 **"@Twitter is now interfering in the 2020 Presidential Election":** Donald Trump (@realDonaldTrump), ".@Twitter is now interfering in the 2020 Presidential Election. They are saying my statement on Mail-In Ballots, which will lead to massive corruption and fraud, is incorrect, based on fact-checking by Fake News CNN and the Amazon Washington Post. . . ." Twitter, May 26, 2020, 4:40 p.m., https://twitter.com/realDonaldTrump/status/1265427538140188676.

116 **"Twitter is completely stifling FREE SPEECH, and I, as President, will not allow it to happen!":** Donald Trump (@realDonaldTrump), ". . . Twitter is completely stifling FREE SPEECH, and I, as President, will not allow it to happen!" Twitter, May 26, 2020, 4:40 p.m., https://twitter.com/realDonaldTrump/status/1265427539008380928.

116 **Trump issued an executive order:** Tony Romm and Elizabeth Dwoskin, "Trump Signs Order That Could Punish Social Media Companies for How They Police Content, Drawing Criticism and Doubts of Legality," *Washington Post*, May 28, 2020, https://www.washingtonpost.com/technology/2020/05/28/trump-social-media-executive-order/.

116 **"Somebody in San Francisco go wake him up and tell him he's about to get more followers":** Bobby Lewis (@revrrlewis), "On Fox & Friends, Kellyanne Conway appears to direct online harassment at Twitter's head of site integrity, Yoel Roth: 'Somebody in San Francisco will wake him up and tell him he's about to get a lot more followers.'" Twitter, May 27, 2020, 5:20 a.m., https://twitter.com/revrrlewis/status/1265618948726435842.

116 **ran a separate story that day highlighting all of the negative things Roth had tweeted:** Jason Lemon, "Twitter's Head of Site Integrity Compares Kellyanne Conway to Joseph Goebbels in Resurfaced Tweets: 'Actual Nazis in the White House,'" *Newsweek*, May 27, 2020, https://www.newsweek.com/twitters-head-site-integrity-compares-kellyanne-conway-joseph-goebbels-resurfaced-tweets-1506801.

116 **"personality-free bag of farts":** Gregg Re, "Twitter Exec in Charge of Effort to Fact-Check Trump Has History of Anti-Trump Posts, Called McConnell a 'Bag of Farts,'" Fox News, May 27, 2020, https://www.foxnews.com/politics/twitter-exec-in-charge-of-effort-to-fact-check-trump-has-history-of-anti-trump-posts-called-mcconnell-a-bag-of-farts.

116 **"So ridiculous . . . Tell that to your hater @yoyoel":** Donald Trump (@realDonaldTrump), "So ridiculous to see Twitter trying to make the case that Mail-In Ballots are not subject to FRAUD. How stupid, there are examples, & cases, all over the

place. Our election process will become badly tainted & a laughingstock all over the World. Tell that to your hater @yoyoel." Twitter, May 28, 2020, 9:44 a.m., https://twitter.com/realDonaldTrump/status/1266047584038256640.

117 **Tim Walz activated the National Guard:** Derrick Bryson Taylor, "George Floyd Protests: A Timeline," *New York Times*, November 5, 2021, https://www.nytimes.com/article/george-floyd-protests-timeline.html.

117 **"These THUGS . . . the shooting starts. Thank you!":** Donald Trump (@realDonaldTrump), "These THUGS are dishonoring the memory of George Floyd, and I won't let that happen. Just spoke to Governor Tim Walz and told him that the Military is with him all the way. Any difficulty and we will assume control but, when the looting starts, the shooting starts. Thank you!" Twitter, May 28, 2020, 9:53 p.m., https://twitter.com/realDonaldTrump/status/1266231100780744704.

117 **Dorsey was awake . . . share notes in real time:** Kate Conger, "Twitter Had Been Drawing a Line for Months When Trump Crossed It," *New York Times*, May 30, 2020, https://www.nytimes.com/2020/05/30/technology/twitter-trump-dorsey.html.

118 **"This Tweet violated . . . to remain accessible":** Nate Lanxon and Vlad Savov, "Twitter-Trump Tension Mounts on Warning Over Shooting Tweet," Bloomberg, May 29, 2020, https://www.bloomberg.com/news/articles/2020-05-29/twitter-trump-minneapolis-post-broke-rules-glorified-violence?sref=dZ65CIng.

120 **The vast majority of Twitter's revenue—roughly 85 percent—came from brand advertising:** "Twitter Analyst Day—Transcript," Twitter IR, Twitter, February 25, 2021, https://s22.q4cdn.com/826641620/files/doc_downloads/2021/02/Twitter-Analyst-Day-2021-Prepared-Remarks.pdf.

122 **The user base goal was pared back from around 365 million to 315 million:** Kurt Wagner, "Twitter Aims to Double Revenue in 3 Years; Shares Surge," Bloomberg, February 25, 2021, https://www.bloomberg.com/news/articles/2021-02-25/twitter-sets-target-to-double-annual-revenue-in-next-three-years?sref=dZ65CIng.

122 **Twitter's stock jumped 12 percent when they were eventually revealed at Analyst Day:** Kurt Wagner, "Twitter Aims to Double Revenue in 3 Years; Shares Surge," Bloomberg, February 25, 2021, https://www.bloomberg.com/news/articles/2021-02-25/twitter-sets-target-to-double-annual-revenue-in-next-three-years.

CHAPTER 10: BANNING TRUMP

123 **"Smoking-gun email reveals how Hunter Biden introduced Ukrainian businessman to VP dad":** Emma-Jo Morris and Gabrielle Fonrouge, "Smoking-Gun Email Reveals How Hunter Biden Introduced Ukrainian Businessman to VP Dad," *New York Post*, October 14, 2020, https://nypost.com/2020/10/14/email-reveals-how-hunter-biden-introduced-ukrainian-biz-man-to-dad/.

123 **"Congratulations to the @nypost . . . Disgraceful!":** Donald Trump (@realDonaldTrump), "Congratulations to the @nypost for having exposed the massive corruption surrounding Sleepy Joe Biden and our Country. He's always been a corrupt politician. Disgraceful!" Twitter, October 14, 2020, 8:22 p.m., https://twitter.com/realDonaldTrump/status/1316580278568022016.

124 **succeeding in getting thousands of emails from her campaign chairman, John Podesta:** Raphael Satter, Jeff Donn, and Chad Day, "How Russian Hackers Pried into Clinton Campaign Emails," Associated Press, November 4, 2017, https://apnews.com/article/moscow-north-america-ap-top-news-hillary-clinton-phishing-addc2727b0b04c1d80ab6ca30c4dc77e.

124 **"There was smoke . . . a hack and leak":** Knight Foundation, "Session 10—On with Kara Swisher, Yoel Roth and the Crisis at Twitter," Vimeo, 2022, https://vimeo.com/776426548.

124 **"As discussed . . . from being amplified":** Matt Taibbi (@mtaibbi), "26. By this point 'everyone knew this was fucked,' said one former employee, but the response was essentially to err on the side of . . . continuing to err." Twitter, December 2, 2022, 4:24 p.m., https://twitter.com/mtaibbi/status/1598835411262279680.

125 **"I'm struggling to understand the policy basis for marking this as unsafe":** Matt Taibbi (@mtaibbi), "25. You can see the confusion in the following lengthy exchange, which ends up including Gadde and former Trust and safety chief Yoel Roth. Comms official Trenton Kennedy writes, 'I'm struggling to understand the policy basis for marking this as unsafe.'" Twitter, December 2, 2022, 4:21 p.m., https://twitter.com/mtaibbi/status/1598834882414727168.

125 **"Can we truthfully claim that this is part of the policy?":** Matt Taibbi (@mtaibbi), "27. Former VP of Global Comms Brandon Borrman asks, 'Can we truthfully claim that this is part of the policy?'" Twitter, December, 2, 2022, 4:26 p.m., https://twitter.com/mtaibbi/status/1598836068282814464.

125 **they would be verified by security experts as legitimate:** Craig Timberg, Matt Viser, and Tom Hamburger, "Here's How the Post Analyzed Hunter Biden's Laptop," *Washington Post*, March 30, 2022, https://www.washingtonpost.com/technology/2022/03/30/hunter-biden-laptop-data-examined/.

125 **they wanted to haul Dorsey back to Washington:** Kurt Wagner, "Twitter Allows Links to N.Y. Post Story, Backtracking Again," Bloomberg, October 16, 2020, https://www.bloomberg.com/news/articles/2020-10-16/twitter-allows-links-to-n-y-post-story-backtracking-again?sref=dZ65CIng.

125 **"Content moderation is incredibly . . . along the way":** Vijaya Gadde (@vijaya), "I'm grateful for everyone who has provided feedback and insights over the past day. Content moderation is incredibly difficult, especially in the critical context of an election. We are trying to act responsibly & quickly to prevent harms, but we're still learning along the way." Twitter, October 15, 2020, 7:06 p.m., https://twitter.com/vijaya/status/1316923560175296514.

125 **"Straight blocking of URLs was wrong," he tweeted, "and we updated our policy and enforcement to fix":** Jack Dorsey (@jack), "Straight blocking of URLs was wrong, and we updated our policy and enforcement to fix. Our goal is to attempt to add context, and now we have capabilities to do that." Twitter, October 16, 2020, 5:35 a.m., https://twitter.com/jack/status/1317081843443912706.

126 **"The Committee expressed its confidence in management and recommended that the current structure remain in place":** Kurt Wagner and Scott Deveau, "Dorsey Keeps Twitter CEO Job on Elliott, Silver Lake Review," Bloomberg, November 2, 2020, https://www.bloomberg.com/news/articles/2020-11-02/twitter-s-jack-dorsey-to-keep-ceo-job-after-board-panel-review?sref=dZ65CIng.

127 **Twitter had labeled more than three hundred of the president's tweets:** Zeve Sanderson, Megan A. Brown, Richard Bonneau, Jonathan Nagler, and Joshua A. Tucker, "Twitter Flagged Donald Trump's Tweets with Election Misinformation: They Continued to Spread Both on and off the Platform," Misinformation Review, August 24, 2021, https://misinforeview.hks.harvard.edu/article/twitter-flagged-donald-trumps-tweets-with-election-misinformation-they-continued-to-spread-both-on-and-off-the-platform/.

127 **"This claim about election fraud is disputed":** Todd Spangler, "Twitter Has Flagged 200 of Trump's Posts as 'Disputed' or Misleading Since Election Day. Does It Make a Difference?" *Variety*, November 27, 2020, https://variety.com/2020/digital/news/twitter-trump-200-disputed-misleading-claims-election-1234841137/.

127 **"Every time I put out a tweet . . . Twitter's bad news":** Brian Naylor, "Read Trump's Jan. 6 Speech, a Key Part of Impeachment Trial," NPR, February 10, 2021, https://www.npr.org/2021/02/10/966396848/read-trumps-jan-6-speech-a-key-part-of-impeachment-trial.

129 **which forbade people from sharing "misleading information intended to undermine public confidence in an election":** "Civic Integrity Misleading Information Policy,"

Twitter Help Center, https://help.twitter.com/en/rules-and-policies/election-integrity-policy.

129 **A Capitol Police officer shot and killed one of the protesters:** Kat Lonsdorf, Courtney Dorning, Amy Isackson, Mary Louise Kelly, and Ailsa Chang, "A Timeline of How the Jan. 6 Attack Unfolded—Including Who Said What and When," NPR, June 9, 2022, https://www.npr.org/2022/01/05/1069977469/a-timeline-of-how-the-jan-6-attack-unfolded-including-who-said-what-and-when.

129 **"But you have to go home now . . . you're very special":** Donald Trump (@realDonaldTrump), "[Video]." Twitter, January 6, 2021, 1:17 p.m., https://twitter.com/realDonaldTrump/status/1346928882595885058.

129 **More than 150 police officers were injured in the attack:** Chris Cameron, "These Are the People Who Died in Connection with the Capitol Riot," *New York Times*, January 5, 2022, https://www.nytimes.com/2022/01/05/us/politics/jan-6-capitol-deaths.html.

130 **only accessible via the resort's own private air fleet:** "A World Away, Yet Well Within Reach," The Brando, https://thebrando.com/location/.

130 **"As a result . . . our Civic Integrity policy":** Twitter Safety (@TwitterSafety), "As a result of the unprecedented and ongoing violent situation in Washington, D.C., we have required the removal of three @realDonaldTrump Tweets that were posted earlier today for repeated and severe violations of our Civic Integrity policy." Twitter, January 6, 2021, 4:02 p.m., https://twitter.com/TwitterSafety/status/1346970430062485505.

130 **"Future violations of the Twitter Rules . . . @realDonaldTrump account":** Twitter Safety (@TwitterSafety), "Future violations of the Twitter Rules, including our Civic Integrity or Violent Threats policies, will result in permanent suspension of the @realDonaldTrump account." Twitter, January 6, 2021, 4:02 p.m., https://twitter.com/TwitterSafety/status/1346970432017031178.

131 **"For the last four years . . . shared by @realDonaldTrump":** "Letter to Jack Dorsey from Twitter Employees Asking to Permanently Suspend Donald Trump's Account," *Washington Post*, January 8, 2021, https://www.washingtonpost.com/context/letter-to-jack-dorsey-from-twitter-employees-asking-to-permanently-suspend-donald-trump-s-account/d9b84fa1-c7cb-4c5b-a90a-fdf167ff0c7a/.

131 **"ensuring a smooth, orderly and seamless transition of power":** Donald Trump (@realDonaldTrump), "[Video]." Twitter, January 7, 2021, 4:10 p.m., https://twitter.com/realDonaldTrump/status/1347334804052844550.

131 **"The 75,000,000 . . . shape or form!!!":** Donald Trump (@realDonaldTrump), "The 75,000,000 great American Patriots who voted for me, AMERICA FIRST, and MAKE AMERICA GREAT AGAIN, will have a GIANT VOICE long into the future. They will not be disrespected or treated unfairly in any way, shape or form!!!" Twitter, January 8, 2021, 6:46 a.m., https://twitter.com/realDonaldTrump/status/1347555316863553542.

131 **"To all of those who have asked, I will not be going to the Inauguration on January 20th":** Donald Trump (@realDonaldTrump), "To all of those who have asked, I will not be going to the Inauguration on January 20th." Twitter, January 8, 2021, 7:44 a.m., https://twitter.com/realDonaldTrump/status/1347569870578266115.

131 **"As an fyi, Safety has assessed the DJT Tweet above and determined that there is no violation of our policies at this time":** Bari Weiss (@bariweiss), "16. She does just that: 'as an fyi, Safety has assessed the DJT Tweet above and determined that there is no violation of our policies at this time.'" Twitter, December 12, 2022, 10:23 a.m., https://twitter.com/bariweiss/status/1602368444485148672.

132 **She worried that Trump's language might be "coded incitement to further violence":** Bari Weiss, Isaac Grafstein, Suzy Weiss, Michael Shellenberger, Peter Savodnik, and Olivia Reingold, "Why Twitter Really Banned Trump," The Free Press, December 15, 2022, https://www.thefp.com/p/why-twitter-really-banned-trump.

132 **which forbade people from glorifying a violent act in a way that "could incite or lead to further violence":** "Glorification of Violence Policy," Twitter Help Center, https://help.twitter.com/en/rules-and-policies/glorification-of-violence.

132 **"[it] makes me think he wants to share it publicly":** Bari Weiss (@bariweiss), "31. Dorsey requested simpler language to explain Trump's suspension. Roth wrote, 'god help us [this] makes me think he wants to share it publicly.'" Twitter, December 12, 2022, 10:45 a.m., https://twitter.com/bariweiss/status/1602374115867754496.

CHAPTER 11: MAXI JACK

134 **services like Facebook, YouTube, and Snapchat were quick to cut Trump's microphone:** Sarah Frier, "Trump Banned from Snapchat for Trying to Incite Violence," Bloomberg, January 13, 2021, https://www.bloomberg.com/news/articles/2021-01-14/trump-is-banned-from-snapchat-for-trying-to-incite-violence?sref=dZ65CIng.

134 **Reddit banned one of its popular pro-Trump discussion forums:** Mike Isaac and Kate Conger, "Reddit Bans Forum Dedicated to Supporting Trump, and Twitter Permanently Suspends His Allies Who Spread Conspiracy Theories," *New York Times*, January 8, 2021, https://www.nytimes.com/2021/01/08/us/politics/reddit-bans-forum-dedicated-to-supporting-trump-and-twitter-permanently-suspends-his-allies-who-spread-conspiracy-theories.html.

134 **Lindsey Graham called it "a serious mistake" and threatened regulation against Twitter:** Lindsey Graham (@LindseyGrahamSC), "Twitter may ban me for this but I willingly accept that fate: Your decision to permanently ban President Trump is a serious mistake. The Ayatollah can tweet, but Trump can't. Says a lot about the people who run Twitter." Twitter, January 8, 2021, 5:15 p.m., https://twitter.com/LindseyGrahamSC/status/1347713459874627588.

134 **"It's like a censorship court is being created, like the Holy Inquisition, for the management of public opinion":** Andrea Navarro and Maya Averbuch, "Facebook Ban on Trump Is 'Holy Inquisition,' Mexico's AMLO Says," Bloomberg, January 8, 2021, https://www.bloomberg.com/news/articles/2021-01-08/facebook-ban-on-trump-is-holy-inquisition-mexico-s-amlo-says?sref=dZ65CIng.

135 **"I don't want to live in a democracy where the key decisions . . . *are* decided by a private player, a private social network":** Dave Lawler, "Emmanuel Macron Blasts Social Media Platforms for Banning Trump," Axios, February 4, 2021, https://www.axios.com/2021/02/04/macron-social-media-bans-trump-twitter-facebook.

135 **"I do not celebrate . . . Was this correct?":** Jack Dorsey (@jack), "I do not celebrate or feel pride in our having to ban @realDonaldTrump from Twitter, or how we got here. After a clear warning we'd take this action, we made a decision with the best information we had based on threats to physical safety both on and off Twitter. Was this correct?" Twitter, January 13, 2021, 4:16 p.m., https://twitter.com/jack/status/1349510769268850690.

135 **"I believe this . . . enforcement above all":** Jack Dorsey (@jack), "I believe this was the right decision for Twitter. We faced an extraordinary and untenable circumstance, forcing us to focus all of our actions on public safety. Offline harm as a result of online speech is demonstrably real, and what drives our policy and enforcement above all." Twitter, January 13, 2021, 4:16 p.m., https://twitter.com/jack/status/1349510770992640001.

135 **"That said . . . environment around us":** Jack Dorsey (@jack), "That said, having to ban an account has real and significant ramifications. While there are clear and obvious exceptions, I feel a ban is a failure of ours ultimately to promote healthy conversation. And a time for us to reflect on our operations and the environment around us." Twitter, January 13, 2021, 4:16 p.m., https://twitter.com/jack/status/1349510771928010753.

136 **"Having to take . . . public conversation":** Jack Dorsey (@jack), "Having to take these actions fragment the public conversation. They divide us. They limit the

potential for clarification, redemption, and learning. And sets a precedent I feel is dangerous: the power an individual or corporation has over a part of the global public conversation." Twitter, January 13, 2021, 4:16 p.m., https://twitter.com/jack/status /1349510772871766020.

138 **"Your multitasking skills are *quite impressive*":** Elizabeth Culliford, "Twitter's Dorsey Called out for Trolling Congress during Hearing," Reuters, March 25, 2021, https://www.reuters.com/world/us/twitters-dorsey-called-out-trolling-congress-during -hearing-2021-03-25/.

138 **He walked on the beach with a swimsuit model half his age:** Kate Sheehy, "Twitter CEO Jack Dorsey Spotted with Swimsuit Model Flora Carter in Miami," Page Six, June 7, 2021, https://pagesix.com/2021/06/07/twitter-ceo-jack-dorsey-spotted-with-swimsuit -model-flora-carter/.

138 **Dorsey had dinner at Grutman's steakhouse, Papi Steak:** Daniel Rodriguez, "Jack Dorsey at Papi Steak," World Red Eye, June 4, 2021, https://worldredeye .com/2021/06/jack-dorsey-at-papi-steak/.

138 **then stayed out late at LIV, one of Grutman's nightclubs:** Samuel Rivas, "Marshmello, G-Eazy, & Jack Dorsey at Liv," World Red Eye, June 4, 2021, https:// worldredeye.com/2021/06/marshmello-g-eazy-jack-dorsey-at-liv/.

138 **where a table can cost upwards of $100,000:** Zachary Weiss, "The Wild, Wild World of David Grutman, the Secret King of Miami," *British GQ*, June 21, 2021, https://www .gq-magazine.co.uk/culture/article/dave-grutman-interview.

138 **the rapper G-Eazy performed followed by the deejay Deadmau5:** Mara Siegler, "Miami Club E11EVEN Rakes in Six Figures of Bitcoin during Convention," Page Six, June 8, 2021, https://pagesix.com/2021/06/08/miami-club-e11even-rakes-in-six-figures -of-bitcoin-during-convention/.

138 **Dorsey and Grutman hung out with Mayweather before the fight:** David Grutman (@DaveGrutman), "TMT Pregame @FloydMayweather @jack @TanzWatson." Twitter, June 6, 2021, 7:16 p.m., https://twitter.com/DaveGrutman/status/1401724796648448002.

138 **Portnoy had chatted with Dorsey and Grutman over dinner one night at one of the Miami mogul's other restaurants, Komodo:** Dave Portnoy (@stoolpresidente), "So about that time I stormed into @twitter HQ's. @DaveGrutman @jack @komodomiami." Twitter, June 4, 2021, 6:10 a.m., https://twitter.com/stoolpresidente /status/1400802162918182912.

138 **"He's a huge Bitcoin guy . . . like pro, pro, pro Bitcoin":** Barstool Sports, "Dave Portnoy Destroys Summer Intern—The Dave Portnoy Show w/ Eddie and Co.—Episode 37," YouTube, 2021, https://www.youtube.com/watch?v=XpIEVWwVEJo.

139 **Bitcoin would be worth $100,000 per coin by the end of the year, and $1 million per coin by 2024:** Full Send Podcast, "The Secret King of Miami Talks Nightlife & Relationship with Kim Kardashian," YouTube, 2021, https://www.youtube.com/watch?v= 1zwSZwPlO0c.

139 **"The whole thing was just poetry":** Africa Fintech Summit, "Fireside Chat with Jack Dorsey—Africa Fintech Summit 2020," YouTube, 2021, https://www.youtube.com/watch ?v=fJqq3STBTgg.

139 **Square invested $50 million into Bitcoin to hold on its balance sheet:** "Square, Inc. Invests $50 Million in Bitcoin," press release, Square, October 8, 2020, https://squareup .com/us/en/press/2020-bitcoin-investment.

139 **Square was preparing to build its own Bitcoin wallet:** Jay Peters, "Square Is Going to Make a Hardware Wallet for Bitcoin," The Verge, July 8, 2021, https://www.theverge .com/2021/7/8/22569309/square-hardware-wallet-bitcoin-jack-dorsey.

139 **Dorsey was even building an entirely new business division within Square to focus exclusively on Bitcoin:** Jack Dorsey (@jack), "Square is creating a new business (joining Seller, Cash App, & Tidal) focused on building an open developer platform with the

sole goal of making it easy to create non-custodial, permissionless, and decentralized financial services. Our primary focus is #Bitcoin. Its name is TBD." Twitter, July 15, 2021, 1:11 p.m., https://twitter.com/jack/status/1415765941904941061.

140 **she had handcuffed herself to the door of Twitter's New York City office building:** Doha Madani and Shoshana Wodinsky, "Far-Right Activist Laura Loomer Handcuffed Herself to Twitter's NYC Building; Police Removed Her," NBC News, November 29, 2018, https://www.nbcnews.com/news/us-news/far-right-activist-laura-loomer-handcuffs -herself-twitter-s-new-n941891.

140 **"I recognize the fact . . . sure that that happens":** Bitcoin Magazine, "Bitcoin 2021: Banking the Unbanked," YouTube, 2021, https://www.youtube.com/watch?v= rSSnyJpFNZU.

142 **He simply shrugged and said it wasn't his thing:** Casey Newton, "Jack Steps Back," Platformer, November 29, 2021, https://www.platformer.news/p/jack-steps-back.

142 **"My hope is that it creates world peace":** ARK Invest, "The Ḃ Word," YouTube, 2021, https://www.youtube.com/watch?v=Zwx_7XAJ3p0&t=518s.

142 **Dorsey visited Musk at Starbase:** Jack Dorsey (@jack), "Grateful for @elonmusk & @SpaceX." Twitter, August 29, 2021, 5:24 p.m., https://twitter.com/jack/status /1432137059666378755.

142 **SpaceX had launched a rocket from Florida on a resupply mission to the International Space Station:** Stephen Clark, "SpaceX Launches Resupply Mission to International Space Station," Spaceflight Now, August 29, 2021, https://spaceflightnow .com/2021/08/29/spacex-launches-resupply-mission-to-international-space-station/.

143 **attending a party where Diplo deejayed and the club ran out of tequila:** Evan Real, "Amelia Hamlin 'Looked Ready to Date Again' at Paris Fashion Week Party," Page Six, October 4, 2021, https://pagesix.com/2021/10/04/amelia-hamlin-spotted-flirting-at-paris -fashion-week-party/.

143 **Twitter's stock had nearly doubled since Elliott's investment became public:** Kurt Wagner and Scott Deveau, "Elliott's Cohn Plans to Step Down from Twitter Board," Bloomberg, April 1, 2021, https://www.bloomberg.com/news/articles/2021-04-01/elliott -s-cohn-plans-to-step-down-from-twitter-board?sref=dZ65CIng.

144 **later becoming an expert in machine learning algorithms:** Mike Isaac, Kate Conger, and Cade Metz, "Who Is Parag Agrawal, Twitter's New C.E.O.?," *New York Times*, November 29, 2021, https://www.nytimes.com/2021/11/29/technology/parag-agrawal -twitter.html.

144 **make him the youngest CEO in the S&P 500:** Jeff Green and Kurt Wagner, "Twitter's Agrawal Is Youngest CEO in S&P 500, Nudging Out Zuckerberg," Bloomberg, November 29, 2021, https://www.bloomberg.com/news/articles/2021-11-30/twitter -s-agrawal-is-now-youngest-ceo-in-s-p-500?sref=dZ65CIng.

146 **In true Dorsey fashion . . . "prove this was the right move":** Jack Dorsey (@jack), "not sure anyone has heard but, I resigned from Twitter." Twitter, November 29, 2021, 7:48 a.m., https://twitter.com/jack/status/1465347002426867720.

148 **Musk had photoshopped Agrawal's face onto Stalin's body, and Dorsey's face onto Yezhov's:** Elon Musk (@elonmusk), "[image]." Twitter, December 1, 2021, 8:00 a.m., https://twitter.com/elonmusk/status/1466074646240014340.

148 **It was a play on Stalin's well-documented propaganda strategy of editing his enemies out of his photographs:** Erin Blakemore, "How Photos Became a Weapon in Stalin's Great Purge," History.com, April 20, 2018, https://www.history.com/news/josef -stalin-great-purge-photo-retouching.

CHAPTER 12: IS TWITTER DYING?

151 **"I didn't want to . . . it was Twitter":** Walter Isaacson, "Active Investor," *Elon Musk* (New York: Simon & Schuster, 2023), 442.

151 **On Monday ... for the next two months:** Twitter Inc., Elon Musk Form 13D
     (filed April 5, 2022), Schedule I, https://www.sec.gov/Archives/edgar/data/1418091
     /000110465922042863/tm2211757d1_sc13d.htm.

152 **"My focus ... this role":** Kurt Wagner, "Twitter's New CEO Aims to Move Faster, Not
     Change Course," Bloomberg, February 10, 2022, https://www.bloomberg.com/news
     /articles/2022-02-10/twitter-gains-as-ad-revenue-holds-up-after-apple-changes?sref=
     dZ65CIng.

152 **Twitter added just 25 million new users in 2021—growth of 13 percent:** Wagner,
     "Twitter's New CEO Aims to Move Faster, Not Change Course."

152 **most people were saying "no" to that tracking:** Kurt Wagner, "Facebook Users Said
     No to Tracking. Now Advertisers Are Panicking," Bloomberg, July 14, 2021, https://
     www.bloomberg.com/news/articles/2021-07-14/facebook-fb-advertisers-impacted-by-
     apple-aapl-privacy-ios-14-changes?sref=dZ65CIng.

153 **revenue was up just 37 percent:** Twitter Inc., Annual Report Form 10-K for the Fiscal
     Year Ended December 31, 2021 (filed February 16, 2022), 40–44, https://www.sec.gov/ix
     ?doc=/Archives/edgar/data/0001418091/000141809122000029/twtr-20211231.htm.

153 **Gymnast Simone Biles was on there and so was philanthropist Melinda Gates and
     Vice President Kamala Harris:** "Meet USA TODAY's Women of the Year," *USA
     Today*, March 28, 2022, https://www.usatoday.com/storytelling/grid/women-of-the-year
     -2022/.

153 **Levine was the "nation's highest-ranking openly transgender official":** Suzette
     Hackney, "'Be True to Yourself': A Message from the Nation's Highest-Ranking Openly
     Transgender Official," *USA Today*, March 13, 2022, https://www.usatoday.com/in-depth
     /opinion/2022/03/13/rachel-levine-honoree-usa-today-women-of-the-year/6600134001/.

153 **"Moving from one gender ... was very rewarding":** Katie Zezima, "Meet Rachel
     Levine, One of the Very Few Transgender Public Officials in America," *Washington
     Post*, June 1, 2016, https://www.washingtonpost.com/politics/meet-rachel-levine-one-of
     -the-very-few-transgender-public-officials-in-america/2016/06/01/cf6e2332-2415-11e6
     -8690-f14ca9de2972_story.html.

154 **"Rookie Mistake: Man Becomes Transgender After Holding Wife's Purse for More
     Than 10 Seconds":** "Rookie Mistake: Man Becomes Transgender After Holding Wife's
     Purse for More Than 10 Seconds," Babylon Bee, February 18, 2021, https://babylonbee
     .com/news/man-becomes-transgender-after-accidentally-holding-wifes-purse-for-more
     -than-20-seconds.

154 **"M&Ms Introduces New Trans Character Who Identifies as a Skittle":** "M&Ms
     Introduces New Trans Character Who Identifies as a Skittle," Babylon Bee, January 20,
     2022, https://babylonbee.com/news/mm-introduces-new-trans-character-who-identifies
     -as-a-skittle.

154 **"Who says a dude ... think about him":** "The Babylon Bee's Man of the Year Is
     Rachel Levine," Babylon Bee, March 15, 2022, https://babylonbee.com/news/the
     -babylon-bees-man-of-the-year-is-rachel-levine.

154 **"They want us to bend ... that's not happening":** Seth Dillon, "Twitter Suspends the
     Babylon Bee," Babylon Bee, March 22, 2022, https://babylonbee.com/news/twitter-has
     -shut-down-the-bee.

154 **complaining about them earlier that day with her friend:** Dana Hull and Lisa
     Fleisher, "Musk's Texts Over Twitter Deal Included Ex-Wife Talulah Riley," Bloomberg,
     October 3, 2022, https://www.bloomberg.com/news/articles/2022-10-04/musk-s-texts
     -over-twitter-deal-included-ex-wife-talulah-riley?sref=dZ65CIng.

154 **"Why has everyone become so puritanical?":** Twitter, Inc. v. Elon R. Musk, X
     Holdings I, Inc., and X Holdings II, Inc. (Court of Chancery of the State of Delaware,
     July 12, 2022), Exhibit H, 4.

154 **the second divorce came in 2016:** Oli Coleman, "Elon Musk and Talulah Riley Are Officially Divorced—Again," Page Six, November 17, 2016, https://pagesix.com/2016/11/17/elon-musk-and-talulah-riley-are-officially-divorced-again/.

154 **Riley texted him . . . he replied:** Twitter, Inc. v. Elon R. Musk, X Holdings I, Inc., and X Holdings II, Inc., Exhibit H, 4.

155 **"Free speech . . . adheres to this principle?":** Elon Musk (@elonmusk), "Free speech is essential to a functioning democracy. Do you believe Twitter rigorously adheres to this principle?" Twitter, March 25, 2022, 12:34 a.m., https://twitter.com/elonmusk/status/1507259709224632344.

155 **"The consequences . . . vote carefully":** Elon Musk (@elonmusk), "The consequences of this poll will be important. Please vote carefully." Twitter, March 25, 2022, 1:26 a.m., https://twitter.com/elonmusk/status/1507272763597373461.

155 **required investors to submit paperwork:** "Officers, Directors and 10% Shareholders," U.S. Securities and Exchange Commission, April 6, 2023, https://www.sec.gov/education/smallbusiness/goingpublic/officersanddirectors.

155 **"Given that Twitter . . . What should be done?":** Elon Musk (@elonmusk), "Given that Twitter serves as the de facto public town square, failing to adhere to free speech principles fundamentally undermines democracy. What should be done?" Twitter, March 26, 2022, 10:51 a.m., https://twitter.com/elonmusk/status/1507777261654605828.

155 **"Is a new platform needed?":** Elon Musk (@elonmusk), "Is a new platform needed?" Twitter, March 26, 2022, 10:54 a.m., https://twitter.com/elonmusk/status/1507777913042571267.

155 **Dorsey: Yes a new platform . . . can for a minute:** Twitter, Inc. v. Elon R. Musk, X Holdings I, Inc., and X Holdings II, Inc., Exhibit H, 4–5.

156 **Dorsey: I think . . . But open:** Twitter, Inc. v. Elon R. Musk, X Holdings I, Inc., and X Holdings II, Inc., Exhibit H, 5.

157 **"This is Elon . . . the Twitter board":** Twitter, Inc. v. Elon R. Musk, X Holdings I, Inc., and X Holdings II, Inc., Exhibit H, 5.

157 **"This wins for the weirdest . . . tractors and donkeys":** Twitter, Inc. v. Elon R. Musk, X Holdings I, Inc., and X Holdings II, Inc., Exhibit H, 8.

158 **"Elon—everyone excited . . . next few days":** Twitter, Inc. v. Elon R. Musk, X Holdings I, Inc., and X Holdings II, Inc., Exhibit H, 5.

159 **was then acquired by Marc Benioff's Salesforce for $750 million:** Brody Ford and Kurt Wagner, "Twitter Chairman Keeps Calm in Chaos of Musk's Bid to Scrap Deal," Bloomberg, September 14, 2022, https://www.bloomberg.com/news/features/2022-09-14/who-is-twitter-chairman-bret-taylor-elon-musk-s-opposite?sref=dZ65CIng.

159 **join Twitter's board:** Isaacson, "Active Investor," 445.

159 **"Great dinner :) . . . to the ambiance":** Twitter, Inc. v. Elon R. Musk, X Holdings I, Inc., and X Holdings II, Inc., Exhibit H, 9.

159 **"What Twitter needs is a fire-breathing dragon . . . Parag is not that":** Isaacson, "Active Investor," 445.

160 **"I heard good things are happening":** Twitter, Inc. v. Elon R. Musk, X Holdings I, Inc., and X Holdings II, Inc., Exhibit H, 10.

160 **Musk owned more than 73 million shares, or 9.2 percent of the company:** Twitter, Inc., Elon Musk Form 13G (filed April 4, 2022), 2–3, https://www.sec.gov/Archives/edgar/data/1418091/000110465922041911/tm2211482d1_sc13g.htm.

160 **it was estimated that Musk saved himself well over $150 million:** Reed Albergotti, "Elon Musk Delayed Filing a Form and Made $156 Million," *Washington Post*, April 6, 2022, https://www.washingtonpost.com/technology/2022/04/06/musk-twitter-sec/.

160 **"Excited to see . . . plausible deniability!":** Twitter, Inc. v. Elon R. Musk, X Holdings I, Inc., and X Holdings II, Inc., Exhibit H, 10.

161 **"Are you going to liberate Twitter from the censorship happy mob?":** Twitter, Inc. v. Elon R. Musk, X Holdings I, Inc., and X Holdings II, Inc., Exhibit H, 12.

161 **"He's both a passionate . . . Welcome Elon!":** Parag Agrawal (@paraga), "He's both a passionate believer and intense critic of the service which is exactly what we need on @ Twitter, and in the boardroom, to make us stronger in the long-term. Welcome Elon!" Twitter, April 5, 2022, 5:32 a.m., https://twitter.com/paraga/status/1511320964813910017.

161 **"He cares deeply . . . incredible team":** Jack Dorsey (@jack), "I'm really happy Elon is joining the Twitter board! He cares deeply about our world and Twitter's role in it. Parag and Elon both lead with their hearts, and they will be an incredible team." Twitter, April 5, 2022, 6:06 a.m. https://twitter.com/jack/status/1511329369473564677.

161 **"Immensely . . . anything you want":** Twitter, Inc. v. Elon R. Musk, X Holdings I, Inc., and X Holdings II, Inc., Exhibit H, 13.

162 *Fixing Twitter . . . focused on execution*: Twitter, Inc., Proxy Statement Form 14-A (filed May 2022), 44, https://www.sec.gov/Archives/edgar/data/1418091 /000119312522152250/d283119dprem14a.htm.

162 **"They pushed really hard to have me join":** Twitter, Inc. v. Elon R. Musk, X Holdings I, Inc., and X Holdings II, Inc., Exhibit H, 14.

162 **"The whole Twitter thing . . . not quite control":** Twitter, Inc. v. Elon R. Musk, X Holdings I, Inc., and X Holdings II, Inc., Exhibit H, 14.

162 **Musk sent several messages back and forth with Agrawal:** Twitter, Inc. v. Elon R. Musk, X Holdings I, Inc., and X Holdings II, Inc., Exhibit H, 16.

163 **"We know that . . . he can do firsthand":** Elizabeth Dwoskin, "Elon Musk to Address Twitter Staff after Internal Outcry," *Washington Post*, April 7, 2022, https://www .washingtonpost.com/technology/2022/04/07/musk-twitter-employee-outcry/.

163 **at one point swapping credentials to show off how technical they were:** Twitter, Inc. v. Elon R. Musk, X Holdings I, Inc., and X Holdings II, Inc., Exhibit H, 16.

163 **The more time he spent . . . in the midst of an all-nighter:** Isaacson, *Elon Musk*, 451.

164 **"Is Twitter dying?":** Elon Musk (@elonmusk), "Most of these 'top' accounts tweet rarely and post very little content. Is Twitter dying?" Twitter, April 9, 2022, 6:32 a.m., https://twitter.com/elonmusk/status/1512785529712123906.

164 **should convert its San Francisco headquarters into a homeless shelter:** Ginger Adams Otis and Salvador Rodriguez, "Elon Musk Suggests Changes to Twitter, Takes Barbs at Company," *Wall Street Journal*, April 11, 2022, https://www.wsj.com/articles /elon-musk-suggests-changes-to-twitter-blue-subscription-service-11649605777.

164 **"You are free to tweet . . . aren't there right now":** Twitter, Inc. v. Elon R. Musk, X Holdings I, Inc., and X Holdings II, Inc., Exhibit H, 17–18.

165 **"I'm not joining the board. This is a waste of time. Will make an offer to take Twitter private":** Twitter, Inc. v. Elon R. Musk, X Holdings I, Inc., and X Holdings II, Inc., Exhibit H, 17–18.

165 **"Please expect . . . Jack's opinion too":** Twitter, Inc. v. Elon R. Musk, X Holdings I, Inc., and X Holdings II, Inc., Exhibit H, 18.

165 **"There will be distractions . . . what we're building":** Parag Agrawal (@paraga), "Elon has decided not to join our board. I sent a brief note to the company, sharing with you all here." Twitter, April 10, 2022, 8:13 p.m., https://twitter.com/paraga/status /1513354622466867201.

CHAPTER 13: @ELONMUSK

166 **He raced dirt bikes . . . undeniably brilliant:** Ashlee Vance, *Elon Musk: Tesla, SpaceX, and the Quest for a Fantastic Future* (New York: Ecco, 2015), 33–39.

166 **He had a photographic memory . . . question thrown his way:** Vance, *Elon Musk*, 23–31.

167 **a mechanical and electrical engineer who could do all kinds of odd jobs with his hands:** Vance, *Elon Musk*, 36.

167 **a finalist in the Miss South Africa pageant:** Derek Blasberg, "Maye Musk: Mother of Elon, Model of the Moment," *Vanity Fair*, March 14, 2017, https://www.vanityfair.com /style/2017/03/maye-musk-model.

167 **"He's good at making life miserable" . . . vowing to keep his own children from ever meeting him:** Vance, *Elon Musk*, 36–38.

167 **routinely send his son emails full of racist rants and conspiracy theories:** Walter Isaacson, *Elon Musk*, 469.

167 **had two more kids of his own with his stepdaughter, who was more than forty years his junior:** Andrew Court, "Elon Musk's Dad, 76, Confirms Secret Second Child—with His Stepdaughter," *New York Post*, July 14, 2022, https://nypost.com/2022/07/14/elon -musks-dad-76-confirms-secret-child-with-stepdaughter/.

167 **pushed down a flight of concrete stairs, a tumble that landed him in the hospital:** Vance, *Elon Musk*, 40.

167 **"People who are worried about words have never been punched in the face":** Full Send Podcast, "Elon Musk Reveals His Knowledge on Aliens, Challenges Putin to UFC, and Predicts WW3," YouTube, 2022, https://www.youtube.com/watch?v=fXS_gkWAIs0.

167 **Musk got his first computer . . . "I had ever seen":** Vance, *Elon Musk*, 38–45.

168 **before enrolling at Queen's University in Ontario:** Robin Keats, "Rocket Man," Queen's Alumni Review, February 2, 2013, https://www.queensu.ca/alumnireview /articles/2013-02-01/elon-musk.

168 **crystallized his desire to work on projects in technology, space, and renewable energy:** Vance, *Elon Musk*, 50–55.

168 **eventually sold to Compaq Computer for more than $300 million:** Lisa Napoli, "Compaq Buys Zip2 to Enhance Altavista," *New York Times*, February 17, 1999, https:// www.nytimes.com/1999/02/17/business/compaq-buys-zip2-to-enhance-altavista.html.

168 **The sale netted him $22 million:** Vance, *Elon Musk*, 72.

168 **he bought was a $1 million McLaren:** CNN, "Watch a Young Elon Musk Get His First Supercar in 1999," YouTube, 2021, https://www.youtube.com/watch?v=s9mczdODqzo.

169 **Musk became CEO and the largest shareholder of the new joint company:** Vance, *Elon Musk*, 86.

169 **Musk learned . . . Musk made $250 million:** Vance, *Elon Musk*, 87–89.

169 **Musk invested . . . was also the CEO:** Vance, *Elon Musk*, 154.

170 **SpaceX's first rocket would take off just fifteen months after the company's founding:** Vance, *Elon Musk*, 115.

170 **it didn't arrive until mid-2008:** Ze'ev Drori, "We Have Begun Regular Production of the Tesla Roadster," *Tesla Blog*. Tesla, March 17, 2008, https://www.tesla.com/blog/we -have-begun-regular-production-tesla-roadster.

170 **closed a round of funding for Tesla on Christmas Eve:** Vance, *Elon Musk*, 187–210.

171 **Tesla was worth more than its top five competitors combined:** Eva Mathews, "Factbox: Tesla Market Cap Eclipses That of Top 5 Rival Carmakers Combined," Reuters, October 26, 2021, https://www.reuters.com/business/autos-transportation/tesla -market-cap-eclipses-that-top-5-rival-carmakers-combined-2021-10-26/.

171 **Tesla delivered more than 1.3 million electric vehicles:** "Tesla Vehicle Production & Deliveries and Date for Financial Results & Webcast for Fourth Quarter 2022," Tesla Investor Relations, January 2, 2023, https://ir.tesla.com/press-release/tesla-vehicle -production-deliveries-and-date-financial-results-webcast-fourth-quarter.

171 **building "brain-computer interfaces":** Chavi Mehta and Rachael Levy, "Factbox: Neuralink: What You Need to Know about Elon Musk's Brain Chip Company," Reuters, December 7, 2022, https://www.reuters.com/technology/what-does-elon-musks-brain-chip-company-neuralink-do-2022-12-05/.

171 **"If people don't have more children, civilization is going to crumble":** Sam Shead, "Elon Musk Says 'Civilization Is Going to Crumble' If People Don't Have More Children," CNBC, December 7, 2021, https://www.cnbc.com/2021/12/07/elon-musk-civilization-will-crumble-if-we-dont-have-more-children.html.

171 **Musk had at least nine kids:** Valeriya Safronova, "How Many Children Does Elon Musk Have?" *New York Times*, July 7, 2022, https://www.nytimes.com/2022/07/07/style/elon-musk-children.html.

171 **His net worth was $270 billion:** Dana Hull, "Tesla Races Against the Clock to Hit Record Deliveries Before the New Year," Bloomberg, December 31, 2021, https://www.bloomberg.com/news/articles/2021-12-31/tesla-has-busy-new-year-s-eve-plans-in-push-to-record-deliveries?sref=dZ65CIng.

171 **after a joke he saw in one of his favorite movies, *Spaceballs*:** Joe Rogan, "*Joe Rogan Experience* #1169—Elon Musk," YouTube, 2018, https://www.youtube.com/watch?v=ycPr5-27vSI.

172 **"The consequences for me and for SpaceX were actually not good":** Full Send Podcast, "Elon Musk Reveals His Knowledge on Aliens, Challenges Putin to UFC, and Predicts WW3," YouTube, 2022, https://www.youtube.com/watch?v=fXS_gkWAIs0.

172 **oftentimes while sitting on the toilet:** TED, "Elon Musk Talks Twitter, Tesla and How His Brain Works—Live at TED2022," YouTube, 2022, https://www.youtube.com/watch?v=cdZZpaB2kDM.

172 **forcing him to give up his role as Tesla's chairman:** Dana Hull and Benjamin Bain, "Elon Musk Can Stay Tesla CEO, but Not Chairman, Under SEC Settlement," Bloomberg, September 29, 2018, https://www.bloomberg.com/news/articles/2018-09-29/elon-musk-and-sec-reach-settlement-on-fraud-charges?sref=dZ65CIng.

173 **Joe Lonsdale . . . set up a meeting:** Twitter, Inc. v. Elon R. Musk, X Holdings I, Inc., and X Holdings II, Inc., Exhibit H, 19–20.

174 **Bankman-Fried was convicted on seven counts:** David Yaffe-Bellany, Matthew Goldstein, and J. Edward Moreno. "Sam Bankman-Fried Is Found Guilty of 7 Counts of Fraud and Conspiracy," *New York Times*, November 2, 2023, https://www.nytimes.com/2023/11/02/technology/sam-bankman-fried-fraud-trial-ftx.html.

174 **later bought the very first Tesla Model S:** Anna Mazarakis and Alyson Shontell, "How a Steak Dinner with Elon Musk in 2008 Scored This Man the Very First Tesla Model S, Serial Number 00001," Business Insider, August 4, 2017, https://www.businessinsider.com/jason-calacanis-owns-first-tesla-model-s-after-dinner-with-elon-musk-2017-8#.

174 **Calacanis had no shortage of ideas . . . "my dream job":** Twitter, Inc. v. Elon R. Musk, X Holdings I, Inc., and X Holdings II, Inc., Exhibit H, 21–26.

174 **how to get his hands on about $46 billion:** Matt Levine, "Elon Got His Deal," Bloomberg, April 26, 2022, https://www.bloomberg.com/opinion/articles/2022-04-26/elon-got-his-deal?sref=dZ65CIng#footer-ref-footnote-1.

175 **calling other banks and investors to line up the funding:** Lauren Hirsch, "Elon Musk Races to Secure Financing for Twitter Bid," *New York Times*, April 19, 2022, https://www.nytimes.com/2022/04/19/technology/elon-musk-twitter.html.

175 **promised to make dramatic cost cuts:** Liana Baker, Michelle F. Davis, and Kurt Wagner, "Musk's Twitter Pitch Featured Job Cuts, Ways to Make Money," Bloomberg, April 28, 2022, https://www.bloomberg.com/news/articles/2022-04-28/musk-s-twitter-pitch-featured-job-cuts-other-ways-to-make-money?sref=dZ65CIng.

175 **Musk: Any interest . . . absolutely :):** Twitter, Inc. v. Elon R. Musk, X Holdings I, Inc., and X Holdings II, Inc., Exhibit H, 22–23.

175　**whose net worth was around $100 billion:** Brian Chappatta, Jack Witzig, Pei Yi Mak, Andrew Heathcote, and Tom Maloney, eds., "Bloomberg Billionaires Index: Larry Ellison," Bloomberg, accessed June 13, 2023, https://www.bloomberg.com/billionaires/profiles/lawrence-j-ellison/?sref=dZ65CIng.

175　**invested $1 billion:** Twitter, Inc., Elon Musk Form 13D (filed May 5, 2022), 2–3, https://www.sec.gov/Archives/edgar/data/1418091/000110465922056055/tm2214608-1_sc13da.htm.

175　**"My Plan B . . . 0,1 Doge":** Twitter, Inc. v. Elon R. Musk, X Holdings I, Inc., and X Holdings II, Inc., Exhibit H, 19.

176　**"As a public company . . . the real issue":** Jack Dorsey (@jack), "as a public company, twitter has always been 'for sale,' that's the real issue." Twitter, April 15, 2022, 7:46 a.m., https://twitter.com/jack/status/1514978366558019598.

176　**"consistently been the dysfunction of the company":** Jack Dorsey (@jack), "it's consistently been the dysfunction of the company." Twitter, April 16, 2022, 9:35 p.m., https://twitter.com/jack/status/1515549577352564740.

176　**Musk had his financing in order:** X Holdings I, Inc., Project X Commitment Letter, Exhibit C (filed April 20, 2022), https://www.sec.gov/Archives/edgar/data/1418091/000110465922048128/tm2213229d1_ex99-c.htm

176　**The arrangement outlined $46.5 billion in funding from several different sources:** Matt Levine, "Elon Got His Money," Bloomberg, April 21, 2022, https://www.bloomberg.com/opinion/articles/2022-04-21/elon-got-his-money?sref=dZ65CIng.

177　**The Federal Trade Commission was already suing Facebook:** "FTC Sues Facebook for Illegal Monopolization," Federal Trade Commission, December 9, 2020, https://www.ftc.gov/news-events/news/press-releases/2020/12/ftc-sues-facebook-illegal-monopolization.

177　**Justice Department was preparing to sue Google:** "Justice Department Sues Google for Monopolizing Digital Advertising Technologies," press release, January 24, 2023, https://www.justice.gov/opa/pr/justice-department-sues-google-monopolizing-digital-advertising-technologies.

177　**Twitter management estimated the company's revenue would be $7.2 billion:** Twitter, Inc., Proxy Statement Form 14-A (filed May 2022), 81, https://www.sec.gov/Archives/edgar/data/1418091/000119312522152250/d283119dprem14a.htm.

178　**he'd been at a party with friends and had too much Red Bull:** Isaacson, *Elon Musk*, 459.

178　**added another clause known as "specific performance":** Twitter, Inc., Form 8-K (filed April 25, 2022), 70, https://www.sec.gov/Archives/edgar/data/1418091/000119312522120474/d310843ddefa14a.htm.

178　**Twitter's board had voted unanimously:** Twitter, Inc., Proxy Statement Form 14-A (filed May 2022), 54, https://www.sec.gov/Archives/edgar/data/1418091/000119312522152250/d283119dprem14a.htm.

179　**"It has been owned . . . correct first step":** Jack Dorsey (@jack), "The idea and service is all that matters to me, and I will do whatever it takes to protect both. Twitter as a company has always been my sole issue and my biggest regret. It has been owned by Wall Street and the ad model. Taking it back from Wall Street is the correct first step." Twitter, April 25, 2022, 7:03 p.m., https://twitter.com/jack/status/1518772754782187520.

179　**"Elon is the singular solution . . . light of consciousness":** Jack Dorsey (@jack), "In principle, I don't believe anyone should own or run Twitter. It wants to be a public good at a protocol level, not a company. Solving for the problem of it being a company however, Elon is the singular solution I trust. I trust his mission to extend the light of consciousness." Twitter, April 25, 2022, 7:03 p.m., https://twitter.com/jack/status/1518772756069773313.

179 **Dorsey: Thank you . . . make it work:** Twitter, Inc. v. Elon R. Musk, X Holdings I, Inc., and X Holdings II, Inc., Exhibit H, 27.

CHAPTER 14: DEAL ON HOLD

180 **Jack Dorsey messaged Elon Musk . . . the Google Meet link for the call:** Twitter, Inc. v. Elon R. Musk, X Holdings I, Inc., and X Holdings II, Inc., Exhibit H, 29–30.

181 **"You and I . . . that was clarifying":** Twitter, Inc. v. Elon R. Musk, X Holdings I, Inc., and X Holdings II, Inc., Exhibit H, 30.

181 **"Suspending the Twitter account . . . incredibly inappropriate":** Elon Musk (@ elonmusk), "Suspending the Twitter account of a major news organization for publishing a truthful story was obviously incredibly inappropriate." Twitter, April 26, 2022, 2:56 p.m., https://twitter.com/elonmusk/status/1519073003933515776.

181 **a meme claiming that Twitter had "left wing bias" and mocked an appearance:** Elon Musk (@elonmusk), "[image]." Twitter, April 27, 2022, 11:06 a.m., https://twitter.com /elonmusk/status/1519377424437243904.

181 **her account was quickly flooded with criticism:** Kurt Wagner and Maxwell Adler, "Twitter Legal Executive Hit with Online Abuse Following Musk Tweet," Bloomberg, April 27, 2022, https://www.bloomberg.com/news/articles/2022-04-27/musk-s-tweet-on -twitter-legal-executive-presages-wave-of-abuse?sref=dZ65CIng.

181 **"Bullying is not leadership . . . harassment and threats":** Dawn Chmielewski and Hyunjoo Jin, "Musk's Criticism of Twitter Staff Triggers Backlash," Reuters, April 27, 2022, https://www.reuters.com/article/twitter-musk-moderation-idCAKCN2MK00U.

181 **"Just to say . . . people I know":** Ev Williams (@ev), "Just to say, there are many defensible _nuanced_ perspectives on content moderation and, also, @vijaya is one of the most thoughtful, principled people I know." Twitter, April 26, 2022, 10:05 p.m., https://twitter.com/ev/status/1519180793729363968.

182 **"Every decision we made was ultimately my responsibility*":** Jack Dorsey (@jack), "I have tried taking a break from Twitter recently, but I must say: the company has always tried to do its best given the information it had. Every decision we made was ultimately my responsibility*. In the cases we were wrong or went too far, we admitted it and worked to correct." Twitter, April 29, 2022, 1:40 p.m., https://twitter.com/jack/status /1520140974801924096.

182 **"*it's also crazy and wrong that individuals or companies bear this responsibility":** Jack Dorsey (@jack), "*it's also crazy and wrong that individuals or companies bear this responsibility. As I've said before, I don't believe any permanent ban (with the exception of illegal activity) is right, or should be possible. This is why we need a protocol that's resilient to the layers above." Twitter, April 29, 2022, 1:40 p.m., https://twitter.com/jack /status/1520140996641624064.

182 **Twitter reversed the decision on the laptop story as soon as he found out:** Jack Dorsey (@jack), "when I found out we took that action, we reversed it almost immediately. we should have also reinstated the account without requiring a delete of the tweet." Twitter, April 29, 2022, 2:10 p.m., https://twitter.com/jack/status /1520148497252552705.

182 **fought against unions at Tesla:** Josh Eidelson, "Tesla Is Ordered to Rehire Worker, Make Musk Delete Tweet," Bloomberg, March 25, 2021, https://www.bloomberg.com /news/articles/2021-03-25/tesla-illegally-fired-worker-and-must-kill-musk-tweet-nlrb -says?sref=dZ65CIng.

182 **openly mocked people who put their pronouns in their Twitter bios:** Jo Yurcaba, "Some Trans Twitter Users Say Platform under Elon Musk Would Be 'Terrifying,'" NBC News, April 27, 2022, https://www.nbcnews.com/nbc-out/out-news/trans-twitter-users -say-platform-elon-musk-terrifying-rcna26085.

183 **Several voiced their concerns about Musk on the company's internal Slack:** Andy Ngo, "Twitter Workers Freaking Out over Elon Musk in Internal Slack Messages," *New York Post*, April 27, 2022, https://nypost.com/2022/04/27/twitter-workers-freak-out-over -elon-musk-in-internal-slack-messages/.

184 **"I could have . . . Should have done better":** Casey Newton, "Inside Twitter's Emotional Friday All-Hands," Platformer, April 29, 2022, https://www.platformer.news /p/inside-twitters-emotional-friday?s=w.

184 **The title slide read "Why Bother?" and did little to inspire:** Kurt Wagner and Dana Hull, "Twitter Works to Soothe Anxious Staffers Wondering 'Why Bother?'" Bloomberg, May 4, 2022, https://www.bloomberg.com/news/articles/2022-05-04/twitter -works-to-soothe-anxious-staffers-wondering-why-bother?sref=dZ65CIng.

184 **Blake Lively wore a Versace dress:** "Blake Lively Transforms Her Met Gala 2022 Dress on the Red Carpet," NBC New York, 2022, https://www.nbcnewyork.com/news /local/blake-lively-transforms-her-met-gala-2022-dress-on-the-red-carpet/3671879/.

185 **after losing sixteen pounds in just three weeks:** Emily Kirkpatrick, "Kim Kardashian Lost 16 Pounds in 3 Weeks to Fit into Marilyn Monroe's Dress for the 2022 Met Gala," *Vanity Fair*, May 2, 2022, https://www.vanityfair.com/style/2022/05/kim-kardashian -2022-met-gala-marilyn-monroe-dress-jfk-happy-birthday-diet-weight-loss.

185 **wore a white dress with the words "Tax the Rich" written in bright red on the back:** Christi Carras, "AOC Defends Polarizing 'Tax the Rich' Met Gala Dress: 'The Medium Is the Message,'" *Los Angeles Times*, September 14, 2021, https://www.latimes.com /entertainment-arts/story/2021-09-14/met-gala-2021-aoc-tax-the-rich-dress.

185 **"like I'm from *Downton Abbey* or something":** Jada Yuan, "In Austere Times, the Met Gala Returns to 'Gilded' Era," *Washington Post*, May 3, 2022, https://www .washingtonpost.com/lifestyle/2022/05/02/met-gala-gilded-age-2022/.

185 **"I admire good style so we're just going to walk around and sort of see the great outfits":** NBC New York, "Elon Musk at 2022 Met Gala: 'I Love Fashion,'" YouTube, 2022, https://www.youtube.com/watch?v=-VC1SKD9e6Q.

185 **"I'm going to ask people in there, 'Please! Please! Please help me buy Twitter!'":** Yuan, "In Austere Times."

185 **Musk sold $8.5 billion in Tesla stock:** Dana Hull, "Musk's Tesla-Stock Sales Double to $8.5 Billion in Latest Tally," Bloomberg, April 29, 2022, https://www.bloomberg.com /news/articles/2022-04-29/musk-s-tesla-stock-sales-top-8-billion-with-latest-filings?sref =dZ65CIng.

185 **"No further TSLA sales planned after today":** Elon Musk (@elonmusk), "No further TSLA sales planned after today." Twitter, April 28, 2022, 6:25 p.m., https://twitter.com /elonmusk/status/1519850299757846530.

185 **"Ultra Genius . . . laborious blockchain debate":** Twitter, Inc. v. Elon R. Musk, X Holdings I, Inc., and X Holdings II, Inc., Exhibit H, 29.

185 **He exchanged texts . . . open to an investment:** Twitter, Inc. v. Elon R. Musk, X Holdings I, Inc., and X Holdings II, Inc., Exhibit H, 31–33.

186 **Jason Calacanis offered to fundraise on Musk's behalf:** Twitter, Inc. v. Elon R. Musk, X Holdings I, Inc., and X Holdings II, Inc., Exhibit J, 2–3.

186 **Musk would promise Dorsey:** Isaacson, *Elon Musk*, 510.

186 **including 13 percent in a single week:** Dana Hull, "Musk's Tesla-Stock Sales Double to $8.5 Billion in Latest Tally," Bloomberg, April 29, 2022, https://www.bloomberg.com /news/articles/2022-04-29/musk-s-tesla-stock-sales-top-8-billion-with-latest-filings?sref= dZ65CIng.

186 **Musk's net worth shrank:** Brian Chappatta, Tom Maloney, Jack Witzig, Pei Yi Mak, and Andrew Heathcote, "Bloomberg Billionaires Index: Elon Musk," Bloomberg, accessed June 13, 2023, https://www.bloomberg.com/billionaires/profiles/elon-r-musk/ ?sref=dZ65CIng.

186 **largest one-year jump since 1981:** "Consumer Prices up 8.6 Percent over Year Ended May 2022," U.S. Bureau of Labor Statistics, June 14, 2022, https://www.bls.gov/opub/ted /2022/consumer-prices-up-8-6-percent-over-year-ended-may-2022.htm.

186 **He was now personally responsible for coming up with $27.25 billion:** Matt Levine, "Elon Called Off His Margin Loan," Bloomberg, May 26, 2022, https://www.bloomberg .com/opinion/articles/2022-05-26/elon-called-off-his-margin-loan?sref=dZ65CIng.

186 **was in for $800 million:** Shaun Maguire, "Partnering with the Boring Company: The Promise of Subspace," Sequoia Capital, April 2, 2022, https://www.sequoiacap.com /article/partnering-with-the-boring-company-the-promise-of-subspace/.

187 **Musk had rounded up a total of $7.1 billion in pledges:** Twitter, Inc., Elon Musk Form 13D (filed May 5, 2022), 2–3, https://www.sec.gov/Archives/edgar/data/1418091 /000110465922056055/tm2214608-1_sc13da.htm.

187 **He flew to San Francisco for the meeting all the way from San Jose:** Elon Musk Jet (@elonmuskjet), "Landed in San Francisco, California, US. Apx. flt. time 9 Mins." Instagram, May 6, 2022, https://www.instagram.com/p/CdPBHz2s1Yb.

187 **encouraged the company to cut costs and head count:** Twitter, Inc. v. Elon R. Musk, X Holdings I, Inc., and X Holdings II, Inc., 54.

187 **"It was the worst diligence meeting I have ever witnessed in my life":** Isaacson, *Elon Musk*, 463.

188 **On May 8, Grimes sent Musk a message . . . Twitter wasn't lying:** Twitter, Inc. v. Elon R. Musk, X Holdings I, Inc., and X Holdings II, Inc., Exhibit J, 4.

188 **"Twitter deal temporarily on hold . . . 5% of users":** Elon Musk (@elonmusk), "Twitter deal temporarily on hold pending details supporting calculation that spam/fake accounts do indeed represent less than 5% of users." Twitter, May 13, 2022, 2:44 a.m., https://twitter.com/elonmusk/status/1525049369552048129.

189 **after his lawyer, Alex Spiro, and his business manager, Jared Birchall, pleaded with him:** Isaacson, *Elon Musk*, 464.

189 **reviewers combed through a list of 100 accounts per day, or roughly 9,000 per quarter:** Twitter, Inc. v. Elon R. Musk, X Holdings I, Inc., and X Holdings II, Inc., 31.

189 **"My team will do a random sample of 100 followers of @twitter":** Elon Musk (@ elonmusk), "To find out, my team will do a random sample of 100 followers of @twitter. I invite others to repeat the same process and see what they discover. . . ." Twitter, May 13, 2022, 6:47 p.m., https://twitter.com/elonmusk/status/1525291586669531137.

190 **"Twitter legal . . . this actually happened":** Elon Musk (@elonmusk), "Twitter legal just called to complain that I violated their NDA by revealing the bot check sample size is 100! This actually happened." Twitter, May 14, 2022, 4:15 p.m., https://twitter.com /elonmusk/status/1525615849167589380.

190 **"There is some chance [bots] might be over 90% of daily active users":** Elon Musk (@elonmusk), "There is some chance it might be over 90% of daily active users, which is the metric that matters to advertisers. Very odd that the most popular tweets of all time were only liked by ~2% of daily active users." Twitter, May 14, 2022, 11:39 p.m., https:// twitter.com/elonmusk/status/1525727450872926209.

190 **"It's like, as unknowable . . . out of the question":** Dana Hull, Nathan Crooks, and Kurt Wagner, "Musk Says Twitter Deal at Lower Price Is 'Not Out of the Question,'" Bloomberg, May 16, 2022, https://www.bloomberg.com/news/articles/2022-05-16/musk -says-twitter-bots-likely-account-for-at-least-20-of-users?sref=dZ65CIng.

190 **"The hard challenge . . . on the surface":** Parag Agrawal (@paraga), "The hard challenge is that many accounts which look fake superficially – are actually real people. And some of the spam accounts which are actually the most dangerous – and cause the most harm to our users – can look totally legitimate on the surface." Twitter, May 16, 2022, 9:26 a.m., https://twitter.com/paraga/status/1526237583843287040.

190 **Musk replied to Agrawal by posting a poop emoji:** Elon Musk (@elonmusk), "[poop emoji]." Twitter, May 16, 2022, 10:03 a.m., https://twitter.com/elonmusk/status /1526246899606601730.

193 **he even "offered to buy her a horse":** Rich McHugh, "A SpaceX Flight Attendant Said Elon Musk Exposed Himself and Propositioned Her for Sex, Documents Show. The Company Paid $250,000 for Her Silence," Business Insider, May 19, 2022, https://www .businessinsider.com/spacex-paid-250000-to-a-flight-attendant-who-accused-elon-musk -of-sexual-misconduct-2022-5.

193 **called the allegations "utterly untrue":** Elon Musk (@elonmusk), "No, it was clear that their only goal was a hit price to interfere with the Twitter acquisition. The story was written before they even talked to me." Twitter, May 19, 2022, 10:19 p.m., https://twitter .com/elonmusk/status/1527519328245059592.

194 **"Jack off the board!":** Elon Musk (@elonmusk), "Jack off the board!" Twitter, May 26, 2022, 10:00 a.m., https://twitter.com/elonmusk/status/1529869999803965446.

194 **only included one character: a horse emoji:** Jack Dorsey (@jack), "[Horse emojis]." Twitter, May 26, 2022, 12:16 p.m., https://twitter.com/jack/status/1529904396292739082.

194 **federal regulators from the SEC were investigating his Twitter stock purchases:** Lydia Beyoud and Nicola M. White, "SEC Sent Query to Musk Last Month Over Major Twitter Stake," Bloomberg, May 27, 2022, https://www.bloomberg.com/news/articles /2022-05-27/sec-sent-query-to-musk-last-month-over-his-major-twitter-stake?sref= dZ65CIng.

195 **had forced Twitter executives to meet with the entire company:** Kurt Wagner and Maxwell Adler, "Elon Musk's Twitter Deal Is Proceeding, Not 'On Hold,' Executives Tell Staff," Bloomberg, May 19, 2022, https://www.bloomberg.com/news/articles/2022 -05-19/twitter-deal-is-proceeding-not-on-hold-executives-tell-staff?sref=dZ65CIng.

197 **repeatedly used a hashtag of the far-right conspiracy group QAnon:** Andrew Kaczynski, "Newly Elected GOP Congresswoman Spread Capitol Riot Conspiracies and QAnon Hashtags in Now-Deleted Tweets," CNN, June 23, 2022, https://www.cnn.com /2022/06/23/politics/mayra-flores-capitol-riot-qanon-kfile/index.html.

197 **"y'all told me . . . a DRINK?":** Project Veritas, "Leaked Internal Slack Messages Show Twitter Employees Reaction to Elon Musk's #TwitterAllHands Call," YouTube, 2022, https://www.youtube.com/watch?v=jvYF4HpitEU.

CHAPTER 15: *TWITTER V. ELON R. MUSK*

198 **quietly slipped in the back door at the Sun Valley Lodge:** Jennifer Maas, "Elon Musk Makes Long-Awaited Arrival at Sun Valley Conference," Variety, July 7, 2022, https:// variety.com/2022/tv/news/elon-musk-sun-valley-twitter-1235311152/.

198 **Facebook's Mark Zuckerberg, Fox chairman Rupert Murdoch, and legendary investor Warren Buffett:** Jennifer Maas, "Sun Valley Scene Day 2: Elon Musk Watch Begins, Rupert Murdoch and Mark Zuckerberg Lay Low," Variety, July 6, 2022, https://variety.com/2022/tv/news/sun-valley-elon-musk-murdoch-zuckerberg-sandberg -1235310007/.

198 **a 20,000-square-foot spa:** "Sun Valley Lodge," SunValley.com, accessed June 13, 2023, https://www.sunvalley.com/lodging/sun-valley-lodge/.

198 **Comcast mapped out a deal to acquire NBCUniversal:** Andrew Ross Sorkin and Tim Arango, "In Secret Meetings, Comcast Wooed G.E. and Won NBC," New York Times, December 2, 2009, https://www.nytimes.com/2009/12/03/business/media/03nbc.html.

199 **the seed was planted for Disney's $19 billion acquisition of ABC:** Geraldine Fabrikant, "The Media Business: The Merger; Walt Disney to Acquire ABC in $19 Billion Deal to Build a Giant for Entertainment," New York Times, August 1, 1995, https://www.nytimes.com/1995/08/01/business/media-business-merger-walt-disney -acquire-abc-19-billion-deal-build-giant-for.html.

199 **Jeff Bezos met secretly at Sun Valley with Donald Graham:** Paul Farhi, "Washington Post to Be Sold to Jeff Bezos, the Founder of Amazon," *Washington Post*, August 5, 2013, https://www.washingtonpost.com/national/washington-post-to-be-sold-to-jeff -bezos/2013/08/05/ca537c9e-fe0c-11e2-9711-3708310f6f4d_story.html?hpid=z1.

199 **terminating his $44 billion deal to buy the company:** Twitter, Inc., Letter from Elon Musk Lawyers (filed July 8, 2022), 1–3, https://www.sec.gov/Archives/edgar/data /1418091/000110465922078413/tm2220599d1_ex99-p.htm.

199 **failed to "conduct its business in the ordinary course":** Twitter, Inc., Letter from Elon Musk Lawyers (filed July 8, 2022), 1–3.

200 **Twitter's stock fell 7 percent:** Kurt Wagner and Sarah Frier, "Musk Backs Out of $44 Billion Twitter Deal Over Bot Accounts," Bloomberg, July 8, 2022, https://www .bloomberg.com/news/articles/2022-07-08/musk-says-he-s-terminating-44-billion-deal -to-buy-twitter?sref=dZ65CIng.

200 **which he referred to as a "civilian life insurance":** Edward Ludlow and Sonali Basak, "Musk Dodges Twitter Questions in Hot Sun Valley Speech," Bloomberg, July 8, 2022, https://www.bloomberg.com/news/articles/2022-07-09/twitter-deal-collapse-makes -musk-a-hot-ticket-at-sun-valley?sref=dZ65CIng.

201 **Musk had even mentioned "defeating the spam bots":** Twitter, Inc., "Elon Musk to Acquire Twitter," PR Newswire, April 25, 2022.

201 **"Having mounted . . . and walk away":** Twitter, Inc. v. Elon R. Musk, X Holdings I, Inc., and X Holdings II, Inc., 1.

201 **"These decisions aligned with Musk's own stated priorities":** Twitter, Inc. v. Elon R. Musk, X Holdings I, Inc., and X Holdings II, Inc., 54.

201 **had once driven a cab in New York to pay the bills:** Katrina Dewey, "Lawyer Limelight: William Savitt," Lawdragon, November 20, 2015, https://www.lawdragon .com/lawyer-limelights/2015-11-20-william-savitt.

201 **taking a clerkship with Supreme Court justice Ruth Bader Ginsburg:** "William Savitt," Wachtell, Lipton, Rosen & Katz, accessed June 13, 2023, https://www.wlrk.com /attorney/wsavitt/.

202 **Charter Communications, which faced litigation after its merger with Time Warner in 2015:** Ed Hammond and Jef Feeley, "Twitter Assembles Legal Team to Sue Musk Over Dropped Takeover," Bloomberg, July 10, 2022, https://www.bloomberg.com/news /articles/2022-07-10/twitter-assembles-legal-team-to-sue-musk-over-dropped-takeover ?sref=dZ65CIng.

202 **"If you read the *Wall Street Journal*, you might as well be looking at Bill Savitt's daily calendar":** Dewey, "Lawyer Limelight: William Savitt."

202 **featured in the *New York Times* real estate section:** Tim McKeough, "Prewar, with a Twist," *New York Times*, December 8, 2017, https://www.nytimes.com/2017/12/08 /realestate/prewar-with-a-contemporary-twist.html.

202 **"we plan to hold . . . we will prevail":** Twitter, Inc., Proxy Statement Schedule 14A (filed July 12, 2022), https://www.sec.gov/Archives/edgar/data/1418091 /000119312522192972/d367858ddefa14a.htm219

204 **working for other A-listers like Jay-Z or billionaire Robert Kraft:** Dan Adler, "How Alex Spiro Became Elon Musk's (and Megan Thee Stallion's and Jay-Z's) Go-To Lawyer," *Vanity Fair*, March 6, 2023, https://www.vanityfair.com/style/2023/03/alex -spiro-lawyer-elon-musk-megan-thee-stallion-jay-z.

204 **Musk was a significant underdog:** Tom Hals, "Analysis: Twitter Has Legal Edge in Deal Dispute with Musk," Reuters, July 11, 2022, https://www.reuters.com/technology /twitter-has-legal-edge-deal-dispute-with-musk-2022-07-09/.

204 **"The reality is, continued delays threaten imminent harm":** Jef Feeley, "Twitter Gets a Win Over Musk with Trial Fast-Tracked for October," Bloomberg, July 19, 2022,

https://www.bloomberg.com/news/articles/2022-07-19/twitter-gets-fast-track-for-musk
-lawsuit-over-canceled-buyout?sref=dZ65CIng.

204 **Twitter reported disappointing earnings:** Kurt Wagner, "Twitter Pares Office Space
to Save Cash, Deepen Remote-Work Tilt," Bloomberg, July 27, 2022, https://www
.bloomberg.com/news/articles/2022-07-27/twitter-pares-back-office-space-in-new-york
-san-francisco-in-remote-work-shift?sref=dZ65CIng.

205 **attrition at Twitter was up to 18 percent:** Sheila Dang and Nivedita Balu, "Twitter
Staff Exodus Accelerates amid Musk Battle, Whistleblower Complaint," Reuters, August
24, 2022, https://www.reuters.com/technology/twitter-ceo-tells-staff-whistleblower
-claims-are-inaccurate-internal-meeting-2022-08-24/.

206 **"I've been a vocal critic of Twitter's management, maybe they don't want me
talking about these issues":** Bloomberg, "David Sacks Calls Twitter Subpoena
'Harassment,'" YouTube, 2022, https://www.youtube.com/watch?v=qzbS2Cwe0vo.

206 **Twitter's subpoena requests were overly broad:** Jef Feeley, "Musk Says Twitter Is
Hounding Him Over Every Chat About Buyout," Bloomberg, August 18, 2022, https://
www.bloomberg.com/news/articles/2022-08-18/musk-says-twitter-is-hounding-him-over
-every-chat-about-buyout?sref=dZ65CIng.

206 **sold another $6.9 billion of Tesla stock:** Peter Vercoe, "Musk Sells Another $6.9
Billion of Tesla Ahead of Twitter Trial," Bloomberg, August 9, 2022, https://www
.bloomberg.com/news/articles/2022-08-10/elon-musk-sells-4-3-billion-of-tesla-shares
-first-since-april?sref=dZ65CIng.

206 **"In the (hopefully unlikely) . . . Tesla stock":** Elon Musk (@elonmusk), "Yes.
In the (hopefully unlikely) event that Twitter forces this deal to close *and* some
equity partners don't come through, it is important to avoid an emergency sale of
Tesla stock." Twitter, August 9, 2022, 7:53 p.m., https://twitter.com/elonmusk/status
/1557198421206769664.

206 **including time running cyber programs for the research-and-development agency
for the U.S. Department of Defense:** Senate Judiciary Committee and Zatko Peiter,
Written Statement of Peiter ("Mudge") Zatko § (2022), https://www.judiciary.senate.gov
/imo/media/doc/Testimony%20-%20Zatko%20-%202022-09-13.pdf.

206 **a seventeen-year-old hacker from Florida gained access to some of Twitter's most
important accounts:** Nathaniel Popper, Kate Conger, and Kellen Browning, "From
Minecraft Tricks to Twitter Hack: A Florida Teen's Troubled Online Path," *New York
Times*, August 2, 2020, https://www.nytimes.com/2020/08/02/technology/florida
-teenager-twitter-hack.html.

207 **estimated that Dorsey said just fifty words to him:** John N. Tye and Andrew P. Bakaj,
"Whistleblower Report: Peiter 'Mudge' Zatko," Whistleblower Aid, July 6, 2022, 53.

207 **Agrawal fired Mudge shortly after he replaced Dorsey as CEO:** Jeff Stone, "Twitter
Whistle-Blower Won Hacker Kudos, Fired Over Performance," Bloomberg, August
23, 2022, https://www.bloomberg.com/news/articles/2022-08-23/twitter-whistleblower
-mudge-has-distinguished-cyber-career?sref=dZ65CIng.

207 **a section titled "Lying about Bots to Elon Musk:** Tye and Bakaj, "Whistleblower
Report," 9.

207 **Twitter executives didn't actually know how many bots there were:** Tye and Bakaj, 11.

207 **"It all comes down to . . . a few more weeks":** Jef Feeley and Kurt Wagner, "Twitter
Whistle-Blower Never Flagged Spam, Company Tells Judge in Buyout Case,"
Bloomberg, September 6, 2022, https://www.bloomberg.com/news/articles/2022-09-06
/twitter-whistle-blower-never-flagged-spam-company-tells-judge?sref=dZ65CIng.

208 **called the timing of the allegations "very, very strange":** Feeley and Wagner.

208 **"Twitter is already doing a decent job excluding spam bots and other worthless
accounts from its calculation":** Tye and Bakaj, "Whistleblower Report," 15.

208 **fined $150 million just a few months earlier:** "FTC Charges Twitter with Deceptively Using Account Security Data to Sell Targeted Ads," press release, Federal Trade Commission, May 25, 2022, https://www.ftc.gov/news-events/news/press-releases/2022 /05/ftc-charges-twitter-deceptively-using-account-security-data-sell-targeted-ads.

208 **"I am convinced that even four weeks' delay would risk further harm to Twitter too great to justify":** Jef Feeley, "Musk Can Use Twitter Whistle-Blower Claims in Buyout Fight," Bloomberg, September 7, 2022, https://www.bloomberg.com/news/articles/2022 -09-07/musk-can-use-twitter-whistle-blower-complaint-in-buyout-fight?sref=dZ65CIng.

208 **McCormick slammed Musk for failing to hand over his personal text messages:** Jef Feeley, "Judge Slams Musk for Not Handing Over Texts in Twitter Fight," Bloomberg, September 7, 2022, https://www.bloomberg.com/news/articles/2022-09-07/judge-slams. -musk-for-not-handing-over-records-in-twitter-fight?sref=dZ65CIng.

209 **98.6 percent of votes cast were in favor of the deal:** Kurt Wagner, "Twitter Shareholders Approve Musk's $44 Billion Buyout as Trial Looms," Bloomberg, September 13, 2022, https://www.bloomberg.com/news/articles/2022-09-13/twitter -shareholders-approve-elon-musk-s-44-billion-buyout?sref=dZ65CIng.

209 **"What is so illuminating . . . Elon Musk's phone":** Charlie Warzel, "Elon Musk's Texts Shatter the Myth of the Tech Genius," *Atlantic*, September 30, 2022, https://www .theatlantic.com/technology/archive/2022/09/elon-musk-texts-twitter-trial-jack-dorsey /671619/.

210 **a new album that Dorsey couldn't stop playing:** Jack Dorsey (@jack), "this is an opera. @kendricklamar is a poet and a teacher. I learn something new each listen . . . and I can't listen to anything else. constant spin." Twitter, June 7, 2022, 2:54 p.m., https:// twitter.com/jack/status/1534292777537884165.

210 **Dorsey sat just a few seats away from Lamar:** Louis Vuitton, "Louis Vuitton Men's Spring-Summer 2023 Show," YouTube, 2022, https://www.youtube.com/watch?v= 6SX50BOmArI&t=661s.

210 **Dorsey even made a brief cameo:** Kendrick Lamar, "Kendrick Lamar—Count Me Out," YouTube, 2022, https://www.youtube.com/watch?v=5GhhVHpPR_M.

210 **Their client wanted to revive the original deal:** Twitter, Inc., Letter from Elon Musk Lawyers (filed October 3, 2022), https://www.sec.gov/Archives/edgar/data/1418091 /000110465922105787/tm2227435d1_ex99-s.htm.

CHAPTER 16: LET THAT SINK IN

213 **"Entering Twitter HQ—let that sink in!":** Elon Musk (@elonmusk), "Entering Twitter HQ – let that sink in!" Twitter, October 26, 2022, 11:45 a.m., https://twitter.com /elonmusk/status/1585341984679469056.

215 **"For Elon Musk . . . bought it anyway":** Manu Cornet, "Bye Twitter," Manu Cornet's Website, November 1, 2022, https://ma.nu/blog/bye-twitter.

215 **approached by a scrum of curious employees:** Walter Isaacson (@walterisaacson), "At Twitter headquarters' coffee bar, @elonmusk." Twitter, October 27, 2022, 9:13 a.m., https://twitter.com/walterisaacson/status/1585666128713371649.

216 **reported that Musk was planning to fire 75 percent of Twitter's workforce:** Elizabeth Dwoskin, Faiz Siddiqui, Gerrit De Vynck, and Jeremy B. Merrill, "Documents Detail Plans to Gut Twitter's Workforce," *Washington Post*, October 20, 2022, https:// www.washingtonpost.com/technology/2022/10/20/musk-twitter-acquisition-staff-cuts/.

216 *No,* **Musk replied:** Ed Hammond and Edward Ludlow, "Musk Tells Twitter Staff He Doesn't Plan to Cut 75% of Jobs," Bloomberg, October 26, 2022, https://www.bloomberg .com/news/articles/2022-10-27/musk-tells-twitter-employees-he-doesn-t-plan-to-cut-75 -of-jobs?sref=dZ65CIng.

216 **even commissioned a glass skybridge connecting the two buildings:** "Twitter Skybridge," Bohlin Cywinski Jackson, accessed June 13, 2023, https://www.bcj.com /projects/corporate/twitter-skybridge/.

216 **hosting Musk at his house in San Francisco:** Isaacson, *Elon Musk*, 529.

217 **showed up to meet with Twitter engineers and review the company's code:** Kurt Wagner and Edward Ludlow, "Elon Musk Asks Tesla Engineers to Meet with Product Leaders at Twitter," Bloomberg, October 27, 2022, https://www.bloomberg.com/news /articles/2022-10-27/tesla-engineers-visit-twitter-office-to-review-code-for-musk?sref= dZ65CIng.

217 **actually living in the office with his partner and newborn child:** Becky Peterson and Erin Woo, "Musk May Have Found a Hardcore Leader for Twitter," The Information, December 23, 2022, https://www.theinformation.com/articles/musk-may-have-found -a-hardcore-leader-for-twitter.

217 **"He's here to win . . . He wins everywhere":** Kurt Wagner, Sarah Frier, and Brad Stone, "Elon Musk's Twitter Is a Shakespearean Psychodrama Set in Silicon Valley," Bloomberg, December 14, 2022, https://www.bloomberg.com/news/features/2022-12-14 /elon-musk-twitter-ownership-full-of-firings-ad-cuts-chaos?sref=dZ65CIng.

218 **"Software engineering, server operations & design will rule the roost":** Elon Musk (@elonmusk), "Software engineering, server operations & design will rule the roost." Twitter, October 6, 2022, 5:42 p.m., https://twitter.com/elonmusk/status /1578184037776216064.

220 **where Tesla had a factory in Shanghai:** Dana Hull and Chunying Zhang, "Elon Musk Set Up His Shanghai Gigafactory in Record Time," Bloomberg, October 23, 2019, https://www.bloomberg.com/news/articles/2019-10-23/elon-musk-opened-tesla -s-shanghai-gigafactory-in-just-168-days.

221 **Gadde was fired immediately . . . was also fired and escorted out:** Kurt Wagner and Ed Hammond, "Twitter CEO Among Top Executives Departing as Musk Takes Over," Bloomberg, October 27, 2022, https://www.bloomberg.com/news/articles/2022-10-28 /twitter-ceo-among-top-executives-departing-as-musk-takes-over?sref=dZ65CIng.

221 **he had zero confidence in Twitter's management:** Twitter, Inc., Amendment No. 2 to Schedule 13D/A (filed April 13, 2022), https://www.sec.gov/Archives/edgar/data/1418091 /000110465922045641/tm2212748d1_sc13da.htm#ex-b_001.

221 **would vest immediately:** Twitter, Inc., Proxy Statement Form 14-A (filed May 2022), 9, https://www.sec.gov/Archives/edgar/data/1418091/000119312522152250 /d283119dprem14a.htm.

221 **Agrawal alone was set to make roughly $50 million:** Anders Melin, "Twitter's Top Executives Are Set to Exit with $100 Million Payout as Musk Takes Over," Bloomberg, October 28, 2022, https://www.bloomberg.com/news/articles/2022-10-28/twitter-s-twtr -top-bosses-poised-to-exit-with-100-million-as-musk-takes-over?sref=dZ65CIng.

222 **"the bird," he wrote, "is freed":** Elon Musk (@elonmusk), "the bird is freed." Twitter, October 27, 2022, 8:49 p.m., https://twitter.com/elonmusk/status/1585841080431321088.

224 **interviewed the "employees" and ran stories:** Thomas Barrabi and Theo Wayt, "Pranksters Posing as Laid-off Twitter Employees Trick Media Outlets: 'Rahul Ligma,'" *New York Post*, October 28, 2022, https://nypost.com/2022/10/28/pranksters-posing-as -laid-off-twitter-employees-trick-media-outlets/.

224 **"Important to admit when I'm wrong & firing them was truly one of my biggest mistakes":** Elon Musk (@elonmusk), "Important to admit when I'm wrong & firing them was truly one of my biggest mistakes." Twitter, November 15, 2022, 12:43 p.m., https://twitter.com/elonmusk/status/1592619267803185152.

224 **"Please print out 50 . . . UPDATE: Stop printing":** Casey Newton, "Elon Takes Over Twitter," Platformer, October 28, 2022, https://www.platformer.news/p/elon-takes-over -twitter.

225 **"Let the good times roll"**: Elon Musk (@elonmusk), "let the good times roll." Twitter, October 28, 2022, 5:09 a.m., https://twitter.com/elonmusk/status/1585966869122457600.

225 **he would investigate whether it was being shadow-banned**: Elon Musk (@elonmusk), "I will be digging in more today." Twitter, October 28, 2022, 4:41 a.m., https://twitter .com/elonmusk/status/1585959864454459393.

225 **pledged to form a "content moderation council"**: Elon Musk (@elonmusk), "Twitter will be forming a content moderation council with widely diverse viewpoints. No major content decisions or account reinstatements will happen before that council convenes." Twitter, October 28, 2022, 11:18 a.m., https://twitter.com/elonmusk/status /1586059953311137792.

225 **"anyone suspended for minor & dubious reasons will be freed from Twitter jail"**: Elon Musk (@elonmusk), "Anyone suspended for minor & dubious reasons will be freed from Twitter jail." Twitter, October 28, 2022, 2:21 p.m., https://twitter.com/elonmusk /status/1586105918143406080.

225 **"Comedy is now legal on Twitter"**: Elon Musk (@elonmusk), "Comedy is now legal on Twitter." Twitter, October 28, 2022, 2:16 p.m., https://twitter.com/elonmusk/status /1586104694421659648.

226 **he wanted to cut Twitter's engineering teams by more than 90 percent**: Isaacson, *Elon Musk*, 521.

227 **Musk would often sleep on a beanbag by his desk**: Vance, *Elon Musk*, 63.

227 **"I wanted my circumstance . . . mine to be worse"**: Tom Randall, "'The Last Bet-the-Company Situation': Q&A With Elon Musk," Bloomberg, July 13, 2018, https://www .bloomberg.com/news/features/2018-07-13/-the-last-bet-the-company-situation-q-amp -a-with-elon-musk?sref=dZ65CIng.

227 **"He preferred a scrappy . . . rather than comfort"**: Isaacson, *Elon Musk*, 557.

228 **"an insane piece of shit"**: Twitter, Inc. v. Elon R. Musk, X Holdings I, Inc., and X Holdings II, Inc., Exhibit H, 21.

229 **he wanted to charge $20 per month**: Alex Heath, "Twitter Is Planning to Start Charging Soon for Verification," The Verge, October 30, 2022, https://www.theverge .com/2022/10/30/23431931/twitter-paid-verification-elon-musk-blue-monthly -subscription.

229 **"$20 a month . . . I'm gone like Enron"**: Stephen King (@StephenKing), "$20 a month to keep my blue check? Fuck that, they should pay me. If that gets instituted, I'm gone like Enron." Twitter, October 31, 2022, 4:23 a.m., https://twitter.com/StephenKing/status /1587042605627490304.

229 **"We need to pay . . . How about $8?"**: Elon Musk (@elonmusk), "We need to pay the bills somehow! Twitter cannot rely entirely on advertisers. How about $8?" Twitter, October 31, 2022, 10:16 p.m., https://twitter.com/elonmusk/status/1587312517679878144.

229 **"lords & peasants system"**: Elon Musk (@elonmusk), "Twitter's current lords & peasants system for who has or doesn't have a blue checkmark is bullshit. Power to the people! Blue for $8/month." Twitter, November 1, 2022, 10:36 a.m., https://twitter.com /elonmusk/status/1587498907336118274.

230 **everyone would be fired**: Heath, "Twitter Is Planning to Start Charging Soon for Verification."

230 **"When your team . . . #SleepWhereYouWork"**: Esther Crawford (@esthercrawford), "When your team is pushing round the clock to make deadlines sometimes you #SleepWhereYouWork." Twitter, November 2, 2022, 12:34 a.m., https://twitter.com /esthercrawford/status/1587709705488830464.

230 **"Since some people . . . order to deliver"**: Esther Crawford (@esthercrawford), "I love my family and I'm grateful they understand that there are times where I need to go into overdrive to grind and push in order to deliver. Building new things at Twitter's scale is very hard to do. I'm lucky to be doing this work alongside some of the best people in

tech." Twitter, November 2, 2022, 7:53 a.m., https://twitter.com/esthercrawford/status /1587820101893378049.

231 **"I think of life . . . on Hard Mode":** Esther Crawford (@esthercrawford), "Like seemingly everyone on this app I have plenty of opinions about Twitter > X and figure now is a good time to open up a bit about my experience at the company." Twitter, July 26, 2023, 12:54 p.m., https://twitter.com/esthercrawford/status/1684291048682684416.

231 **"We just won't pay those . . . We just won't pay rent":** Wolfram Arnold, Erik Froese, Tracy Hawkins, Joseph Killian, Laura Chan Pytlarz, and Andrew Schlaikjer v. X Corp. f/k/a Twitter, Inc. (U.S. District Court for the District of Delaware May 16, 2023), 26, https://int.nyt.com/data/documenttools/twitter-employee-lawsuit-v/e5d27a60a7b7d51e /full.pdf.

CHAPTER 17: THERMONUCLEAR

232 **Elon Musk's Gulfstream jet touched down at Teterboro Airport:** Elon Jet (@ ElonJet), "2,456 mile (2,134 NM) flight from HHR to TEB ~ 2,247 gallons (8,505 liters). ~ 15,058 lbs (6,830 kg) of jet fuel used. ~ $14,829 cost of fuel. ~ 24 tons of CO2 emissions." Twitter, October 31, 2022, 10:54 p.m., https:/twitter.com/ElonJet/status /1586959701840830464.

232 **There was a 1,300 percent increase in users tweeting the N-word:** Davey Alba, "Has Twitter Changed since Elon Musk Bought It?" Bloomberg, October 29, 2022, https:// www.bloomberg.com/news/articles/2022-10-29/musk-s-twitter-roils-with-hate-speech-as -trolls-test-new-limits.

232 **"explicitly drawing inspiration from @elonmusk's takeover of the company":** Anti-Defamation League (@ADL), "The ADL Center on Extremism has identified a coordinated effort to spread #antisemitic content on @Twitter, explicitly drawing inspiration from @elonmusk's takeover of the company. In the past 24 hours, over 1200 tweets and retweets have spread antisemitic memes." Twitter, October 28, 2022, 2:02 p.m., https://twitter.com/adl/status/1586101227041230848.

232 **congresswoman Marjorie Taylor Greene saw an immediate spike in followers:** Gerrit De Vynck, Jeremy B. Merrill, and Luis Melgar, "High-Profile Republicans Gain Followers in First Weeks of Musk's Reign," *Washington Post*, November 28, 2022, https://www.washingtonpost.com/technology/2022/11/27/musk-followers-bernie-cruz/.

233 **the result of a dispute Paul Pelosi had with a male escort:** Davey Alba and Daniel Zuidijk, "Elon Musk Posts Then Deletes Tweet Spreading Conspiracy Theory on Pelosi Attack," Bloomberg, October 30, 2022, https://www.bloomberg.com/news/articles/2022 -10-30/musk-posts-then-deletes-tweet-spreading-conspiracy-theory-on-pelosi-attack.

233 **"Twitter obviously cannot . . . welcoming to all":** Elon Musk (@elonmusk), "Dear Twitter Advertisers." Twitter, October 27, 2022, 6:08 a.m., https://twitter.com/elonmusk /status/1585619322239561728.

233 **roughly 90 percent of Twitter's annual revenue:** @TwitterIR, "Q4 and Fiscal Year 2021 Letter to Shareholders," Twitter, February 10, 2022.

234 **he also brought his mother, Maye Musk:** Kurt Wagner, Sarah Frier, and Brad Stone, "Elon Musk Twitter Ownership Full of Firings, Ad Cuts, Chaos," Bloomberg, December 14, 2022, https://www.bloomberg.com/news/features/2022-12-14/elon-musk-twitter -ownership-full-of-firings-ad-cuts-chaos.

234 **WPP controlled billions of advertising dollars for clients:** "WPP 2022 Preliminary Results," WPP, February 23, 2023, https://www.wpp.com/-/media/project/wpp/files /investors/2023/wpp-preliminary-results-2022-v2.pdf.

235 **JP Maheu, objected to the idea:** Wagner, Frier, and Stone, "Elon Musk Twitter Ownership."

235 **Musk just laughed and posted it anyway:** Elon Musk (@elonmusk), "If I had a dollar for every time someone asked me if Trump is coming back on this platform, Twitter

would be minting money!" Twitter, October 31, 2022, 10:10 a.m., https://twitter.com/elonmusk/status/1587129795732770824.

236 **had resigned and was officially gone:** Sarah Personette (@SEP), "Hi folks, I wanted to share that I resigned on Friday from Twitter and my work access was officially cut off last night." Twitter, November 1, 2022, 4:28 a.m., https://twitter.com/SEP/status/1587406184650358784.

238 **repeated plans to create a content moderation council:** Rebecca Kern and Mark Scott, "Musk Personally Led Call with Civil Rights Groups to Address Hate Speech on Twitter," *Politico*, November 2, 2022, https://www.politico.com/news/2022/11/02/musk-twitter-hate-speech-00064690.

238 **advised all its clients:** Lora Kolodny, "Ad Giant IPG Advises Brands to Pause Twitter Spending after Musk Takeover," CNBC, November 1, 2022, https://www.cnbc.com/2022/11/01/ad-giant-ipg-advises-brands-to-pause-twitter-spending.html.

238 **"Freedom of speech" or "Political 'correctness'":** Elon Musk (@elonmusk), "Advertisers should support: Freedom of speech Political 'correctness.'" Twitter, November 2, 2022, 1:09 p.m., https://twitter.com/elonmusk/status/1587899771091566595.

240 **"massive drop in revenue":** Elon Musk (@elonmusk), "Twitter has had a massive drop in revenue, due to activist groups pressuring advertisers, even though nothing has changed with content moderation and we did everything we could to appease the activists. Extremely messed up! They're trying to destroy free speech in America." Twitter, November 4, 2022, 7:28 p.m., https://twitter.com/elonmusk/status/1588538640401018880.

240 **"A thermonuclear name & shame is exactly what will happen if this continues":** Elon Musk (@elonmusk), "Thank you. A thermonuclear name & shame is exactly what will happen if this continues." Twitter, November 4, 2022, 4:37 p.m., https://twitter.com/elonmusk/status/1588676939463946241.

241 **wasn't signed by an actual person, but rather just "Twitter":** Kurt Wagner and Edward Ludlow, "Read the Twitter Memo Sent to Employees Ahead of Layoffs," Bloomberg, November 4, 2022, https://www.bloomberg.com/news/articles/2022-11-04/twitter-layoff-email-read-the-full-letter-as-elon-musk-cuts-jobs.

242 **The employee was booted from the call without warning:** Kate Conger, Ryan Mac, and Mike Isaac, "Confusion and Frustration Reign as Elon Musk Cuts Half of Twitter's Staff," *New York Times*, November 4, 2022, https://www.nytimes.com/2022/11/04/technology/elon-musk-twitter-layoffs.html.

243 **including tons of engineers focused on critical infrastructure projects:** Kurt Wagner and Davey Alba, "Twitter Cuts Spur Concerns About US Midterms, Human Rights," Bloomberg, November 4, 2022, https://www.bloomberg.com/news/articles/2022-11-04/twitter-cuts-spur-concerns-about-us-midterms-human-rights?sref=dZ65CIng.

244 **tweeted that just 15 percent of his group was laid off:** Yoel Roth (@yoyoel), "Yesterday's reduction in force affected approximately 15% of our Trust & Safety organization (as opposed to approximately 50% cuts company-wide), with our front-line moderation staff experiencing the least impact." Twitter, November 4, 2022, 3:19 p.m., https://twitter.com/yoyoel/status/1588657228462317568.

244 **Musk finally addressed the layoffs:** Elon Musk (@elonmusk), "Regarding Twitter's reduction in force, unfortunately there is no choice when the company is losing over $4M/day. Everyone exited was offered 3 months of severance, which is 50% more than legally required." Twitter, November 4, 2022, 4:14 p.m., https://twitter.com/elonmusk/status/1588671155766194176.

244 **claimed Musk didn't pay employees what they were contractually owed:** Ashley Belanger, "Twitter Offering Some Laid-off Staff Only Half What They're Owed, Lawsuit Says," Ars Technica, November 9, 2022, https://arstechnica.com/tech-policy/2022/11/twitter-offering-some-laid-off-staff-only-half-what-theyre-owed-lawsuit-says/.

244 **"Folks at Twitter . . . I apologize for that":** Jack Dorsey (@jack), "Folks at Twitter past and present are strong and resilient. They will always find a way no matter how difficult the moment. I realize many are angry with me. I own the responsibility for why everyone is in this situation: I grew the company size too quickly. I apologize for that." Twitter, November 5, 2022, 8:17 a.m., https://twitter.com/jack/status/1588913276980633600.

245 **"You threw Twitter's investors, employees, and users under a bus in a fit of pique. GTFO":** Ian Brown (@igb), "You threw Twitter's investors, employees, and users under a bus in a fit of pique. GTFO." Twitter, November 5, 2022, 10:05 a.m., https://twitter.com /igb/status/1588940613063704576.

245 **"Fuck you . . . Bitcoin ass bitch":** Shiraz Siddiqui (@shiraz), "fuck you and yo sneaker game weak bitcoin ass bitch." Twitter, November 5, 2022, 12:12 p.m., https://twitter.com /shiraz/status/1588972462955704321.

245 **included United Airlines, REI, and Volkswagen:** Tiffany Hsu, "Twitter's Advertisers Pull Back as Layoffs Sweep Through Company," *New York Times*, November 4, 2022, https://www.nytimes.com/2022/11/04/technology/twitter-advertisers.html.

CHAPTER 18: TWITTER BLUES

247 **Behnam Rezaei, a senior engineering manager, was now running engineering for the entire company:** Kurt Wagner, "Musk Starts Assembling New Cadre of Leaders Inside Twitter," Bloomberg, November 10, 2022, https://www.bloomberg.com/news /articles/2022-11-10/musk-starts-assembling-new-cadre-of-leaders-inside-twitter.

247 **He woke up and tweeted two jokes about masturbation:** Kurt Wagner (@ KurtWagner8), "Multiple masturbation jokes so far from Twitter CEO Elon Musk and it's not even 9 am PT. Happy Monday!" Twitter, November 7, 2022, 8:30 a.m., https://twitter .com/KurtWagner8/status/1589656470114959360.

248 **"Twitter usage is at an all-time high lol":** Elon Musk (@elonmusk), "Twitter usage is at an all-time high lol." Twitter, November 7, 2022, 4:57 p.m., https://twitter.com /elonmusk/status/1589784134691741696.

248 **"I just hope the servers don't melt!":** Elon Musk (@elonmusk), "I just hope the servers don't melt!" Twitter, November 7, 2022, 5:00 p.m., https://twitter.com/elonmusk/status /1589784884666859520.

249 **people would eventually connect their bank accounts to Twitter:** "Elon Musk Speaks at Twitter Advertiser Town Hall," Bloomberg, November 9, 2022, https://www .bloomberg.com/news/live-blog/2022-11-09/elon-musk-speaks-at-advertiser-town-hall ?sref=dZ65CIng.

253 **"BREAKING: A second Tesla has hit the World Trade Center":** Johnna Crider, "Tesla's Twitter Impersonator Tells Tiktok Followers He Wanted to Create an Account for SpaceX," Teslarati, November 11, 2022, https://www.teslarati.com/teslas-twitter -impersonator-spacex/.

253 **posted that he "missed killing Iraqis":** Lee Moran, "Verified Bush and Blair Profiles Work to Make Musk's Twitter 'Completely Unusable,'" HuffPost, November 10, 2022, https://www.huffpost.com/entry/twitter-tony-blair-george-w-bush-iraq-fake _n_636cdclee4b021a403915b65.

254 **the pharmaceutical company decided to pause all ad spending on Twitter:** Drew Harwell, "A Fake Tweet Sparked Panic at Eli Lilly and May Have Cost Twitter Millions," *Washington Post*, November 14, 2022, https://www.washingtonpost.com/technology /2022/11/14/twitter-fake-eli-lilly/.

254 **"We apologize to those who have been served a misleading message from a fake Lilly account":** Eli Lilly (@LillyPad), "We apologize to those who have been served a misleading message from a fake Lilly account. Our official Twitter account is @LillyPad." Twitter, November 10, 2022, 1:09 p.m., https://twitter.com/LillyPad/status /1590813806275469333.

254 **Musk tried to adjust Twitter's policies on the fly:** Elon Musk (@elonmusk), "To
be more precise, accounts doing parody impersonations. Basically, tricking people is
not ok." Twitter, November 10, 2022, 5:56 p.m., https://twitter.com/elonmusk/status
/1590886170543915009.

254 **recommending that they pause spending:** "Major AD Firm Omnicom Recommends
Clients Pause Twitter Ad Spend—Memo," Reuters, November 12, 2022, https://www
.reuters.com/technology/major-ad-firm-omnicom-recommends-clients-pause-twitter-ad
-spend-verge-2022-11-11/.

255 **"Quite the day! . . . Some epically funny tweets":** Elon Musk (@elonmusk), "Quite
the day!" Twitter, November 10, 2022, 11:30 p.m., https://twitter.com/elonmusk/status
/1590970255064854529.

255 **Twitter suspended the subscription offering until further notice:** Zoë Schiffer (@
zoeschiffer), "NEW: Twitter has suspended the launch of Twitter Blue and is actively
trying to stop people from subscribing 'to help address impersonation issues,' per an
internal note. 1/." Twitter, November 11, 2022, 6:54 a.m., https://twitter.com/ZoeSchiffer
/status/1591081913166745601.

255 **"battleground of ideas . . . achieve for humanity":** Alex Heath, "Inside Elon Musk's
First Meeting with Twitter Employees," The Verge, November 11, 2022, https://www
.theverge.com/2022/11/10/23452196/elon-musk-twitter-employee-meeting-q-and-a.

257 **recessions require tough decisions:** Edward Ludlow, Kurt Wagner, Davey Alba, and
Paula Seligson, "Elon Musk Warns Twitter Bankruptcy Possible as Senior Executives
Exit," Bloomberg, November 10, 2022, https://www.bloomberg.com/news/articles/2022
-11-10/musk-tells-twitter-staff-social-network-s-bankruptcy-is-possible?sref=dZ65Cing.

257 **Musk had sold $4 billion worth of Tesla stock:** Anders Melin, "Musk Sells Another
Batch of Tesla Shares Despite Vow to Stop," Bloomberg, November 9, 2022, https://www
.bloomberg.com/news/articles/2022-11-09/musk-sells-3-95-billion-of-tesla-stock-after
-twitter-takeover?sref=dZ65CIng.

257 **"It was excruciatingly difficult . . . we're going to survive":** Heath, "Inside Elon
Musk's First Meeting."

257 **"Basically, if you can . . . End of story":** Heath.

258 **penalized by the Federal Trade Commission for a series of privacy missteps:** "FTC
Accepts Final Settlement with Twitter for Failure to Safeguard Personal Information,"
Federal Trade Commission, March 11, 2011, https://www.ftc.gov/news-events/news
/press-releases/2011/03/ftc-accepts-final-settlement-twitter-failure-safeguard-personal
-information-0.

258 **Twitter was required to beef up its privacy programs and participate in third-
party audits:** "Twitter to Pay $150 Million Penalty for Allegedly Breaking Its Privacy
Promises—Again," Federal Trade Commission, May 25, 2022, https://www.ftc.gov
/business-guidance/blog/2022/05/twitter-pay-150-million-penalty-allegedly-breaking-its
-privacy-promises-again.

258 **It created a five-person Data Governance Committee:** Damien Kieran and Rinki
Sethi, "Our Continued Work to Protect Your Privacy and Security," *Twitter Blog*,
Twitter, November 10, 2021, https://blog.twitter.com/en_us/topics/company/2021/our
-continued-work-to-protect-your-privacy-and-security.

259 **"I don't watch Game of Thrones. I certainly don't want to play it at work":**
Marianne Fogarty (@mariannefogarty), "I don't watch Game of Thrones. I certainly
don't want to play it at work." Twitter, November 7, 2022, 12:59 p.m., https://twitter.com
/mariannefogarty/status/1589724275510226944.

259 **Spiro later denied the statement:** Dan Adler, "How Alex Spiro Became Elon Musk's
(and Megan Thee Stallion's and Jay-Z's) Go-To Lawyer," *Vanity Fair*, March 6, 2023,
https://www.vanityfair.com/style/2023/03/alex-spiro-lawyer-elon-musk-megan-thee
-stallion-jay-z.

261　**Musk opened Twitter and posted an apology:** Elon Musk (@elonmusk), "Btw, I'd like
to apologize for Twitter being super slow in many countries. App is doing > 1000 poorly
batched RPCs just to render a home timeline!" Twitter, November 13, 2022, 10:00 a.m.,
https://twitter.com/elonmusk/status/1591853644944932865.

261　**not for the reasons Musk was claiming:** Eric Frohnhoefer, "'Elon Musk Fired Me in
a Tweet,'" *Newsweek*, December 4, 2022, https://www.newsweek.com/eric-frohnhoefer
-fired-elon-musk-tweet-reaction-where-now-1764290.

261　**"I have spent . . . this is wrong":** Eric Frohnhoefer (@EricFrohnhoefer), "I have spent
~6yrs working on Twitter for Android and can say this is wrong." Twitter, November 13,
2022, 1:14 p.m., https://twitter.com/EricFrohnhoefer/status/1591902285403418624.

261　**Leib was also fired for the criticism:** Kurt Wagner, "Musk Steps Up Purge of Twitter
Engineers Who Criticize Him," Bloomberg, November 14, 2022, https://www.bloomberg
.com/news/articles/2022-11-14/musk-publicly-punishes-twitter-engineers-who-call-him
-out-online?sref=dZ65CIng.

261　**"It sucked . . . would still have a job":** Frohnhoefer, "'Elon Musk Fired Me in a Tweet.'"

262　**scoured the company's internal systems:** Isaacson, *Elon Musk*, 549.

262　**"We will be scheduling multiple all-hands every day until morale improves":** Sasha
Solomon (@sachee), "we will be scheduling multiple all-hands every day until morale
improves." Twitter, November 10, 2022, 11:59 a.m., https://twitter.com/sachee/status
/1590796308998422530.

262　**"You don't get . . . you laid off":** Sasha Solomon (@sachee), "You don't get to shit on
our infra if you don't know what the fuck it does while you're also scrambling to rehire
folks you laid off." Twitter, November 13, 2022, 10:17 a.m., https://twitter.com/sachee
/status/1591857907184070656.

262　**"Kiss my ass elon":** Wagner, "Musk Steps Up Purge."

263　**"Twitter will survive and thrive but it will take some time":** Jack Dorsey (@jack),
"both the common misconception and your stated reality are wrong. Twitter will survive
and thrive but it will take some time." Twitter, November 16, 2022, 3:47 p.m., https://
twitter.com/jack/status/1593027984575037440.

263　**"I did":** Jack Dorsey (@jack), "I did." Twitter, November 16, 2022, 4:04 p.m., https://
twitter.com/jack/status/1593032351671803906.

264　**nearly 1,200 employees took the buyout:** Ryan Mac, Mike Isaac, and Kellen Browning,
"Elon Musk's Twitter Teeters on the Edge After Another 1,200 Leave," *New York Times*,
November 18, 2022, https://www.nytimes.com/2022/11/18/technology/elon-musk-twitter
-workers-quit.html.

265　**Musk had even started sleeping on a couch at the office:** Isaacson, *Elon Musk*, 547.

CHAPTER 19: VOX POPULI, VOX DEI

266　**At a private room inside the New Orleans Museum of Art:** Claire Gatinois and
Philippe Ricard, "Emmanuel Macron's Unexpected Conversation with Elon Musk in
New Orleans," *Le Monde*, December 3, 2022, https://www.lemonde.fr/en/international
/article/2022/12/03/emmanuel-macron-s-new-orleans-trip-included-street-bands
-promoting-the-french-language-and-an-unexpected-conversation-with-elon-musk
_6006490_4.html.

266　**"clear and honest discussion":** Emmanuel Macron (@EmmanuelMacron), "I'll
say it here, on Twitter, because it's all about the blue bird. This afternoon I met with
@elonmusk and we had a clear and honest discussion." Twitter, December 2, 2022,
3:48 p.m., https://twitter.com/EmmanuelMacron/status/1598826588367470592.

266　**flew back to the Bay Area:** Elon Musk Jet (@elonmuskjet), "Landed in Oakland,
California, US. Apx. flt. time 4 Hours : 15 Mins." Instagram, December 2, 2022, https://
www.instagram.com/p/ClsWLItIvNL/.

267 **was living in New Zealand to avoid extradition to the U.S.:** Nick Perry, "2 Make Deal, Leaving Just Kim Dotcom Facing US Extradition," Associated Press, May 9, 2022, https://apnews.com/article/technology-business-new-zealand-copyright-extradition-be77 a708b74bb972048bb14f44a31615.

267 **asked his 117 million followers if Trump should be reinstated:** Elon Musk (@ elonmusk), "Reinstate former President Trump." Twitter, November 18, 2022, 4:47 p.m., https://twitter.com/elonmusk/status/1593767953706921985.

267 **"The people have spoken":** Elon Musk (@elonmusk), "The people have spoken. Trump will be reinstated. Vox Populi, Vox Dei." Twitter, November 19, 2022, 4:53 p.m., https:// twitter.com/elonmusk/status/1594131768298315777.

268 **welcoming him back to Twitter:** Vlad Savov, "Musk Welcomes Ye Back to Twitter After Inviting Trump's Return," Bloomberg, November 20, 2022, https://www.bloomberg .com/news/articles/2022-11-21/musk-welcomes-ye-back-to-twitter-after-inviting-trump -s-return?sref=dZ65CIng.

268 **before he suspended West again:** Vlad Savov, "Musk Suspends Ye from Twitter After Offensive Image Post," Bloomberg, December 1, 2022, https://www.bloomberg.com /news/articles/2022-12-02/musk-to-suspend-ye-s-twitter-account-after-offensive-image -post?sref=dZ65CIng.

269 **Musk had personally invited the journalists to Twitter's offices:** Bari Weiss, "Our Reporting at Twitter," Free Press, December 15, 2022, https://www.thefp.com/p/why-we -went-to-twitter.

269 **"We're double checking some facts":** Elon Musk (@elonmusk), "We're double-checking some facts, so probably start live tweeting in about 40 mins." Twitter, December 2, 2022, 2:21 p.m., https://twitter.com/elonmusk/status /1598804557722972160.

270 **The first dump looked at Twitter's handling of the Hunter Biden laptop incident:** Kurt Wagner, "Musk Hails Release of Twitter Emails on Hunter Biden Story," Bloomberg, December 2, 2022, https://www.bloomberg.com/news/articles/2022-12-03 /musk-hails-release-of-twitter-emails-on-hunter-biden-story?sref=dZ65CIng.

270 **keeping their accounts from trending on the service without telling them:** Bari Weiss, Abigail Shrier, Michael Shellenberger, and Nellie Bowles, "Twitter's Secret Blacklists," Free Press, December 15, 2022, https://www.thefp.com/p/twitters-secret -blacklists.

271 **"Can high school students ever meaningfully consent to sex with their teachers?":** Yoel Roth (@yoyoel), "Can high school students ever meaningfully consent to sex with their teachers? http://bit.ly/bbpH68." Twitter, November 20, 2010, 5:41 a.m., https:// twitter.com/yoyoel/status/5979003856879617.

272 **"Looks like Yoel . . . his PhD thesis":** Elon Musk (@elonmusk), "Looks like Yoel is arguing in favor of children being able to access adult Internet services in his PhD thesis." Twitter, December 10, 2022, 11:29 a.m., https://twitter.com/elonmusk/status /1601660414743687169.

272 **were forced to leave their home:** Cat Zakrzewski, Joseph Menn, and Naomi Nix, "Twitter Dissolves Trust and Safety Council," *Washington Post*, December 12, 2022, https://www.washingtonpost.com/technology/2022/12/12/musk-twitter-harass-yoel-roth/.

274 **"I'm rich, bitch!":** Matt Novak, "Elon Musk Gets Booed by the Crowd at Dave Chappelle's San Francisco Show (Part 3 of 4)," YouTube, 2022, https://www.youtube .com/shorts/u1cl8U0UCMQ.

274 **Musk pushed back:** Jill Goldsmith, "Elon Musk Tweets 'The Woke Mind Virus Is Either Defeated or Nothing Else Matters' After Being Booed at a Dave Chappelle Show," Deadline, December 12, 2022, https://deadline.com/2022/12/elon-musk-booed-dave -chappelle-comedy-show-twitter-1235196727/.

274 **the "crazy stalker" had followed his Tesla thinking that Musk was inside:** Elon Musk (@elonmusk), "Last night, car carrying lil X in LA was followed by crazy stalker (thinking it was me), who later blocked car from moving & climbed onto hood. Legal action is being taken against Sweeney & organizations who supported harm to my family." Twitter, December 14, 2022, 4:48 p.m., https://twitter.com/elonmusk/status /1603190155107794944.

274 **he also admitted that he believed Grimes was sending him coded messages in her Instagram posts:** Drew Harwell and Taylor Lorenz, "Musk Blamed a Twitter Account for an Alleged Stalker. Police See No Link," *Washington Post*, December 18, 2022, https://www.washingtonpost.com/technology/2022/12/18/details-of-musk-stalking -incident/.

275 **he made a swift policy change at Twitter:** Elon Musk (@elonmusk), "Any account doxxing real-time location info of anyone will be suspended, as it is a physical safety violation. This includes posting links to sites with real-time location info. Posting locations someone traveled to on a slightly delayed basis isn't a safety problem, so is ok." Twitter, December 14, 2022, 4:13 p.m., https://twitter.com/elonmusk/status /1603181423787380737.

275 **the gas station itself was twenty-six miles from the airport:** Drew Harwell and Taylor Lorenz, "Musk Blamed a Twitter Account for an Alleged Stalker. Police See No Link," *Washington Post*, December 18, 2022, https://www.washingtonpost.com/technology /2022/12/18/details-of-musk-stalking-incident/.

275 **so was the sports commentator Keith Olbermann:** Kurt Wagner, Davey Alba, and Vlad Savov, "Twitter Suspends Journalists Who Musk Says Imperiled His Safety," Bloomberg, December 15, 2022, https://www.bloomberg.com/news/articles/2022-12-16 /twitter-suspends-accounts-of-mastodon-journalists-covering-musk?sref=dZ65CIng.

275 **"They posted my exact real-time location, basically assassination coordinates":** Elon Musk (@elonmusk), "They posted my exact real-time location, basically assassination coordinates, in (obvious) direct violation of Twitter terms of service." Twitter, December 15, 2022, 7:09 p.m., https://twitter.com/elonmusk/status/1603587970832793600.

275 **"My commitment to free speech . . . personal safety risk":** Elon Musk (@elonmusk), "My commitment to free speech extends even to not banning the account following my plane, even though that is a direct personal safety risk." Twitter, November 6, 2022, 4:30 p.m., https://twitter.com/elonmusk/status/1589414958508691456.

276 **which had invested $375 million into Musk's Twitter deal:** Twitter, Inc., Elon Musk Form 13D (filed May 5, 2022), 2–3, https://www.sec.gov/Archives/edgar/data/1418091 /000110465922056055/tm2214608-1_sc13da.htm.

277 **Musk had agreed to attend the match as part of the investment:** Isaacson, *Elon Musk*, 461.

277 **met briefly with Turkey's president, Recep Tayyip Erdogan:** Dalton Bennett, Samuel Oakford, Gerrit De Vynck, and Monique Woo, "From Jared Kushner to Salt Bae: Here's Who Elon Musk Was Seen with at the World Cup," *Washington Post*, December 20, 2022, https://www.washingtonpost.com/investigations/2022/12/20/elon-musk-spotted -world-cup-final/.

277 **"Goal by Argentina!":** Elon Musk (@elonmusk), "Great goal by Argentina!" Twitter, December 18, 2022, 7:27 a.m., https://twitter.com/elonmusk/status /1604498679234273286.

277 **"Evenly matched game!!":** Elon Musk (@elonmusk), "Well done France! Evenly-matched game!!" Twitter, December 18, 2022, 8:54 a.m., https://twitter.com/elonmusk /status/1604520419515662337.

277 **against Twitter's rules to post links to other social media sites:** "Promotion of Alternative Social Platforms Policy," Twitter Help Center, Twitter, n.d., https:/help .twitter.com/en/rules-and-policies/social-platforms-policy.

277 **"This is just sad":** Aaron Levie (@levie), "This is just sad." Twitter, December 18, 2022, 10:15 a.m., https://twitter.com/levie/status/1604540771951968260.

277 **"This is a bad policy and should be reversed":** Edward Snowden (@Snowden), "Twitter seemingly banned @paulg for this tweet. A major account that was obviously not 'solely created to promote other social media platforms,' And he didn't even post the link! As @balajis said, this is a bad policy and should be reversed." Twitter, December 18, 2022, 2:37 p.m., https://twitter.com/Snowden/status/1604606914372984832.

277 **at first he tried to defend it:** Elon Musk (@elonmusk), "Exactly. Twitter should be easy to use, but no more relentless free advertising of competitors. No traditional publisher allows this and neither will Twitter." Twitter, December 18, 2022, 1:26 p.m., https://twitter.com/elonmusk/status/1604588904828600320.

278 **"Policy will be adjusted . . . no spam rule":** Elon Musk (@elonmusk), "Policy will be adjusted to suspending accounts only when that account's *primary* purpose is promotion of competitors, which essentially falls under the no spam rule." Twitter, December 18, 2022, 3:12 p.m., https://twitter.com/elonmusk/status/1604615711036407809.

278 **"Going forward . . . won't happen again":** Elon Musk (@elonmusk), "Going forward, there will be a vote for major policy changes. My apologies. Won't happen again." Twitter, December 18, 2022, 3:17 p.m., https://twitter.com/elonmusk/status/1604616863673208832.

278 **"Should I step down as head of Twitter?":** Elon Musk (@elonmusk), "Should I step down as head of Twitter? I will abide by the results of this poll." Twitter, December 18, 2022, 3:20 p.m., https://twitter.com/elonmusk/status/1604617643973124097.

278 **"As the saying goes, be careful what you wish, as you might get it":** Elon Musk (@elonmusk), "As the saying goes, be careful what you wish, as you might get it." Twitter, December 18, 2022, 3:43 p.m., https://twitter.com/elonmusk/status/1604623424164282368.

278 **"The question is not finding a CEO, the question is finding a CEO who can keep Twitter alive":** Elon Musk (@elonmusk), "The question is not finding a CEO, the question is finding a CEO who can keep Twitter alive." Twitter, December 18, 2022, 3:34 p.m., https://twitter.com/elonmusk/status/1604621101245419520.

278 **"No one wants the job who can actually keep Twitter alive. There is no successor":** Elon Musk (@elonmusk), "No one wants the job who can actually keep Twitter alive. There is no successor." Twitter, December 18, 2022, 4:04 p.m., https://twitter.com/elonmusk/status/1604628761395138561.

278 **"You must like pain a lot . . . still want the job?":** Elon Musk (@elonmusk), "You must like pain a lot. One catch: you have to invest your life savings in Twitter and it has been in the fast lane to bankruptcy since May. Still want the job?" Twitter, December 18, 2022, 3:54 p.m., https://twitter.com/elonmusk/status/1604626103326253056.

279 **"Those who want power are the ones who least deserve it":** Elon Musk (@elonmusk), "Those who want power are the ones who least deserve it." Twitter, December 18, 2022, 5:29 p.m., https://twitter.com/elonmusk/status/1604650028999405568.

279 **Musk's jet took off for the United States:** Elon Musk's Jet "Tracking," "Took off from Doha, Ad-Dawhah Municipality, QA," Facebook, December 18, 2022, https://www.facebook.com/ElonJet/posts/pfbid025GvRHacGZgVvk88KnRV4Rt8Cy7BvvBu4WAUfXchu75VBM9VSXiJifJyT7dSvw5tMl.

279 **57.5 percent—were in favor of Musk stepping down:** Elon Musk, (@elonmusk), "Should I step down as head of Twitter? I will abide by the results of this poll." Twitter, December 18, 2022, 3:20 p.m., https://twitter.com/elonmusk/status/1604617643973124097.

279 **"I will resign . . . servers teams":** Elon Musk (@elonmusk), "I will resign as CEO as soon as I find someone foolish enough to take the job! After that, I will just run the

software & servers teams." Twitter, December 20, 2022, 5:20 p.m., https://twitter.com /elonmusk/status/1605372724800393216.

279 **revenue was down 40 percent in December 2022:** Alexander Saeedy, Laura Cooper, and Alexa Corse, "Twitter's Revenue, Adjusted Earnings Fell about 40% in Month of December," *Wall Street Journal*, March 3, 2023, https://www.wsj.com/articles/twitters -revenue-adjusted-earnings-fell-about-40-in-month-of-december-ee91f1eb?mod=latest _headlines.

279 **which was estimated at $300 million:** Paula Seligson, "Musk Has 'More to Lose' If He Tries to Skip Twitter Debt Payment," Bloomberg, January 18, 2023, https://www .bloomberg.com/news/articles/2023-01-18/elon-musk-has-more-to-lose-if-he-tries-to -skip-twitter-debt-payment?sref=dZ65CIng.

279 **sold another $3.6 billion worth of Tesla stock:** Dana Hull, "Elon Musk's Tesla Share Sales Approach the $40 Billion Mark," Bloomberg, December 14, 2022, https://www .bloomberg.com/news/articles/2022-12-15/elon-musk-sells-at-least-3-6-billion-of-tesla -shares?sref=dZ65CIng.

279 **Fidelity cut the value of its Twitter holdings in half:** Dan Primack, "Fidelity Slashes Twitter Value by 56%," Axios, December 30, 2022, https://www.axios.com/2022/12/30 /twitter-fidelity-valuation.

279 **made an impromptu flight north to Sacramento:** Isaacson, "Christmas Capers." *Elon Musk*, 584.

280 **Musk would later say he regretted the haphazard decision:** Isaacson, *Elon Musk*, 590.

280 **it converted several conference rooms into bedrooms:** Cyrus Farivar and Katharine Schwab, "Elon Musk Has Outfitted Twitter's Headquarters with Bedrooms for Employees," *Forbes*, December 5, 2022, https://www.forbes.com/sites/cyrusfarivar/2022 /12/05/elon-musk-twitter-bedrooms/?sh=4dfabcf3d791.

280 **its office leases were estimated at $130 million annually:** Wolfram Arnold, Erik Froese, Tracy Hawkins, Joseph Killian, Laura Chan Pytlarz, and Andrew Schlaikjer v. X Corp. f/k/a Twitter Inc. (U.S. District Court for the District of Delaware, May 16, 2023), 29–30, https://int.nyt.com/data/documenttools/twitter-employee-lawsuit -v/e5d27a60a7b7d51e/full.pdf

280 **later sued by the landlord for its San Francisco headquarters:** Roland Li, "Twitter Sued by Landlord at S.F. HQ after Alleged $6.8 Million in Missed Rent Payments," *San Francisco Chronicle*, January 23, 2023, https://www.sfchronicle.com/tech/article/Twitter -sued-by-landlord-at-S-F-HQ-after-alleged-17737102.php.

281 **allegedly told Killian that Twitter didn't need to follow those rules:** Wolfram Arnold, Erik Froese, Tracy Hawkins, Joseph Killian, Laura Chan Pytlarz, and Andrew Schlaikjer v. X Corp. f/k/a Twitter Inc., 31.

281 **demanded that Killian install new locks and space heaters in the rooms even though they weren't up to code:** Wolfram Arnold, Erik Froese, Tracy Hawkins, Joseph Killian, Laura Chan Pytlarz, and Andrew Schlaikjer v. X Corp. f/k/a Twitter Inc., 34–35.

281 **were subpoenaed and interviewed by the FTC shortly after they resigned:** Kurt Wagner and Leah Nylen, "Musk's Twitter Draws Deeper FTC Scrutiny Over Rising Privacy, Security Concerns," Bloomberg, December 20, 2022, https://www.bloomberg .com/news/articles/2022-12-20/musk-s-twitter-draws-deeper-ftc-scrutiny-over-rising -privacy-security-concerns?sref=dZ65CIng.

281 **"The giant elephant in the room was that he was acting like a fucking idiot":** Isaacson, *Elon Musk*, 580–86.

281 **both SpaceX and Tesla had less than a 10 percent chance of survival:** Rory Cellan-Jones, "Tesla Chief Elon Musk Says Apple Is Making an Electric Car," BBC News, January 11, 2016, https://www.bbc.com/technology-35280633.

282 **"Where are the people that work there?":** All-In Podcast, "E109: 2022 Bestie Awards Live from Twitter HQ," YouTube, 2022, https://www.youtube.com/watch?v= HE5CTKqWEV0&t=4481s.

282 **"I can just go . . . embarrassing and sad":** All-In Podcast, "E109."

CONCLUSION

283 **notified the company it was violating safety codes:** Lauren McCarthy, "After Investigation and Complaints, Twitter Removes 'X' on Headquarters," *New York Times*, August 1, 2023, https://www.nytimes.com/2023/08/01/us/twitter-x-logo-sf-headquarters .html.

284 **He applied for money transfer licenses:** Pedro Solimano, "Twitter Awarded Three State Money Transmitter Licenses," Yahoo! Finance, July 5, 2023, https://finance.yahoo .com/news/twitter-awarded-three-state-money-022410075.html.

284 **started sharing advertising revenue with some popular users:** Sarah Frier, "Musk Offers to Share Twitter Ad Revenue with Blue Subscribers," Bloomberg, February 3, 2023, https://www.bloomberg.com/news/articles/2023-02-03/musk-offers-to-share -twitter-ad-revenue-with-blue-subscribers?sref=dZ65CIng.

284 **eliminated the service's Covid-19 misinformation policies:** Taylor Lorenz, "Twitter Ends Its Ban on Covid Misinformation," *Washington Post*, November 29, 2022, https:// www.washingtonpost.com/technology/2022/11/29/twitter-covid-misinformation-policy/.

284 **Both were promptly suspended again:** Nikki McCann Ramirez, "Kanye's 2024 Brain Trust Booted from Twitter (Again)," *Rolling Stone*, January 25, 2023, https://www .rollingstone.com/politics/politics-news/ali-alexander-nick-fuentes-rebanned-twitter -1234668251/.

284 **he brought his popular talk show onto X:** Gerry Smith, "Tucker Carlson Says He's Launching a New Show on Twitter," Bloomberg, May 9, 2023, https://www.bloomberg .com/news/articles/2023-05-09/tucker-carlson-says-he-s-launching-a-new-show-on -twitter.

284 **he tweeted his mug shot:** Dan Mangan and Kevin Breuninger, "Trump Arrest Full Recap: Mugshot, Surrender, What's Next in Georgia Election Case," CNBC, August 25, 2023, https://www.cnbc.com/2023/08/24/donald-trump-to-be-arrested-in-georgia-live -updates.html.

284 **Musk retweeted the post to all of his followers:** Elon Musk (@elonmusk), "Next-level." Twitter, August 24, 2023, 7:46 p.m., https://twitter.com/elonmusk/status /1694903930981884041.

285 **"You have said the actual truth":** Elon Musk (@elonmusk), "You have said the actual truth," Twitter, November 15, 2023, 1:52 p.m., https://twitter.com/elonmusk/status /1724908287471272299.

285 **Apple, IBM, Disney and several other major brands paused advertising:** Sara Fischer, "What Makes the X Advertiser Revolt Different from Other Boycotts," Axios, November 18, 2023, https://www.axios.com/2023/11/18/twitter-x-boycott-apple-ibm -advertisers.

285 **advertising revenue was down 50 percent:** Elon Musk (@elonmusk), "We're still negative cash flow, due to ~50% drop in advertising revenue plus heavy debt load. Need to reach positive cash flow before we have the luxury of anything else." Twitter, July 14, 2023, 10:08 p.m., https://twitter.com/elonmusk/status/1680082007873953794.

285 **U.S. ad revenue was down 60 percent:** Elon Musk (@elonmusk), "Our US advertising revenue is still down 60%, primarily due to pressure on advertisers by @ADL (that's what advertisers tell us), so they almost succeeded in killing X/ Twitter!" Twitter, September 4, 2023, 10:52 a.m., https://twitter.com/elonmusk/status /1698755938541330907.

285 **the company was worth just $20 billion:** Kate Conger and Ryan Mac, "Elon Musk Values Twitter at $20 Billion," *New York Times*, March 26, 2023, https://www.nytimes.com/2023/03/26/technology/elon-musk-twitter-value.html.

285 **"Say what you want . . . for $44B lol":** Elon Musk (@elonmusk), "Say what you want about me, but I acquired the world's largest non-profit for $44B lol." Twitter, February 21, 2023, 6:41 p.m., https://twitter.com/elonmusk/status/1628117788857405461.

286 **"It's evident that verified checkmarks no longer represent authority and expertise":** Oliver Darcy, "News Organizations Reject Elon Musk's Demand of Paying to Keep Checkmarks on Twitter," CNN, March 31, 2023, https://www.cnn.com/2023/03/30/media/news-organizations-elon-musk-twitter-checkmark/index.html.

286 **Musk himself encouraged people to follow accounts known for spreading false information:** Davey Alba, Daniel Zuidijk, and Isabella Ward, "Israel-Hamas Conflict Was a Test for Musk's X, and It Failed," Bloomberg, October 9, 2023, https://www.bloomberg.com/news/articles/2023-10-10/israel-hamas-conflict-was-a-test-for-musk-s-x-and-it-failed?sref=dZ65CIng.

286 **After attending the Super Bowl . . . with Musk's posts:** Zoë Schiffer and Casey Newton, "Yes, Elon Musk Created a Special System for Showing You All His Tweets First," Platformer, February 14, 2023, https://www.platformer.news/p/yes-elon-musk-created-a-special-system.

287 **Musk thought AI was dangerous, and Zuckerberg thought Musk was being alarmist:** Cade Metz, "Mark Zuckerberg, Elon Musk and the Feud Over Killer Robots," *New York Times*, June 9, 2018, https://www.nytimes.com/2018/06/09/technology/elon-musk-mark-zuckerberg-artificial-intelligence.html.

287 **Instagram made people depressed and sad:** Beatrice Nolan, "Elon Musk Says Instagram Makes People Depressed and Twitter Makes Them Angry," Business Insider, January 16, 2023, https://www.businessinsider.com/elon-musk-instagram-depressed-twitter-angry-2023-1.

287 **"I think we can all agree Elon isn't serious and it's time to move on":** Mark Zuckerberg (@Zuck), "I think we can all agree Elon isn't serious and it's time to move on." Threads, August 13, 2023, https://www.threads.net/@zuck/post/Cv5CV3-rMKb/?igshid=MTc4MmM1YmI2Ng%3D%3D.

287 **"I have rarely seen evil in as pure a form as Yoel Roth":** Elon Musk (@elonmusk), "I have rarely seen evil in as pure a form as Yoel Roth and Kara Swisher's heart is filled with seething hate." Twitter, October 2, 2023, 6:58 p.m., https://twitter.com/elonmusk/status/1709025216578335003.

288 **"I learned a ton . . . social-emotional intelligence":** Esther Crawford (@esthercrawford), "Like seemingly everyone on this app I have plenty of opinions about Twitter > X and figure now is a good time to open up a bit about my experience at the company. . . ." Twitter, July 26, 2023, 12:54 p.m., https://twitter.com/esthercrawford/status/1684291048682684416?s=46&t=FY5LfS3Q1bvn3Df5aoImCQ.

INDEX

ABOUT THE AUTHOR

KURT WAGNER is an award-winning business and technology journalist covering social media for Bloomberg, where he has worked since 2019. He's been covering social media since 2013, and previously worked at Recode, Mashable, and *Fortune*. Kurt grew up near Seattle, went to college at Santa Clara University, and now lives in Denver, Colorado, with his wife and two children. Follow him on X, formerly Twitter, at @KurtWagner8.